Mastering NServiceBus and Persistence

Design and build various enterprise solutions using NServiceBus while utilizing persistence enterprise objects

Rich Helton

BIRMINGHAM - MUMBAI

Mastering NServiceBus and Persistence

First published: August 2014

Production reference: 1200814

Published by Packt Publishing Ltd.
Livery Place
35 Livery Street
Birmingham B3 2PB, UK.

ISBN 978-1-78217-381-6

www.packtpub.com

Cover image by Zarko Piljak (zpiljak@gmail.com)

Credits

Author
Rich Helton

Reviewers
Andrew Church
Eben Roux

Commissioning Editor
Usha Iyer

Acquisition Editor
Neha Nagwekar

Content Development Editor
Shaon Basu

Technical Editor
Manal Pednekar

Copy Editors
Sarang Chari
Mradula Hegde
Gladson Monteiro
Alfida Paiva
Adithi Shetty

Project Coordinator
Sanghamitra Deb

Proofreaders
Simran Bhogal
Stephen Copestake
Linda Morris

Indexer
Rekha Nair

Production Coordinators
Manu Joseph
Conidon Miranda
Alwin Roy
Nitesh Thakur

Cover Work
Manu Joseph

About the Author

Rich Helton is the Principal Software Engineer at the Colorado Department of Labor and Employment (CDLE) in their IT office. He works on several projects, such as Unemployment Insurance's WyCAN (Wyoming-Colorado-Arizona-North Dakota) and CDLE's Internet Self-Service (ISS). He has spent time as a technical manager, as an information security officer, and an enterprise services manager for the state. Rich has an experience of more than 2 decades in building large-scale enterprise systems, working as the principal architect for a customer list that includes ADP, Jeppesen, J.B. Hunt, Schneider Logistics, US West, DCN, and many more. He has implemented Java and C# projects since these languages were in beta, and he has built many projects in frameworks to include Spring, ORMs, NoSQL, and multiple ESB frameworks since their beginning.

He has several patents in the field of mobile video from when he was the VP of Technology of Digital Camera Networks. He holds many certifications in security and software development and a Master's degree in software. He has taught many software and application security classes as a consultant in both the public and private sectors. He posts some of his classes on `http://www.slideshare.net/rhelton_1`. Rich has built many monitoring systems, network tools, and mobile tools for decades as an independent consultant to include C# system tools and Java Android applications.

I would like to thank the ongoing support of my wife, Johennie, and my daughters, Ashley and Courtney.

About the Reviewers

Andrew Church is a senior software engineer and alumni of the Rochester Institute of Technology. Andrew has 5 years of experience working on enterprise-distributed systems for large companies, including a large retailer, as well as product systems for small start-ups. Andrew has also spent time in product development and innovation for a start-up in Rochester, NY.

I would like to acknowledge my parents for always telling me that I could do anything that I set out to do. I would also like to acknowledge my best friend, my wife Taylor, whose unwavering support for all of my crazy ambitions is nothing but inspiring.

Eben Roux has been an IT professional since 1995 and has acted as a developer, consultant, and architect within many industries. He has also provided strategies and solutions that have contributed to the successful implementation of various systems, which includes an NServiceBus solution for an insurance firm.

He is the owner of the free open source Shuttle Service Bus project and believes firmly in the development of quality software that empowers users to get their job done.

Having come from a Visual Basic background, Eben first became a Microsoft Certified Professional in 1998, and by 2003, had completed three Microsoft Certified Solution Developer certifications (VB5, VB6, and VB.NET). Since moving exclusively to C# development in 2007, he has focused on a domain-driven design implemented within an event-driven architecture based on message-oriented middleware.

Eben can be contacted at `me@ebenroux.co.za` or via his blog at `www.ebenroux.co.za`.

I would like to thank my wife, Amanda, and our sons, Reynard and Reynier, for allowing me to contribute to the community.

www.PacktPub.com

Support files, eBooks, discount offers, and more

You might want to visit www.PacktPub.com for support files and downloads related to your book.

Did you know that Packt offers eBook versions of every book published, with PDF and ePub files available? You can upgrade to the eBook version at www.PacktPub.com and as a print book customer, you are entitled to a discount on the eBook copy. Get in touch with us at service@packtpub.com for more details.

At www.PacktPub.com, you can also read a collection of free technical articles, sign up for a range of free newsletters and receive exclusive discounts and offers on Packt books and eBooks.

http://PacktLib.PacktPub.com

Do you need instant solutions to your IT questions? PacktLib is Packt's online digital book library. Here, you can access, read and search across Packt's entire library of books.

Why subscribe?

- Fully searchable across every book published by Packt
- Copy and paste, print and bookmark content
- On demand and accessible via web browser

Free access for Packt account holders

If you have an account with Packt at www.PacktPub.com, you can use this to access PacktLib today and view nine entirely free books. Simply use your login credentials for immediate access.

Instant updates on new Packt books

Get notified! Find out when new books are published by following @PacktEnterprise on Twitter, or the *Packt Enterprise* Facebook page.

Table of Contents

Preface

Starting with the basics of NServiceBus (NSB), this book will provide you with all the skills you need to successfully design, develop, and architect C# enterprise systems with NSB. We will walk through many enterprise NSB scenarios with different persistence models. Some of these enterprise solutions will include additional frameworks, such as Model-View-Controller, Entity Frameworks, NHibernate, SFTP, and WCF. There will be discussions on MongoDB, RavenDB, and NHibernate as they relate to NSB. The Particular Service Platform, including ServiceControl, ServicePulse, and ServiceInsight, will be discussed at length with examples.

You will be taken through IBus characteristics, followed by the Persistent and NServiceBus saga architectures. You will get to know about the basics of persistence and the supporting frameworks for persistence, followed by SQL queuing and database logging. This will be followed by an in-depth look at the saga architecture, covering the mechanics, message mapping, and internal configuration, as well as tips on how to avoid certain common errors.

We will discuss how NSB provides an enhanced quality of software through the use of security, logging, monitoring, notification, and persisting objects and messages. There will be many examples. We will end the book with future enhancements to NSB, how NSB is part of the cloud space, and how it finds itself in use in the mobile world.

What this book covers

Chapter 1, NServiceBus Persistence Introduction, will discuss NSB and the basic persistence design pattern it uses, which include the sagas, gateways, subscriptions, messages, and timeout design patterns. We will also discuss the benefits of using NSB, and what it brings to the table in terms of software design.

Chapter 2, The *NServiceBus Architecture*, will focus on the NServiceBus architecture. We will also discuss the different message and storage types supported in NSB. This discussion will include an introduction to some of the tools and advantages of using NSB as we conceptually look at how some of the pieces fit together. We will back up the discussions with code examples.

Chapter 3, *Particular Service Platform*, will focus on Particular Service Platform that includes ServicePulse, ServiceControl, ServiceInsight, and ServiceMatrix. As the name implies, ServicePulse gives us a pulse on the messages, services, and endpoints. ServiceControl is the control API that ServicePulse and ServiceInsight depend on to get their internal information. ServiceInsight gives us graphical and message-level drilldown into the services, endpoints, and messages that also include a saga drilldown. ServiceMatrix is the graphical interface into code generation for NServiceBus endpoints, services, and messages in a Visual Studio canvas.

Chapter 4, *Knowing Your IBus*, will discuss various configurations and examples of the NSB IBus. In Enterprise Service Bus (ESB), the bus is the backbone of the sagas, subscriptions, sending, timeouts, and gateways. For NServiceBus, the bus interface is known as the IBus. Knowing your IBus is the most important part of NServiceBus.

Chapter 5, *Persistence Architecture*, will cover persisting items to the database, including messages and logging. For the ESB bus, persistence is the key element for the storing of messages, which could be associated as business objects that run through the ESB workflow. The metadata comprises other persistent elements that define how the messages and workflow are being handled in the ESB through configuration. Persistence can also be considered the feedback that the ESB gives back to the system in the form of logging, errors, and audits.

Chapter 6, *SQL Server Examples*, will focus on snippets about SQL Server examples. We will discuss queuing in SQL Server. More advanced features for Entity Framework will be discussed, as will MVC-EF examples. This chapter is for developers who are working with SQL Server and Entity Frameworks with NServiceBus.

Chapter 7, *Persistent Snippets*, will focus on snippets about persistence. We will discuss NHibernate, RavenDB, and MongoDB. We will dive into code to accomplish some database tasks related to NServiceBus. This code could be applied to many tasks that are not ESB-specific. But this is a much needed chapter on database code itself. We will create SQL Server databases without the use of SQL code and read tables that NServiceBus created in RavenDB. We will show how to create tables with code, read tables, and display tables in NHibernate and RavenDB.

Chapter 8, The NSB Cloud, will focus on snippets about NServiceBus in the Azure cloud after an introduction to various components about the Azure cloud services. NSB has a lot of support for the Azure cloud. Be it SQL Storage, Azure Queues, or the Azure Service Bus, NSB is headed in a direction of working more with Cloud Services. We will briefly discuss Salesforce and even NSB integration into mobile devices.

What you need for this book

Beginner-level knowledge of Visual Studio 2012 with C# will be required. This could be the Visual Studio 2012 Express Edition from Microsoft.

Who this book is for

This book is for any person who wishes to develop, design, or architect NServiceBus's ESB systems in C# as a possible solution. We discuss many items that go beyond NSB, such as MVC-EF frameworks and databases such as RavenDB, SQL Server, and MongoDB.

Conventions

In this book, you will find a number of styles of text that distinguish between different kinds of information. Here are some examples of these styles, and an explanation of their meaning.

Code words in text, database table names, folder names, filenames, file extensions, pathnames, dummy URLs, user input, and Twitter handles are shown as follows: "First, run the `Install` commands for the pieces that are accomplished in PowerShell commandlets."

A block of code is set as follows:

```
using System;
using System.IO;
using ServiceControl.Plugin.CustomChecks;
using ServiceControl.Plugin.CustomChecks.Messages;
using ServiceControl.Plugin.CustomChecks.Internal;
namespace PaymentEngine.ECommerce
```

```
{
    public class MyCustomCheck : CustomCheck
    {
        public MyCustomCheck()
            : base("ECommerce SubmitPayment check", "ECommerce")
        {
            ReportPass();
        }
    }}
```

Any command-line input or output is written as follows:

```
"PM> Get-NserviceBusLocalMachineSettings"
```

New terms and **important words** are shown in bold. Words that you see on the screen, in menus or dialog boxes for example, appear in the text like this: "Go to the **Component Services** option under the **Administrative Tools** menu."

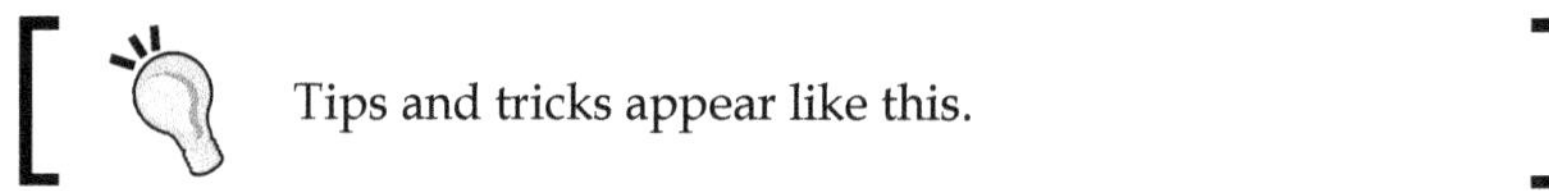

Tips and tricks appear like this.

Reader feedback

Feedback from our readers is always welcome. Let us know what you think about this book—what you liked or may have disliked. Reader feedback is important for us to develop titles that you really get the most out of.

To send us general feedback, simply send an e-mail to `feedback@packtpub.com`, and mention the book title through the subject of your message.

If there is a topic that you have expertise in and you are interested in either writing or contributing to a book, see our author guide on `www.packtpub.com/authors`.

Customer support

Now that you are the proud owner of a Packt book, we have a number of things to help you to get the most from your purchase.

Downloading the example code

You can download the example code files for all Packt books you have purchased from your account at `http://www.packtpub.com`. If you purchased this book elsewhere, you can `http://www.packtpub.com/support` and register to have the files e-mailed directly to you.

Errata

Although we have taken every care to ensure the accuracy of our content, mistakes do happen. If you find a mistake in one of our books—maybe a mistake in the text or the code—we would be grateful if you would report this to us. By doing so, you can save other readers from frustration and help us improve subsequent versions of this book. If you find any errata, please report them by visiting `http://www.packtpub.com/support`, selecting your book, clicking on the **errata submission form** link, and entering the details of your errata. Once your errata are verified, your submission will be accepted and the errata will be uploaded to our website, or added to any list of existing errata, under the Errata section of that title.

Piracy

Piracy of copyright material on the Internet is an ongoing problem across all media. At Packt, we take the protection of our copyright and licenses very seriously. If you come across any illegal copies of our works, in any form, on the Internet, please provide us with the location address or website name immediately so that we can pursue a remedy.

Please contact us at `copyright@packtpub.com` with a link to the suspected pirated material.

We appreciate your help in protecting our authors, and our ability to bring you valuable content.

Questions

You can contact us at `questions@packtpub.com` if you are having a problem with any aspect of the book, and we will do our best to address it.

Downloading the example code

[illegible]

1
NServiceBus Persistence Introduction

In this chapter, we will discuss **NServiceBus** (**NSB**) and the basic persistence design pattern it uses, which includes the saga, gateway, subscription, messages, and timeout design patterns. We will also discuss the benefits of using NSB and what it brings to the table in software design. Finally, we will discuss the following topics:

- Introduction to SOA
    - The need for metadata
    - The need for persistence patterns
    - The need for enterprise frameworks
    - Fallacies of distributed computing
    - The need for sagas
    - A real-life saga
- Beginning an NServiceBus saga
- Beginning NServiceBus assemblies

Introduction to SOA

Service Oriented Architecture (**SOA**) is a very important architectural concept (`http://en.wikipedia.org/wiki/Service-oriented_architecture`). To understand what services it brings to the table, we bring up the four tenets of services, also known as the Principles of Service Oriented Design (for more details refer to `http://msdn.microsoft.com/en-us/library/bb972954.aspx`). They are **autonomous, boundaries, share schema and class**, and **compatibility**.

- **Autonomous**: Services are autonomous; this means that each individual service takes care of its own self-contained life cycle independent of other services, and changing a particular service will not have any side effects on other services.
- **Boundaries**: Boundaries to services are explicit. There are distinct entry and exit points for messaging; it is well defined where these points are in the service.
- **Share schema and class**: Services share schema and contract, but not their classes. This means that the internals of the services are not exposed. Again, the messaging interface is defined, but the internals of what is going on are not exposed across the platform. This adds a layer of abstraction to services that define a business requirement, say an order service, without having to go into every detail of the business.
- **Compatibility**: A service's compatibility is based on its policy. The policy defines the nonfunctional requirements of what the service must conform to while it is being produced. For example, what is the level of encryption, maintenance, and effort required? For instance, in an order service, what data needs to be saved to the disk, what data needs to be encrypted, and what is the level of fault tolerance of the service?

A simple example comes from ordering websites that need to send payments to third-party servers to receive the payment. Assume a pizza-ordering site; there are a number of issues that may occur at the time of credit card processing, which include insufficient funds as well as network and connectivity issues. If SOA or ESB is not used, the customer may be asked not to refresh the page. This is required so that the payment request is sent to the third-party processing server, and the customer may even receive a network error. When an error is received, the customer is asked to retry again.

There are many major ordering websites that function in this way today. As a customer, some of the concerns include the integrity of how a website handles orders since it requires customer validation and intervention to process payments. Even ensuring that a page does not refresh relies on the customer, which makes the site less appealing in comparison to those that do not require customer intervention for issues the customer does not need to be made aware of.

Instead, the responsibility to ensure the funds are processed should be on the system rather than on the customer. Of course, in order for a website to take on the responsibility of firing off the message to an SOA, there has to be an SOA in place to take on the responsibility of processing the message for the payment.

While developing an SOA or ServiceBus system, many software architects consider starting it from scratch. However, they soon realize that there are many unstated requirements that are expected to be incorporated. These requirements assume a specific behavior and do not explicitly call them out. It is a given fact that a good design takes these non-business functional requirements into account.

Some examples of these requirements include second-level retries for when a credit card isn't processed the first time. When this happens, the system stores the messages along the way; keeps track of the state of the services; and integrates into other company systems network errors, the encryption of the credit card number, and the access control level that different users and systems may need.

These requirements become complex quickly, as the following diagram implies. It may take years to resolve some of the issues but most of the time, the business allocates months rather than years to address them. In order to resolve these non-business functional requirements and to address the associated issues that may arise, it is best to study solutions that other architects have provided for similar situations.

For instance, use a ServiceBus product such as NServiceBus as a guide to performance-enhanced products with built-in message reliability and integrity.

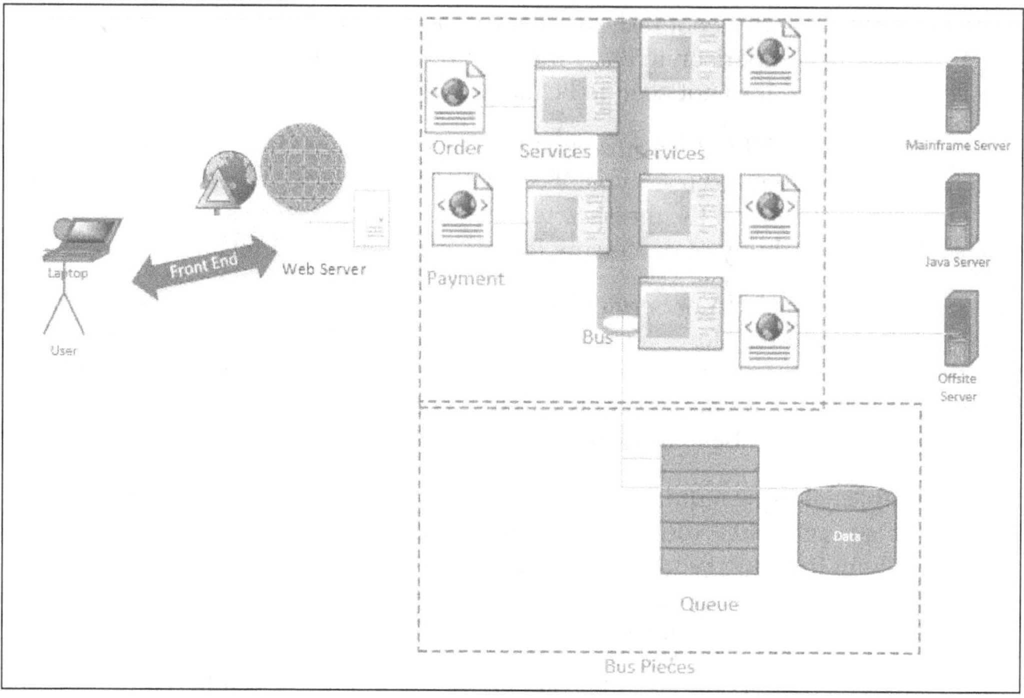

Continuing with the order system for a pizza establishment, the website would process the order and hand off the message to ServiceBus to process the payment. Then, the system takes the ownership of the payment message instead of relying on the customer.

The messages need to accommodate the partner's systems. However, the bus handles data and queues internally and saves the state, messages, and objects if something goes wrong. This is important since payments affect the bottom line, and the company has a business need to keep track of its payments.

The hand-off of messaging allows a customer to continue to the next action or website page. The payment response is later processed as the system takes on the responsibility for the payment.

The messages are sent between services as autonomous tasks, and the messages need to be made durable, scalable, reliable, secure, transactional, and capable of being distributed among different systems. This backbone, the pieces as a whole, is by definition an **Enterprise Service Bus** (**ESB**). ESB is simply a common bus across the enterprise, with the preceding characteristics (durable, scalable, reliable, secure, transactional, and distributable).

A saga is a mechanism that evolved in ESBs to save the state of messages. A saga also keeps track of the originating message's endpoints so that it can respond to the originator with changes to the message.

Just as an accountant must keep track of receivable payments and orders in a company, so must a company's systems—record keeping is of paramount concern. Once a user creates an account, they become a customer; as a customer, they assume that the company protects their information, unless told otherwise.

Throughout history, many companies that are no longer in existence neither protected users' data, nor adequately kept track of payments and orders. Security and sales are an overall concern in the industry. A company's main goal is to make more money than it spends, which includes keeping track of the company's data. Losing sales and data can be expensive. Reporting where data is and its current state (be it a sale or customer's data) is important. Therefore, of course, it is better to have a system that never has an issue. Though, if a system has an issue (such as losing data or funds), it is best to know the magnitude of the issue and as much information as possible. Therefore, when building payment engines, it is not uncommon to require daily reports of dollar totals, the number of successes or failures, reasons for failures, root cause of failures, and more.

In order to provide such reports, there needs to be an end-to-end tracking of messages. A message is nothing more than a piece of data that travels through a system as the system completes a transaction.

A transaction is a completed unit of work, such as completing a payment. A message can be saved after a transaction is completed in order to keep a record and be able to provide feedback on what happened through the workflow.

A workflow is the end-to-end processing of transactions as the message moves through the system to complete its life cycle. During a message's life cycle, some data may be mutated. An example is payment in part or additional fees. The system uses the message's metadata to determine how the message moves through the workflow.

Metadata is information about the message itself, such as a message ID or header information. Header information is used to keep information that may show, for instance, the originating system and destination.

A saga uses a message ID to save and lookup the state of the message at a given point using the originator of the message to respond, with the status of the message, to the originator.

All of the previous work is performed in order to do reporting; also, instead of creating a solution from the ground up, NServiceBus is built explicitly to simplify and assist with the amount of work within a system. NServiceBus uses queuing to pass messages to other services, such as MSMQ, which includes error queues and audit queues.

For example, a simple report may be there to send a daily message of how many messages were sent to the error queue. Since messages can be created in XML, there could be an error field to be easily parsed out for error details. However, in no way does this replace logging.

Products such as ServicePulse and other reporting mechanisms are used to assist in giving reports of the company's messages and data. This simple example could be expanded to send messages that contain payments above a threshold ($100 for instance) to one queue and under the threshold to a different queue. A report could be made daily based on timestamps. Since sagas are saved in databases before a message is completed, another report could be generated to report on all the payments over $100 that are not processed.

There are many ways to provide reports of messages, and because sagas and queues are used, it can be drilled down to very detailed information. It is obvious that there is extensive work to be done to create and implement a solution from scratch.

The need for metadata

During the course of building enterprise systems, there are functional and nonfunctional requirements. Functional requirements describe the business rules, and nonfunctional requirements are system characteristics with non-business rules. A simple nonfunctional requirement for a system is, for instance, that any SSN must be encrypted both at rest and in-transient states. Nonfunctional requirements simply go beyond security requirements; nonfunctional requirements include notifications, alerts, monitoring, logging, and other software qualities.

Nonfunctional requirements include many of the components that make up software quality `http://en.wikipedia.org/wiki/Software_quality`. Software quality includes some of the software characteristics already mentioned, such as maintainability, security, code quality, reliability, integrity, and so on. Software quality is the ideal state for software to achieve; nonfunctional requirements form the specifics of how to achieve certain pieces.

The problem is that, while business requirements may be clearly spelled out, nonfunctional requirements may not be defined clearly or negotiated enough ahead of time. Therefore, tweaks are required along the way during the application life cycle, including development or maintenance. Metadata and precreated frameworks are the key players of this tweaking.

Consider an administration application that **business analysts** (**BAs**) and operational teams use to check the current state of an enterprise application. The application takes orders for aircraft maps and equipment, and **customer service representatives** (**CSRs**) have an interface for working with the customers and changing their data at will. Operations use an administration application to monitor the end-to-end throughput from a browser to a database and receive notifications if the levels are not achieved.

In the previous example, notifications and monitoring are nonfunctional requirements. BAs may use the administration application to handle special customer cases and monitor the number of orders, customers, and other reports. The generation of the reports, the data for monitoring, is based on the business data and generates metadata. This metadata is used to check the business data.

The following is a common 3-tier diagram for an application that gathers sales information:

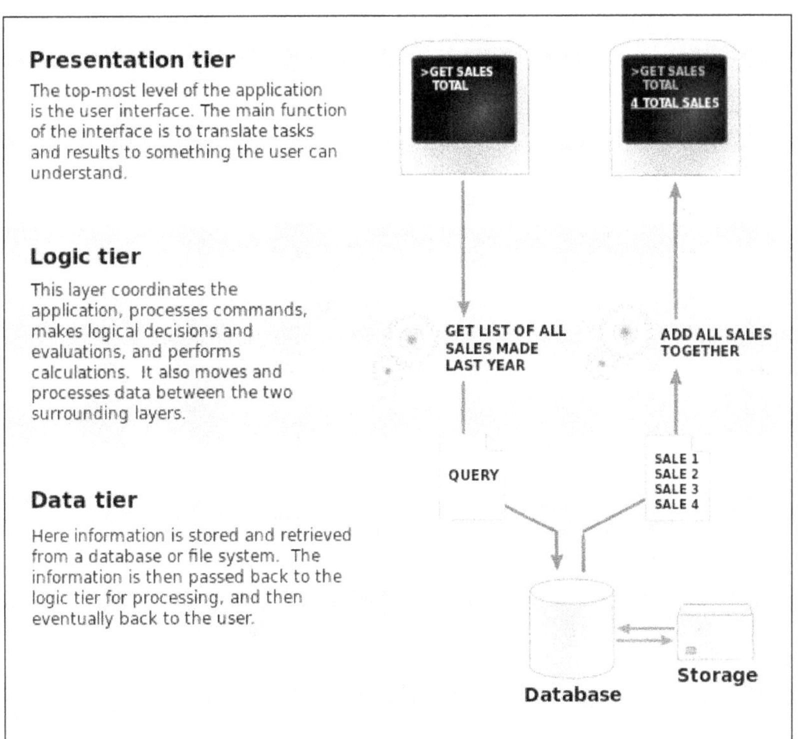

The application has a frontend, a logic tier (middle tier), and a data tier. So far, this is a very common design for an application. The frontend is done in HTML or ASP.NET to control the presentation layer in a browser. The logic tier contains the workflow and messaging to handle business logic. Finally, the data tier is the storage to hold the information in a persisted repository—usually a database, mainframe, file I/O, or third-party server among other options.

When you look at this basic application, you'll realize that many endpoints are missing. These endpoints are used to monitor the application, to log the application, and perform other operational and administration tasks previously mentioned. Therefore, this model is incomplete since it does not address nonfunctional requirements.

Many software projects seem to need continuous enhancements because the developer keeps on adding components for security, operational reports, and other application characteristics that were not mentioned in the list of business requirements, even though they are components required to ensure the integrity of the application itself.

The need for persistence patterns

To paraphrase what's written in `http://en.wikipedia.org/wiki/Service_oriented_architecture`, the idea behind **Service-oriented Architecture** (**SOA**) is to decouple the end-to-end application functionality between discreet services.

So far, we have discussed sagas and some metadata of applications. There are other types of data that are saved to the data store, including business objects that contain the information used for business rules. Business rules run the business engines and are used to execute business logic.

In the ESB world, the bus transports (moves) objects that could be considered business objects; these business objects move through sagas. These objects are the pieces of NSBs that are used for notifications, timeouts, gateways for message distribution, **Second-level Retries** (**SLRs**), and even endpoints to where the messages are sent.

The preceding objects make up many of the application metadata. Many of these are the configurations of the services that make up the distribution of the messages and the behavior of the transactions. The metadata that NSB keeps track of during a publish-subscribe message pattern is the same subscription information required for NSB to keep track of the publish-subscribe endpoints. The subscription information is needed for the subscribers to keep track of the message types and queue endpoints. This is needed to subscribe to the publishers. NSB uses the database to keep track of these types of endpoints.

A small table of what is available can be seen at `http://docs.particular.net/nservicebus/persistence-in-nservicebus`.

	InMemory	RavenDB	NHibernate	MSMQ
Timeout	√	√	√	Not supported begining version 3.3,0
Subscription	√	√	√	√
Saga	√	√	√	
Gateway	√	√	√	
Distributor			√	√
Second Level Retry				√
Fault Management	√			√
Notifications				√

The persistence configurations are just some of the typical ESB service configurations in NSB. There are many more configurations as NSB is meant to do so much more as a complete automation framework for the middleware. We will be discussing the various features and their associated configurations on the bus called IBus throughout this book.

Through this table, we know that the timeout for sagas, the saga object itself, the subscription information for publish-subscribe, the second-level retries, the fault management, notification, the gateway, and distributor can be supported in MSMQ. Some of these pieces can be stored in the local memory of the host application; it cannot be saved when the application is not running. Pieces can be saved in the RavenDB database, which is a NoSQL document-oriented database. Pieces can also be saved using the NHibernate database connecter, which is an ORM mapper to various relational databases, such as SQL Server, MySQL, and Oracle. Some of the items have been referred to as data, which is data that describes the messages versus the messages themselves that will be part of the ESB workflow. The workflow itself makes up the business logic, while the messages themselves could be considered as business objects.

The benefit of NServiceBus is that it will handle the persisting of the object's messages and various pieces for the developer, as long as the developer has configured NSB correctly.

For instance, when using NHibernate, NSB will perform the mapping of the messages to the relational database, and the developer does not have to configure the NHibernate-mapping properties to map the objects to the relational database. This saves the developer a lot of time and effort. The messages themselves can also be persisted through various means using the settings for using the transport in IBus configurations. These message queues include MSMQ, Azure queues, SQL Server queues, ActiveMQ, and RabbitMQ.

Fallacies of distributed computing

Many books are written on just various troubleshooting issues over networks and servers. There are many issues that come up in operations and maintenance that were never conceived as potential issues, anywhere from intermittent routers due to a power cord not being plugged in all the way, patches that left the servers in a hung state, DNS errors from a domain controller, and so on. There is no guarantee that the networks, or servers, are secure, remain unchanged, and all the routes remain reliable for the application that was built. Not having to deal with these abnormal issues by having someone else deal with the uptime issues is what makes cloud computing so attractive. In many enterprise applications, as in this usage, we discuss where uptime is critical, and where it is normal to have to code, notification, and monitoring, for failure along every step of the way between services and clients. There are many assumptions that we can make, including the one that it is someone else's concern; however, in the end, it becomes a piece of the application's responsibility to describe how it is working.

Because the network may not be reliable, there may be a changeover in staff and servers. The need for persistent enterprise objects, such as bus technology and persistent messaging, has evolved. Also, the need for instrumentation has grown to track the messages and objects. Not knowing where payments and orders are in a system can be bad for any organization that needs to track them. In the end, the data that runs through applications is owned by the organization; if it is hacked, if financial data is lost, or if employees are not paid, it is their responsibility, rather than considering that it lives in the cloud or it is the fault of a bad network or any other condition. Because of this need for reporting on the systems, there is a need for metadata, which is just another form of persisting the company's data, except for business data such as a customer's address. Metadata is a form of reporting data, such as the current state of a message or if there was an error with a message reaching its endpoint. It is a snapshot in the organization's operations of applications. Sometimes these snapshots are very important; in many cases, where money and personal identifying information are involved, they are used to provide information, even to courts, on what happened when the money goes missing. We will start on this journey of running through the designing of systems with a common SOA design pattern called saga that will assist us in providing these pieces discussed thus far.

The need for sagas

A saga is a design pattern that was originally coined in a paper by Hector Garcia-Molina in 1987, `http://www.amundsen.com/downloads/sagas.pdf`. To quote a piece:

> *"A long-lived transaction (LLT) is a saga if it can be written as a sequence of transaction that can be interleaved with other transactions."*

In Arnon Rotem-Gal-Oz's book on SOA Patterns, page 137 says:

> *"Sagas are a way for services to reach distributed consensus without relying on distributed transactions."*

It is expressed by many references that sagas may be built differently, depending on the need.

A saga pattern is supported by NServiceBus; for more information see `http://docs.particular.net/nservicebus/sagas-in-nservicebus`. A saga handles the persisting of pieces of messages as part of an ESB. During a workflow of messages, a message is sent to a saga; the saga persists the needed data and responds to the original client with messages. A saga itself is a data object with an ID, getters, and setters. As messages are passed back and forth between services, the saga is an intermediate to save valuable data. The data are message parts.

The messages of a service bus are persisted by nature and can be replayed when there is an issue with the delivery of the message with the endpoint; however, the saga keeps track of the originator and can store other data to be associated with the original message. This updated data, which is defined by the developer, may be the state of the message, the session information related to the message, or any other data needed by the application. The saga correlates messages it receives, synchronizes the activity using the corresponding ID, and deals with other features such as timeouts and lookups.

The saga evolves in the ServiceBus architecture as a pattern; it is discussed in greater detail in the next chapters.

Many common frameworks such as Microsoft MVC and EF are designed for business requirements only, with additional frameworks to assist in nonfunctional requirements; this point is stressed throughout this book. Also, we emphasize the concept of ServiceBus.

ServiceBus is a messaging workflow; it stores messages along the way. It is a workflow since it incorporates both business and nonfunctional requirements. ServiceBus does have transactional persistence to perform second-level retries if there is an error in the server or the network. The saga pattern extends that concept by giving feedback to services along the way to the originator and timing out messages. Also, it provides feedback on which operations business analysts and CSRs normally require to perform day-to-day operations. This information is used to correct issues that are of interest to the business. Remember that the saga pattern is a framework that is easily extensible, and so it is not a stress to use it for more than just retries.

A real-life saga

NServiceBus simplifies the implementation of the concepts in the previous section; the following is a real-life scenario to illustrate them and multiple services that communicate with each other.

Recall the pizza-ordering example we discussed earlier where the **Please do not refresh the page and wait for the order to complete** message is displayed when a user places an order. We discussed the concern that the user may have doubts about whether the order is completed, and there is the implication that a browser refresh could cause order issues. Obviously, an ASP or JSP web page waits for some web service to go out and charge my card as it waits for the result. To avoid this behavior, a better solution is needed. One such solution is a workflow for passing messages around so that the system fires off a transaction to process the payments, allowing user interaction to continue; eventually, the system is to receive an update once the payment is processed.

There are a few possible solutions for the preceding example, and all of them have one thing in common: combining a workflow with a middle layer simplifies the solution.

One possible solution is to have several services that are responsible for different actions. We need to save data entered by a user to a database; this can be accomplished via some backend services. These services handle all the transactions needed. A service, say Service1, can pick up the data and pass it into a MSMQ for processing. This provides the separation of knowing which messages are in the state of processing. Another service, say Service2, can be responsible for the interaction with a payment engine.

Continuing with the pizza-ordering example, Service1 is responsible for getting the data entered by the customer and Service2 is responsible for processing the credit card payment. If there are errors with the payment engine, Service2 and the ServiceBus have the logic to retry again. However, Service1 remains unaware that there are errors with the payment. Service2 is atomic and does not provide notifications and feedback to the user. The payment service may place the error in an error queue, but some information, such as why the payment was not processed, will remain missing.

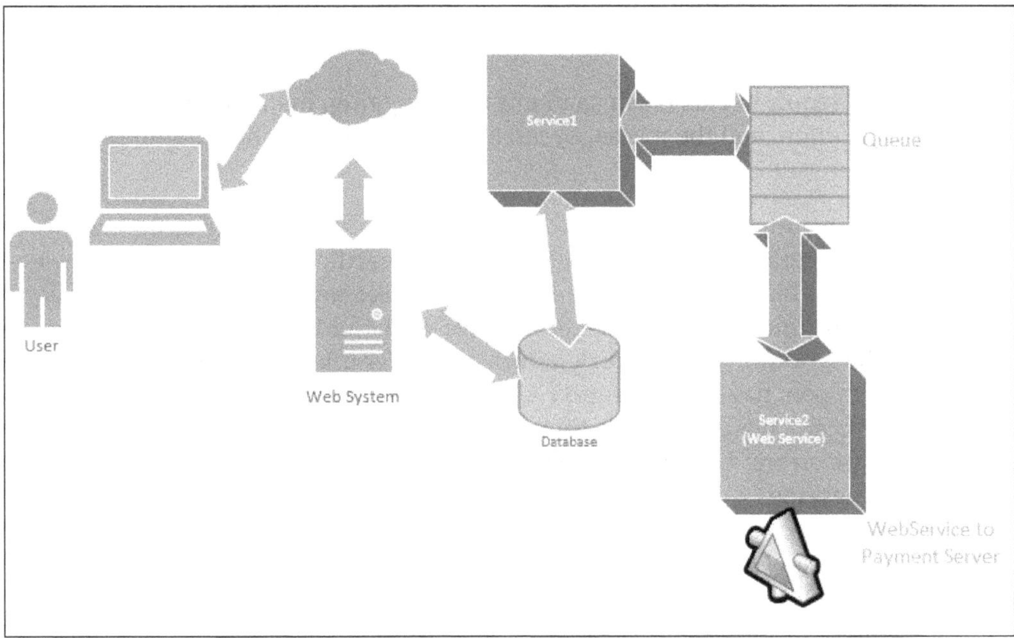

Using the saga pattern provides many of the features that are currently missing in the solution presented thus far. The saga is the end-to-end message workflow that can be used to save the state in an intermediate process. This can be accomplished by saving an intermediate saga data object. This persistence typically is done to a database and looked up when the same message is passed back through. Sagas can get complicated but, because very little code is required—since the ServiceBus handles most of the work—sagas can be simple to use.

As hinted previously, a saga can be created as an intermediate between the services to keep the client, in our example Service1, informed about the progress of the message.

The saga can update other endpoints of the message status and change the message if it needs updating as it moves through the workflow. The important piece of a saga is the one-to-one lookup of the data related to the message and the message itself. This allows the workflow to follow a message's progress and know where it is at a given moment along multiple services. We could define a timer to fail the message if it continually errors out, since we don't want messages to live forever.

Returning back to the pizza-ordering example, instead of waiting and not refreshing the page, we can create a page where the user can go to and check the status as the order progresses through the ServiceBus workflow. Notice that this allows many nonfunctional requirements to be addressed.

Nonfunctional requirements (such as monitoring, logging, manual retries, timeouts, checking encryption, and the message) can be addressed by monitoring the services and messages.

To recap, we can address the payment engine errors by adding logic to the saga to notify the user, operations, and the organization of specific errors. For instance, we could add logic to the saga to send an e-mail to the user saying that the order was denied due to insufficient funds. In addition, we could add another error-checking option into the workflow for network failure and other unexpected events. When such events happen, have a notification sent to operations stating that the payment engine server is not available at this time. Notice that the user does not need to be notified of these errors. Therefore, the saga becomes the focal point for checking the status of the message.

Beginning an NServiceBus saga

As mentioned earlier, sagas are a design pattern. They are not unique to NServiceBus but are common in most enterprise service bus systems. There are many references to sagas, for instance, `http://vasters.com/clemensv/2012/09/01/Sagas.aspx` and `http://msdn.microsoft.com/en-us/library/jj591569.aspx`. These details are discussed in greater detail later. For now, we will expand on the payment engine example we have been exploring.

First, a saga in NServiceBus is always started and updated by a message.

Even when a timer is fired, a message is created. This timeout message is to be handled by the saga—refer to the following class diagram.

In the class diagram, there is message that starts the saga container from Service1; this means that the message is originated from the service that communicates with the frontend. A saga data is created and saved to the database. This data may be retrieved when the message passes the saga again; this means that the data that was saved for a message from Service1 may be retrieved on the return trip from Service2. Therefore, when returning from the payment service, persisted data can be retrieved and the message can be updated with data that is not directly passed to the message.

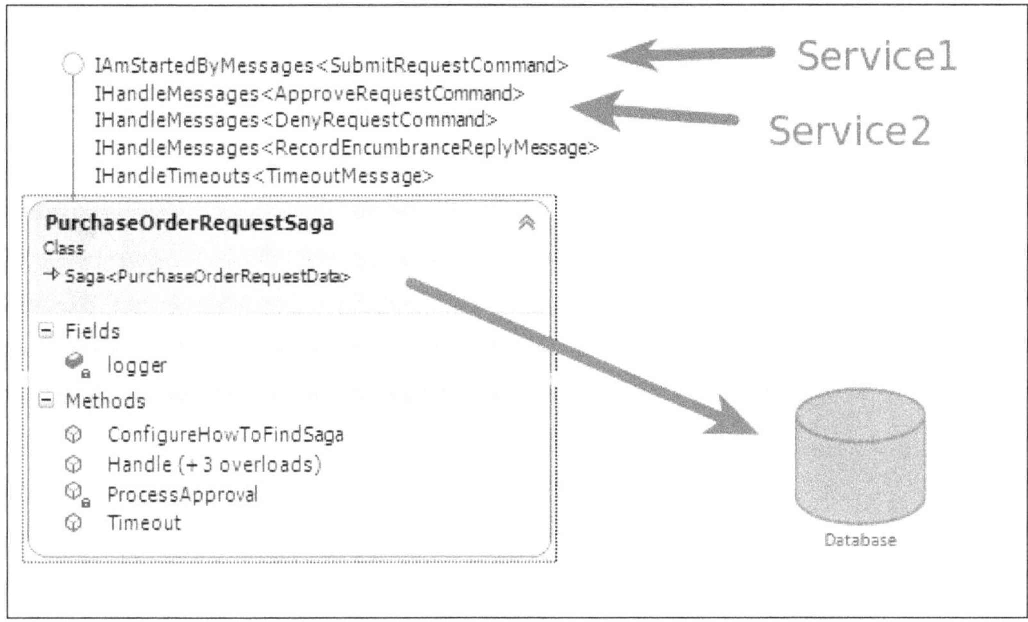

There is a lot of debate on how sagas are used, mostly relating to how sagas can be extended and used in multiple ways. However, the basics remain the same. A message starts a saga, a saga saves the data that is associated with the message, a saga handles other types of messages, a saga is able to lookup the original message that it started with, a saga is able to add data to the original message, and a saga routes messages to different destinations.

Beginning NServiceBus assemblies

You can start your first NServiceBus installation from Visual Studio. There are some preconditions that must be satisfied before NServiceBus is installed on the machine:

- **Install DTC**: **Distributed Transaction Coordinator** (DTC) is responsible for ensuring that the transaction is committed or rolled back in Microsoft technologies, such as SQL Server and MSMQ
- **Install MSMQ**: Microsoft Message Queuing (MSMQ is the messaging system for Microsoft operating systems
- **Install RavenDB**: RavenDB is a NoSQL document-oriented database that stores internal information for NServiceBus, such as the endpoint subscription information
- **Install performance counters**: The performance counters are calls into the Microsoft performance management system so that Microsoft operating systems can give performance reports on NServiceBus

Before setting up NServiceBus itself, vanilla NServiceBus makes a lot of use of MSMQ, DTC, RavenDB, and even performance counters to monitor NServiceBus's performance.

We will need to install the PowerShell commandlets through Package Manager.

Many items can be managed in the Package Manager console program of Visual Studio, 2012. We will need a solution, and we can start by using the MSMQ solution from GitHub. It is available at `https://github.com/Particular/NServiceBus.Msmq.Samples/tree/master/VideoStore.Msmq`. We will need to install the various NserviceBus references by using NuGet, as in the following screenshot:

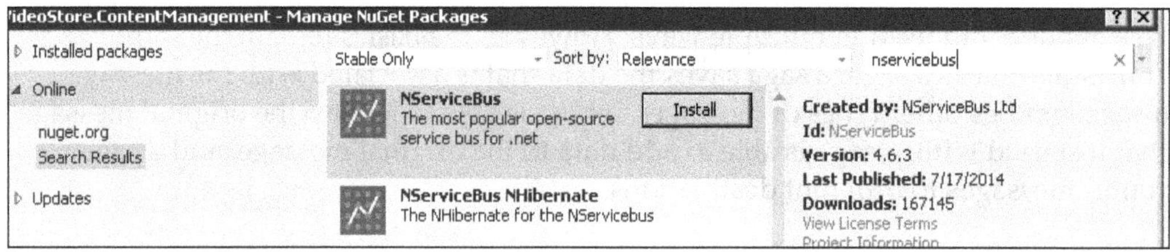

We need to make sure that the PowerShell commandlets are installed correctly first. We do this by using Package Manager:

- Install the package, `NServiceBus.PowerShell`
- Import the module, `.\packages\NServiceBus.PowerShell.4.3.0\lib\net40\NServiceBus.PowerShell.dll`
- Test `NServiceBusPerformanceCountersInstallation`

The "import module" step is dependent on where `NService.PowerShell.dll` was installed during the "install package" process. The "Install-package" command will add the `.dll` module into a package directory related to the solution. We can find out more on PowerShell commandlets at `http://docs.particular.net/nservicebus/managing-nservicebus-using-powershell` and even by reviewing the help section in Package Manager. Here, we see that we can insert configurations into the `App.config` file when we look at the help section, `PM> get-help about_NServiceBus`.

NServiceBus provides instructions for preparing your machine on `http://docs.particular.net/nservicebus/preparing-your-machine-to-run-nservicebus`. First, run the `Install` commands for the pieces that are accomplished in PowerShell commandlets.

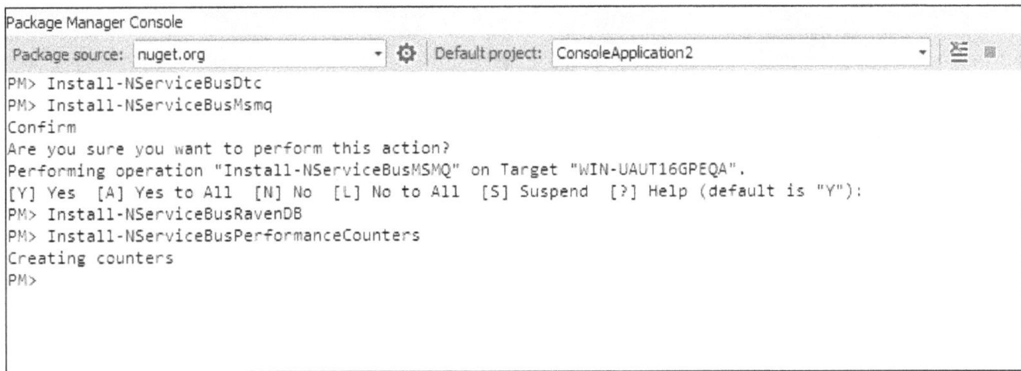

We can then run various `Test` commands to see whether the installations succeeded.

```
PM> Test-NServiceBusDTCInstallation
True
PM> Test-NServiceBusMSMQInstallation
True
PM> Test-NServiceBusRavenDBInstallation
True
PM> Test-NServiceBusPerformanceCountersInstallation
True
PM> |
```

This verifies that everything is set up correctly. I like using C# and NServiceBus because I can then use other products to verify the correctness. We can verify many pieces using services that come with Windows Server. These instructions will be specific to Windows-operating systems, and we will use the Windows 2008 server for these instructions. For instance, to verify that DTC is set up, we can check to see how it's set up:

1. Go to the **Component Services** option under the **Administrative Tools** menu.
2. Expand the **Computers** mode under the **Component Services** node.
3. Right-click on **Properties** and select the **MSDTC** tab.
4. Hit the **Security** configuration button, as shown in the following screenshot:

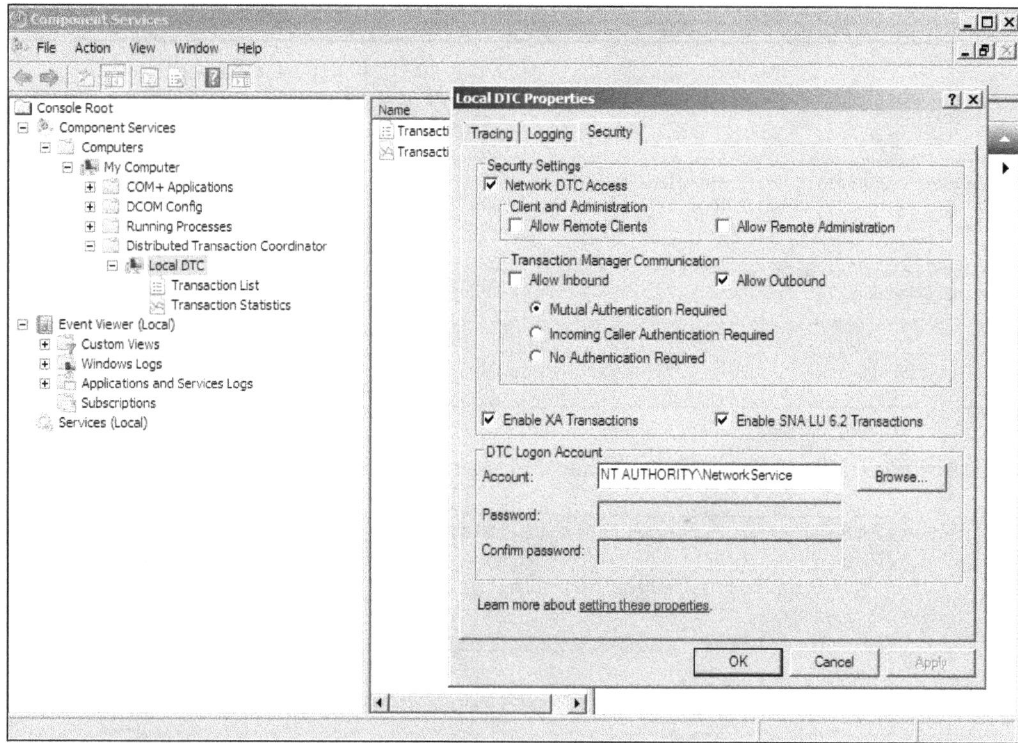

This way, there is verification from Windows Server's tools that DTC is configured. However, this does not mean that the firewall ports are open to ensure that DTC is in operation. For example, a firewall may block the interaction of the DTC protocol between machines.

Due to firewalls not being allowed to open up all the ports between machines, it is often a best practice to minimize the ports to run the transactions between ports 5000 and 6000. This can be done by setting the **Ports Ranges** value under **Component Service** | **My Computer** | **Default Protocols** | **Properties** to `5000-6000`.

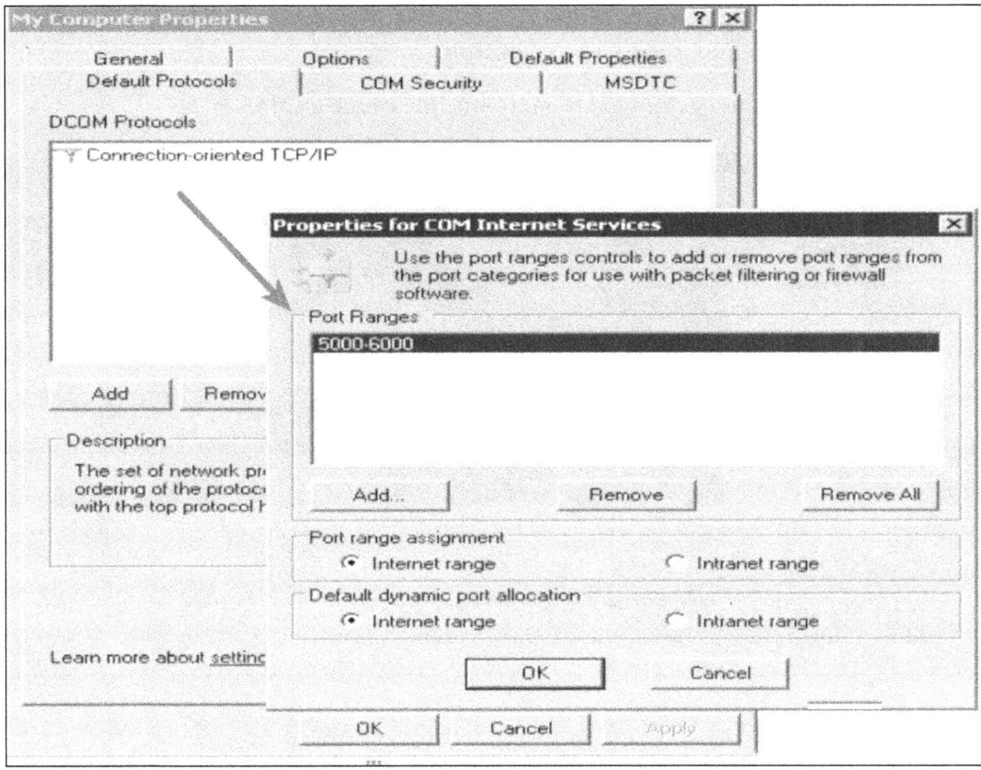

DTC can be used to verify that the system is working before running a program. Both machines have to be set up to run DTC, and there are many articles related to troubleshooting DTC, such as `http://blogs.msdn.com/b/distributedservices/archive/2008/11/12/troubleshooting-msdtc-issues-with-the-dtcping-tool.aspx` and `http://docs.particular.net/nservicebus/transactions-message-processing`. Note that DTC is very dependent on the protocols that run between machines and can cause many errors when not configured properly.

Even if we know that MSMQ is set up correctly (because we have tested it), we may need to know which queues it is currently using.

Using the PowerShell `PM> Get-NServiceBusLocalMachineSettings` command, we can see which queues it currently wishes to reference. Also, by viewing Visual Studio Server Explorer, we can verify that they are present.

One of the many features I really like about NServiceBus is its ability to create message queues, services, and DTC pieces. This is less work than what the server staff does to maintain and install an application.

Here is a look at the queues now in Visual Studio Server Explorer:

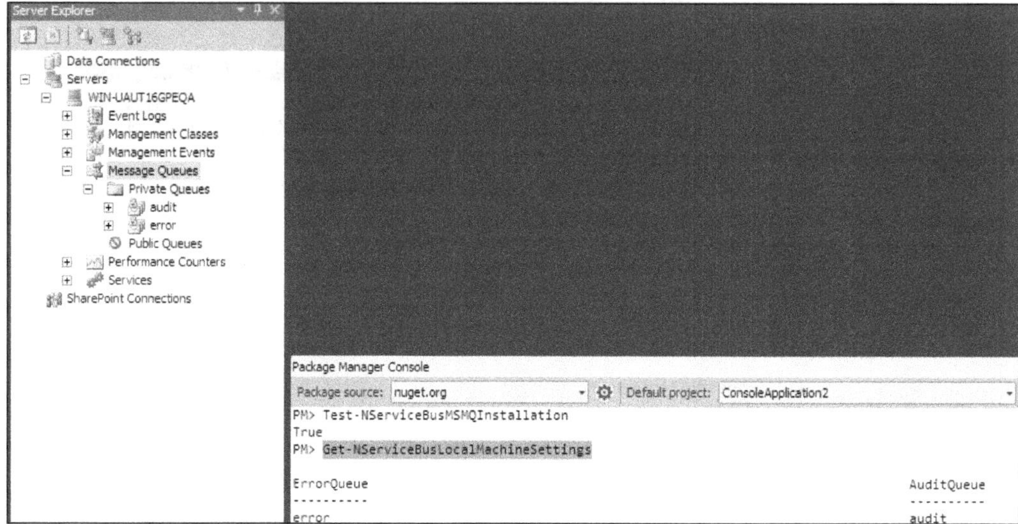

We can see the RavenDB service is running without even leaving Visual Studio by looking into the services section of the same Visual Studio Server Explorer in which it was installed.

RavenDB is a document-oriented database that can operate completely independent of NServiceBus. This means that you are now working on NoSQL development, and it has an interface to save the collections of objects.

RavenDB must be running as NServiceBus uses it to store internal information such as subscription endpoint information and message types. The following screenshot is of Server Explorer in Visual Studio and shows that RavenDB is running:

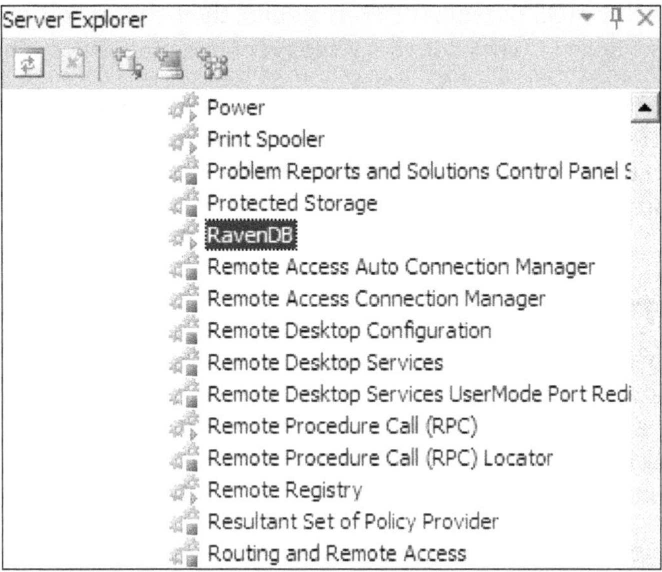

In addition, we can see that RavenDB is installed by its web interface. When running one of the NServiceBus video store examples, we can see that it creates associated tables in RavenDB for internal use. We can view it through the default port `8080` and access it using `http://localhost:8080/raven/studio.html`.

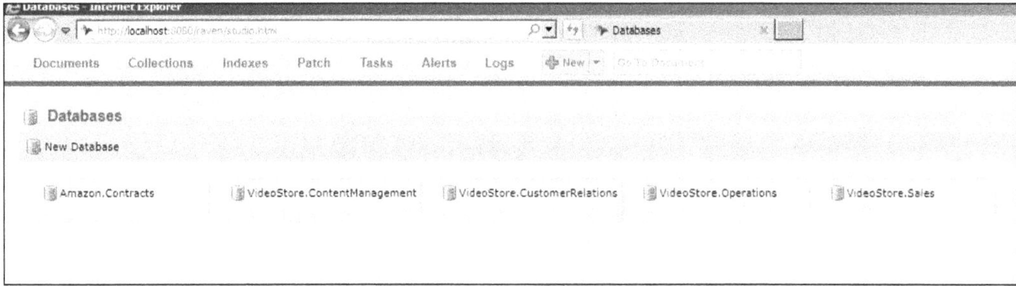

At this point, we have the basics to set up pieces that NServiceBus utilizes. We have a data store for sagas and another persistence, RavenDB. Also, we have queues in MSMQ that uses DTC to handle transactions. These are not the only options, but they are the default options for NServiceBus.

RavenDB, a NoSQL database, comes standard with NServiceBus as a persister for sagas and other NServiceBus controls. It is worth mentioning that the licensing of RavenDB is part of NServiceBus.

If you are to use RavenDB outside of NServiceBus, then you must license RavenDB for your own use: `http://ravendb.net/nservicebus-and-ravendb`.

An alternate solution to RavenDB is to use other databases, such as SQL Server, through an open source ORM connector (called NHibernate). This does not negate the need to have RavenDB running, but it can offload many of the tables from RavenDB to other databases.

Summary

In this chapter, we introduced and explained the need for the saga pattern. We discussed how saga handles nonfunctional requirements that are commonly overlooked. We also discussed the fallacies of distributed computing. We briefly discussed the need for NServiceBus, its installation, and how it helps to improve the quality of software while it provides support for nonfunctional requirements.

In the next chapter, we will discuss a particular service platform that includes ServicePulse, ServiceControl, ServiceInsight, and ServiceMatrix.

2

The NServiceBus Architecture

In this chapter, we will focus on the NServiceBus architecture. We will discuss the different message and storage types supported in NSB. This discussion will include an introduction to some of the tools and advantages of using NSB. We will conceptually look at how some of the pieces fit together while backing up the discussions with code examples.

In this chapter, we will cover the following topics:

- Benefits of NSB
    - More on endpoints
    - The application security perspective
- Message exchange patterns
    - The publish/subscribe pattern
    - The request-response pattern
    - Saga services
    - Message mutations
    - Message encryption
    - Cluster messaging
    - Performance monitoring
    - Gateway messages
- Storage patterns
    - Timeout storage
    - Subscription storage
    - Backing it up

- Monitoring
    - A sample e-mail notification
- Recap

NSB is the cornerstone of automation. As an **Enterprise Service Bus** (**ESB**), NSB is the most popular C# ESB solution. NSB is a framework that is used to provide many of the benefits of implementing a **service-oriented architecture** (**SOA**). It uses an IBus and its ESB bus to handle messages between NSB services, without having to create custom interaction. This type of messaging between endpoints creates the bus. The services, which are autonomous Windows processes, use both Windows and NSB hosting services. NSB-hosting services provide extra functionalities, such as creating endpoints; setting up **Microsoft Queuing** (**MSMQ**), DTC for transactions across queues, subscription storage for publish/subscribe message information, NSB sagas; and much more. Deploying these pieces for messaging manually can lead to errors and a lot of work is involved to get it correct. NSB takes care of provisioning its needed pieces.

NSB is not a frontend framework, such as Microsoft's **Model-View-Controller** (**MVC**). It is not used as an **Object-to-Relationship Mapper** (**ORM**), such as Microsoft's Entity Frameworks, to map objects to SQL Server tables. It is also not a web service framework, such as Microsoft's **Windows Communication Foundation** (**WCF**). NSB is a framework to provide the communication and support for services to communicate with each other and provide an end-to-end workflow to process all of these pieces.

Benefits of NSB

NSB provides many components needed for automation that are only found in ESBs. ESBs provide the following:

- **Separation of duties**: From the frontend to the backend by allowing the frontend to fire a message to a service and continue with its processing not worrying about the results until it needs an update. Also, you can separate workflow responsibilities by separating NSB services. One service could be used to send payments to a bank, and another service can be used to provide feedback of the current status of the payment to the MVC-EF database so that a user may see the status of their payment.
- **Message durability**: Messages are saved in queues between services so that if the services are stopped, they can start from the messages saved in the queues when they are restarted. This is done so that the messages will persist, until told otherwise.

- **Workflow retries**: Messages, or endpoints, can be told to retry a number of times until they completely fail and send an error. The error is automated to return to an error queue. For instance, a web service message can be sent to a bank, and it can be set to retry the web service every 5 minutes for 20 minutes before giving up completely. This is useful while fixing any network or server issues.
- **Monitoring**: NSB's ServicePulse can keep a check on the heartbeat of its services. Other monitoring checks can be easily performed on NSB queues to report the number of messages.
- **Encryption**: Messages between services and endpoints can be easily encrypted.
- **High availability**: Multiple services, or subscribers, could be processing the same or similar messages from various services that live on different servers. When one server, or a service, goes down, others could be made available to take over that are already running.

More on endpoints

While working with a service-to-service interaction, messages are transmitted in the form of XML through queues that are normally part of Microsoft Server such as MSMQ, SQL Server such as SQL queuing, or even part of Microsoft Azure queues for cloud computing.

There are other endpoints that services use to process resources that are not part of service-to-service communications. These endpoints are used to process commands and messages as well, for instance, sending a file to non-NSB-hosted services, sending SFTP files to non-NSB-hosted services, or sending web services, such as payments, to non-NSB services. While at the other end of these communications are non-NSB-hosted services, NSB offers a lot of integrity by checking how these endpoints were processed. NSB provides information on whether a web service was processed or not, with or without errors, and provides feedback and monitoring, and maintains the records through queues. It also provides saga patterns to provide feedback to the originating NSB services of the outcome while storing messages from a particular NSB service to the NSB service of everything that has happened.

In many NSB services, an audit queue is used to keep a backup of each message that occurred successfully, and the error queue is used to keep track of any message that was not processed successfully.

The application security perspective

From the application security perspective, OWASP's top ten list of concerns, available at `https://www.owasp.org/index.php/Top_10_2013-Top_10`, seems to always surround injection, such as SQL injection, broken authentication, and **cross-site scripting** (**XSS**). Once an organization puts a product in production, they usually have policies in place for the company's security personnel to scan the product at will. Not all organizations have these policies in place, but once an organization attaches their product to the Internet, there are armies of hackers that may try various methods to attack the site, depending on whether there is money to be gained or not. Money comes in a new economy these days in the form of using a site as a proxy to stage other attacks, or to grab usernames and passwords that a user may have for a different system in order to acquire a user's identity or financial information. Many companies have suffered bankruptcy over the last decades thinking that they were secure.

NSB offers processing pieces to the backend that would normally be behind a firewall to provide some protection. Firewalls provide some protection as well as **Intrusion Detection Systems** (**IDSes**), but there is so much white noise for viruses and scans that many real hack attacks may go unnoticed, except by very skilled antihackers. NSB offers additional layers of security by using queuing and messaging. The messages can be encrypted, and the queues may be set for limited authorization from production administrators.

NSB hosting versus self-hosting

`NServiceBus.Host` is an executable that will deploy the NSB service. When the NSB service is compiled, it turns into a Windows DLL that may contain all the configuration settings for the IBus. If there are additional settings needed for the endpoint's configuration that are not coded in the IBus's configuration, then it can be resolved by setting these configurations in the Host command.

However, `NServiceBus.Host` need not be used to create the program that is used in NServiceBus. As a developer, you can create a console program that is run by a Window's task scheduler, or even create your own services that run the NSB IBus code as an endpoint. We can see samples of this type of code in the MVC samples in other chapters. Not using the NSB-hosting engine is normally referred to as self-hosting.

The NServiceBus host streamlines service development and deployment, allows you to change technologies without code, and is administrator friendly when setting permissions and accounts. It will deploy your application as an NSB-hosted solution. It can also add configurations to your program at the `NServiceBus.Host.exe` command line. If you develop a program with the `NServiceBus.Host` reference, you can use `EndpoinConfig.cs` to define your IBus configuration in this code, or add it as part of the command line instead of creating your own `Program.cs` that will do a lot of the same work with more code. When debugging with the `NServiceBus.Host` reference, the Visual Studio project is creating a windows DLL program that is run by the `NserviceBus.Host.exe` command.

Here's an example form of the properties of a Visual Studio project:

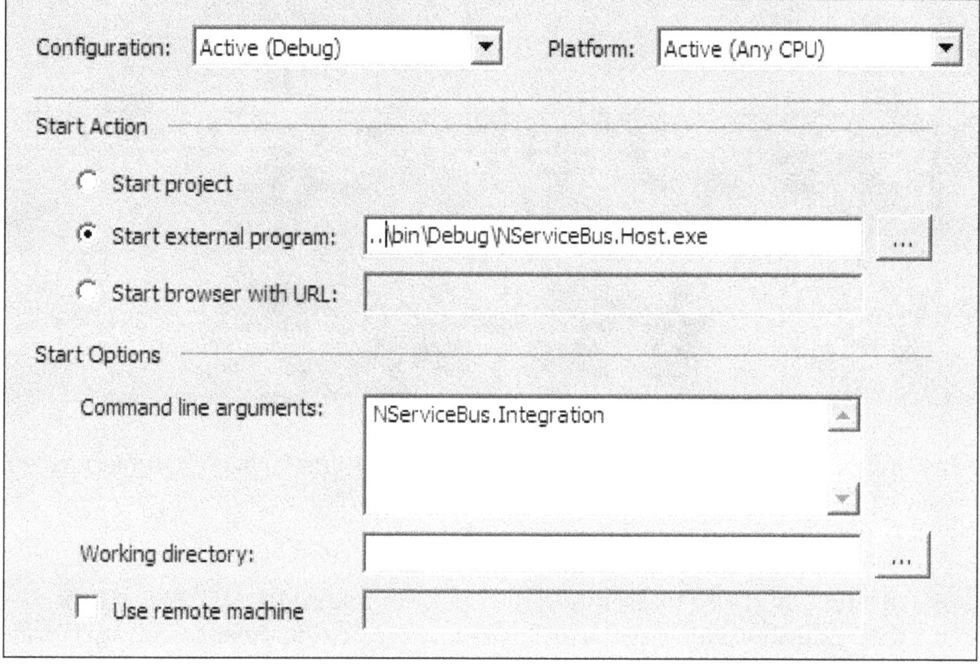

The `NServiceBus.Host.exe` command line has support for deploying Window's services as NSB-hosted services:

```
C:\Program Files (x86)\Particular Software\NServiceBus\v4.3\Binaries>NServiceBus
.Host.exe -?
NServiceBus Endpoint Host Service

USAGE:
   NServiceBus.Host.exe [-install] [options]
   NServiceBus.Host.exe [-uninstall] [options]


INSTALL OPTIONS:

  -?, -h, -help                 Help about the command line options.
  -install                      Install the endpoint as a Windows service.
  -serviceName=VALUE            Specify the service name for the installed
                                  service.
  -displayName=VALUE            Friendly name for the installed service.
  -description=VALUE            Description for the service.
  -endpointConfigurationType=VALUE
                                Specify the type implementing
                                  IConfigureThisEndpoint that should be used.
  -dependsOn=VALUE              Specifies the names of services or groups which
                                  must start before this service.
  -sideBySide                   Install the service with the version included in
                                  the service name. This allows running multiple
                                  endpoints side by side when doing hot
                                  deployments.
  -endpointName=VALUE           The name of this endpoint.
  -username=VALUE               Username for the account the service should run
                                  under.
  -password=VALUE               Password for the service account.
  -startManually                Specifies that the service should start manually.
  -installInfrastructure        This setting is no longer in use. Please see
                                  http://particular.net/articles/managing-
                                  nservicebus-using-powershell for the replacement.

  -scannedAssemblies=VALUE      Configures NServiceBus to use the types found in
                                  the given assemblies.
```

These configurations are typically referred to as the profile for which the service will be running. Here are some of the common profiles:

- **MultiSite**: This turns on the gateway.
- **Master**: This makes the endpoint a "master node endpoint". This means that it runs the gateway for multisite interaction, the timeout manager, and the distributor. It also starts a worker that is enlisted with the distributor. It cannot be combined with the worker or distributor profiles.
- **Worker**: This makes the current endpoint enlist as a worker with its distributor running on the master node. It cannot be combined with the master or distributor profiles.
- **Distributor**: This starts the endpoint only as a distributor. This means that the endpoint does no actual work and only distributes the load among its enlisted workers. It cannot be combined with the Master and Worker profiles.

- **Performance counters**: This turns on the NServiceBus-specific performance counters. Performance counters are installed by default when you run a Production profile.
- **Lite**: This keeps everything in memory with the most detailed logging.
- **Integration**: This uses technologies closer to production but without a scale-out option and less logging. It is used in testing.
- **Production**: This uses scale-out-friendly technologies and minimal file-based logging. It is used in production.

Using Powershell commands

Many items can be managed in the Package Manager console program of Visual Studio 2012. Just as we add commands to the `NServiceBus.Host.exe` file to extend profiles and configurations, we may also use VS2012 Package Manager to extend some of the functionalities while debugging and testing. We will use the **ScaleOut** solution discussed later just to double check that the performance counters are installed correctly. We need to make sure that the PowerShell commandlets are installed correctly first. We do this by using Package Manager:

Install the package, `NServiceBus.PowerShell`

Import the module, `.\packages\NServiceBus.PowerShell.4.3.0\lib\net40\NServiceBus.PowerShell.dll`

Test `NServiceBusPerformanceCountersInstallation`

The "Import module" step is dependent on where `NService.PowerShell.dll` was installed during the "Install package" process. The "Install-package" command will add the DLL into a package directory related to the solution. We can find out more on PowerShell commandlets at `http://docs.particular.net/nservicebus/managing-nservicebus-using-powershell` and even by reviewing the help section of Package Manager.

Here, we see that we can insert configurations into `App.config` when we look at the help section, `PM> get-help about_NServiceBus`.

```
PM>  get-help about_NServiceBus
TOPIC
  about_NServiceBus

SHORT DESCRIPTION
  Provides information about NServiceBus commands.

LONG DESCRIPTION
  This topic describes the NServiceBus commands.
  http://docs.particular.net/

  The following NServiceBus cmdlets are included:

  Cmdlet                                            Description
  ------------------------------------------------------------------------------------------
  Add-NServiceBusMessageForwardingInCaseOfFaultConfig  Adds the required configuration section to
                                                    the config file.

  Add-NServiceBusUnicastBusConfig                   Adds the required configuration section to
                                                    the config file.

  Add-NServiceBusTransportConfig                    Adds the required configuration section to
                                                    the config file.

  Add-NServiceBusSecondLevelRetriesConfig           Adds the required configuration section to
                                                    the config file.

  Add-NServiceBusLoggingConfig                      Adds the required configuration section to
                                                    the config file.

  Add-NServiceBusMasterNodeConfig                   Adds the required configuration section to
                                                    the config file.

  Add-NServiceBusNHibernateConfig                   Adds the NHibernate supported config settings
                                                    as a comment.
```

Message exchange patterns

Let's discuss the various exchange patterns now.

The publish/subscribe pattern

One of the biggest benefits of using the ESB technology is the benefits of the publish/subscribe message pattern; refer to `http://en.wikipedia.org/wiki/Publish-subscribe_pattern`.

The publish/subscribe pattern has a publisher that sends messages to a queue, say a MSMQ `MyPublisher` queue. Subscribers, say `Subscriber1` and `Subscriber2`, will listen for messages on the queue that the subscribers are defined to take from the queue. If `MyPublisher` cannot process the messages, it will return them to the queue or to an error queue, based on the reasons why it could not process the message. The queue that the subscribers are looking for on the queue are called endpoint mappings. The publisher endpoint mapping is usually based on the default of the project's name. This concept is the cornerstone to understand NSB and ESBs. No messages will be removed, unless they are explicitly told to be removed by a service. Therefore, no messages will be lost, and all are accounted for from the services. The configuration data is saved to the database. Also, the subscribers can respond back to `MyPublisher` with messages indicating that everything was alright or not using the queue.

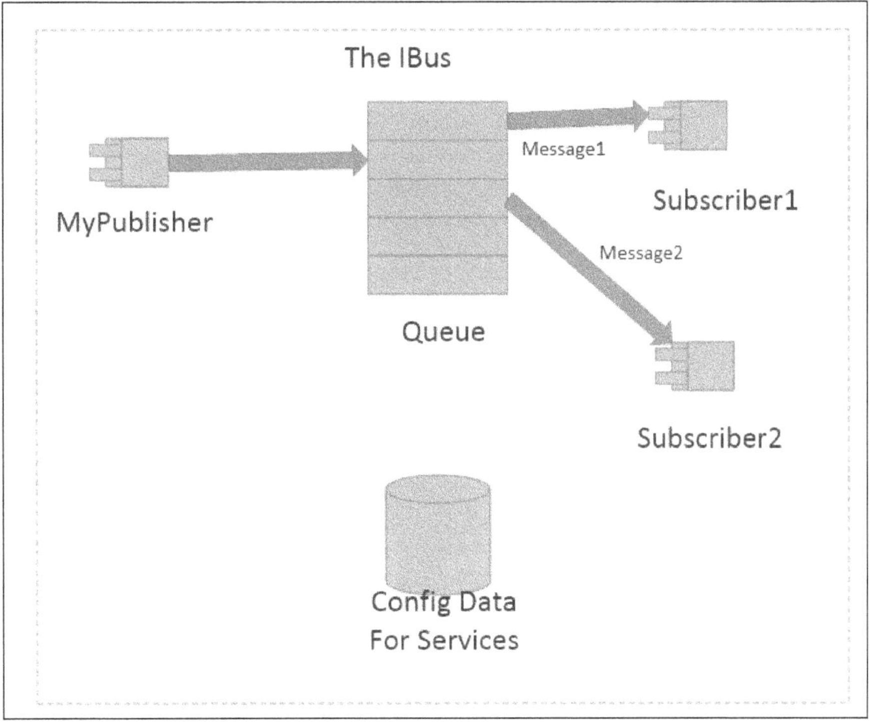

So why is this important? It's because all the messages can then be accounted for, and feedback can be provided to all the services. A service is a Windows service that is created and hosted by the NSB host program. It could also be a Windows command console program or even an MVC program, but the service program is always up and running on the server, continuously checking queues and messages that are sent to it from other endpoints.

These messages could be commands, such as instructions to go and look at the remote server to see whether it is still running, or data messages such as sending a particular payment to the bank through a web service. For NSB, we formalize that events are used in publish/subscribe, and commands are used in a request-response message exchange pattern.

Windows Server could have too many services, so some of these services could just be standing by, waiting to take over if one service is not responding or processing messages simultaneously. This provides a very high availability.

Request-response messages

There is also the message exchange pattern of request-response; you can refer to `http://en.wikipedia.org/wiki/Request-response`. The concept is simple: we send a request to a specific endpoint and get a response only from that endpoint. There are no additional subscribers listening in to process the message. This is done using a `Bus.Send(command)` function, where command is a type of message, in NSB. In the request-response pattern, we send a message to a specific queue indicating that only one endpoint is being listened to and no one else. We can send a message to each service as a heartbeat or to get an update of the status of each service.

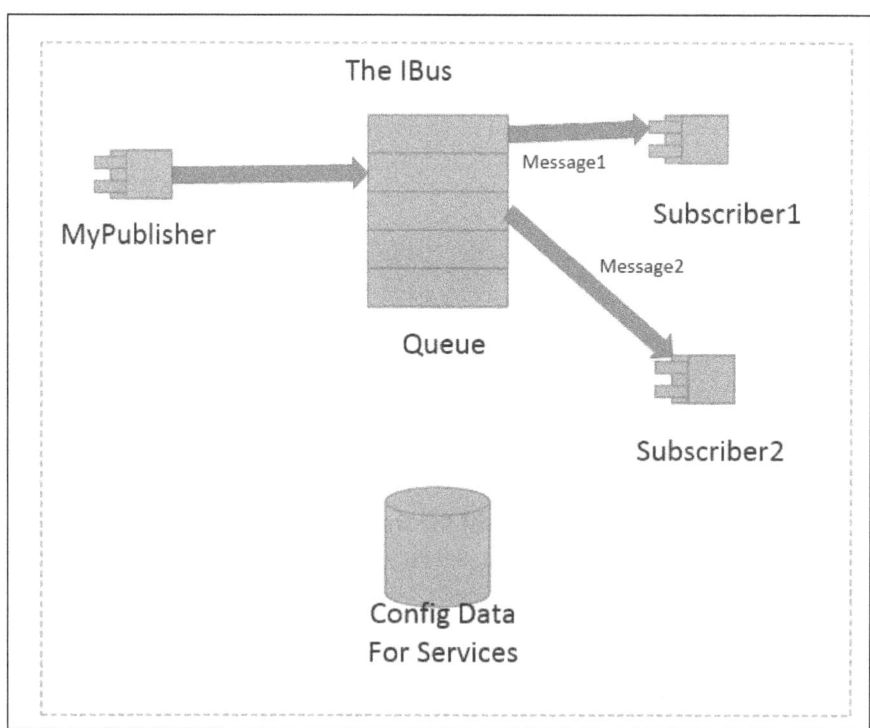

Saga services

As messages move through the workflow of service-to-service, new messages are created and sent to the next service. There is a need to keep track of the relationship of messages when responses are sent back to the service. A lookup of message states, or sessions, needs to be done in a saga entity object saved to a database. This concept is like a session cookie for session state information when a user moves from web page to web page. A service needs to respond to the original service to provide a progress of the original message. In order to do this, the saga entity also stores the originator of the message to be able to provide a response to the original message.

The saga entity is an interface derived from IContainSagaData that will contain the mandatory getter/setter fields of `Id`, `Originator` and `OriginalMessageId`. These properties are needed to reply to the client with information from the original message.

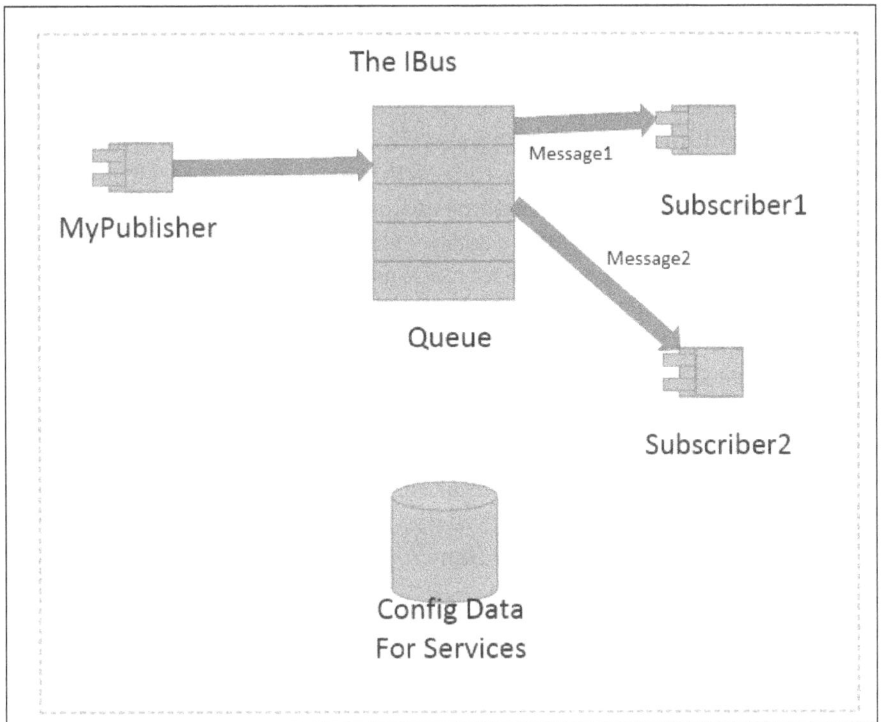

Some saga features

As we have mentioned, sagas are design patterns. This means that they are reusable patterns used in designing software for the purpose of saving different states in messages, as they are processed through an end-to-end workflow. They have many features and characteristics:

- Sagas are started by a message, maybe more than one. A saga is started by a message in the interface, for example, `"IAmStartedByMessage<Message1>"`.
- Sagas contain **long-lived transactions** (**LLTs**) that contain database information for the messages for relatively long periods of time. LLT is used when conditions such as short-lived transactions are not adequate. A short-lived transaction is when a call to a database, or MSQM, performs a straightforward rollback or commit. For queues, NServiceBus performs **second-level retries** (**SLRs**) to try to commit a number of times before performing a rollback. In LLT, there can be multiple conditions and actions that need to take place for a message to be fully completed, or operations performed to start the message right from the beginning. LLT is used for messages where a simple short-term transaction may not suffice. In an SOA, there are multiple endpoints and services. Most messages will start with a starting type and will continue to pass through different services in an SOA, all the while completing operations and updating information. They will start as one type and pass through a service when they change to a different type of message. During these transformations of the message, a saga can globally keep track of the message's state through this workflow of services. It can respond back to the different originating services indicating that everything was processed successfully, or respond that there were errors and that there is a need to rollback the message to each client.
- Sagas contain timeout. There is a condition where a message needs to have a timer to interrupt its actions regardless of what it is doing. Going back to the pizza-ordering example, we may want to check with the customer whether the order takes longer than 20 minutes to see if they still wish to order the pizza. For this reason, you may want to interrupt the order in progress, which is in the form of a message, and time it out and check with the customer before proceeding.
- Sagas contain state-related information. Sagas save saga data to the database. Saga data is initially started with a message, and it is also updated with messages that are passed in with the same identification information. When a message passes between different services in an end-to-end workflow, saving the state information before the next service is wise if it needs to change back to its original state.

- Sagas handle messages. A saga is started by a message and passes it through its message handler. As messages are passed into the saga that are not the started message, the saga updates its saga data from these messages through a message handler. The message doesn't normally end at the saga; the saga forwards it to its next endpoint.

Timeout messages

There is the need in ESBs to set timers for various messages to ensure that they do not live in the services and queues for an infinite period of time. Even most production databases require an archive and purging schedule to clean up old data that may not be relevant anymore. Since messages live on queues as a form of data, there also needs to be archiving and purging plans to revisit any messages that could reside in the system when there is no longer a need for them to do so. For this reason, as NSB is all about automation, timers can be set to relook at a message to check its status or even delete some resident messages that are no longer needed.

Sagas support timeout messages that are set using the `RequestTimeout` function of a saga. This code will look as follows:

```
public void Handle(SubmitRequestCommand message)
{

    logger.Info("--------MySaga Handle-------" + message);


    RequestTimeout<TimeoutMessage>(TimeSpan.FromSeconds(60));
```

`TimeoutMessage` is a user-defined message from the interface `IMessage` that will be sent when the timer is expired. In this case, it will be 60 seconds. A timeout message will be received on the saga instance like any other message handler, and the code is put in the timeout message handler to perform any cleanup required to get rid of the message information that is no longer required. The timeout message may be an empty message:

```
namespace MySaga
{
    public class TimeoutMessage : IMessage
    {
    }
```

The saga process does not have to be used to set timeouts in NSB. For similar tasks, as the one described previously, we may also use `NServiceBus.Schedule` as well.

In this section, we will be using the `TimeoutManager` solution with the following projects:

- `TimeoutManager`: This project will perform several timeout functions.

Running the `TimeoutManager` project, we will be presented with a couple of options:

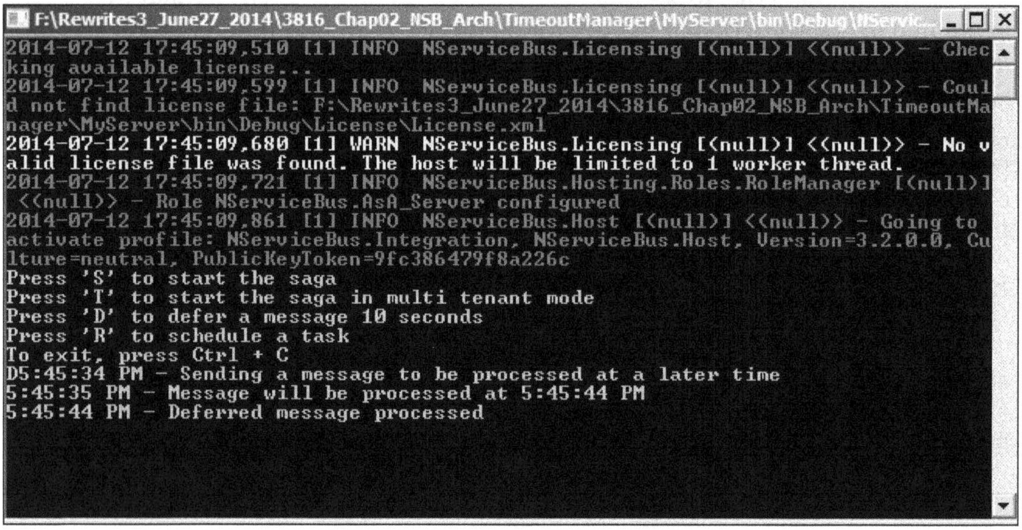

```
F:\Rewrites3_June27_2014\3816_Chap02_NSB_Arch\TimeoutManager\MyServer\bin\Debug\NServic...
2014-07-12 17:45:09,510 [1] INFO  NServiceBus.Licensing [(null)] <(null)> - Chec
king available license...
2014-07-12 17:45:09,599 [1] INFO  NServiceBus.Licensing [(null)] <(null)> - Coul
d not find license file: F:\Rewrites3_June27_2014\3816_Chap02_NSB_Arch\TimeoutMa
nager\MyServer\bin\Debug\License\License.xml
2014-07-12 17:45:09,680 [1] WARN  NServiceBus.Licensing [(null)] <(null)> - No v
alid license file was found. The host will be limited to 1 worker thread.
2014-07-12 17:45:09,721 [1] INFO  NServiceBus.Hosting.Roles.RoleManager [(null)]
 <(null)> - Role NServiceBus.AsA_Server configured
2014-07-12 17:45:09,861 [1] INFO  NServiceBus.Host [(null)] <(null)> - Going to
activate profile: NServiceBus.Integration, NServiceBus.Host, Version=3.2.0.0, Cu
lture=neutral, PublicKeyToken=9fc386479f8a226c
Press 'S' to start the saga
Press 'T' to start the saga in multi tenant mode
Press 'D' to defer a message 10 seconds
Press 'R' to schedule a task
To exit, press Ctrl + C
D5:45:34 PM - Sending a message to be processed at a later time
5:45:35 PM - Message will be processed at 5:45:44 PM
5:45:44 PM - Deferred message processed
```

We can delay the processing of a message or schedule a task with NSB. This is done in support of the `NServiceBus.Schedule` function where we can schedule actions or send messages based on time. Here, we are showing the support of scheduling a task to be performed after a minute:

```
namespace MyServer.Scheduling
{
    public class ScheduleATaskHandler : IHandleMessages<ScheduleATask>
    {
        private readonly IBus bus;

        public ScheduleATaskHandler(IBus bus)
        {
            this.bus = bus;
        }
```

```
        public void Handle(ScheduleATask message)
        {
            Console.WriteLine("Scheduling a task to be executed every
1 minute");
            Schedule.Every(TimeSpan.FromMinutes(1)).Action(() => bus.
SendLocal(new ScheduledTaskExecuted()));
        }
    }
}
```

Downloading the example code

You can download the example code files for all Packt books you have purchased from your account at `http://www.packtpub.com`. If you purchased this book elsewhere, you can `http://www.packtpub.com/support` and register to have the files e-mailed directly to you.

By default, the timeout data will be persisted in RavenDB but may be stored in other databases, such as SQL Server, using the NHibernate connector as well. Here's what a document entry for a timeout would look like in RavenDB:

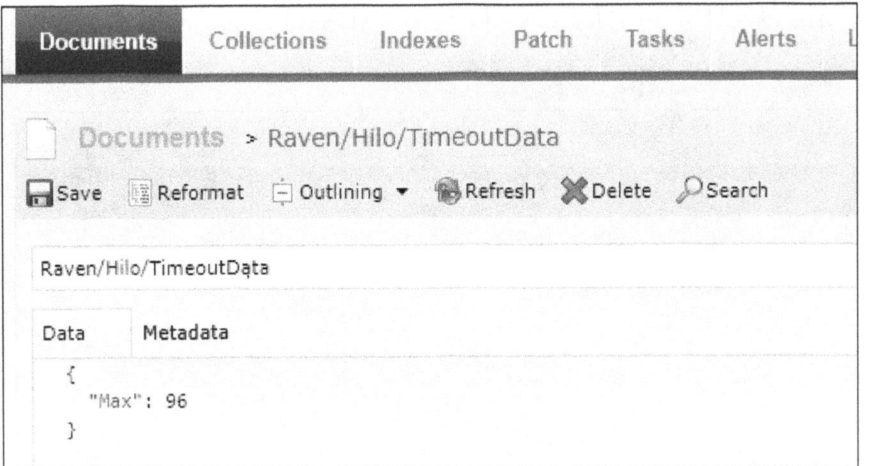

Message mutations

Message mutators allow you to change messages by plugging custom logic into a couple of simple interfaces. For instance, you can encrypt all or part of a message. The encryption message mutator is part of the NServiceBus library and can be used at any time. You can intercept the incoming message, then mutate it before sending it as an outgoing message. This is the process of changing messages; they leave a client and enter a server.

In this section, we will be using the `MessageMutators` solution with the following projects:

- `Client`: The client will send messages to the server.
- `Server`: The server will receive the mutated message.
- `Messages`: This refers to the message format that is being passed between the client and the server.
- `MessageMutators`: This project will contain the mutation code to compress and uncompress the messages in `TransportMessageCompressionMutator.cs` and validate the message annotation in `ValidateMessageMutator.cs`.

The client and server needs to be running. The client will prompt to send a good or bad message. The good message is compressed so that it will pass the 4 MB MSMQ buffer size:

```
F:\Rewrites3_June27_2014\3816_Chap02_NSB_Arch\MessageMutators\Client\bin\Debug\NServiceB...
lessageDrivenSubscriptions [4.6.1] - Enabled

2014-07-13 10:40:21,717 [1] INFO  NServiceBus.Features.FeatureInitializer [(null
)] <(null)> - Feature categories:
  - Serializers
      * BinarySerialization - Disabled
      * BsonSerialization - Disabled
      * JsonSerialization - Disabled
      * XmlSerialization - Enabled

2014-07-13 10:40:21,758 [1] INFO  NServiceBus.Unicast.Config.FinalizeUnicastBusC
onfiguration [(null)] <(null)> - Number of messages found: 4
2014-07-13 10:40:21,764 [1] INFO  NServiceBus.Config.InfrastructureServices [(nu
ll)] <(null)> - Infrastructure service NServiceBus.AutomaticSubscriptions.IAutoS
ubscriptionStrategy was found in the container and will be used instead of the d
efault
2014-07-13 10:40:21,770 [1] INFO  NServiceBus.Configure [(null)] <(null)> - Invo
cation of NServiceBus.Config.IFinalizeConfiguration completed in 0.10 s
2014-07-13 10:40:22,321 [1] INFO  NServiceBus.Installation.PerformanceMonitorUse
rsInstaller [(null)] <(null)> - Skipped adding user 'WIN-UAUT16GPEQA\Administrat
or' to group 'Performance Monitor Users' because the user is already in group.
Press 's' to send a valid message, press 'e' to send a failed message. To exit,
'q'
```

The queue will be validated and compressed from the client before processing it on the MSMQ:

```
Client → send message → Validate (Outgoing) → TransportCompression
(Outgoing) ---> To MSMQ
```

Then, the server will receive the message from MSMQ, but before processing it, this will decompress and validate the message before the server processes the message. It will unmutate the message that the client mutated:

```
From MSMQ → TransportCompression (Incoming)→ Validate (Incoming) →
Server
```

This is just a simple compressing and data annotation validation to ensure that MSMQ will process the message. There may be many other reasons for mutating the message; one of them may be to encrypt the credit card within a payment message.

Message encryption

NSB supports the AES or Rijndael encryption algorithm. This is a symmetric key algorithm, so both the program encrypting the data and decrypting the data must share a secret key for their effort; see `http://en.wikipedia.org/wiki/Advanced_Encryption_Standard`.

Encrypting data will depend on the needs of the organization, but common items could be any passwords, financial information, or customer's personal identification information. AES is the strongest symmetric encryption algorithm, and most languages, such as Java and C#, provide API support to use it.

We know that part of the configuration on both sides will be a secret key.

In this section, we will be using the `Encryption` solution with the following projects:

- `Client`: The client will send encrypted credit card messages to the server.
- `Server`: The server will receive the credit card message and decrypt it.
- `Messages`: This refers to the message format that is being passed between the client and the server.

Both the client and server must be running. The client will have a prompt to send messages to the server:

```
F:\Rewrites3_June27_2014\3816_Chap02_NSB_Arch\EnterpriseDevWithNSB\samples\Encryption\Cli...
king available license...
2014-07-13 12:01:29,933 [1] INFO  NServiceBus.Licensing [(null)] <(null)> - Coul
d not find license file: F:\Rewrites3_June27_2014\3816_Chap02_NSB_Arch\Enterpris
eDevWithNSB\samples\Encryption\Client\bin\Debug\License\License.xml
2014-07-13 12:01:30,185 [1] WARN  NServiceBus.Licensing [(null)] <(null)> - No v
alid license file was found. The host will be limited to 1 worker thread.
2014-07-13 12:01:30,250 [1] INFO  NServiceBus.Hosting.Roles.RoleManager [(null)]
 <(null)> - Role NServiceBus.AsA_Client configured
2014-07-13 12:01:30,274 [1] WARN  MessageForwardingInCaseOfFault [(null)] <(null
)> - Could not find configuration section 'MessageForwardingInCaseOfFaultConfig'
. Going to try to find the error queue defined in 'MsmqTransportConfig'.
2014-07-13 12:01:30,323 [1] INFO  NServiceBus.Host [(null)] <(null)> - Going to
activate profile: NServiceBus.Production, NServiceBus.Host, Version=3.2.0.0, Cul
ture=neutral, PublicKeyToken=9fc386479f8a226c
2014-07-13 12:01:30,326 [1] INFO  NServiceBus.Host [(null)] <(null)> - Going to
activate profile: NServiceBus.PerformanceCounters, NServiceBus.Host, Version=3.2
.0.0, Culture=neutral, PublicKeyToken=9fc386479f8a226c
2014-07-13 12:01:46,913 [1] WARN  NServiceBus.Utils.MsmqUtilities [(null)] <(nul
l)> - Queue win-uaut16gpeqa\private$\error does not exist.
2014-07-13 12:01:47,626 [1] WARN  NServiceBus.Utils.MsmqUtilities [(null)] <(nul
l)> - Queue win-uaut16gpeqa\private$\client.retries does not exist.
2014-07-13 12:01:47,817 [1] WARN  NServiceBus.Utils.MsmqUtilities [(null)] <(nul
l)> - Queue win-uaut16gpeqa\private$\client does not exist.
Press 'Enter' to send a message.
```

Once you press *Enter*, you will see that the message is encrypted on the server queue:

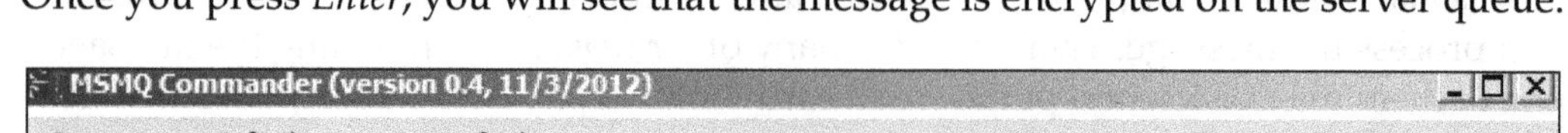

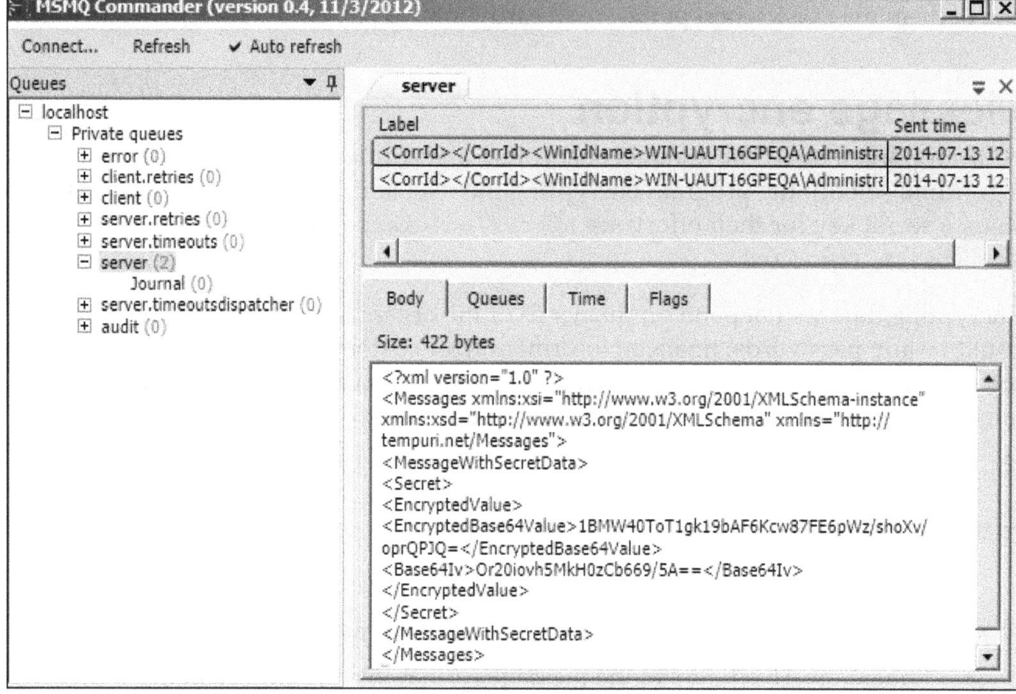

When running the server, NSB will decrypt the message before it passes it to the server's message handler.

All that is really needed is that both the ends should be enabled for AES in IBus using the configuration, `.RijndaelEncryptionService();`. We set a part of the message that we want to encrypt using `public WireEncryptionString Secret { get;set; }` where `WireEncryptionString` defines that the string will be encrypted. Also, the secret key has to be in `App.config` of both the client and the server.

```
<?xml version="1.0"?>
<configuration>
  <configSections>
     <section name="UnicastBusConfig" type="NServiceBus.Config.UnicastBusConfig, NServiceBus.Core"/>
    <section name="RijndaelEncryptionServiceConfig" type="NServiceBus.Config.RijndaelEncryptionServiceConfig, NServiceBus.Core"/>
  </configSections>
  <MsmqTransportConfig ErrorQueue="error" NumberOfWorkerThreads="1" MaxRetries="5"/>
  <UnicastBusConfig>
    <MessageEndpointMappings>
      <add Messages="Messages" Endpoint="Server"/>
    </MessageEndpointMappings>
  </UnicastBusConfig>
  <RijndaelEncryptionServiceConfig Key="gdDbqRpqdRbTs3mhdZh8qCaDaxJXl+e7"/>
  <startup>
    <supportedRuntime version="v4.0" sku=".NETFramework,Version=v4.0"/>
  </startup>
</configuration>
```

Cluster messaging

As mentioned earlier, one of the many benefits of using NSB is that you can distribute the load or the NSB services or processes. This is commonly known as scaling out the services. The idea is that you can copy a service, say an order handler, and copy the exact code or DLL to be a worker to distribute the work. The worker will be exactly the same as the order handler, except for its configuration. The configuration of the original order handler would normally be labeled as the **master**, and the subsequent extra workers will be labeled as **worker** processes. The worker processes could be running locally, but that wouldn't be helpful if the local server is overtaxed with work already, or they could be framed out to other servers that have process speed to spare.

This model is a form of round-robin clustering, where a handler can distribute its workload to additional workers doing exactly the same kind of work. A distributor is used with MSMQ. If an endpoint has a critical time set for performance and requires more processing help, this clustering could be used to spawn off work to the same services that live on other machines to share the load. If the machine processing the message crashes, the message would be rolled back to the queue and other machines could then process it accordingly.

Worker services send messages through a control queue saying that they are ready for work. The distributor stores these messages, and when it receives the messages, it farms them out of the available queues. All the pending work stays in the distributor's queue so that messages can be timed for performance.

In this section, we will be using the `ScaleOut` solution with the following projects:

- `Orders.Messages`: This refers to the common messages for the sender and handlers.
- `Orders.Sender`: This will send messages to `Orders.Handler` to be handled across the workers, `worker1` and `worker2`.
- `Orders.Handler.Worker1`: This is one of the worker services that uses a worker profile to send a response back to the sender. This will be an additional worker copy of `Orders.Handler`.
- `Orders.Handler.Worker2`: This is one of the worker services that uses a worker profile to send a response back to the sender. This will be an additional worker copy of `Orders.Handler`.
- `Orders.Handler`: This is an endpoint that processes the message and configures it to the distributor. This will be the master profile that the sender will send the place order command to in the `orders.handler` MSMQ. In the Visual Studio 2012 debugger, `NServiceBus.Integration NserviceBus.Master` is set in the command line to be used instead of `Configure.Instance.RunDistributor()`.

The solution for the ordering will look like the following:

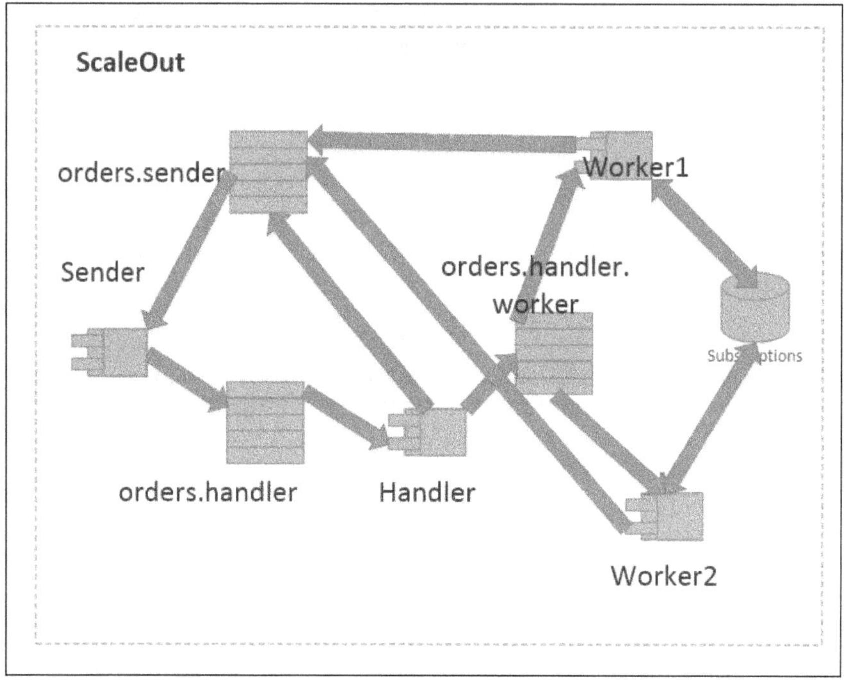

If there are too many place orders for `Orders.Handler` to receive, then a round-robin effect will happen to the worker services across the `orders.handler.worker` MSMQ. The control queue is `orders.handler.distibutor.control` and the data queue is `orders.handler.distibutor.storage`. The `DataInputQueue`, or the data queue, is the queue where the client processes send their applicative messages. `ControlInputQueue`, or the control queue, is the queue where the worker nodes send their control messages. The control queue is the distributor queue that the workers will signal to the handler indicating that they are available to process the message. These queues and worker processes could be spanned across machines or used on the same machine to distribute the load of the messages. If no workers are available for the handler to distribute the messages, then the handler will process the message and respond back to the sender. The workers are duplicated code for the handler and perform the same function; their purpose is just to take the workload off the handler to distribute the load.

By default, there will be subscription storage information saved in the RavenDB database. This information is for the worker processes to understand whom to respond back to when responding. The master node is the handler, which receives messages from the sender client. So, it knows that it has to respond to the sender client. However, the handler, which is the master, sends the messages to the worker processes. So, the workers are only aware of the handler. The handler will create subscription information so that the workers know that they have to respond back to the sender client. This will be the subscription storage information that will be stored by default in the RavenDB, but the subscription storage's configuration can be changed to save it to other databases as well.

Performance monitoring

When using clustering, an important practice is to monitor the performance of the handlers and workers. This is needed to determine whether workers are even needed, and if so, how many.

The first step is to ensure that the solution has the performance counters installed. We discussed this in the use of PowerShell to test the installation of the performance counters.

There are two main types of performance counters in NSB. The first is the critical time performance that is more of an end-to-end performance, and the other is the endpoint **Service-level agreement** (**SLA**) that monitors the mean time of the endpoint to ensure it meets the service level. The SLA endpoint has to specify a time that it must meet in the performance. In order to do this, the endpoint SLQ must be set in code. The monitor will show the seconds left until you breach your SLA time. Let's look at adding the code into the handler's `EndpointConfig.cs:`.

```
namespace Orders.Handler
{
    [EndpointSLA("00:00:10")]
    class EndpointConfig : IConfigureThisEndpoint, AsA_Publisher { }
```

In this section, we will be using the `ScaleOut - Performance` solution, which is the same as the `ScaleOut` solution, except for the fact that some performance settings have been added to this solution.

The performance counters are used by default if the profile of the deployment is in production mode. This mode is set by default, but it needs to be specified if other parameters such as master or worker are used. Let's look at the handler's deployment properties:

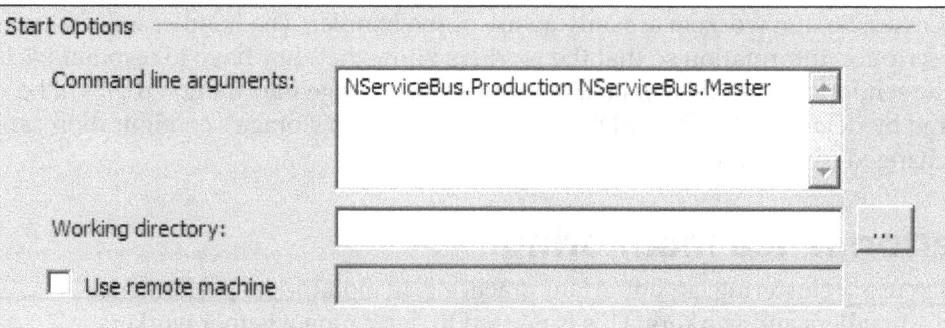

We can see that the performance counters are installed at startup:

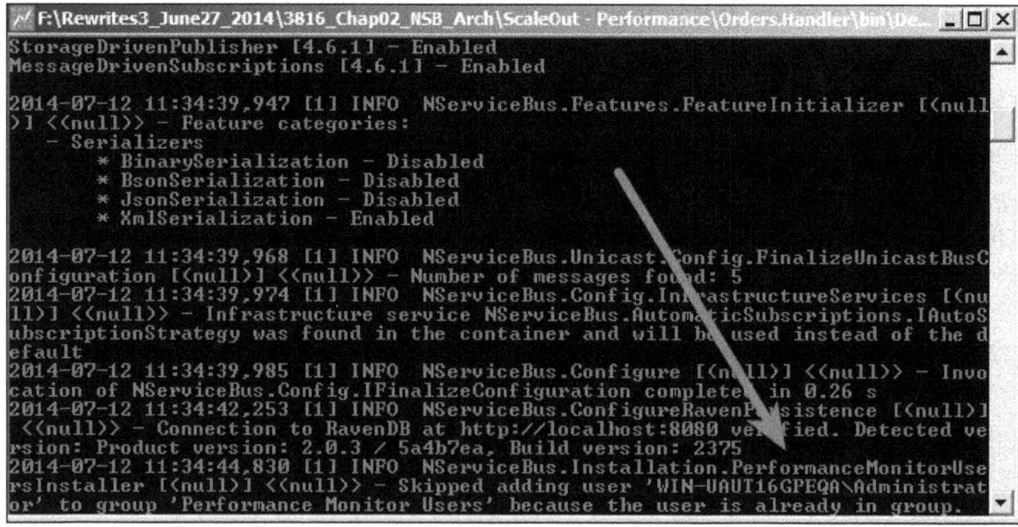

Then, all we have to do is start the server's performance monitor and start adding the services that we wish to monitor and specify the SLA, critical times, and "# of the messages":

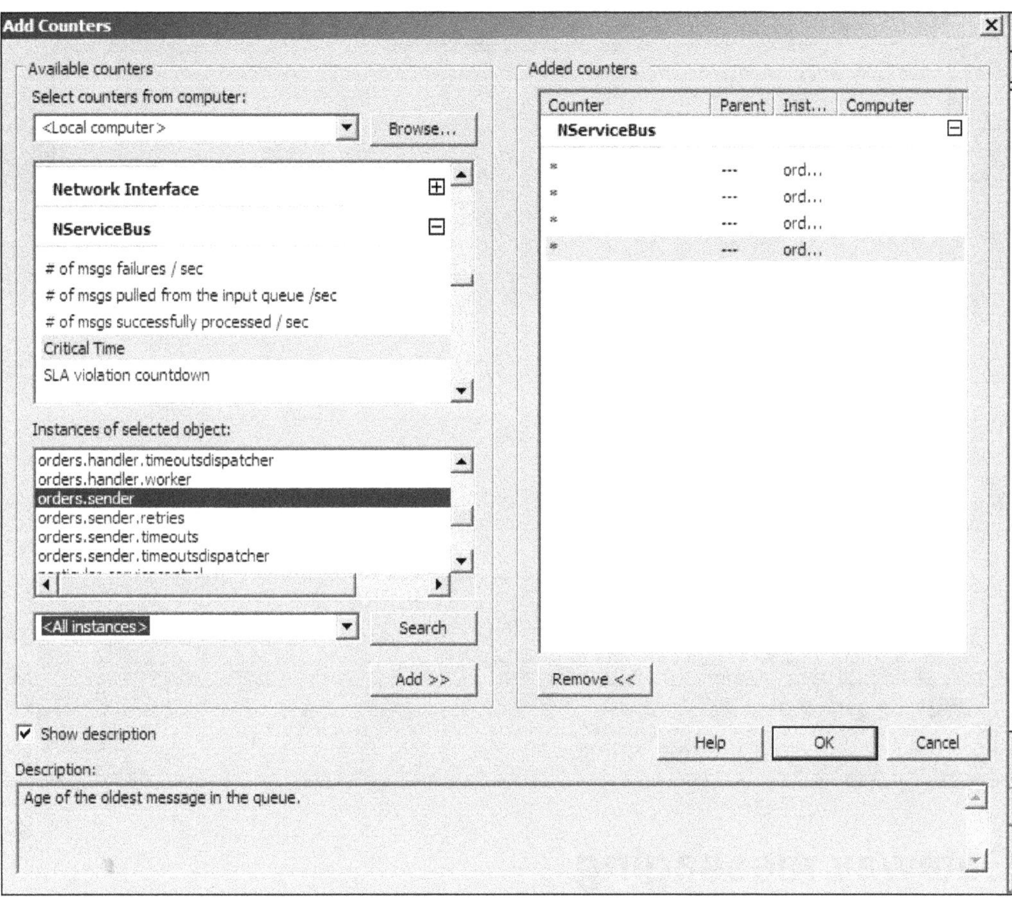

Running the performance monitor, we can drill down into the specifics of the NSB process and even see whether the SLA has any issues that need to be met:

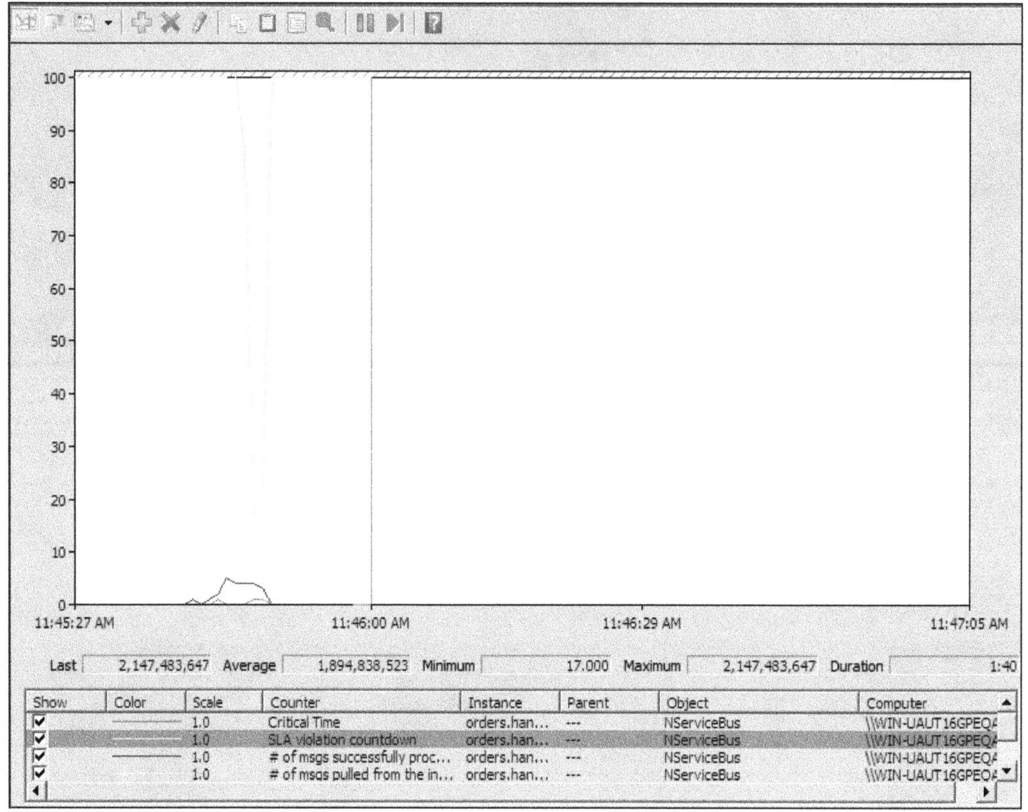

Gateway messaging

There are cases for when one part of the services may be stored on one part of an organization's LAN, while other services are stored on another LAN; the only mode of transport that both these parts have to pass messages to NSB is through the use of an HTTP or HTTPS tunnel.

The main purpose of the gateway is to allow you to perform the same durable fire-and-forget messaging that you are accustomed to with NServiceBus across physically separated sites, where sites are locations where you run the IT infrastructure and not the websites.

The gateway only comes into play when you can't use the normal LAN-to-LAN VPN tunnels or internal LAN servers to communicate MSMQ to MSMQ. The purpose of the gateway is to create messages that communicate through HTTP, but it would be preferable to use HTTPS to ensure that messages are secured.

In this section, we will be using the `Gateway` solution:

- `Headquarter.Messages`: This refers to the common messages for `Headquarters`, `SiteA` and `SiteB`.
- `Headquarter`: This will receive messages from `http://localhost:25899/Headquarter/` and `http://localhost:25899/Headquarter2/`, and send messages to `http://localhost:25899/SiteA/` and `http://localhost:25899/SiteB/`.
- `SiteA`: This is a project that will receive the update price information from `Headquarters` via `http://localhost:25899/SiteA/` and respond that it was successful back to the `Headquarters` via `http://localhost:25899/Headquarter2/`.
- `SiteB`: This is a project that will receive the update price information from `Headquarters` via `http://localhost:25899/SiteB/`.
- `WebClient`: This will have an `Index.htm` page to send a JSON script to `http://localhost:25899/Headquarter/`.

These were run in VS2012 in Windows Server 2012 with MSMQ, DTC, NServiceBus references, and SQL Server 2012 Express LocalDB installed.

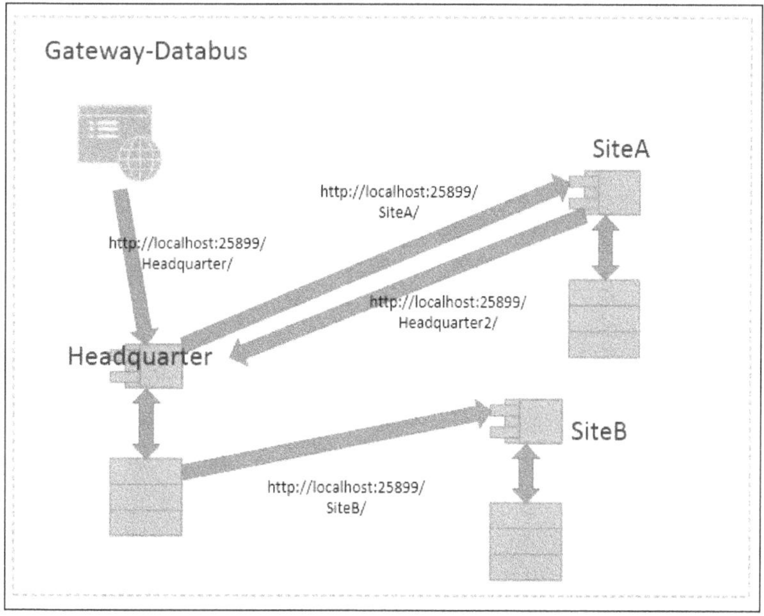

In a gateway, there are incoming channels and defined site keys to send outgoing messages to their sites. We can see in `App.config` of the headquarters that the receiving channels for the headquarters are `http://localhost:25899/Headquarter/` and `http://localhost:25899/Headquarter2/`.

There will be a site keys set for the sending sites that make up `SiteA` and `SiteB`:

```
<GatewayConfig>
  <Sites>
    <Site Key="SiteA" Address="http://localhost:25899/SiteA/" ChannelType="Http" />
    <Site Key="SiteB" Address="http://localhost:25899/SiteB/" ChannelType="Http" LegacyMode="false" />
  </Sites>
  <Channels>
    <Channel Address="http://localhost:25899/Headquarter/" ChannelType="Http" />
    <Channel Address="http://localhost:25899/Headquarter2/" ChannelType="Http" Default="true" />
  </Channels>
</GatewayConfig>
<UnicastBusConfig>
```

The site keys are used for `Bus.SendToSites(new[] { "SiteA", "SiteB"}`, which will take in an array of keys to send the messages to their sites. For instance, the parameter of `SiteA` will send the message to `http://localhost:25899/SiteA/`.

Going across alternate channels such as HTTP means that you lose out on MSMQ's safety guarantee of exactly one message. This means that communication errors resulting in retries can lead to receiving messages more than once. To avoid burdening you with deduplication, the NServiceBus gateway supports this out of the box. You just need to store the message IDs of all the received messages so it can detect potential duplicates. The deduplication code can be stored in SQL Server using the NHibernate persistence configuration. This will be configured on IBus using `.UseNHibernateGatewayDeduplication()`. Of course, settings always need to be applied in the `App.config` file to define the database connection. Here, we are connecting to the local `SQLExpress` instance.

```
<connectionStrings>
  <add name="NServiceBus/Transport" connectionString="cacheSendConnection=true" />
  <add name="NServiceBus/Persistence" connectionString="Data Source=.\SQLEXPRESS;Initial Catalog=nservicebus;Integrated Security=True" />
</connectionStrings>
<!-- specify the other needed NHibernate settings like below in appSettings:-->
<appSettings>
  <!-- dialect is defaulted to MsSql2008Dialect, if needed change accordingly -->
  <add key="NServiceBus/Persistence/NHibernate/dialect" value="NHibernate.Dialect.MsSql2008Dialect" />
  <!-- other optional settings examples -->
  <add key="NServiceBus/Persistence/NHibernate/connection.provider" value="NHibernate.Connection.DriverConnectionProvider" />
  <add key="NServiceBus/Persistence/NHibernate/connection.driver_class" value="NHibernate.Driver.Sql2008ClientDriver" />
</appSettings>
<runtime>...</runtime>
```

This is the deduplication table in SQL Server.

WIN-UAUT16GP...Deduplication

	Id	TimeReceived
▶	c66-a36401482562	2014-07-11 01:54:56.000
*	NULL	NULL

Data bus messaging

Data bus is used to send large chunks of data or files across as an attachment because of the limitations of MSMQ to 4 MB. For this reason, a reference can be passed on to a local file to transfer data using the data bus method.

In this section, we will continue to use the `Gateway` solution.

The path of the data bus has to be set in the configuration of the endpoint. We will be using a relative path to where the gateway project is running. Both `SiteA` and `SiteB` will also have relative paths. There will be a relative path to the binary data with a data bus subdirectory that contains the files that will have large data.

```
public void Init()
{
    Configure.With()
        .DefaultBuilder()
        .FileShareDataBus(".\\databus");
}
```

When we execute the gateway project, it will have `SomeLargeString` to simulate data that is larger than 4 MB.

```
Bus.SendToSites(new[] { "SiteA", "SiteB" }, new PriceUpdated
{
    ProductId = 2,
    NewPrice = 100.0,
    ValidFrom = DateTime.Today,
    SomeLargeString = new DataBusProperty<string>("This is a random large string " + Guid.NewGuid())
});
```

If we execute the gateway project, it will create a message to the relative path of its binary, save the message under `databus`, and use it as a reference to send to `SiteA` and `SiteB`. Here, we see the message saved to the local relative path.

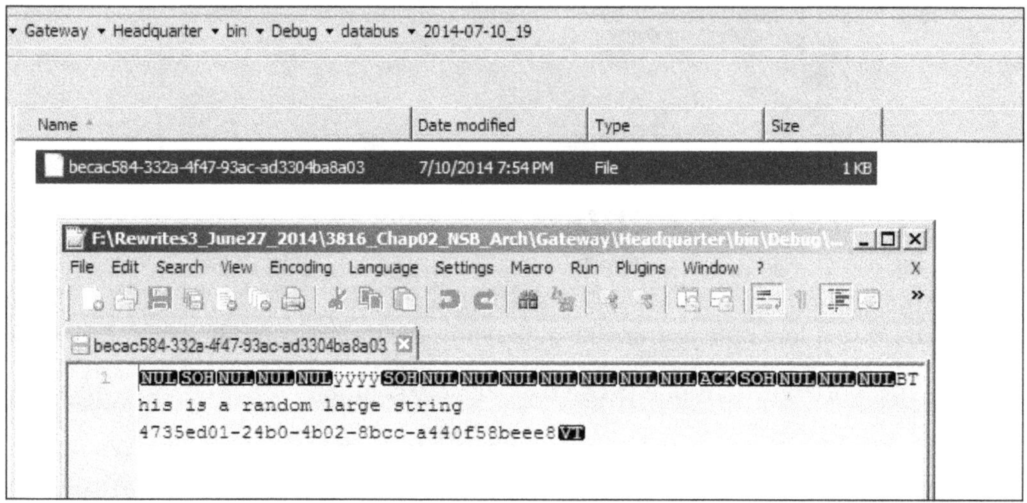

The data bus is very useful to move the files around or for data that is too large for MSMQ.

Storage patterns

Here is a very important chart that we will continuously refer to:

Type	InMemory	RavenDB	NHibernate	MSMQ
Timeout	X	X	X	Not supported beginning with V3.3,0
Subscription	X	X	X	X
Saga	X	X	X	-
Gateway	X	X	X	-
Distributor	-	-	-	X

The type is the various persistence storage properties that can be persisted. For instance, when performing publish/subscribe messaging, there is subscription information that needs to be saved to a database that details the subscribers and the message types that they are listening for in their queues.

We can have various configurations for these persistence stores: InMemory, RavenDB, NHibernate and MSMQ. The following bullet list provides a brief explanation of these stores:

- **InMemory**: This refers to the data that is persisted only to the local memory of the NSB service. This also means that when a service is stopped or restarted, the data is no longer saved. A reboot will cause the data to disappear.
- **RavenDB**: This refers to the data that is persisted to a Raven database. RavenDB is a document-oriented NoSQL database. Regardless of a reboot, the data in RavenDB will be persisted. It uses JSON documents for communication; see `http://ravendb.net/docs/intro/ravendb-in-a-nutshell`. The default for almost all persistences, except the distributor, which is just MSMQ, is RavenDB.
- **NHibernate**: This is ORM that connects objects to relational databases, such as SQL Server, MySQL, and Oracle. It normally needs a mapper properties file usually in the form of XML to map the objects to the SQL. In NSB, it will handle any mapping that it requires with NHibernate, otherwise you will have to use the mapping interface; see `http://nhforge.org/`. Regardless of a reboot, the data will be persisted. For NSB configurations, see `http://docs.particular.net/nservicebus/relational-persistence-using-nhibernate`.
- **MSMQ**: This refers to the data that is persisted to **Microsoft Message Queues** (**MSMQs**). MSMQ is an installation of the Windows server that is used for queuing messages; see `http://en.wikipedia.org/wiki/Microsoft_Message_Queuing`. Regardless of a reboot, the messages will be persisted in this configuration.

The data that is typically persisted in these methods have to deal with message information such as Timeouts, Subscriptions, sagas' objects, Gateways, and Distributors. The following bullet list provides a brief explanation of this message information:

- **Timeouts**: Timeout entities is the message information that has to be stored when a timer message is used. Sagas use timeouts, and timers can also be set when scheduling NSB tasks and messages. This is used with the timeout persister, such as `.UseNHibernateTimeoutPersister()`, to persist the data in the SQL Server database, as shown in the following screenshot:

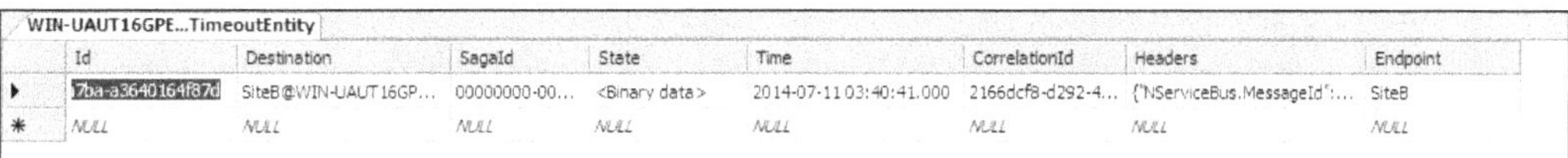

WIN-UAUT16GPE...TimeoutEntity

	Id	Destination	SagaId	State	Time	CorrelationId	Headers	Endpoint
▶	7ba-a3640164f87d	SiteB@WIN-UAUT16GP...	00000000-00...	<Binary data>	2014-07-11 03:40:41.000	2166dcf8-d292-4...	{"NServiceBus.MessageId":...	SiteB
*	NULL	NULL	NULL	NULL	NULL	NULL	NULL	NULL

- **Subscription**: Subscription information is used in publish/subscribe scenarios to keep track of the subscribers' information. This will typically be the queues that they are subscribing to and the messages that the subscribers are looking for. By viewing a publish/subscribe example that is defaulted to RavenDB for the subscription information, we can see the client queues and the message types that they process.

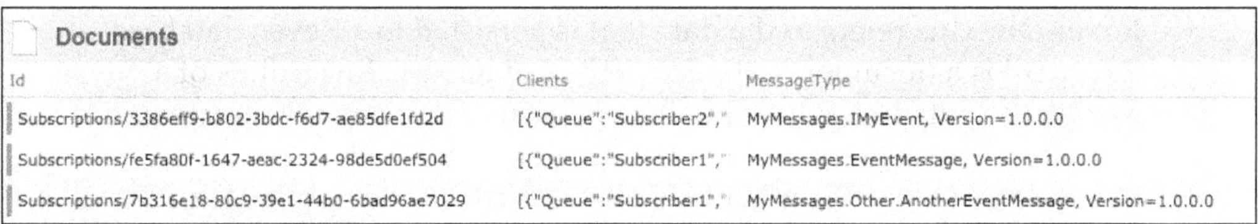

Documents

Id	Clients	MessageType
Subscriptions/3386eff9-b802-3bdc-f6d7-ae85dfe1fd2d	[{"Queue":"Subscriber2","	MyMessages.IMyEvent, Version=1.0.0.0
Subscriptions/fe5fa80f-1647-aeac-2324-98de5d0ef504	[{"Queue":"Subscriber1","	MyMessages.EventMessage, Version=1.0.0.0
Subscriptions/7b316e18-80c9-39e1-44b0-6bad96ae7029	[{"Queue":"Subscriber1","	MyMessages.Other.AnotherEventMessage, Version=1.0.0.0

- **Sagas**: Sagas store their message information in a saga data object that will contain at least the `Id`, `Originator`, and `OriginalMessageId`. This is the generated information from the saga engine to respond to the client with a relationship to the original message. If a timeout is set, it will also persist the timeout information as well. We can configure `.UseNHibernateSagaPersister()` to persist the saga entity information to SQL Server as follows:

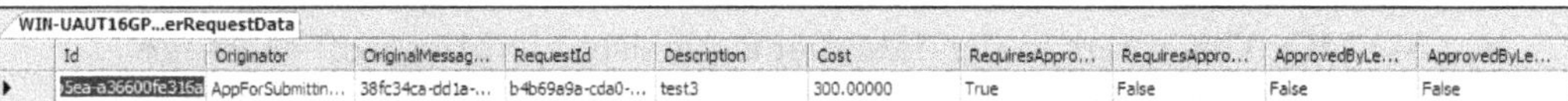

WIN-UAUT16GP...erRequestData

Id	Originator	OriginalMessag...	RequestId	Description	Cost	RequiresAppro...	RequiresAppro...	ApprovedByLe...	ApprovedByLe...
5ea-a36600fe316a	AppForSubmittin...	38fc34ca-dd1a-...	b4b69a9a-cda0-...	test3	300.00000	True	False	False	False

- **Gateway storage**: Gateway acts like a router to remote sites through HTTP and HTTPS to forward and receive messages that are remote and cannot use IPSEC or VPN tunnels. Using `.UseNHibernateGatewayPersister( );` in the `Headquarters` project for SQL Server will store the gateway messaging results, as follows, for persistence:

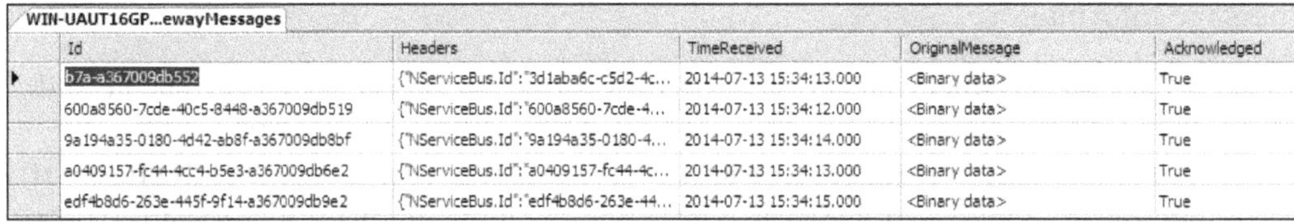

WIN-UAUT16GP...ewayMessages

Id	Headers	TimeReceived	OriginalMessage	Acknowledged
b7a-a367009db552	{"NServiceBus.Id":"3d1aba6c-c5d2-4c...	2014-07-13 15:34:13.000	<Binary data>	True
600a8560-7cde-40c5-8448-a367009db519	{"NServiceBus.Id":"600a8560-7cde-4...	2014-07-13 15:34:12.000	<Binary data>	True
9a194a35-0180-4d42-ab8f-a367009db8bf	{"NServiceBus.Id":"9a194a35-0180-4...	2014-07-13 15:34:14.000	<Binary data>	True
a0409157-fc44-4cc4-b5e3-a367009db6e2	{"NServiceBus.Id":"a0409157-fc44-4c...	2014-07-13 15:34:13.000	<Binary data>	True
edf4b8d6-263e-445f-9f14-a367009db9e2	{"NServiceBus.Id":"edf4b8d6-263e-44...	2014-07-13 15:34:15.000	<Binary data>	True

- **Distributor Storage**: In the scale-out example, we needed to store distributor data to get the necessary workers available. This data is stored in MSMQ.

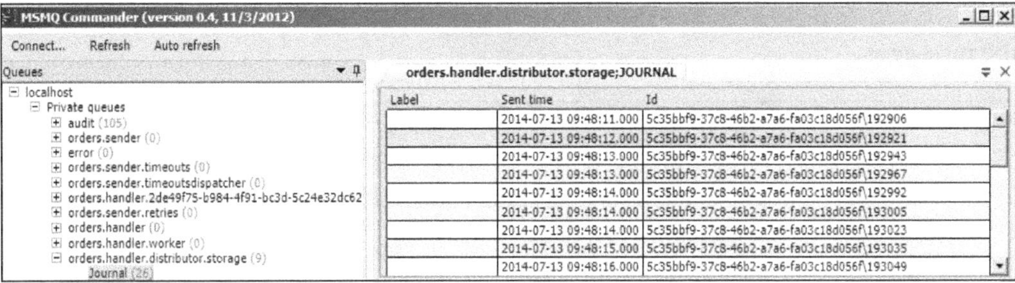

Backing it up

NSB utilizes a lot of the storage mechanisms that other C# enterprise applications would normally utilize in the Microsoft world. If data and messages are stored in SQL Server, then the organization's normal operations for backing up SQL Server would suffice. For MSMQ, and all the services running in the Windows Server, a daily backup of the server itself will be advisable. Another method of backing up MSMQ is that all the messages in the queues are in XML, and daily saving of messages through MSMQ tools to files could be accomplished. Another method when sending a file to MSMQ is to save a copy of the message to the disk; alternatively, you can turn on the auditing function and then create a console program with a daily task scheduler to save all the new audit messages of the day to the disk. There are many different ways to do this using the NSB framework or other SQL Server and MSMQ utilities. Because these are normal Microsoft C# processes, there are many, many different ways to automate these tasks.

Monitoring

This form of architecture may be referred to as an event-driven SOA where the events drive the design of the architecture, and the numerous services make up the flow of the disparate events that drive the workflow; please refer to `http://en.wikipedia.org/wiki/Event-driven_SOA`,. In an event-driven workflow, business users monitor the events.

In this case, the events are messages; one way to monitor the messages in the queues is to examine the queues. If SQL Server queues are being used, then the tables can be examined. If MSMQ is being used, then products such as MSMQCommander (`https://github.com/sverrehundeide/MSMQCommander`) can be used to examine the messages.

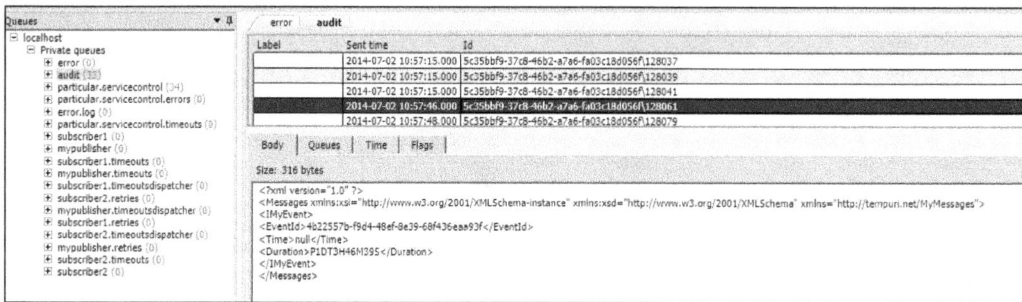

There are many examples to look at MSMQ and SQL Server queues. Another one can be found at `http://blog.halan.se/page/Service-Bus-MQ-Manager.aspx` that will work like the following:

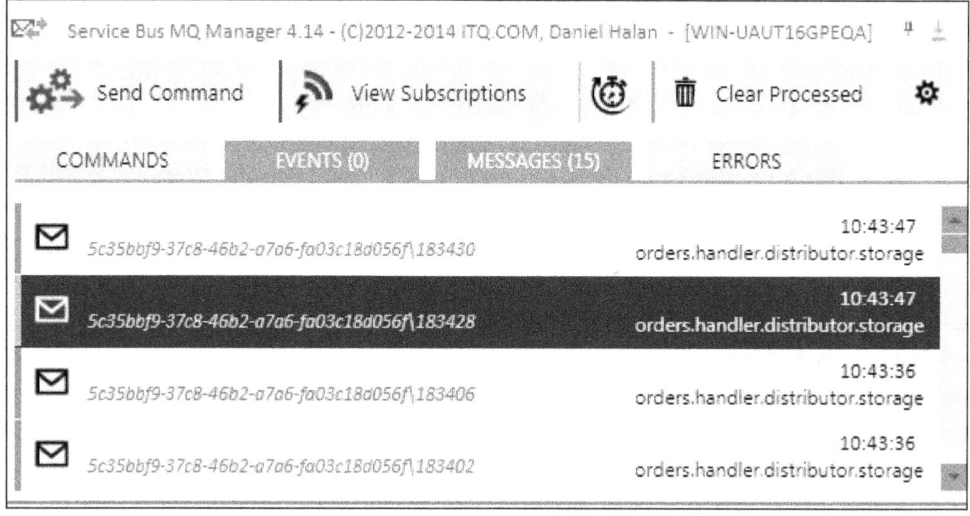

However, the preferred method is to use the NSB ServicePulse tool found at `http://particular.net/servicepulse`, which can check the heartbeat of an NSB-hosted service by accessing the browser at `http://localhost:9090/#/dashboard`. ServicePulse is monitored through a web browser.

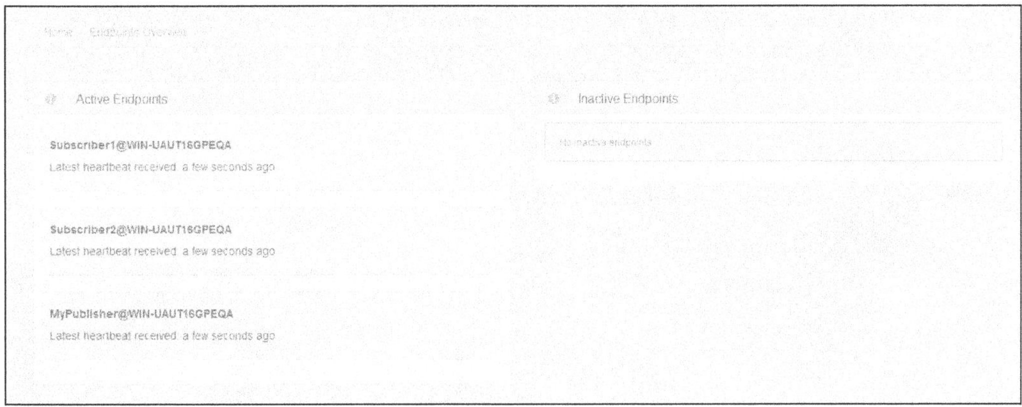

Another NSB tool that offers more insight into the services, endpoints, and messages is NSB's ServiceInsight. It allows you to have a detailed look into the messages, visual diagrams of the message flows, and detailed endpoint information.

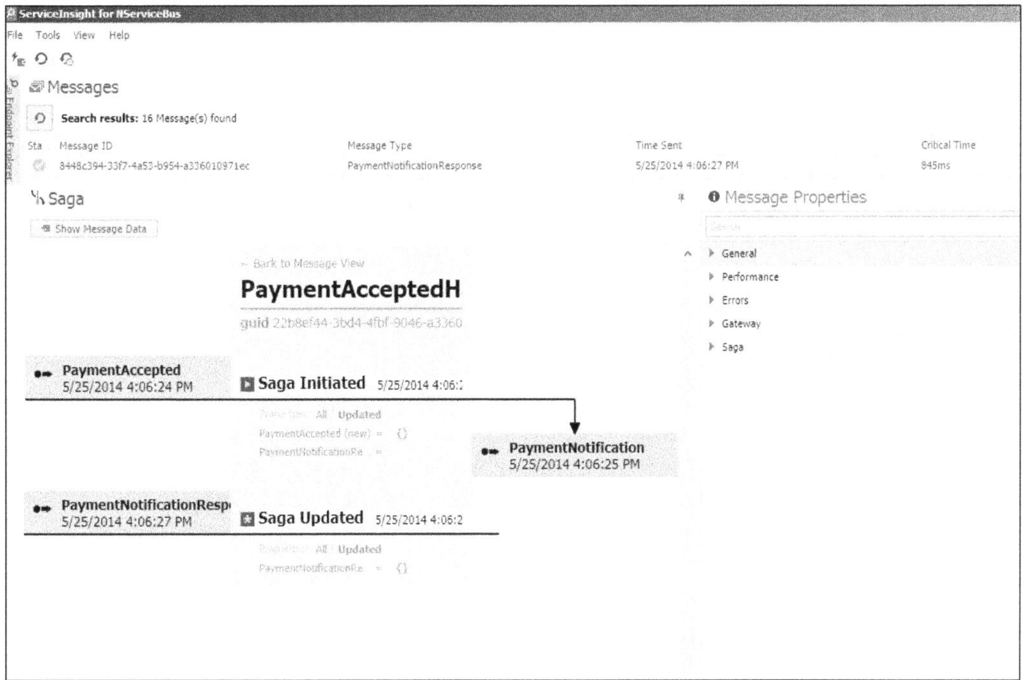

There are many features in the NSB product ServiceMatrix that provide standard development features to develop endpoints, services, and messages. ServiceMatrix provides a visual canvas to graphically design endpoints, services, and messages.

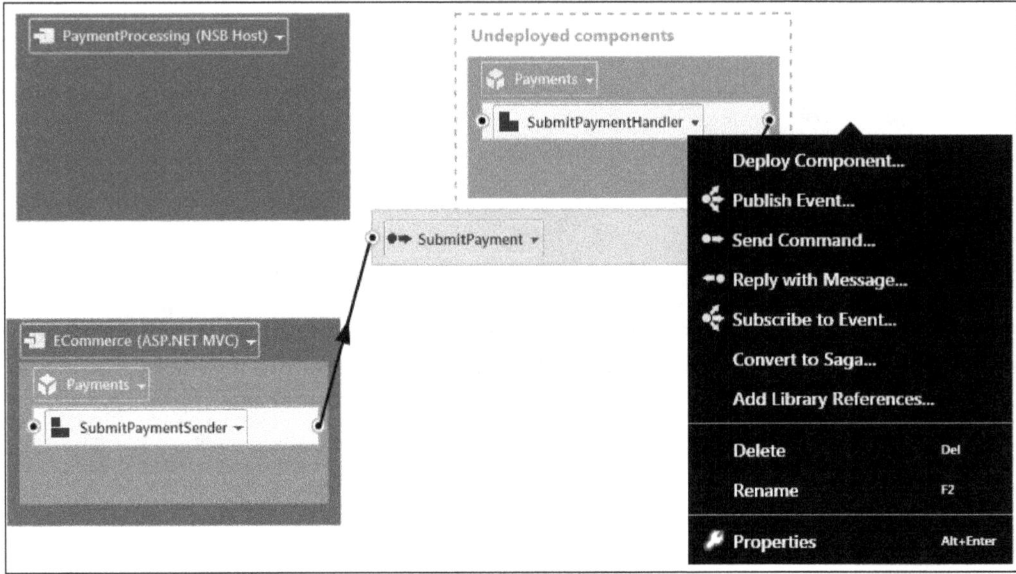

Sample e-mail notification

We mentioned earlier that normal production is filled with notifications related to checking queues, tables, processes, tasks, and more for both businesses and operations. We will create a console program that just formats an e-mail, reads the error queue in MSMQ, saves the number of errors in the queue, and sends it via an e-mail. Programs such as these don't do much work, but they can be added to check tasks, services, and even send log details via e-mail as time progresses. Some people like to only see e-mails if something is not working. However, having a daily e-mail that indicates whether all the systems are working or not is something that is found to be useful; this is because when systems fail, they have a tendency to have issues with notifications as well.

In this section, we will be using the `ConsoleReadTasks` solution:

This will be the `ConsoleReadTasks` solution:

```
using System.Messaging;
using System.Net.Mail;
using System.Text;
using System.Threading.Tasks;

namespace ConsoleReadTasks
{
    class Program
    {
        static void Main(string[] args)
        {

            // Set the machine to read queues and processes
            string machineToRead = System.Environment.MachineName;
            /*****
             * Checking MSMQ status
             * *****/
            StringBuilder sendMessage = new StringBuilder();
            sendMessage.AppendLine(" Message from Daily Status Process
on " + System.Environment.MachineName);
            sendMessage.AppendLine(System.Environment.MachineName + "
Searching on machine  " + machineToRead);
            Console.WriteLine("<--------Checking MSMQ status --------
------->");
            sendMessage.AppendLine("<--------Checking MSMQ status ----
----------->");
            sendMessage.AppendLine(" Reading MSMQ Status");

            // read all the queues
            var queues = MessageQueue.GetPrivateQueuesByMachine(machi
neToRead);
            foreach (MessageQueue queue in queues)
            {

                MessageQueue new_queue = new MessageQueue(queue.Path);
                queue.MessageReadPropertyFilter.SentTime = true;
                queue.MessageReadPropertyFilter.Body = true;
                new_queue.MessageReadPropertyFilter.SentTime = true;
                Message[] msgs = new_queue.GetAllMessages();
                // We will keep track of the error queue
                if (queue.QueueName == "private$\\error")
```

```
                    {
                        sendMessage.AppendLine(" Error Queue :" + msgs.
Length);
                        Console.WriteLine(" Error Queue :" + msgs.Length);
                    }
               }
               sendMessage.AppendLine("-------------End of EMa
il-------------------------");
               MailMessage nMail = new MailMessage();
               nMail.To.Add("test@google.com");
               nMail.From = new MailAddress("test@google.com");
               nMail.Subject = ("Testing A message from " + System.
Environment.MachineName);
               nMail.Body = sendMessage.ToString();
               SmtpClient sc = new SmtpClient("localhost");
               sc.Send(nMail);
          }
     }
}
```

To test the e-mail, here is a simple **Simple Mail Transfer Protocol** (**SMTP**) listener that will intercept the e-mails locally on port `25` to view, or rather test, your e-mail sending scenarios. It can be found at `http://smtp4dev.codeplex.com/`. When the e-mail is sent to the localhost, it will be recorded for review in the smtp4dev software.

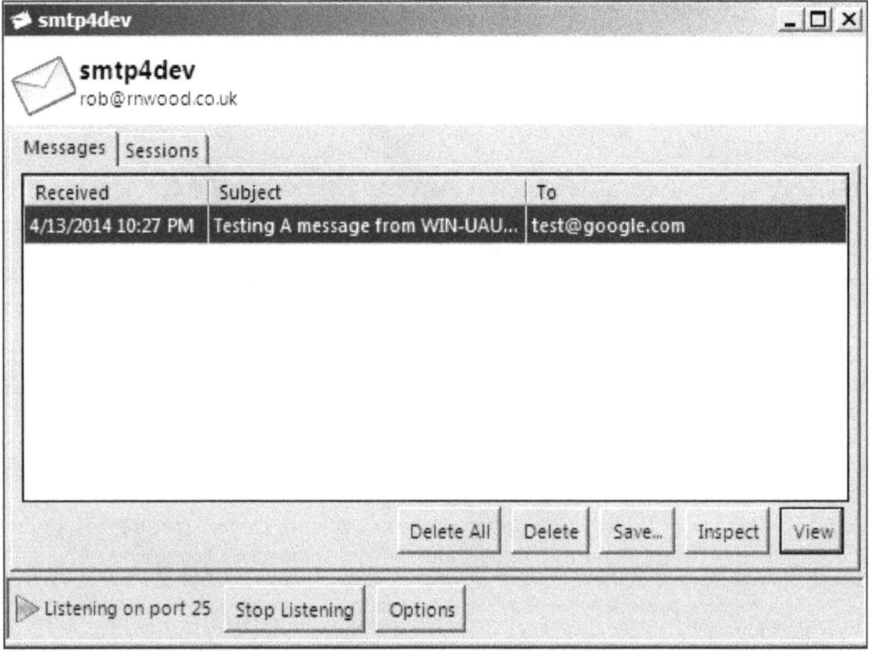

To receive a check only on a daily schedule, say 09:00 A.M, the Windows Task Scheduler normally takes a console program such as this one to set a daily running schedule. It's easy to use Task Scheduler to set up a daily recurring task that will just execute this console program to send a daily e-mail. To use the Task Scheduler, just see `http://technet.microsoft.com/en-us/library/cc766428.aspx`. We could add tasks to check the database table, to see whether RavenDB is running, to get a total of the messages, and more. This is just a beginning sample from a piece of code that monitors many different endpoints that we will cover in the upcoming chapter.

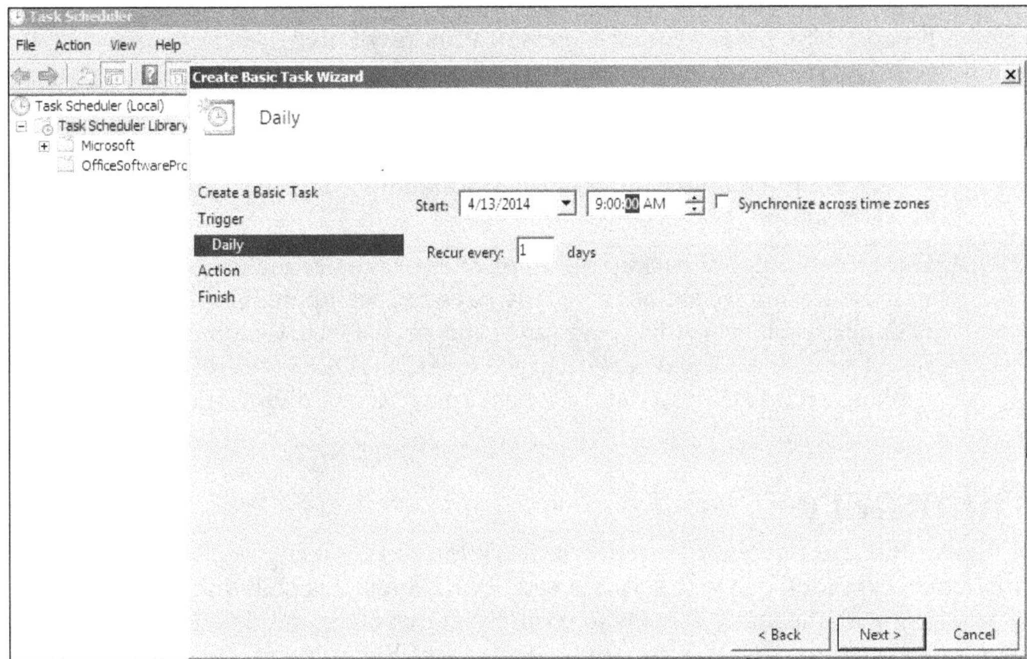

Let's recap

Here are some of the benefits of NSB that we have demonstrated:

1. NSB offers a workflow and can save the message state for services with the use of sagas.
2. NSB can host an NSB service in which NSB can deploy many of the settings to install Windows' services through the `NserviceBus.Host.exe` command line.
3. NSB can distribute or scale out duplicate services to distribute the load across machines. This provides high availability.

4. NSB can deploy its own gateway to send messages across the Intranet, or Internet, to remote services.
5. NSB has a tool called ServiceInsight to provide the insight on messages, endpoints and services.
6. NSB has production tools to check for a heartbeat on an endpoint called ServicePulse.
7. NSB has a tool called ServiceMatrix that helps you work on visual development on a canvas in Visual Studio.
8. Because NSB uses common Microsoft Windows Server services, such as MSMQ and SQL Server, you can take advantage of many tools and deployment techniques in C#.
9. NSB supports many message and storage patterns to build applications to perform full monitoring, reporting, scalability functions, and to never lose a message.
10. There are no special backup mechanisms that are needed for NSB that an organization would not normally have to back up queuing as well as databases. If everything, messages and persistence, is stored in SQL Server, then the normal backup procedures for SQL Server should be applied, such as using a database backup agent or a data vault.

Summary

ESBs like NSB are a necessity to perform workflows in C# using sagas. While there are frameworks for C# in web services and SFTP clients, it is NSB that establishes a workflow with the many benefits to ensure that messages and data is not lost as files are transferred, web services are processed, or SFTP interfaces are established. Without it, file sharing from mainframes to Windows could be easily untraceable and could not be processed with durable integrity. There are many benefits of using NSB. We discussed some of the messaging patterns from encryption, gateways, clustering, and many more, as how they relate to persistence. We also discussed monitoring and availability.

In the next chapter, we are going to take a look at a particular service platform that includes ServicePulse, ServiceControl, ServiceInsight, and ServiceMatrix.

3
Particular Service Platform

In this chapter, we will focus on Particular Service Platform, which includes ServicePulse, ServiceControl, ServiceInsight, and ServiceMatrix.

As the names imply, ServicePulse gives us a pulse of the messages, services, and endpoints; ServiceControl is a control API that ServicePulse and ServiceInsight depend on to get their internal information; ServiceInsight gives us a graphical and message-level drilldown into services, endpoints, and messages, and it includes a Saga drilldown as well.

ServiceMatrix is a graphical interface into code generation for NServiceBus endpoints, services, and messages in a Visual Studio canvas. In this chapter, we will cover the following topics:

- ServicePulse
- ServiceControl
- ServiceInsight
- ServiceMatrix
    - Introducing custom checks
    - Publish-subscribe through ServiceMatrix
- Sagas through ServiceMatrix

There are many tools that can be licensed through `http://particular.net`. These tools work in developing and monitoring NServiceBus and can be found from their download page, `http://particular.net/downloads`. However, one of the benefits of NServiceBus using Microsoft protocols such as DTC and MSMQ and databases such as RavenDB and SQL Server is that other tools from Microsoft and Visual Studio may work as well. The drawback is that a developer or software architect who is developing and designing in NServiceBus will lose many of the benefits of NServiceBus without using additional tools. These tools include ServiceMatrix, ServicePulse, and ServiceInsight.

The names of these services explain their use. ServiceMatrix is a development application in Visual Studio that helps you develop endpoints, messages, and services that include sagas; it has modeling and code generation tools. ServicePulse takes a quick pulse of NServiceBus's endpoints, messages, and services, providing you with an option to quickly monitor them and get their status; it is a monitoring tool for production operations. ServiceInsight provides as much detail as possible of endpoints, messages, and services and allows you to perform enhanced debugging of these pieces.

ServicePulse

ServicePulse is an operation-monitoring tool for applications in NServiceBus. It has three main functions:

- Monitoring heartbeats
- Monitoring errors and retries
- Extensibility for custom checks

Using ServicePulse, we can get a dashboard of failed messages, endpoint heartbeats, successful messages, and custom checks.

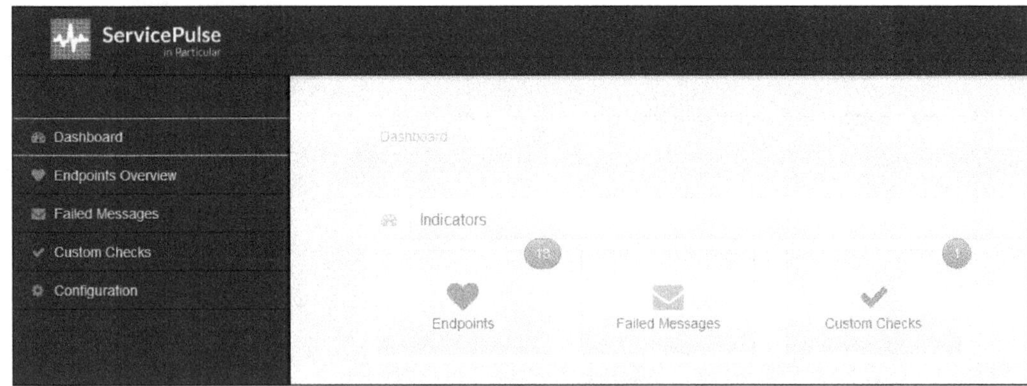

Besides the dashboard, we can get endpoint overviews, failed messages, custom checks, and configurations.

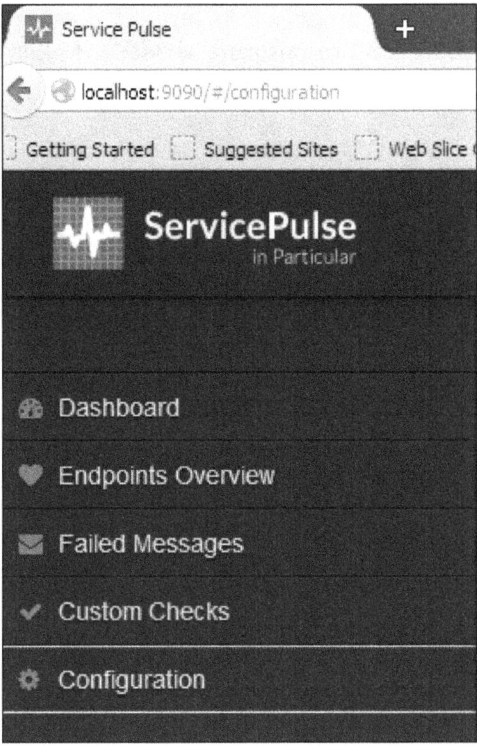

ServiceControl

ServiceControl can be downloaded from `http://particular.net/downloads`. For ServicePulse and ServiceInsight to work, ServiceControl has to be installed. ServiceControl is an auditing and monitoring service for NServiceBus endpoints and applications. This will define the transport type and port number that ServiceControl will be using.

ServiceControl gathers the audited messages forwarded by NServiceBus endpoints and sends them to the configured Audit queue; additionally, it exposes the HTTP API that provides data and functionality services for ServiceInsight and ServicePulse. Many of the ServiceControl configuration and troubleshooting instructions can be found at `http://docs.particular.net/servicecontrol/`.

ServiceControl supports other queuing types, for instance, SQL Server queues, Azure, and RabbitMQ. You will find instructions on this at `http://docs.particular.net/servicecontrol/multi-transport-support`.

ServiceControl, by default, will be installed at `C:\Program Files (x86)\Particular Software\ServiceControl`. ServiceControl has its own RavenDB that keeps track of the messages when it runs as a Windows service. RavenDB for NServiceBus must be installed. Most of the NServiceBus databases are located at `C:\Program Files\NServiceBus.Persistence.v4` by default. ServiceControl is managed through `http://localhost:33333/api`, and its database is defaulted at `C:\ProgramData\Particular\ServiceControl\localhost-33333`. The following is a snippet on how a database may look:

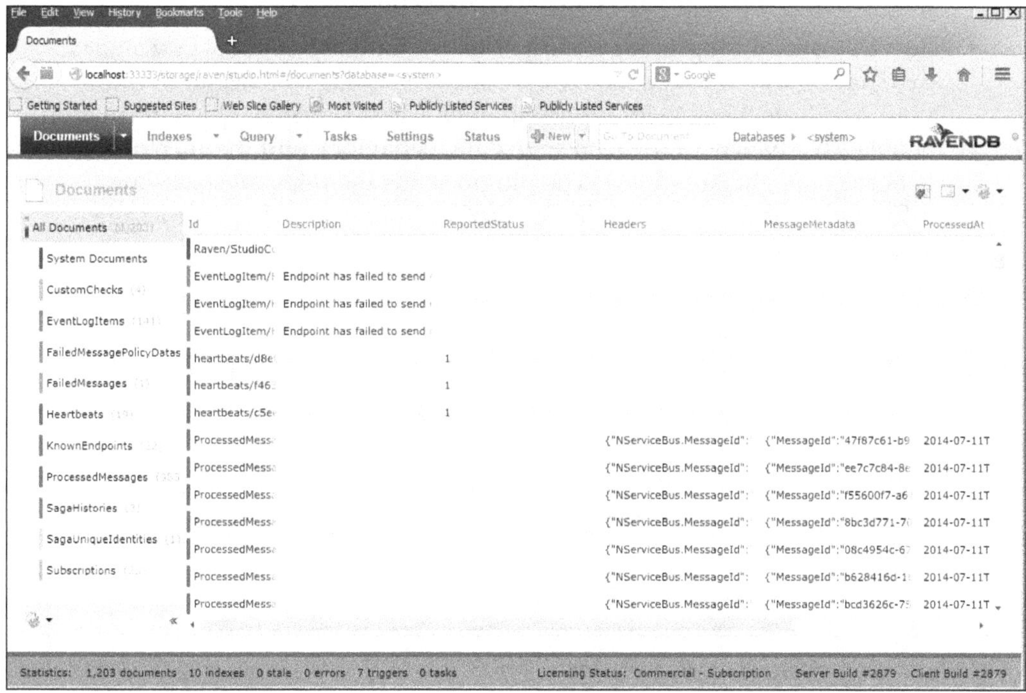

We will be using the **ScaleOut-ServiceControl** solution. This solution is similar to an earlier chapter's example, except that there we added service control plugins through NuGet to generate service control endpoints for monitoring purposes:

- **ServiceControl.Plugin.DebugSession**: This is found at `https://www.nuget.org/packages/ServiceControl.Plugin.DebugSession/`. When deployed, the debug session plugin adds a specified debug session identifier to the header of each message sent by the endpoint. This allows messages sent by debugging or a test run within Visual Studio to be correlated, filtered, and highlighted within ServiceInsight.

- **ServiceControl.Plugin.CustomChecks**: This is found at `https://www.nuget.org/packages/ServiceControl.Plugin.CustomChecks`. The result of a custom check is either a success or a failure (with a detailed description defined by the developer). This result is sent as a message to the ServiceControl queue.
- **ServiceControl.Plugin.Heartbeat**: This is found at `https://www.nuget.org/packages/ServiceControl.Plugin.Heartbeat`. The heartbeat plugin sends heartbeat messages from the endpoint to the ServiceControl queue. These messages are sent every 10 seconds (by default).
- **ServiceControl.Plugin.SagaAudit**: This is found at `https://www.nuget.org/packages/ServiceControl.Plugin.SagaAudit`. The Saga Audit plugin collects the activity information of a saga runtime. This information enables the display of detailed saga data, behaviors, and the current status in ServiceInsight Saga View. The plugin sends the relevant saga state information as messages to the ServiceControl queue whenever a saga state changes.

ServiceControl normally runs through the URL at `http://localhost:33333/api`. If the ServiceControl screen does not come up correctly, you may want to check to see whether the `Particular.ServiceControl` Windows service has started. ServiceInsight and ServicePulse will be looking to read the endpoint information from this port.

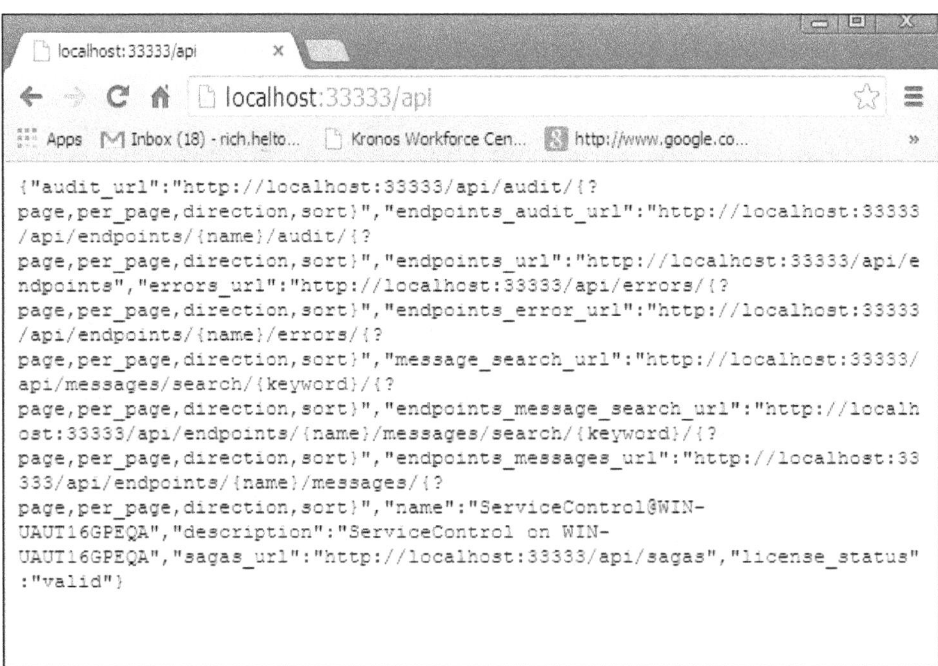

These are the starting URLs to provide the endpoint information. If we look at this page, we can see the URL structure to get further information, such as endpoints via `http://localhost:33333/api/endpoints/`.

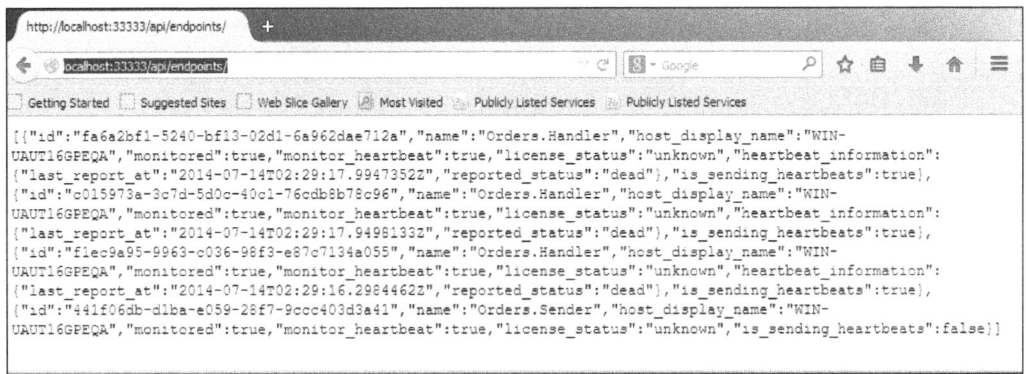

We can also view the messages from ServiceControl via `http://localhost:33333/api/messages/`.

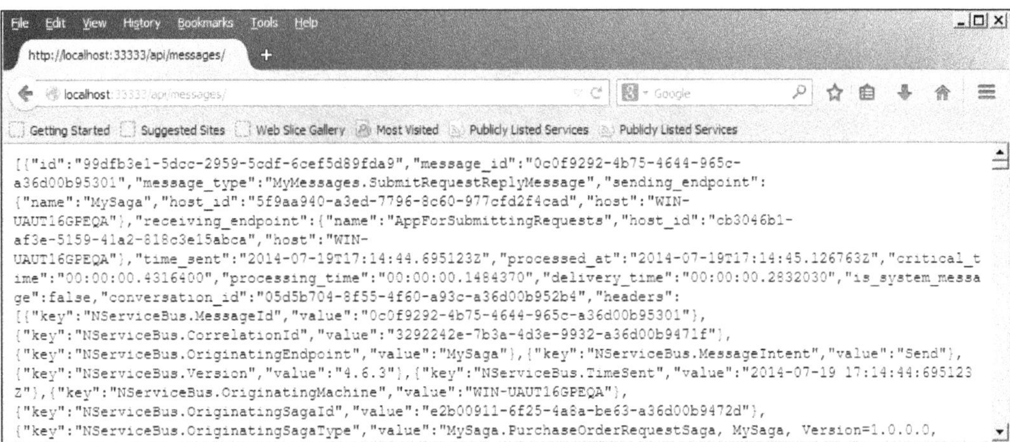

This is our message list with key-value pairs that define the collection of messages that have been captured. Notice that it is a key-value JSON format that is given in the ServiceControl interface. The ServiceControl's RavenDB performs a fetch in storage in JSON as well, so there is very little translation needed from the tables in RavenDB to be posted in HTTP protocol at port `33333`.

We can add the message GUID to the URL in the ServiceControl browser to see the message body from one of the messages listed as shown in the following screenshot:

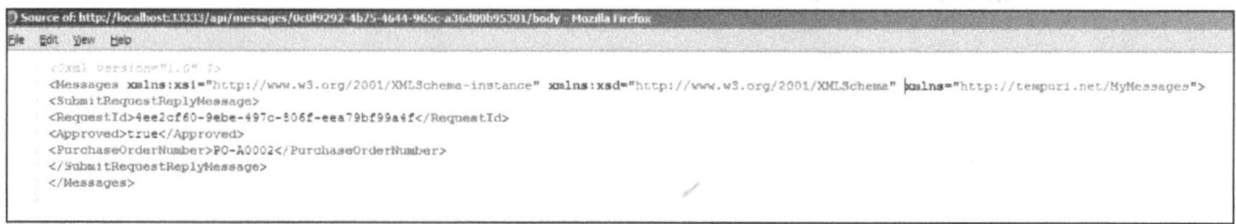

Then, when installing ServicePulse, it will define how it will access ServiceControl.

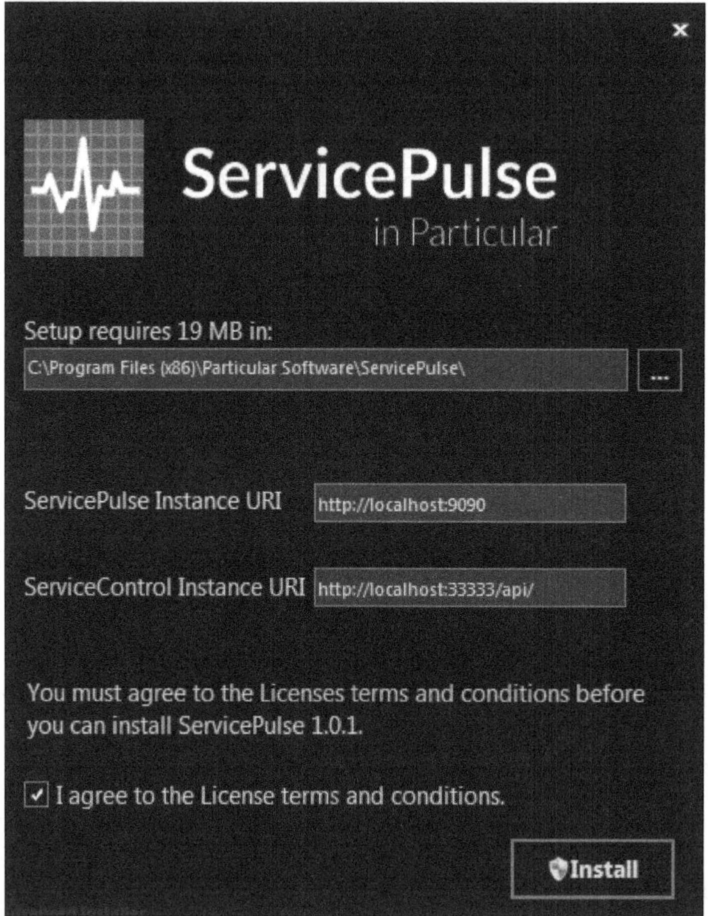

Let's look at a simple example. We can start with the publish-subscribe MSMQ example from `https://github.com/Particular/NServiceBus.Msmq.Samples/tree/master/PubSub`. We will add the ServiceControl plugins for heartbeats and custom checks through NuGet.

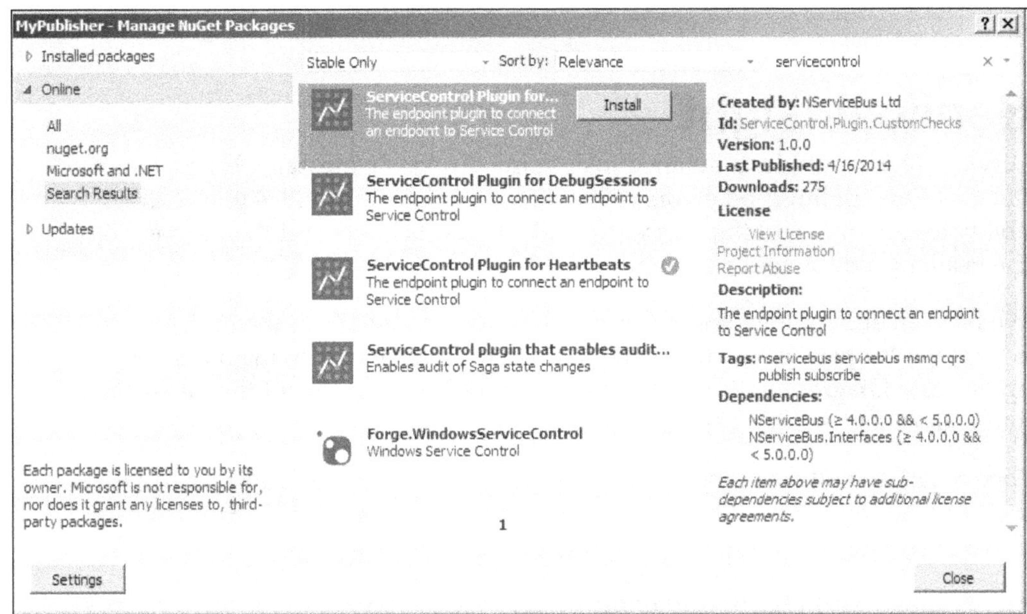

Then, we can check the heartbeats in ServicePulse to validate that the applications are available; this is indicated in the form of heartbeats. We monitor ServicePulse through the URL `http://localhost:9090`.

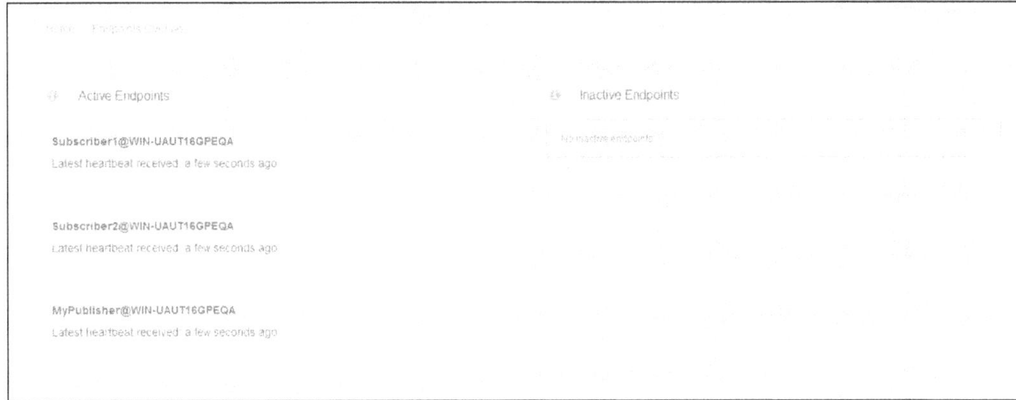

If there are issues with the services, always check that ServiceControl and ServicePulse are running.

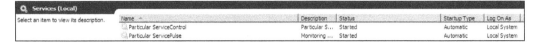

ServiceInsight

ServiceInsight provides a detailed insight into a specific message. It provides a detailed flow, timing, and errors of the message; also, it provides you with the ability to retry and sort the messages, look at their headers and their sagas, copy the headers and the messages, and more.

We have an endpoint explorer that provides us with details of the messages, a **Message Properties** window to drill down into the details of the message, and a **Flow Diagram** window to give us a graphical overview of the messages and endpoints.

ServiceInsight will collect endpoint information from ServiceControl through its web API. ServiceControl is a collector of endpoint information for ServiceInsight and ServicePulse.

The directory for the code is under the `BasicSagas-ServiceControl` directory. We will use this solution to generate some saga messages to look at through ServiceInsight.

The solution was run in VS2012 in Windows Server 2012, with MSMQ, DTC, RavenDB, NServiceBus version 4.0 references, and SQL Server 2012 Express LocalDB installed.

ServiceInsight will have four main parts to view. You have the **Messages** window to select which message to view, the **Message Properties** window to view the properties of the details of a message, the view canvas that currently displays a **Saga View** window, and the **Endpoint Explorer** window to look for messages based on the available endpoints.

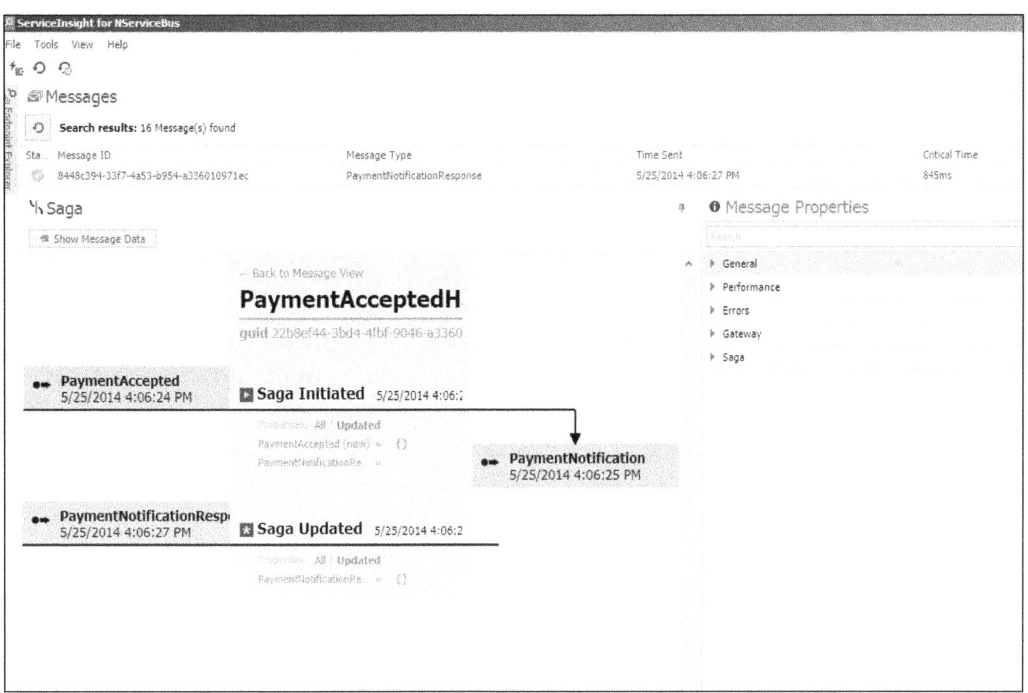

The **Endpoint Explorer** window gives a list of the available endpoints that have been captured in ServiceControl. This list can be used to filter all of the available messages so that you may view just the messages on an endpoint. The following is an example of an Endpoint Explorer tree that is viewed:

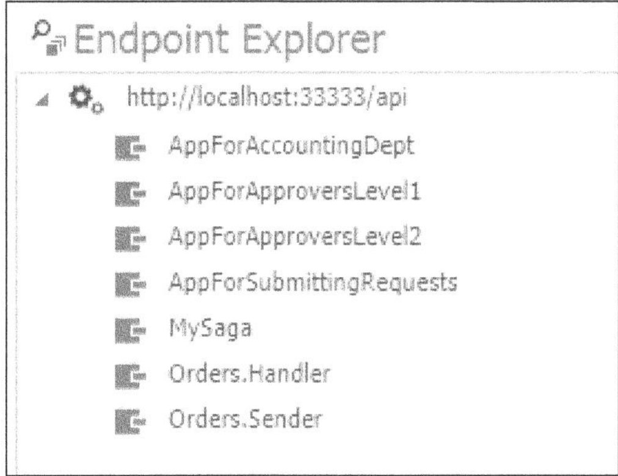

The collection of messages can be viewed for a single endpoint or in total, from the collection of messages available and stored in the ServiceControl RavenDB. This will appear as follows:

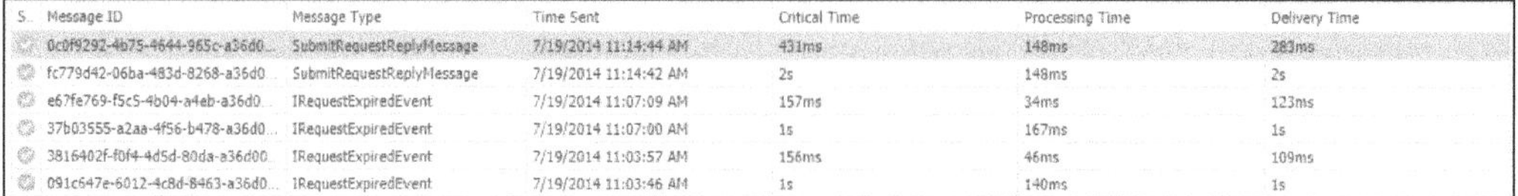

S..	Message ID	Message Type	Time Sent	Critical Time	Processing Time	Delivery Time
	0c0f9292-4b75-4644-965c-a36d0...	SubmitRequestReplyMessage	7/19/2014 11:14:44 AM	431ms	148ms	283ms
	fc779d42-06ba-483d-8268-a36d0...	SubmitRequestReplyMessage	7/19/2014 11:14:42 AM	2s	148ms	2s
	e67fe769-f5c5-4b04-a4eb-a36d0...	IRequestExpiredEvent	7/19/2014 11:07:09 AM	157ms	34ms	123ms
	37b03555-a2aa-4f56-b478-a36d0...	IRequestExpiredEvent	7/19/2014 11:07:00 AM	1s	167ms	1s
	3816402f-f0f4-4d5d-80da-a36d00...	IRequestExpiredEvent	7/19/2014 11:03:57 AM	156ms	46ms	109ms
	091c647e-6012-4c8d-8463-a36d0...	IRequestExpiredEvent	7/19/2014 11:03:46 AM	1s	140ms	1s

In the **Flow Diagram** view, we have selections at the bottom for the flow view of the message, the **Saga** view tab, the **Headers** view tab, the **Body** tab, and the **Logs** tab of ServiceInsight.

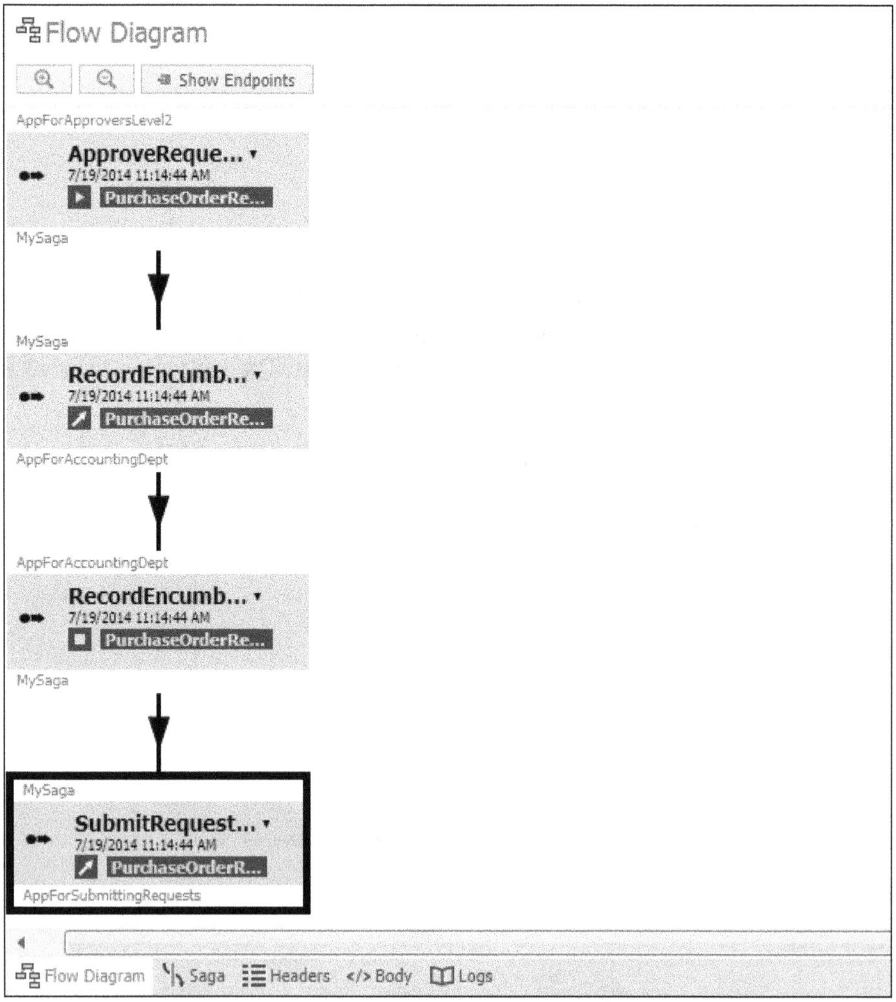

The **Logs** tab of the **Flow Diagram** window displays details of the interactions when ServiceInsight polls ServiceControl for more data, such as the example that appears in the following screen:

Logs

Clear All | Copy All

```
2014-07-24 20:21:50.314 -06:00 [Information] HTTP GET http://localhost:33333/api/
2014-07-24 20:21:50.852 -06:00 [Debug] HTTP Status OK (http://localhost:33333/api)
2014-07-24 20:21:50.854 -06:00 [Debug] Response Header: "Transfer-Encoding" : "chunked"
2014-07-24 20:21:50.854 -06:00 [Debug] Response Header: "Vary" : "Accept"
2014-07-24 20:21:50.854 -06:00 [Debug] Response Header: "X-Particular-Version" : "1.1.0"
2014-07-24 20:21:50.854 -06:00 [Debug] Response Header: "Access-Control-Expose-Headers" : "ETag, Last-Modified, Link, Total-Count, X-Particular-Version"
2014-07-24 20:21:50.854 -06:00 [Debug] Response Header: "Access-Control-Allow-Headers" : "Origin, X-Requested-With, Content-Type, Accept"
2014-07-24 20:21:50.854 -06:00 [Debug] Response Header: "Access-Control-Allow-Methods" : "POST, GET, PUT, DELETE, OPTIONS, PATCH"
2014-07-24 20:21:50.855 -06:00 [Debug] Response Header: "Access-Control-Allow-Origin" : "*"
2014-07-24 20:21:50.855 -06:00 [Debug] Response Header: "Cache-Control" : "private, max-age=0"
2014-07-24 20:21:50.856 -06:00 [Debug] Response Header: "Content-Type" : "application/json; charset=utf-8"
2014-07-24 20:21:50.856 -06:00 [Debug] Response Header: "Date" : "Fri, 25 Jul 2014 02:21:50 GMT"
2014-07-24 20:21:50.857 -06:00 [Debug] Response Header: "ETag" : "\"8d145f930920600\""
2014-07-24 20:21:50.857 -06:00 [Debug] Response Header: "Last-Modified" : "Sun, 25 May 2014 06:25:00 GMT"
2014-07-24 20:21:50.857 -06:00 [Debug] Response Header: "Server" : "Microsoft-HTTPAPI/2.0"
```

The **Body** view tab shows the body of a particular message; notice that we were able to view this in the ServiceControl browser earlier:

XML | Hex

```
<?xml version="1.0"?>
<Messages xmlns:xsi="http://www.w3.org/2001/XMLSchema-instance" xmlns:xsd="http://www.w3.org/2001/XMLSchema" xmlns="http://tempuri.net/MyMessages">
  <SubmitRequestReplyMessage>
    <RequestId>4ee2cf60-9ebe-497c-806f-eea79bf99a4f</RequestId>
    <Approved>true</Approved>
    <PurchaseOrderNumber>PO-A0002</PurchaseOrderNumber>
  </SubmitRequestReplyMessage>
</Messages>
```

The **Headers** view will give the NSB header information related to the message:

Headers

Key	Value
CorrId	3292242e-7b3a-4d3e-9932-a36d00b9471f\0
NServiceBus.ContentType	text/xml
NServiceBus.ConversationId	05d5b704-8f55-4f60-a93c-a36d00b952b4
NServiceBus.CorrelationId	3292242e-7b3a-4d3e-9932-a36d00b9471f
NServiceBus.EnclosedMessageTypes	MyMessages.SubmitRequestReplyMessage, MyMessages, Version=1.0.0.0, Culture=neutral, PublicKeyToken=null
NServiceBus.MessageId	0c0f9292-4b75-4644-965c-a36d00b95301
NServiceBus.MessageIntent	Send
NServiceBus.OriginatingAddress	MySaga@WIN-UAUT16GPEQA
NServiceBus.OriginatingEndpoint	MySaga
NServiceBus.OriginatingMachine	WIN-UAUT16GPEQA
NServiceBus.OriginatingSagaId	e2b00911-6f25-4a8a-be63-a36d00b9472d
NServiceBus.OriginatingSagaType	MySaga.PurchaseOrderRequestSaga, MySaga, Version=1.0.0.0, Culture=neutral, PublicKeyToken=null
NServiceBus.ProcessingEnded	2014-07-19 17:14:45:126763 Z
NServiceBus.ProcessingEndpoint	AppForSubmittingRequests
NServiceBus.ProcessingMachine	WIN-UAUT16GPEQA
NServiceBus.ProcessingStarted	2014-07-19 17:14:44:978326 Z
NServiceBus.RelatedTo	e9ed9522-dded-45f4-94c8-a36d00b952ed
NServiceBus.TimeSent	2014-07-19 17:14:44:695123 Z
NServiceBus.Version	4.6.3
WinIdName	WIN-UAUT16GPEQA\Administrator

So, now that we have covered views and messages, there's more. There are also properties on each message that details NSB properties for the time transmitted, saga IDs, performance information, message IDs, and other distinct details of the NSB message details. The saga information will include the saga ID, originator, and `OriginalMessageId` that the saga needs for the original client. Here's a sample of the properties tab:

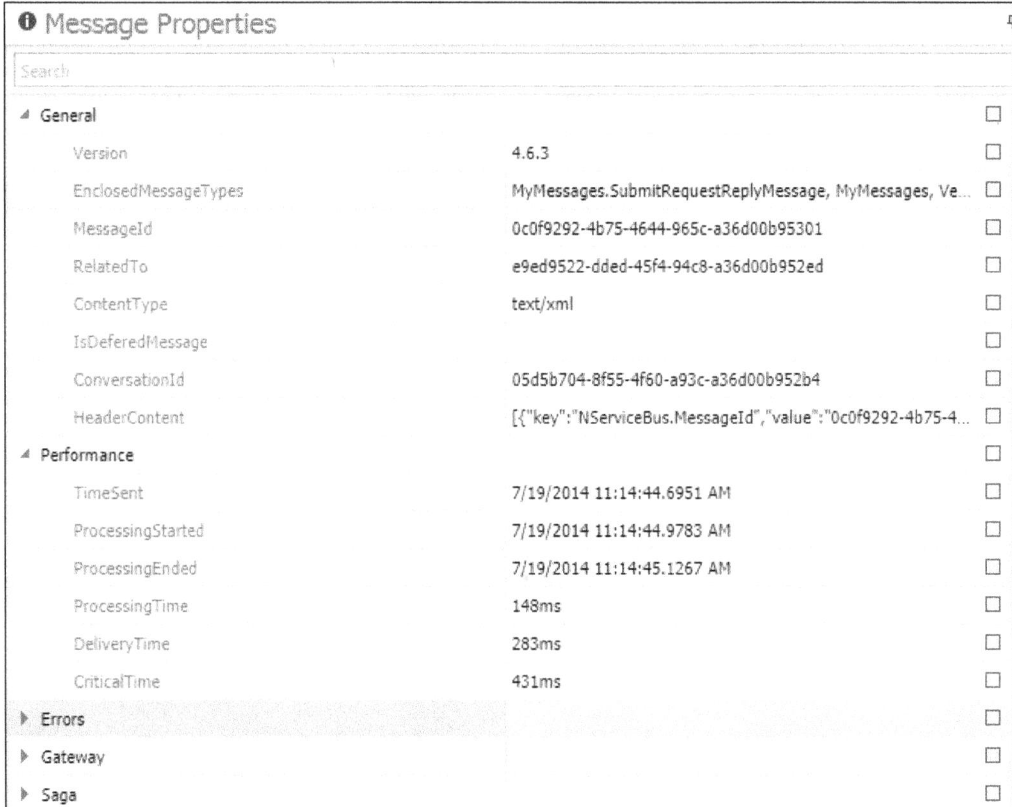

ServiceInsight gives more information than is usually needed to troubleshoot messages, endpoints, or services with some amount of detail. The future of NSB ServiceInsight is to add more detail, such as sequence diagrams to enhance the flow of the views and add more details to view saga information.

ServiceMatrix

ServiceMatrix is a series that can start projects as NServiceBus projects with pieces already integrated for faster development. However, it is not necessary to use ServiceMatrix to build NServiceBus components. A step-by-step guide on how to use ServiceMatrix is available at `http://docs.particular.net/servicematrix/getting-started-with-servicematrix-2.0`, and the process of using code without ServiceMatrix is found at `http://particular.net/articles/NServiceBus-Step-by-Step-Guide`.

We install ServiceMatrix in Visual Studio using the **Extensions and Updates...** option under the **Tools** menu.

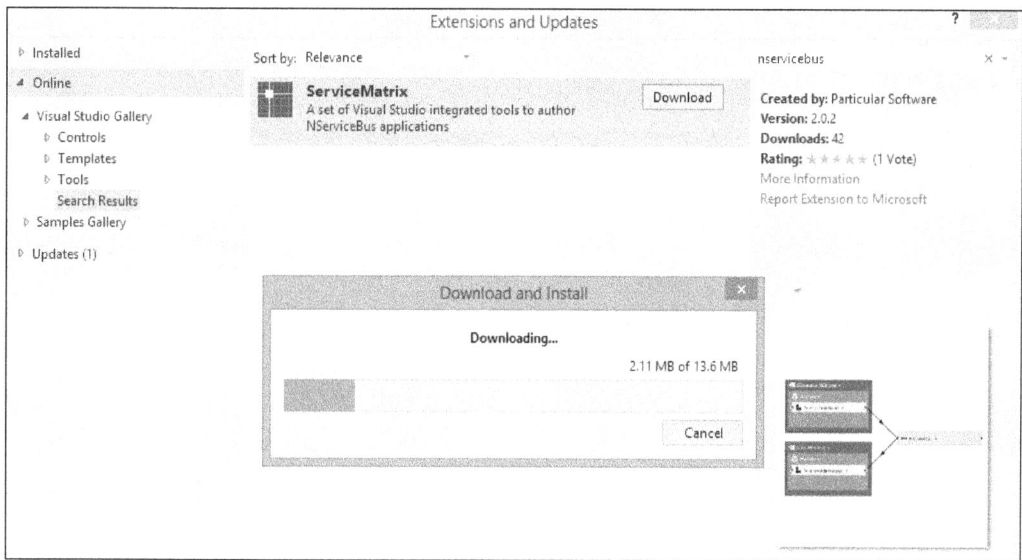

We can create an NServiceBus project by navigating to the **Project** option under the **Files** | **New** menu. Here, we will create a `PaymentEngine` example:

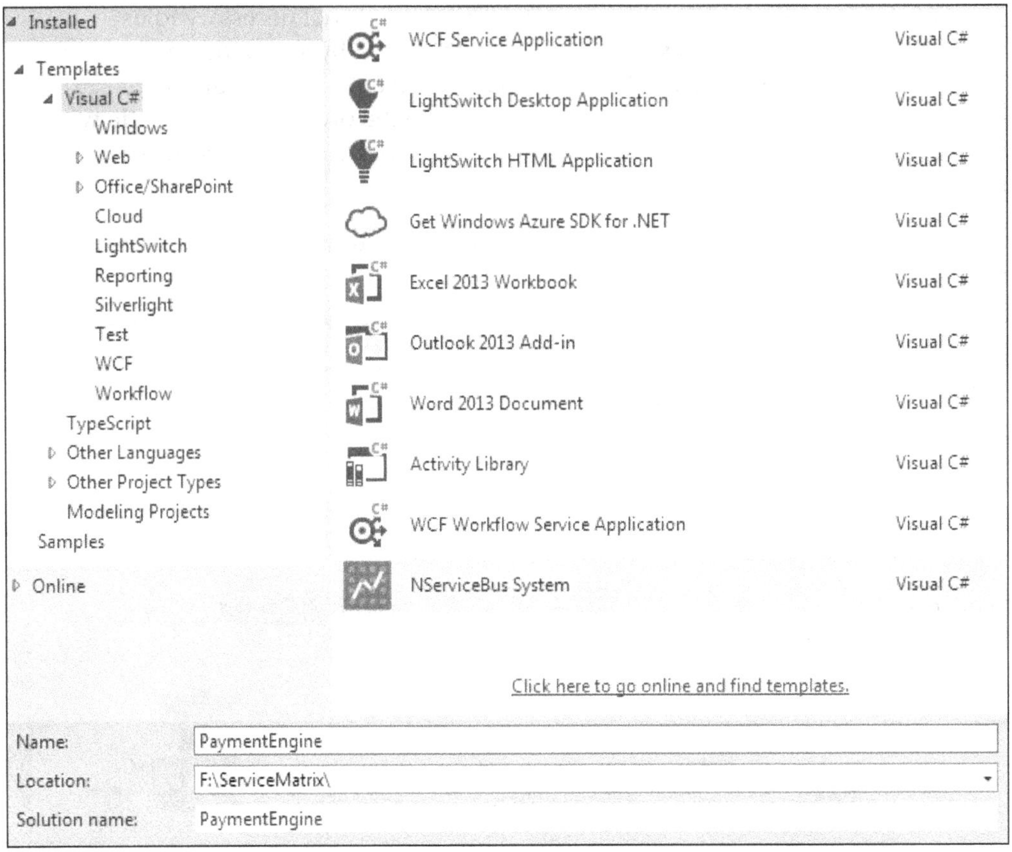

Normally, there will be three different areas for the standard development environment. There will be **Solution Builder** on the left-hand side, **NServiceBus Canvas** in the center, and **Solution Explorer** on the right-hand side.

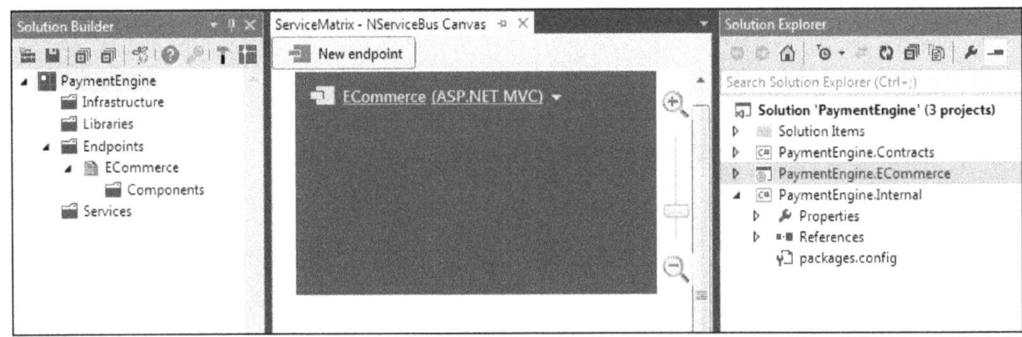

We will create another endpoint called `PaymentProcessing` that will be an NServiceBus host program. The NServiceBus host streamlines service development and deployment, allows you to change technologies without code, and is administrator-friendly when setting permissions and accounts. Refer to `http://docs.particular.net/nservicebus/the-nservicebus-host`.

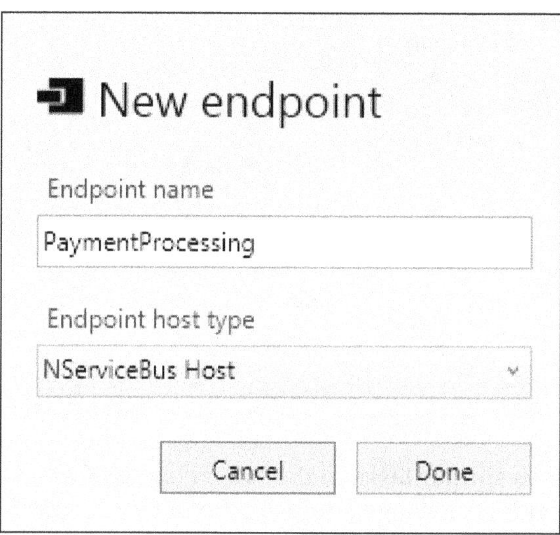

The **Solution Builder** window contains four main sections:

- **Infrastructure**: This is used to create and manage NServiceBus authentication and auditing
- **Libraries**: This is used to create and manage NServiceBus reusable libraries
- **Endpoints**: This is used to create and manage NServiceBus endpoints
- **Services**: This is used to create and manage NServiceBus services

By right-clicking on the elements of these sections, we can add or change their properties.

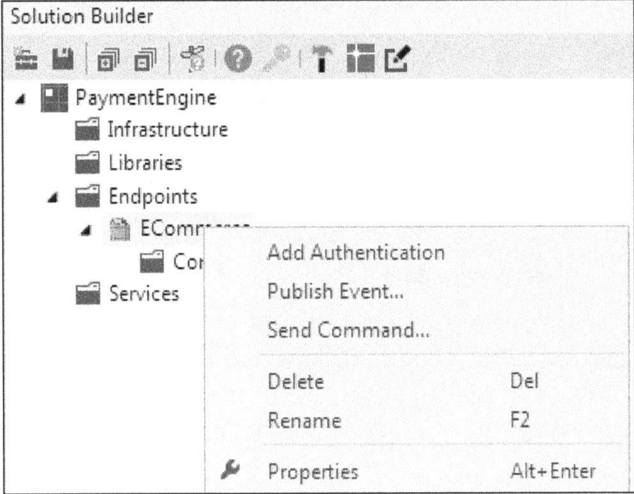

We can also accomplish similar tasks in the **NServiceBus Canvas** window with the difference being that it is a visual graph instead of a tree hierarchy.

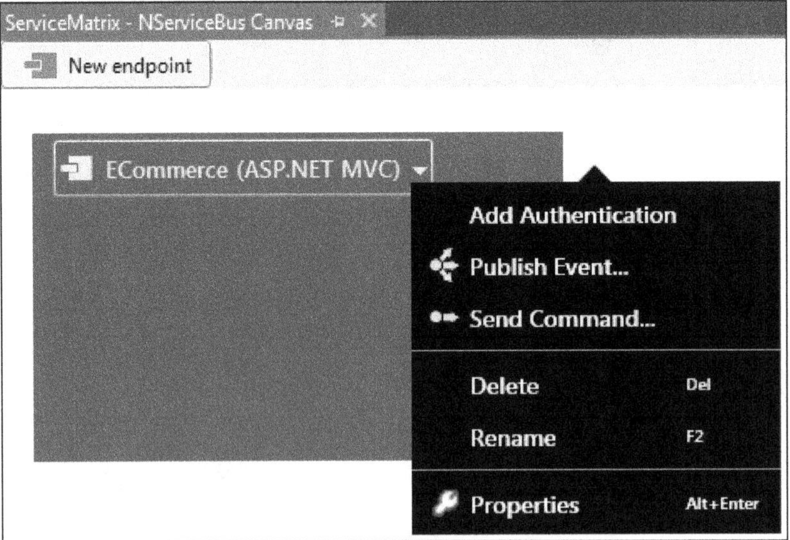

The **Solutions Explorer** window will give the resultant generated code. Some of the code will be stubs that are created to add more detail during development. An event can be created using **Publish Event...**, and a command message can be created using **Send Command....** We can create a send command message. We will create a ServiceName of `Payments` for the command message, `SubmitPayment`.

The **Contracts** section will contain NServiceBus events, and the **Internal** section will contain NServiceBus commands. Notice that `SubmitOrder.cs` was created when we created the **SubmitPayment** command.

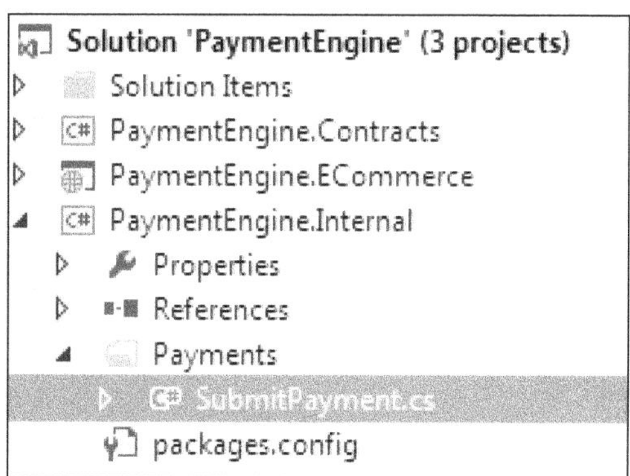

In the following screenshot, we can see the code that would normally contain your command message; at this time, it is nothing but a code stub. Here, we add a string field call data to be passed through the message.

```
using System;

namespace PaymentEngine.Internal.Commands.Payments
{
    9 references
    public class SubmitPayment
    {
        0 references
        public string data { get; set; }
    }
}
```

At this point, the code will not be compiled because the message only has one endpoint. We need to deploy the other endpoint with the **Deploy Component...** command.

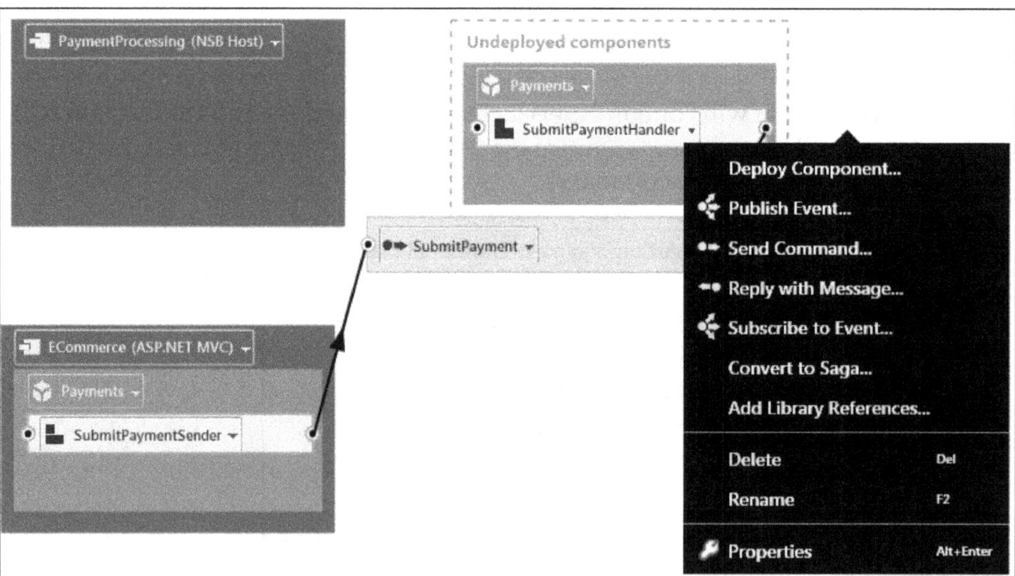

We can select the available endpoints. In this case, we also created an endpoint, `PaymentProcessing`. We also have the ability to create new endpoints.

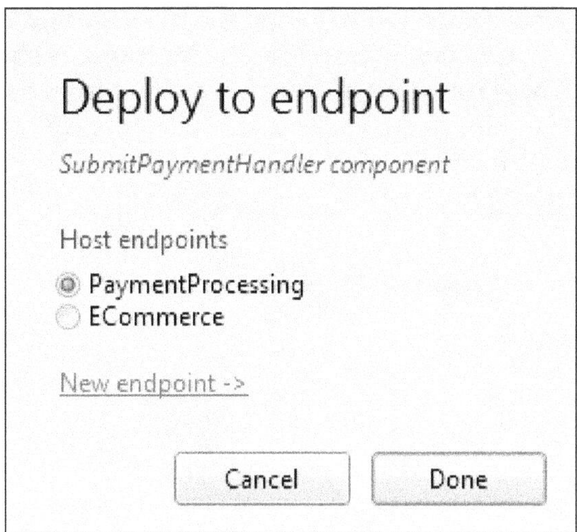

Then, we will have two endpoints with a command message being sent from **ECommerce**, an MVC controller, to **PaymentProcessing**, and an NSB Host; both these endpoints will be created by a command prompt or service.

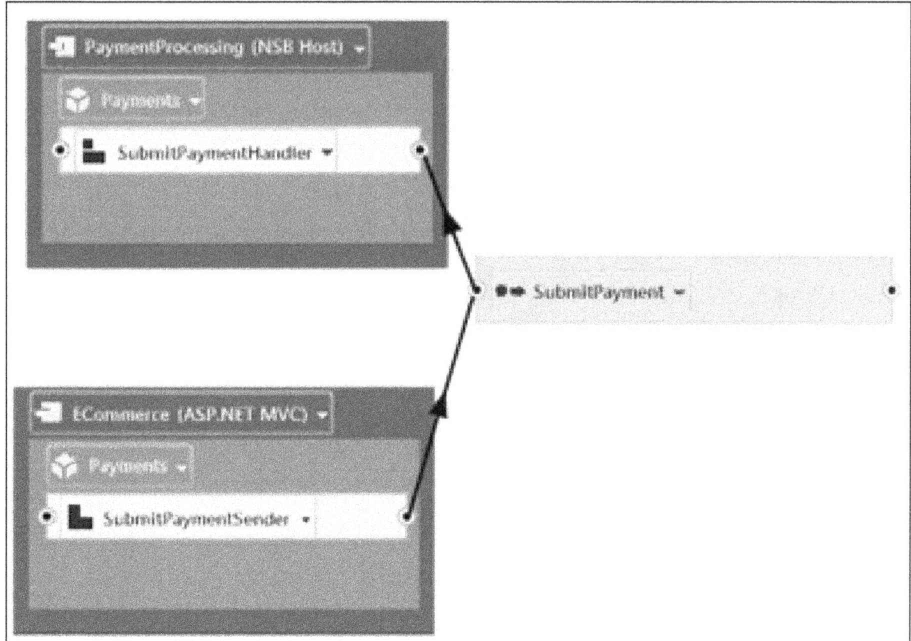

Endpoints

The `SubmitPaymentSender` function will send the message and the `SubmitPaymentHandler` function will receive the message, as shown in the previous screenshot. These functions are already created from ServiceMatrix and can be extended. Looking at `SubmitPaymentHandler`, we can extend the function to print the data field.

```
using System;
using NServiceBus;
using PaymentEngine.Internal.Commands.Payments;

namespace PaymentEngine.Payments
{
    1 reference
    public partial class SubmitPaymentHandler
    {
        2 references
        partial void HandleImplementation(SubmitPayment message)
        {
            // TODO: SubmitPaymentHandler: Add code to handle the SubmitPayment message.
            Console.WriteLine("Payments received " + message.GetType().Name);
            Console.WriteLine("Data " + message.data);
        }
    }
}
```

When we run the project, without adding further code, we get an ASP interface to send the data in the message.

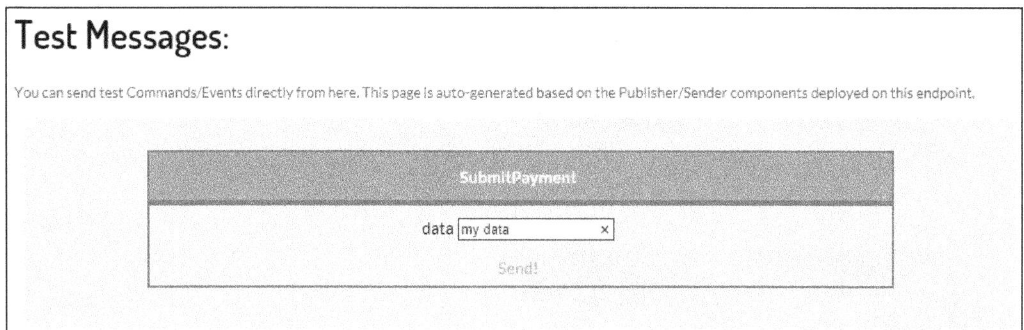

Once you send the message, we receive the data that was sent in `PaymentProcessing`.

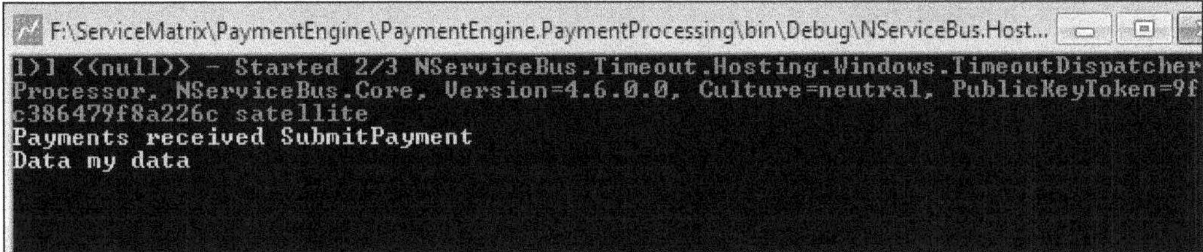

If we open up ServicePulse, at `http://localhost:9090/#/dashboard`, we can see that the message will appear at the two endpoints; however, we will need to install the plugin to monitor the endpoint.

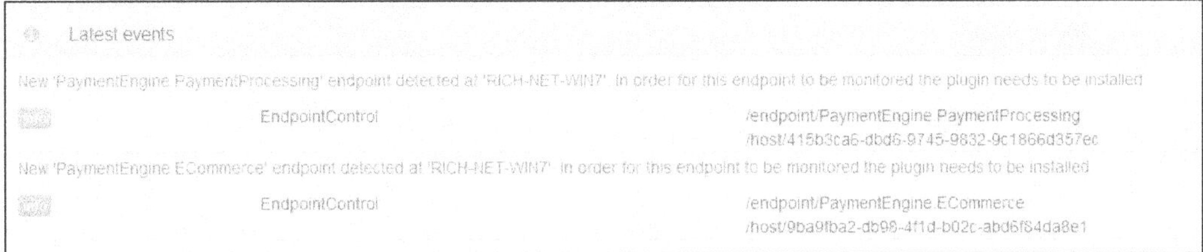

The plugins can be installed via NuGet.

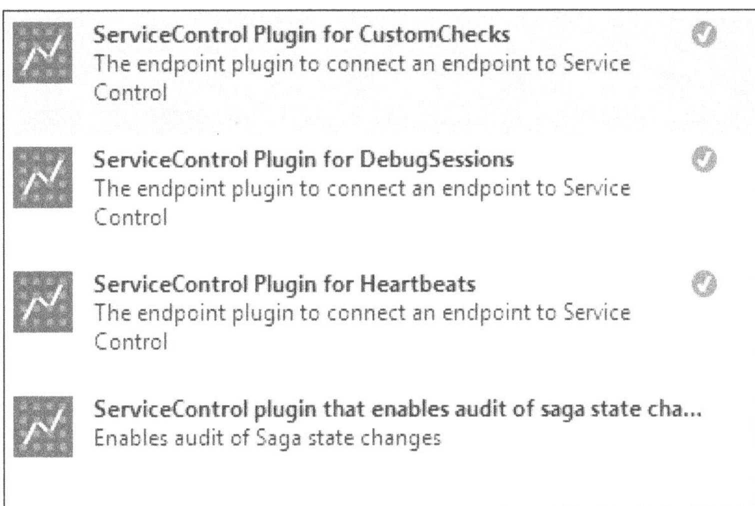

Again, there are four ServiceControl plugins that can be installed:

- **The ServiceControl plugin for CustomChecks**: The custom checks plugin allows the developer of an NServiceBus endpoint to define a set of conditions that are checked periodically or during an endpoint's startup.
- **The ServiceControl plugin for DebugSessions**: Debug session is a dedicated plugin that enables integration between ServiceMatrix and ServiceInsight.
- **The ServiceControl plugin for Heartbeats**: The Heartbeat plugin sends heartbeat messages from the endpoint to the ServiceControl queue. These messages are sent every 10 seconds (by default).
- **The ServiceControl plugin for Saga Audits**: The Saga Audit plugin collects saga runtime activity information. This information enables the display of detailed saga data, behavior, and the current status of the ServiceInsight saga view.

By installing the Heartbeats plugin into the **ECommerce** and **PaymentProcessing** projects, ServicePulse will provide heartbeat information on the uptime of these services.

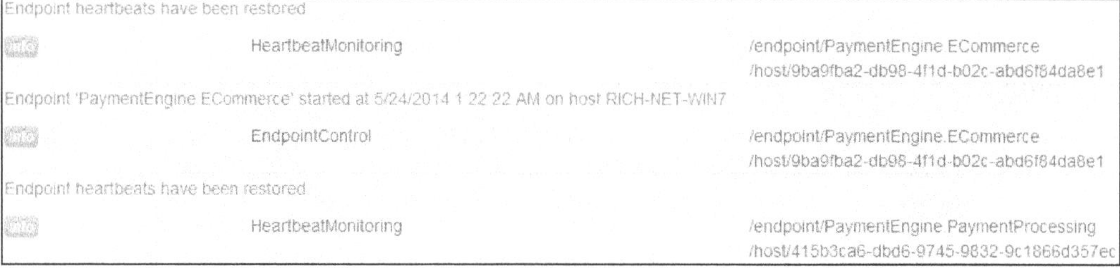

We can also run ServiceInsight to visually see the flow of the **Ecommerce** MVC by sending `SubmitPayment` to **PaymentProcessing**.

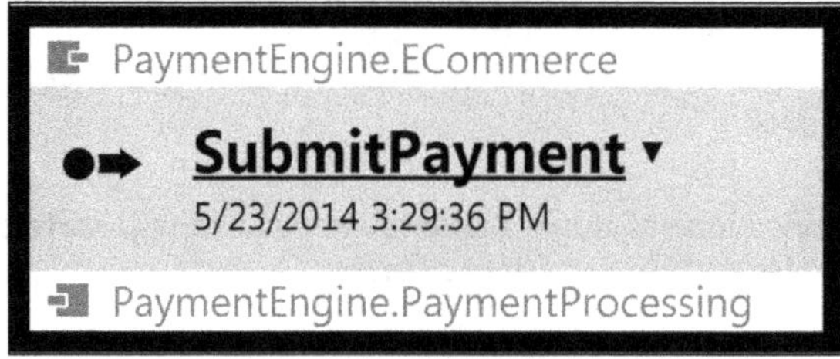

We can walk down the message and drill down into further information to gain insight into the performance and operation of the messages and endpoints.

S..	Message ID	Message Type	Time Sent	Critical Time	Processing Time ▲	Delivery Time
	50101f22-5efa-4c0d-8704-a33400d05586	SubmitPayment	5/23/2014 12:38:31 PM	2s	59ms	2s
	e1b42d5c-c392-4cba-8ab1-a33400ff5295	SubmitPayment	5/23/2014 3:29:36 PM	1s	79ms	1s

Introducing custom checks

With ServiceControl.Plugin.CustomChecks installed, we can perform several checks.

In this section, we will be using the **PubSub--ReportFailure** solution—the **MyPublisher** project reports a failure check that will be reported in ServicePulse. This solution shows custom checks.

In this section, we will also be using the **PubSub--ReportPass** solution—the **MyPublisher** project reports a pass check that will be reported in ServicePulse. This solution shows custom checks.

There are the following base constructors under the `CustomCheck` package—the base constructor is used to define which class is passing or failing:

- `ReportPass`: This will report that the custom check has passed
- `ReportFailed`: This will report that a custom check has failed, passing in the string stating the reason for the failure

Here, we create the code for a custom check object that can be called when we submit a payment as an additional check. It is a simple constructor in a `MyCustomCheck` class that will pass information through the base class of `CustomCheck`. We call this class when we send the `SubmitPayment` command from the **ECommerce** project using `MyCustomCheck myCheck = new MyCustomCheck();`:

```
using System;
using System.IO;
using ServiceControl.Plugin.CustomChecks;
```

```
using ServiceControl.Plugin.CustomChecks.Messages;
using ServiceControl.Plugin.CustomChecks.Internal;
namespace PaymentEngine.ECommerce
{
    public class MyCustomCheck : CustomCheck
    {
        public MyCustomCheck()
            : base("ECommerce SubmitPayment check", "ECommerce")
        {
            ReportPass();
        }
    }
}
```

So, when a submit payment is sent, we get an additional message on ServicePulse.

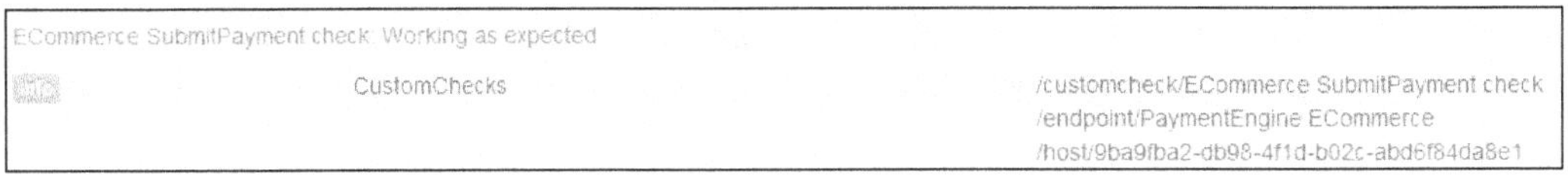

ECommerce SubmitPayment check: Working as expected

CustomChecks /customcheck/ECommerce SubmitPayment check /endpoint/PaymentEngine ECommerce /host/9ba9fba2-db98-4f1d-b02c-abd6f84da8e1

We can use conditional statements to check whether files are present, other messages are present, and a number of conditions that can be reported as either passing or failing while providing status information to ServicePulse for operations to take action.

In the `CustomChecks` class, we can also set a timer to periodically check for files using the `PeriodicCheck` interface. This will set a timer to call the class back and send the condition to ServicePulse. It operates differently from `ReportPass` as the condition here is reported based on a timer. It will use the function `PerformCheck()` that it must override; this will return `CheckResult` (either passed or failed) to inform ServicePulse. We will check the status every 2 minutes in this example; depending on the seconds, it will return a result as either passed or failed:

```
namespace PaymentEngine.PaymentProcessing
{
    class CheckHealth : PeriodicCheck
    {
        public CheckHealth()
            : base("PaymentProcessing Healthcheck",
"PaymentProcessing", TimeSpan.FromMinutes(2))
        {
        }
```

```
        public override CheckResult PerformCheck()
        {
            // Fake a failure once in a while
            if (DateTime.Now.Second % 2 == 0)
            {
                return CheckResult.Failed("PaymentProcessing fake
failure");
            }
            return CheckResult.Pass;
        }
    }
}
```

Passing a failure for a custom check in ServicePulse:

PaymentProcessing Healthcheck: PaymentProcessing fake failure

error CustomChecks /endpoint/PaymentEngine.PaymentProcessing /host/415b3ca6-dbd6-9745-9832-9c1866d357ec /customcheck/PaymentProcessing Healthcheck

Passing a pass for a custom check in ServicePulse:

There are many uses of custom checks in ServicePulse to give operations and the business the internal operations of the services, endpoints, and messages in NServiceBus.

We called the `MyCustomCheck` class when we passed messages to the `MyPublisher` queue using `MyCustomCheck myCheck = new MyCustomCheck();`.

We can then put conditional statements to check the condition and report whether the check has failed or passed. We will show how we can pass a message to ServicePulse to report that it has passed. We can report a failure by replacing the report that has passed with the one that failed, such as `ReportFailed("Testing")`. It will then log the failures in ServicePulse.

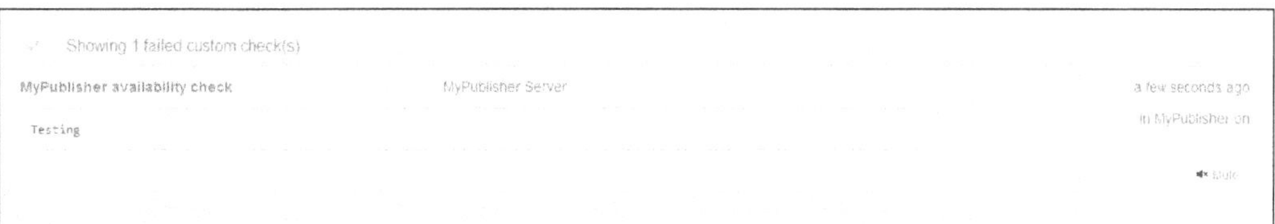

ServicePulse provides a visual interface to show the history of the heartbeats, failures, and custom checks when it is running, and we can configure which available endpoints to check.

Publish/subscribe through ServiceMatrix

The publish/subscribe messaging pattern is where senders, called publishers, send messages without direct receivers; this is because the receivers of the messages, called subscribers, subscribe to the messages that they are interested in receiving.

In this section, we will be using the **Payment-Saga** solution created with ServiceMatrix. So, ServiceMatrix must be installed. This will be a walk-through of ServiceMatrix.

The **Publish Event...** command is used to create the message to be published.

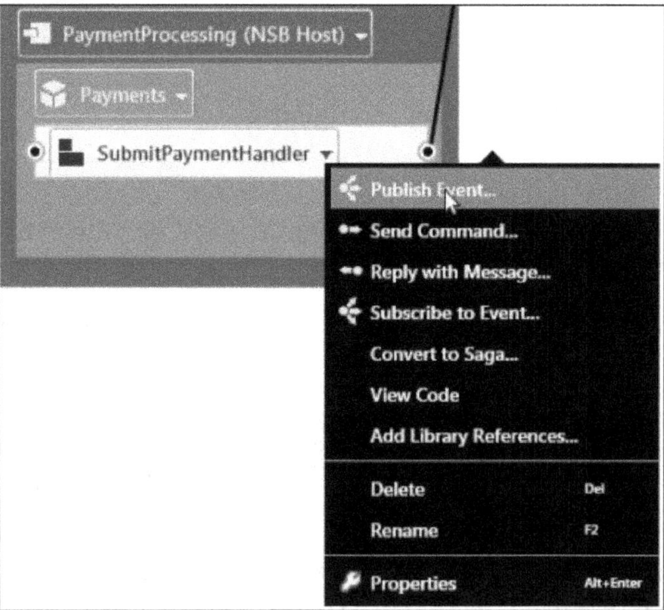

We name the publisher event message `PaymentAccepted` via the **PaymentProcessing** host.

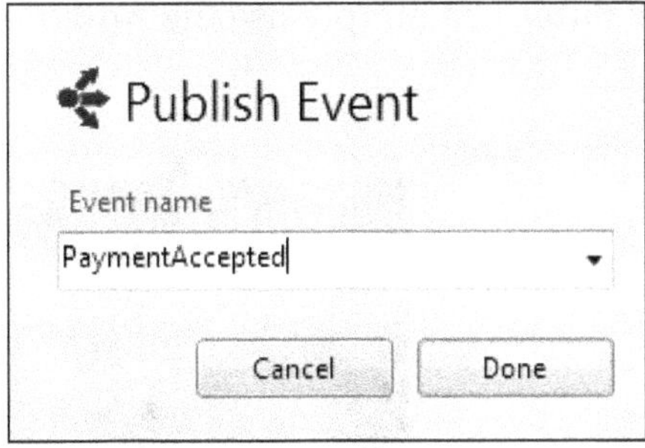

A code-convenient window will be created to review the code before it is deployed.

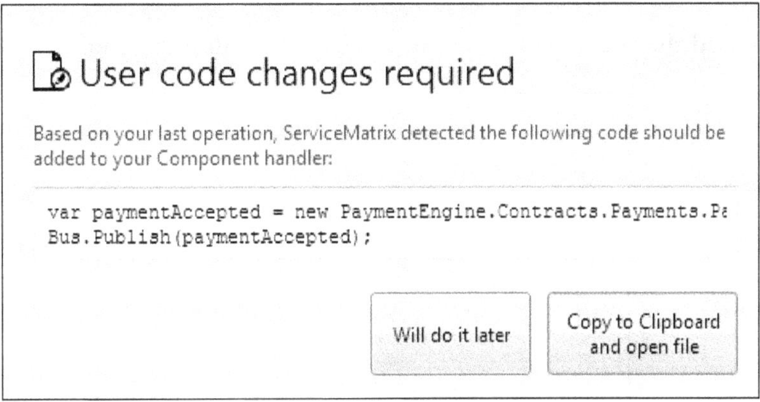

This is so that you can review the code before copying it into the message handler that you will be publishing from:

```
public partial class SubmitPaymentHandler
{
    partial void HandleImplementation(SubmitPayment message)
    {
        // TODO: SubmitPaymentHandler: Add code to handle the
SubmitPayment message.
        Console.WriteLine("Payments received " + message.
GetType().Name);
        Console.WriteLine("Data " + message.data);
        var paymentAccepted = new PaymentEngine.Contracts.
Payments.PaymentAccepted();
        Bus.Publish(paymentAccepted);

    }
}
```

To add a subscriber to the publisher, simply use the **Add Subscriber...** command.

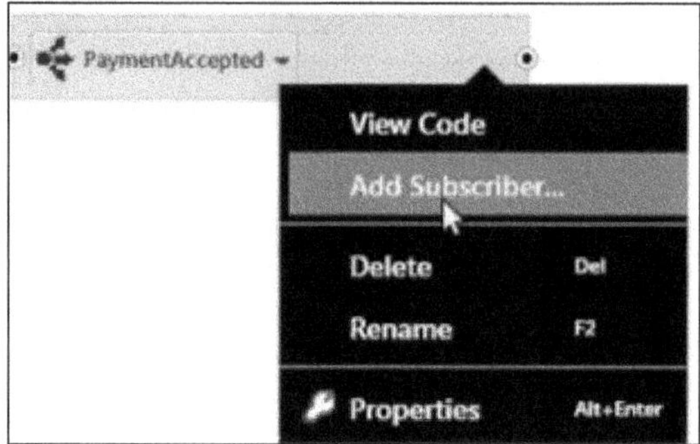

We can then add the subscriber to a new service; let's call it `Paying`.

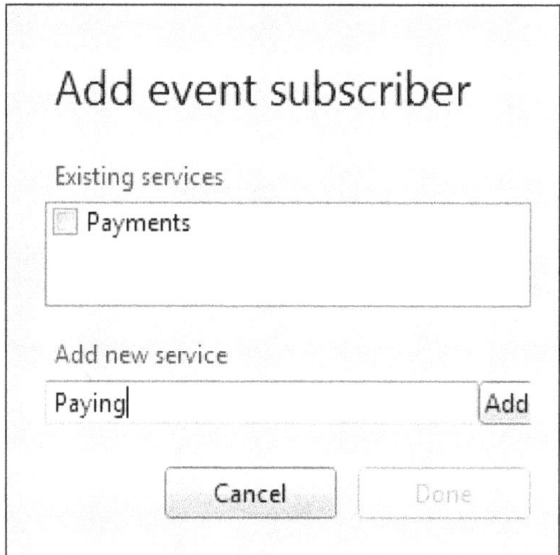

After these changes are made, we should have the following:

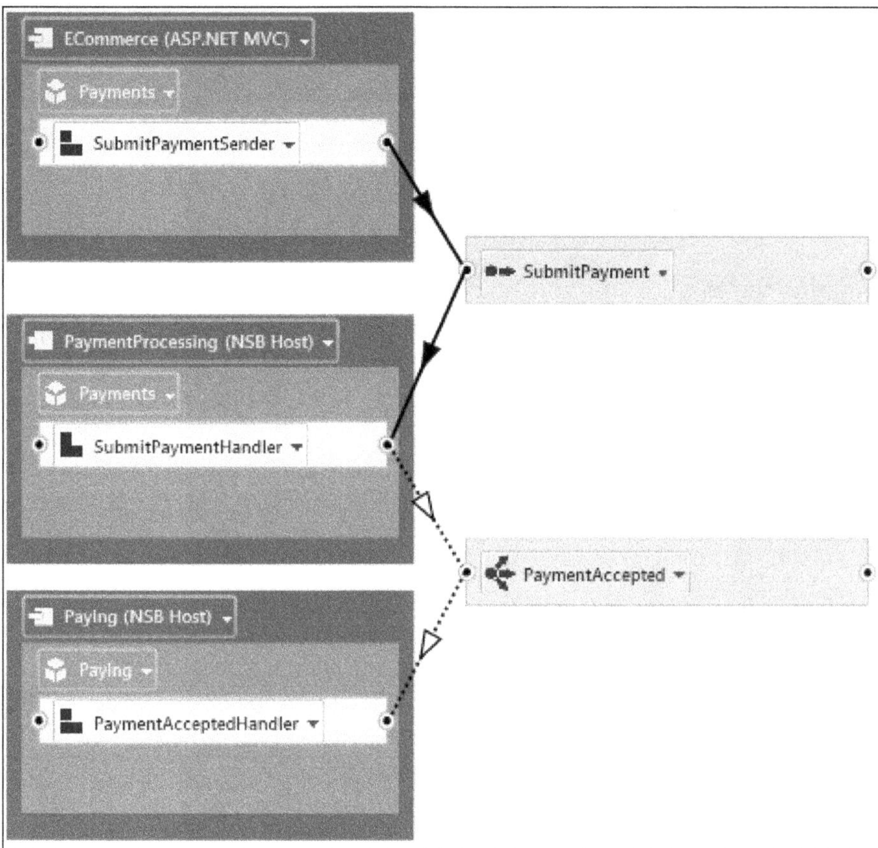

The properties description of the solution will define the error and audit queues:

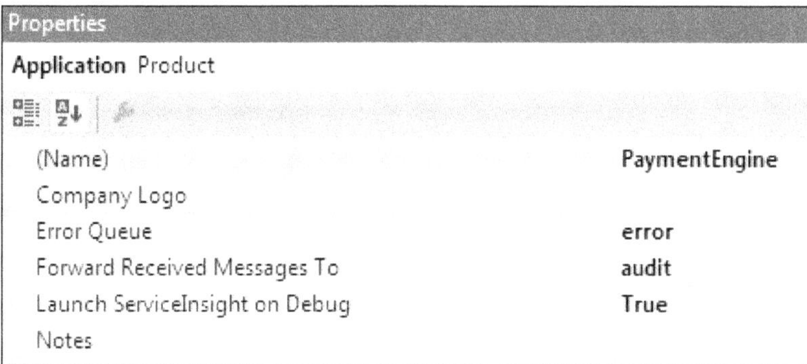

The properties description of the solution will also define the various types of queues that can be used.

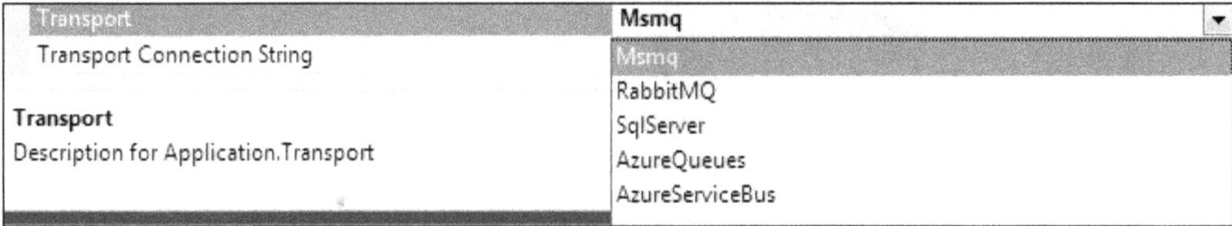

When running the solution and rerunning ServicePulse, we can see the additional **Paying** endpoint created that didn't have the plugins installed.

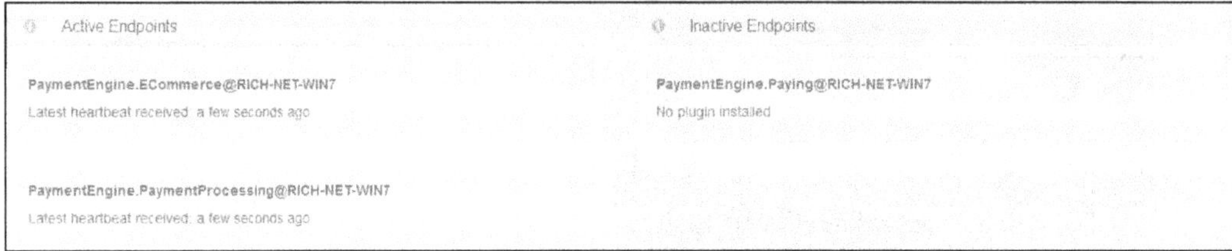

If we review the flow in ServiceInsight, we will see the new flows.

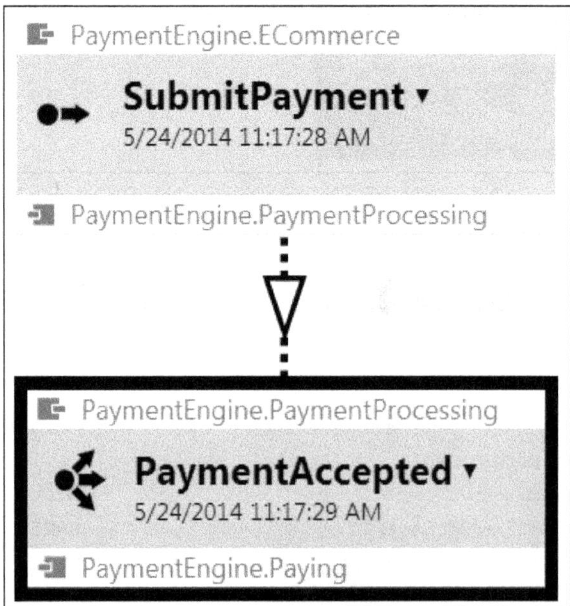

Sagas through ServiceMatrix

Not only can we develop endpoints for command and publish/subscribe messages, but we can also develop sagas in ServiceMatrix. We will start by creating a new command message, `PaymentNotification`.

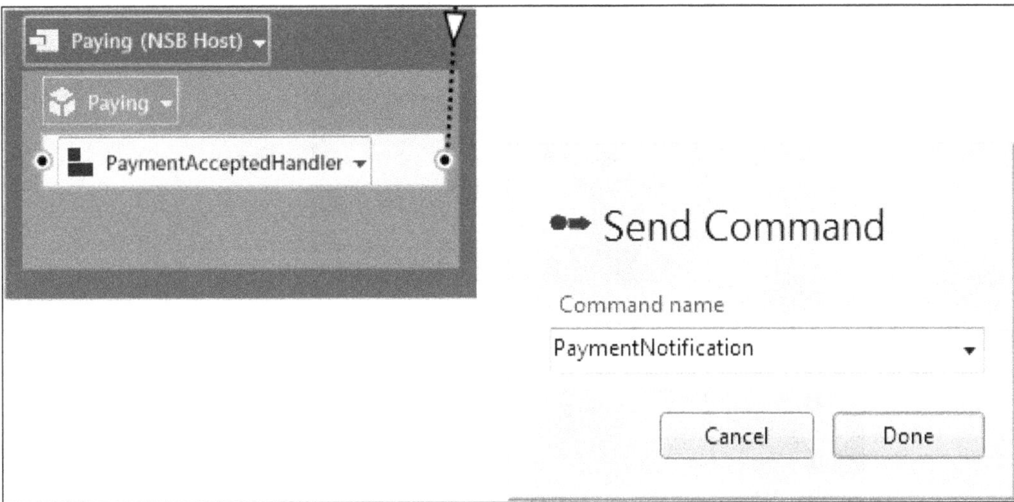

The copy preview box will appear again as we copy the sending of the new command message to the message handler:

```
public partial class PaymentAcceptedHandler
  {

       partial void HandleImplementation(PaymentAccepted message)
       {
           // TODO: PaymentAcceptedHandler: Add code to handle the
PaymentAccepted message.
           Console.WriteLine("Paying received " + message.GetType().
Name);
           var paymentNotification = new PaymentEngine.Internal.
Commands.Paying.PaymentNotification();
           Bus.Send(paymentNotification);
       }
  }
```

We will deploy the receiving endpoint on to a new endpoint called `NotifyProcessing`.

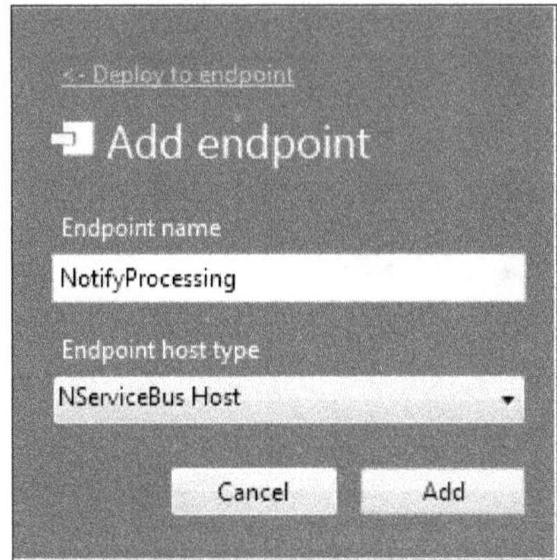

This is what we should have so far:

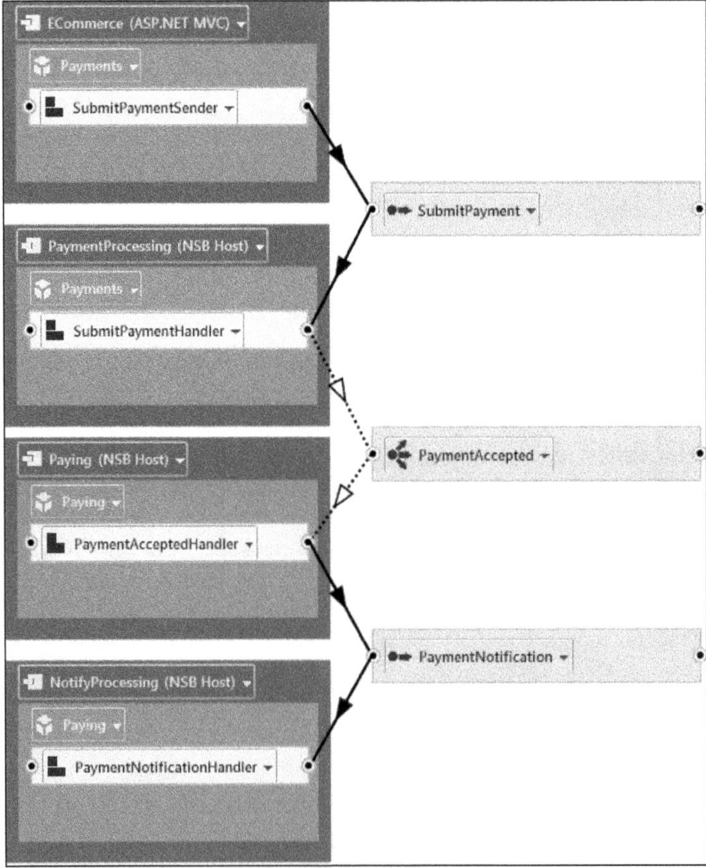

To start the saga process, we need to click on **Reply with Message...**.

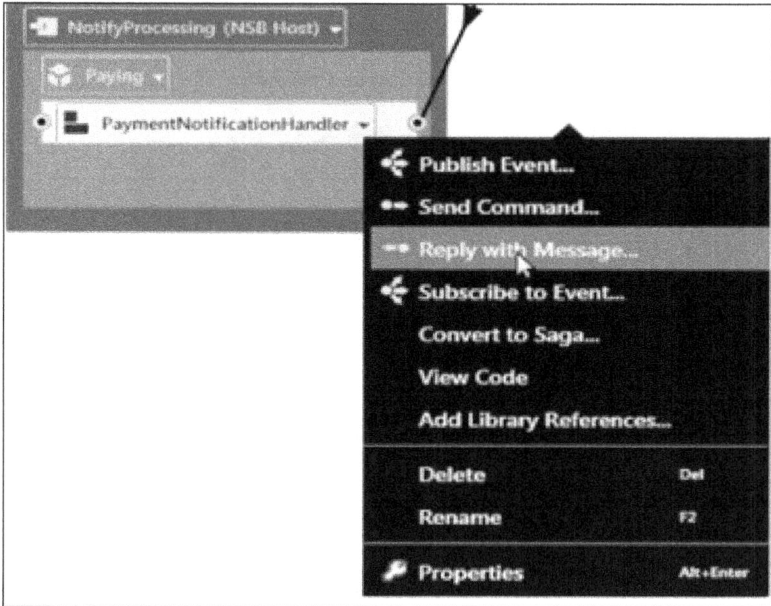

This will allow us to convert `PaymentAcceptedHandler` into a saga.

After the saga is created, we can run the code from Visual Studio. If we look at ServiceInsight, we will see the updated flow diagram that contains all the endpoint components.

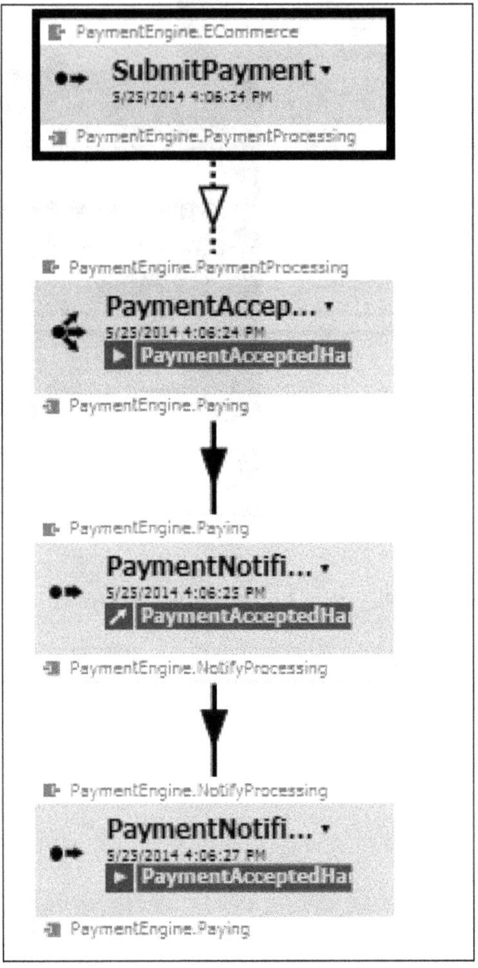

Drill down to the saga component in the `Paying` service and the `PaymentAcceptedHandler` component—where the saga is initiated with `PaymentAccepted`, saving the `PaymentNotification` data—and update the `PaymentNotificationResponse` message.

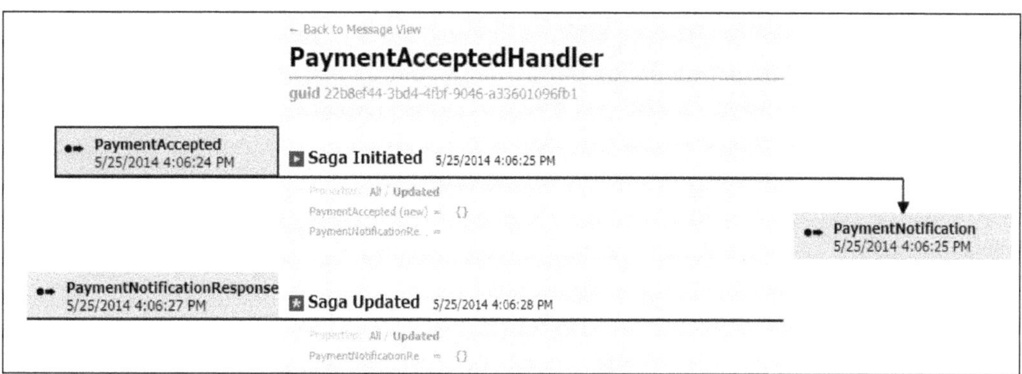

Summary

In this chapter, we looked at the various tools of Particular Service Platform; these included ServiceMatrix, ServicePulse, and ServiceInsight.

We gave a very brief introduction to ServiceMatrix as we walked through a description of building an e-commerce MVC solution that worked with request/reply messages using the send command. This was followed by publish/subscribe messages, showing ServicePulse and ServiceInsight results. Finally, these derived into Saga components to show the result in ServiceInsight.

4

Knowing Your IBus

In **Enterprise Service Bus** (**ESB**), bus is the backbone of the sagas, subscriptions, sending of messages, timeouts, and gateways. For NServiceBus, the bus interface is IBus. Knowing your IBus is the most important part of NServiceBus.

In this chapter, we will cover the following topics:

- The basics of IBus, including the different basic configurations
    - Config
    - Interfaces
    - Configure
- A basic walk-through of saga with NHibernate
    - Logging
- A more advanced NHibernate walk-through with saga
    - Message mutators
    - Encryption
- Services and deployment

Understanding the basics of IBus

Up to this point, it is assumed that you have been exposed to some of the examples in the previous chapters. By now, we know that IBus orchestrates messages in various queues, such as MSMQ, RabbitMQ, and ActiveMQ. Also, messages, sagas, gateways, and timeouts can be stored in the memory; RavenDB; or various databases, specifically SQL Server.

Many examples are available, and knowing a few basic examples will allow one to understand almost all the examples; most are just variations of some of the same code. Many of these samples are similar to that of Video Store examples. Here's just a small breakdown of the various examples from `https://github.com/Particular`. For instance, the source code of NServiceBus.Nhibernate can be found at `https://github.com/Particular/NServiceBus.Nhibernate`. However, NServiceBus.Nhibernate, which appears in the table, is taken from the `https://github.com/Particular` link. The **X** in the table means that the source code is part of the original package.

Package	Samples from `https://github.com/Particular/`	Source from `https://github.com/Particular/`	Nuget installers from `http://www.nuget.org/packages/`
SQL Server	NServiceBus.SqlServer.Samples	NServiceBus.SqlServer	NServiceBus.SqlServer
NHibernate	NServiceBus.Nhibernate.Samples	NServiceBus.Nhibernate	NServiceBus.NHibernate
MSMQ	NServiceBus.MSMQ.Samples	X	X
RabbitMQ	NServiceBus.RabbitMQ.Samples	NServiceBus.RabbitMQ	NServiceBus.RabbitMQ
ActiveMQ	NServiceBus.ActiveMQ.Samples	NServiceBus.ActiveMQ	NServiceBus.ActiveMQ
Azure	NServiceBus.Azure.Samples	NServiceBus.Azure	NServiceBus.Azure
Notifications		NServiceBus.Notifications	NServiceBus.Notifications

IBus will take care of a lot of the mapping; for instance, the developer doesn't need to provide the mapping from objects to tables for NHibernate or from objects to XML to put into MSMQ. This saves you from a lot of work in developing ESB pieces. More information on samples can be found at `https://docs.particular.net/Platform/samples`.

The three main pieces that need to be understood with NServiceBus is IBus, which includes the configurations in the `app.config` file, messages, and message handlers. Knowing this breakdown helps with a lot of the basics. Also, queues and tables are normally created by the namespace names of the applications, which NServiceBus handles using the C# reflection. This basic knowledge is needed to understand sagas, message handling, and persistence understanding.

Configuring IBus

There are several parts to configuring IBus; let me reiterate that the configuration relies on the `app.config` file, IBus, messages, and message handlers as a whole.

We will start with the configurations in the `app.config` file, where many pieces of the code will come from `https://github.com/Particular/NServiceBus/tree/develop/src/NServiceBus.Core/Config`.

Another valuable source to get some of this information is through the sources on NServiceBus, such as `http://www.nudoq.org/#!/Packages/NServiceBus/NServiceBus.Core`.

In the following table, the `app.config` file will be referred to as "config", and IBus will be referred to as "configuration". Here are some of the config sections that will be defined in many of your `app.config` files:

Name	Description	Detailed link
AuditConfig	This is the config section for the auditing feature	`http://docs.particular.net/nservicebus/auditing-with-nservicebus`
GatewayConfig	This is the config section for the gateway	`http://docs.particular.net/NServiceBus/the-gateway-and-multi-site-distribution`
Logging	This the section for logging the configuration	`http://docs.particular.net/NServiceBus/logging-in-nservicebus`
MasterNodeConfig	This is the configuration section to hold the node that is the master	`http://docs.particular.net/NServiceBus/load-balancing-with-the-distributor`
MessageEndpointMappings	This is a configuration element that represents which message types map to which endpoint.	`http://docs.particular.net/nservicebus/how-do-i-specify-to-which-destination-a-message-will-be-sent`

Name	Description	Detailed link
MessageForwardingInCaseOfFaultConfig	This is the section for message forwarding in case of faulty config	`http://docs.particular.net/NServiceBus/msmqtransportconfig`
MsmqMessageQueueConfig	This contains the properties that represent the MsmqMessageQueue configuration section	
MsmqSubscriptionStorage	This contains the properties that represent the MsmqSubscriptionStorage configuration section.	`http://docs.particular.net/NServiceBus/publish-subscribe-configuration`
RijndaelEncryptionServiceConfig	The AES encryption service	`http://docs.particular.net/NServiceBus/encryption-sample`
SecondLevelRetriesConfig	This is the section for retrying multiple times after error	`http://docs.particular.net/NServiceBus//second-level-retries`
TransportConfig		`http://docs.particular.net/NServiceBus/msmqtransportconfig`
UnicastBusConfig	This is a configuration section for UnicastBus-specific settings.	`http://docs.particular.net/NServiceBus/hosting-nservicebus-in-your-own-process`

To view the different sections of the `app.config` file in the code, we can pull out the configurations through the NSB code with something as simple as the following:

```
namespace MyMessages
{
    [Serializable]
// Reading configurations from App configuration
UnicastBusConfig unicastBusCfg = Configure.GetConfigSection<UnicastBu
sConfig>();
Logging loggingCfg = Configure.GetConfigSection<Logging>();
```

```
TransportConfig transportCfg =       Configure.GetConfigSection<Trans
portConfig>();
SecondLevelRetriesConfig secondCfg = Configure.GetConfigSection<Second
LevelRetriesConfig>();
AuditConfig auditCfg = Configure.GetConfigSection<AuditConfig>();
            MsmqSubscriptionStorageConfig endpoinsCfg Configure.GetCon
figSection<MsmqSubscriptionStorageConfig>();
```

We can view the details in Visual Studio as we step through the code.

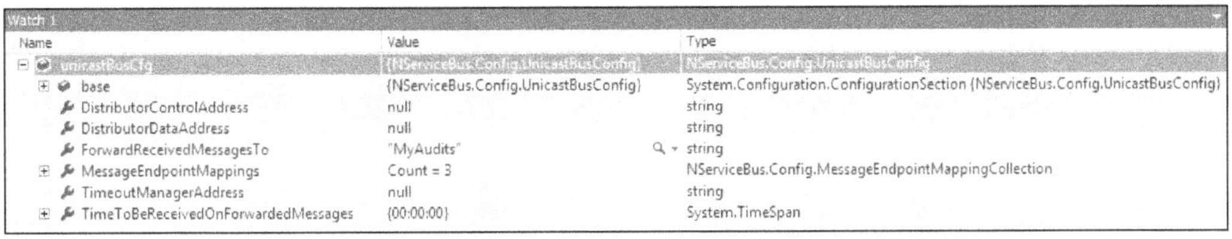

Watch 1

Name	Value	Type
unicastBusCfg	{NServiceBus.Config.UnicastBusConfig}	NServiceBus.Config.UnicastBusConfig
base	{NServiceBus.Config.UnicastBusConfig}	System.Configuration.ConfigurationSection {NServiceBus.Config.UnicastBusConfig}
DistributorControlAddress	null	string
DistributorDataAddress	null	string
ForwardReceivedMessagesTo	"MyAudits"	string
MessageEndpointMappings	Count = 3	NServiceBus.Config.MessageEndpointMappingCollection
TimeoutManagerAddress	null	string
TimeToBeReceivedOnForwardedMessages	{00:00:00}	System.TimeSpan

For instance, in the first line, we have a config object called `UnicastBusConfig` that retrieves the settings that are configured either from the `app.config` file or the code. The structure of `UnicastBusConfig` appears as follows:

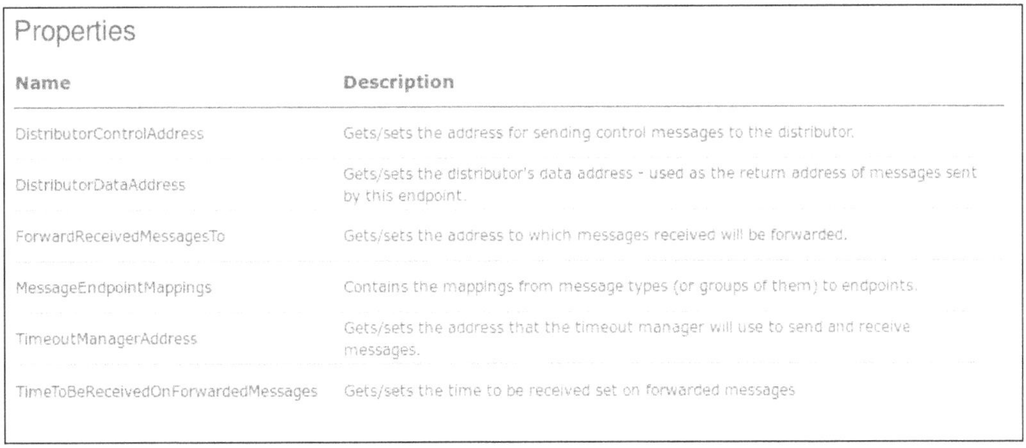

Properties

Name	Description
DistributorControlAddress	Gets/sets the address for sending control messages to the distributor.
DistributorDataAddress	Gets/sets the distributor's data address - used as the return address of messages sent by this endpoint.
ForwardReceivedMessagesTo	Gets/sets the address to which messages received will be forwarded.
MessageEndpointMappings	Contains the mappings from message types (or groups of them) to endpoints.
TimeoutManagerAddress	Gets/sets the address that the timeout manager will use to send and receive messages.
TimeToBeReceivedOnForwardedMessages	Gets/sets the time to be received set on forwarded messages

Inspecting a sample `UnicastBusConfig`, we can see that this section has three mapping endpoints.

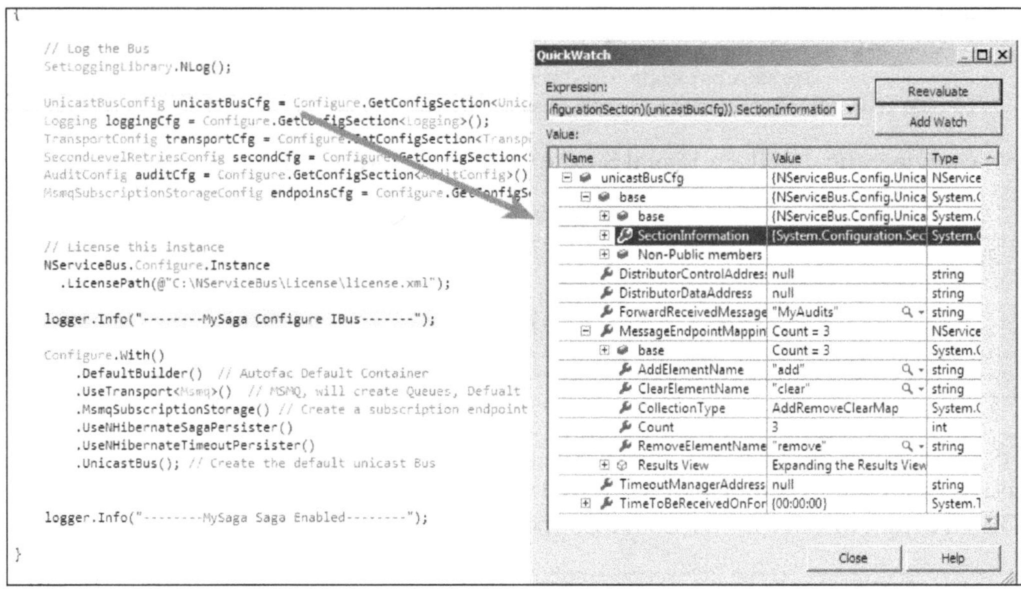

This is a reflection of what is being set in the `app.config` file and possibly any settings that may exist in the code to direct the IBus config settings. In this sample, we had three mapping endpoints in `app.config`. This is very useful in tracing how IBus is intended to operate while debugging. When we view the config file, we see three endpoints.

```
<UnicastBusConfig ForwardReceivedMessagesTo="MyAudits">
  <MessageEndpointMappings>
    <add Endpoint="AppForApproversLevel1" Messages="MyMessages.SolicitApprovalFromLevel1Command, MyMessages" />
    <add Endpoint="AppForApproversLevel2" Messages="MyMessages.SolicitApprovalFromLevel2Command, MyMessages" />
    <add Endpoint="AppForAccountingDept" Messages="MyMessages.RecordEncumbranceCommand, MyMessages" />
  </MessageEndpointMappings>
</UnicastBusConfig>
```

Interface configurations

Instead of using the IBus' configuration, or `app.config` configuration, NSB can use the Host configuration by extending the `EndpointConfigclasses`. These tables are not to be all inclusive, but a starting point to understand the various pieces of IBus:

Name	Description	Detailed link
INeedInitialization	Here, implementers will be called after NServiceBus. Configure.With completes and a container has been set.	`http://docs.particular.net/NServiceBus/the-nservicebus-host`
IWantToRunWhen ConfigurationIsComplete	Here, implementers are invoked when a configuration is complete. Also, implementers are resolved from the container and so have access to full DI.	`http://docs.particular.net/NServiceBus/profiles-for-nservicbus-host`
IWantToRunWhenBus StartsAndStops	In this interface, Start and Stop implementers will be invoked when the endpoint starts up. A dependency injection is provided for these types.	`http://docs.particular.net/NServiceBus/scheduling-with-nservicebus`

We have the addition of the following interfaces defined at the root of the NServiceBus code:

Name	Description	Detailed link
IConfigureThisEndpoint	This indicates that the implementing class will specify the configuration.	`http://docs.particular.net/NServiceBus/the-nservicebus-host` `http://docs.particular.net/NServiceBus/how-to-specify-your-input-queue-name`

Name	Description	Detailed link
IWantCustomInitialization	If you want to specify your own container or serializer, implement this interface on the class that implements `IConfigureThisEndpoint`. Implementers will be invoked before the endpoint starts up. A dependency injection is not provided for these types.	`http://docs.particular.net/NServiceBus/the-nservicebus-host`
IWantCustomLogging	If you want to specify your own logging, implement this interface on the class that implements `IConfigureThisEndpoint`.	`http://docs.particular.net/NServiceBus/the-nservicebus-host`
IWantTheEndPointConfig	In this interface, implementers will be provided with a reference to `IConfigureThisEndpoint`, and they must inherit either `IHandleProfile` or `IWantCustomInitialization`.	`http://docs.particular.net/NServiceBus/profiles-for-the-nservicebus-host`
IWantToRunAtStartup	In this interface, implementers will be invoked when the endpoint starts up. A dependency injection is provided for these types.	`http://docs.particular.net/NServiceBus/NServiceBus-Step-by-Step-Guide`
IWantToRunBefore Configuration	This interface indicates that this class contains logic that needs to be executed before other configurations.	`http://docs.particular.net/NServiceBus/how-do-i-centralize-all-unobtrusive-declarations`

By adding NServiceBus.Hosting, we get the following roles:

Name	Description	Detailed link
AsA_Client	This sets the class as a client role. As a client, every time it starts, it will do so with a new material.	`http://docs.particular.net/NServiceBus/NServiceBus-Step-by-Step-Guide`
AsA_Publisher	This is the same as AsA_Server but subscriptions need to be set. As a server, it is fault tolerant and holds a message for continuous use.	`http://docs.particular.net/NServiceBus//publish-subscribe-sample`
AsA_Server	This sets the class as a server role.	`http://docs.particular.net/NServiceBus/NServiceBus-Step-by-Step-Guide`

Most of the examples will have an `EndpointConfig.cs` file that will define IBus with the endpoint of the application. Here's an example from the `MySaga` project in `EndpointConfig.cs` that is defining an endpoint and configuring IBus:

```
namespace MySaga
{
    public class EndpointConfig : IConfigureThisEndpoint, AsA_Server, IWantCustomInitialization, IWantToRunWhenBusStartsAndStops
    {

        private static Logger logger = LogManager.GetCurrentClassLogger();

        public void Init()
        {
```

In this example, a `MySaga` endpoint will be created as a server via AsA_Server. It will have to implement the overwritten functions' `Start()` and `Stop()` functionalities due to `IWantToRunWhenBusStartsAndStops`. We will use this class to configure the endpoint, and since we did not explicitly configure and name the endpoint in IBus, the namespace `MySaga` will be used because of `IConfigureThisEndpoint`. This class will have an `Init()` function to define IBus because of the use of `IWantCustomInitialization`; otherwise, an IBus will be created with the default values and `app.config`.

Using the Fluent Configure.With()

There are many configuration settings for IBus. We will be discussing several of them as they relate to sagas and persisters. There are too many different configurations to discuss in their entirety and many are not used in most common configurations. NSB can be explicitly configured to accommodate many, many situations. For a more complete listing of some of the configurations, as far as available functions are concerned, please refer to `http://www.nudoq.org/#!/Packages/NServiceBus/NServiceBus.Core/Configure`.

1. Let's start by breaking down a sample IBus configuration:

```
Configure.With()
    .DefaultBuilder()  // Autofac Default Container
    .UseTransport<Msmq>()  // MSMQ, will create Queues, Defualt
    .MsmqSubscriptionStorage() // Create a subscription endpoint
    .UseNHibernateSagaPersister()  // NHibernate Saga
    .UseNHibernateTimeoutPersister() // NHibernate Timeout
    .UnicastBus(); // Create the default unicast Bus
```

2. For IBus, the first piece to define is the IoC, we have to set the container, `http://docs.particular.net/NServiceBus/containers`:
    - `DefaultBuilder()`: This is the default Autofac
    - `NinjectBuilder()`: This is the most popular C# IoC container found at `http://www.ninject.org/`
    - `StructureMapBuilder()`: This can be found at `http://docs.structuremap.net/`
    - `UnityBuilder()`: This can be found at `http://unity.codeplex.com/`
    - `SpringBuilder()`: This can be found at `http://www.spring.net/`
    - `CastleWindsorBuilder()`: This can be found at `http://www.castleproject.org/`
    - `AutofacBuilder()`: This can be found at `http://code.google.com/p/autofac/`
3. We have to ensure that the proper reference is installed; for instance, NHibernate.Unity must be installed to use `UnityBuilder`.

4. Next, we want to ensure that the serialization is set. By default, XML serialization is used. In Version 4.0, the serialization is set in front of the IBus' configuration, `Configure.With()`.

```
public void Init()
{
    Configure.Serialization.Xml();// or BinarySerializer()

    Configure.With()
        .CastleWindsorBuilder();
}
```

By default, IBus uses the XML serialization, but it could be set directly by using the following:

```
public class EndpointConfig : IConfigureThisEndpoint, AsA_Server, IWantCustomInitialization
{
    public void Init()
    {
        Configure.Serialization.Xml();// or BinarySerializer()

        Configure.With()
            .CastleWindsorBuilder();
    }
}
```

The options for the IBus serialization are as follows:

- XmlSerialization: This is set by default, and it serializes data into an XML form.
- BinarySerialization: This is a serialization in binary form.
- BsonSerialization: This is a serialization for binary-encoded serialization for JSON-like documents; for more information, refer to `http://codebetter.com/karlseguin/2010/03/05/bson-serialization/`.
- JsonSerialization: This is a JavaScript Object Notation (JSON) format; for more information, refer to `http://msdn.microsoft.com/en-us/library/bb410770%28v=vs.110%29.aspx`.

The transport storage

We need to set the transport information using the `.UseTransport()` configured portion of the IBus. This will be the transportation method that will be followed across the bus, and remember that the endpoints that you want to communicate together must all communicate across the transport method. In other words, a message on MSMQ and message in SQL will not see each other. An example is already given previously, but here are some of the following choices:

- `UseTransport<Msmq>`: You can use MSMQ transport for messages.
- `UseTransport<SqlServer>`: You can use a `SqlServer` table to queue messages.
- `UseTransport<ActiveMQ>`: You can use ActiveMQ to queue messages.
- `UseTransport<RabbitMQ>`: You can use RabbitMQ to queue messages.
- `UseTransport<AzureServiceBus>`: You can use Azure ServiceBus; see `http://docs.particular.net/NServiceBus/windows-azure-transport`. A sample of this is found at `https://github.com/Particular/NServiceBus.Azure.Samples`.
- `UseTransport<AzureStorageQueue>`: You can use Azure queues; see `http://docs.particular.net/NServiceBus/windows-azure-transport`. A sample of this is found at `https://github.com/Particular/NServiceBus.Azure.Samples`.

The saga persister

The saga persister is where the saga message data will be saved. It is just data, but it is handled like a message in many cases. When setting up saga data, we have a few choices on whether to save it to a database or not, and there are many databases that NHibernate will support. By default, the RavenDB database will be used. Here are some of the saga persister choices:

- `UseNHibernateSagaPersister()`: You can use NHiberntae based on the connection string in `app.config` to store the saga instance
- `UseInMemorySagaPersister()`: You can use volatile memory storage to store the saga instance
- `RavenSagaPersister()`: You can use RavenDB to store the saga instance

The timeout persister

The procedure to set up a timeout persister can be found in many documents, such as the saga documentation at `http://docs.particular.net/NServiceBus/sagas-in-nservicebus`. When designing a saga message handler, the timeout creation is entered early on in the functions to ensure that any code beforehand is not a concern. For example, we are setting up the saga timeout code; while doing this, the creation code will create a timeout message, say of 60 seconds, and the question that will remain is where the timer and timeout messaging code will be saved. If it is in the memory, and obviously if the system is rebooted and the application shuts down, it is no longer persisted as it was in memory. Many NSB services are designed in a way that when a server is completely rebooted and the services are restarted, they would start from where they had left off, including timeouts that would still be running in sagas. For this reason, the timeout messaging has to be persisted to a database, thus enters RavenDB and the NHibernate interface of databases for the timeout persister. By default, the RavenDB database will be used. Here are a few variations on how the timeout message can be persisted as it is timing down:

- `UseNHibernateTimeoutPersister()`: Using the implementation of the NHibernate package for Timeout Manager
- `UseInMemoryTimeoutPersister()`: Using the volatile local memory to store Timeout Manager
- `UseRavenTimeoutPersister()`: Using RavenDB to store Timeout Manager
- `DisableTimeoutManager()`: As Timeout Manager is on by default for server roles, use this method to turn off Timeout Manager

The gateway persister

Another persister for NServiceBus is the gateway pieces of NSB; see `http://docs.particular.net/NServiceBus/the-gateway-and-multi-site-distribution`. An instance of a gateway example can be found at `https://github.com/Particular/NServiceBus.Msmq.Samples`. The persister will keep track of message IDs for duplication. Some persisters that are offered are as follows:

- `UseRavenGatewayPersister()`: This uses the RavenDB message persistence via the gateway.
- `UseRavenGatewayDeduplication()`: This uses RavenDB for message deduplication via the gateway.
- `RunGateway()`: This is used as a configuration to run the gateway. By default, a gateway will use RavenPersistence (see the `GatewayDefaults` class).

- `UseInMemoryGatewayPersister()`: This uses the in-memory and volatile message persistence via the gateway.
- `UseInMemoryGatewayDeduplication()`: This uses an in-memory message deduplication for the gateway.
- `UseNHibernateGatewayPersister()`: This configuration will use the NHibernate framework to persist the NSB gateway data.
- `DisableGateway()`: The gateway is turned on by default for the master role. Call the `DisableGateway()` method to turn the gateway off.

By default, the RavenDB database will be used.

The subscription storage

The subscription storage is an IBus configuration to set where the subscription metadata information will reside. It will define the subscription endpoint information in publish/subscribe. The subscription storage keeps track of publish/subscribe endpoint information. More information on subscription storage can be found at `http://docs.particular.net/NServiceBus/publish-subscibe-configuration`. This is not the messaging process itself, that is, the publisher message being sent and saved, because that will be the transport setting, but this is the information saved for NSB saying that specific messages are sent and received by each subscription endpoint. Without this information, subscription message routing will not work, but the host programs will normally set these settings when they are started by default. Again, RavenDB stores the data by default. However, these persisters are also available:

- `RavenSubscriptionStorage()`: Uses subscription storage using RavenDB
- `MsmqSubscriptionStorage()`: Uses subscription storage using MSMQ
- `UseNHibernateSubscriptionPersister()`: Uses subscription storage using NHibernate; see `http://docs.particular.net/NServiceBus/relational-persistence-using-nhibernate—nservicebus-4.x`
- `InMemorySubscriptionStorage()`: Uses subscription storage in the local memory, which is volatile

Finding more configuration settings

These are just some basic settings. Going through the settings and then adding on the many other variations of configurations from sources such as Nudoq documentation with the many different configurations, `http://www.nudoq.org/#!/Packages/NServiceBus/NServiceBus.Core/Configure`, as an example defining the endpoint, the various messages, and more, can seem overwhelming. NSB offers a lot of default settings that are most commonly used.

NSB offers many common examples that could be used out of the box for many designs. An easy way to learn is to take an MSMQ example, and if you wish to learn RabbitMQ instead, just change the settings for RabbitMQ. The samples are free and offer a great learning experience.

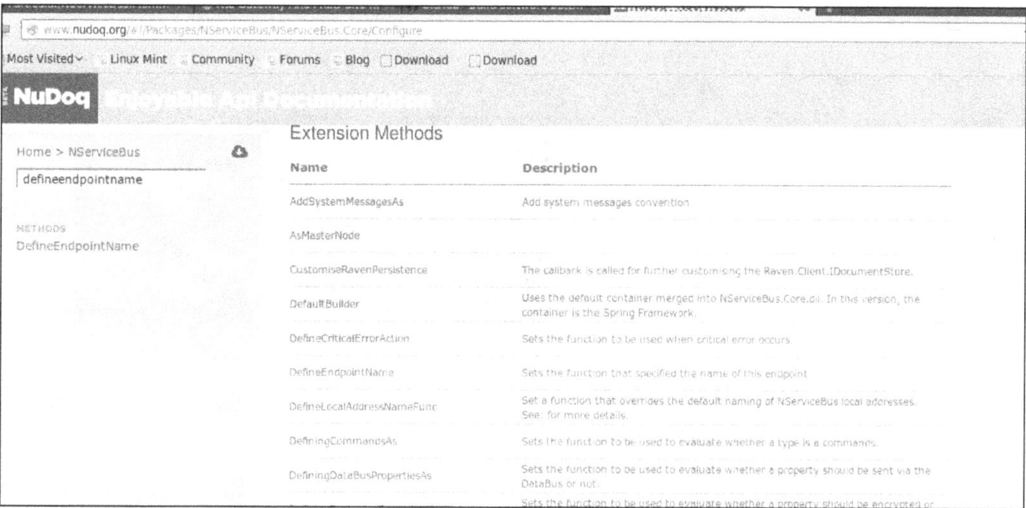

Using saga and NHibernate

We will walk through a modified example of a basic saga, originally from `https://github.com/jkillingsworth/NServiceBus-BasicSagas`. However, this example has been modified to use NHibernate, which uses a local SQL Express database. NHibernate was added using some of the steps from `http://docs.particular.net/NServiceBus/relational-persistence-using-nhibernate-nservicebus-4.x`. We also added logging using the NLog framework to log the functionality as we go. The NHibernate ORM framework was chosen because it can connect to a multitude of different databases using the same code, the difference being to the different databases is the connection string in the `app.config` file.

To elaborate on this Saga example, there is a `MySaga` program that directs the messages using message handlers that creates new messages to send and respond through the workflow. The saga object is persisting the message states to be used during these message handlers. The saga persistence keeps track of the information that we defined to be saved in a saga entity object. It is the state and session information of the message that we deem relevant.

The saga acts as an anchor that we can persist as we orchestrate messages moving across the bus. We can retrieve the instance of the saga associated with the message, update it, and keep it stored, as even the original message morphs into different types of messages. The following screenshot demonstrates this orchestration:

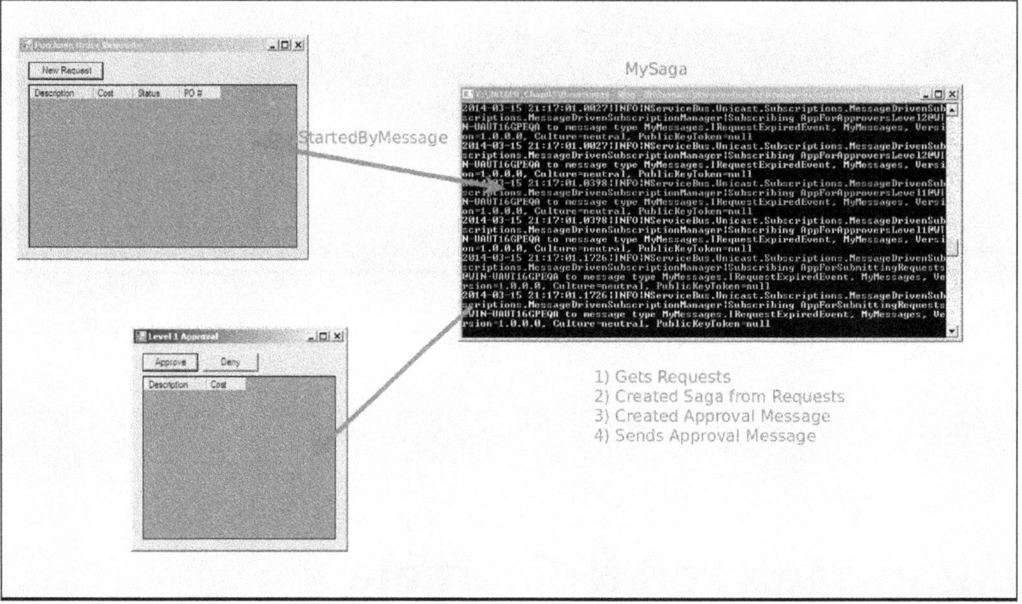

In this application, we sent `IAmStartedByMessages<SubmitRequestCommand>` from an `AppSubmittingRequests` application that is seen here as **Purchase Order Requests**. It creates and submits `SubmitRequestCommand` that takes the data from this message and creates a saga on the bus, along with a unique ID. It also sets a 60-second timer that will send a timeout message from the bus once 60 seconds are over.

```
public void Handle(SubmitRequestCommand message)
{

    logger.Info("--------MySaga Handle-------" + message);

    RequestTimeout<TimeoutMessage>(TimeSpan.FromSeconds(60));

    Data.RequestId = message.RequestId;
    Data.Description = message.Description;
    Data.Cost = message.Cost;
    Data.RequiresApprovalByLevel1 = message.Cost > 100.00m;
    Data.RequiresApprovalByLevel2 = message.Cost > 1000.00m;
    Data.ApprovedByLevel1 = false;
    Data.ApprovedByLevel2 = false;

    ProcessApproval();
}
```

Then, it sends an approval that creates the level 1 approval, which is an application called `AppForApprovalsLevel1`. After the **Approve** or **Deny** button is selected, it creates a new message that is sent back to the saga, and the saga handles the messages. Depending on the return message, it will either call the `IHandleMessages<ApproveRequestCommand>` or `IHandleMessages<DenyRequestCommand>` handler. The saga will be pulled up by the bus, as we had the mapping code in this example to map the messages to `RequestID`.

```
public override void ConfigureHowToFindSaga()
{
    logger.Info("--------Start MySaga ConfigureMapping-------");
    /*****
     When the infrastructure is handling a message of the given type
    this specifies which message property should be matched to
     which saga entity property in the persistent saga store.
     * ****/
    ConfigureMapping<ApproveRequestCommand>(x => x.RequestId).ToSaga(x => x.RequestId);
    ConfigureMapping<DenyRequestCommand>(x => x.RequestId).ToSaga(x => x.RequestId);
    logger.Info("--------End MySaga ConfigureMapping-------");
}
```

We can pull up the saga that matches the message and routes it based on some logic—in this case, the cost—or returns it to the originating client. The saga may contain a huge part of the original message, so all of it doesn't need to be propagated through messages.

```
public void Handle(ApproveRequestCommand message)
{
    logger.Info("--------MySaga Handle-------" + message);
    if (message.Approver == Approver.Level1)
    {
        Data.ApprovedByLevel1 = true;
    }

    if (message.Approver == Approver.Level2)
    {
        Data.ApprovedByLevel2 = true;
    }

    ProcessApproval();
}

public void Handle(DenyRequestCommand message)
{
    logger.Info("--------MySaga Handle-------" + message);
    var reply = new SubmitRequestReplyMessage
    {
        RequestId = Data.RequestId,
        Approved = false
    };

    ReplyToOriginator(reply);
    MarkAsComplete();
}
```

The saga is aware of its originator; it knows that it needs to match `RequestId` because of the mapping, and the bus keeps an internal ID to keep all the sagas unique. All the sagas must have the `Id`, `Originator`, and `OriginalMessageId` fields that the bus will use to keep track of the saga. Here, we also have a `[Unique]` attribute to ensure that `RequestId` is kept unique to ensure that the map is made to return to the correct saga.

```
public class PurchaseOrderRequestData : IContainSagaData
{
    /***
     * Gets/sets the Id of the process. Do NOT generate this value in your code.
       The value of the Id will be generated automatically to provide the
       best performance for saving in a database.
     * ***/
    public virtual Guid Id { get; set; }  // Required
    /***
     * Contains the return address of the endpoint that caused the process to run.
     * ***/
    public virtual string Originator { get; set; }  //Required
    /***
     * Contains the Id of the message which caused the saga to start.
       This is needed so that when we reply to the Originator, any
       registered callbacks will be fired correctly.
     * ***/
    public virtual string OriginalMessageId { get; set; }  //Required

    [Unique]
    public virtual Guid RequestId { get; set; }  // Unique ID to lookup Request message
    public virtual string Description { get; set; }
    public virtual decimal Cost { get; set; }
    public virtual bool RequiresApprovalByLevel1 { get; set; }
    public virtual bool RequiresApprovalByLevel2 { get; set; }
    public virtual bool ApprovedByLevel1 { get; set; }
    public virtual bool ApprovedByLevel2 { get; set; }
}
```

The `EndpointConfig.cs` file of the `MySaga` project contains the `Init()` method. This function contains the initial configuration of the endpoint for the IBus. The endpoint will default to the namespace of the project; for instance, in this case, `MySaga` will be the endpoint as it is associated with the namespace.

```
namespace MySaga
{
    public class EndpointConfig : IConfigureThisEndpoint, AsA_Server, IWantCustomInitialization, IWantToRunWhenBusStartsAndStops
    {

        private static Logger logger = LogManager.GetCurrentClassLogger();

        public void Init()
        {
```

However, you may explicitly define your endpoints on IBus with `Configure.With().DefineEndpointName("MyEndpoint");`, where `MyEndpoint` is the IBus' endpoint to be defined.

As always, the NSB IBus will create the appropriate endpoints if defined correctly. Here, we have it based on the different projects' namespaces in the solution. The different projects are `MySaga`, `AppforApprovalsLevel1`, `AppforApprovalsLevel2`, `AppForSubmittingRequests`, and `AppForAccountingDept`. Note that NSB will create them in lowercase and it will also create the appropriate timeout, error, and audit queues.

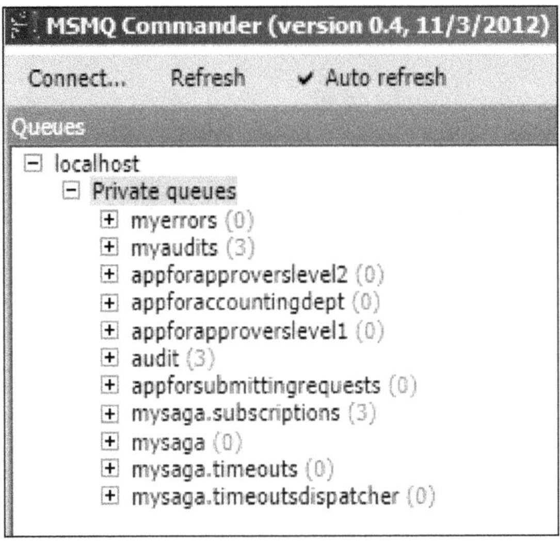

We are going to configure IBus in the `EndpointConfig.cs` file, which in most cases is where IBus will be configured to use saga and timeout persistence in NHibernate.

```
Configure.With()
    .DefaultBuilder()  // Autofac Default Container
    .UseTransport<Msmq>()  // MSMQ, will create Queues, Defualt
    .MsmqSubscriptionStorage() // Create a subscription endpoint
    .UseNHibernateSagaPersister()
    .UseNHibernateTimeoutPersister()
    .UnicastBus(); // Create the default unicast Bus
```

Defining NHibernate

NHibernate is configured in the `app.config` file for the `MySaga` project to configure the NHibernate interface to connect to the local SQL Express Server instance.

```
<!--  NHibernate Settings-->
<connectionStrings>
  <add name="NServiceBus/Transport" connectionString="cacheSendConnection=true" />
  <add name="NServiceBus/Persistence" connectionString="Data Source=.\SQLEXPRESS;Initial Catalog=nservicebus;Integrated Security=True" />
</connectionStrings>

<!-- specify the other needed NHibernate settings like below in appSettings:-->
<appSettings>
  <!-- dialect is defaulted to MsSql2008Dialect, if needed change accordingly -->
  <add key="NServiceBus/Persistence/NHibernate/dialect" value="NHibernate.Dialect.MsSql2008Dialect" />
  <!-- other optional settings examples -->
  <add key="NServiceBus/Persistence/NHibernate/connection.provider" value="NHibernate.Connection.DriverConnectionProvider" />
  <add key="NServiceBus/Persistence/NHibernate/connection.driver_class" value="NHibernate.Driver.Sql2008ClientDriver" />
</appSettings>
```

Here, we can see the NServiceBus NHibernate connection strings and its app settings. Now that we have NHibernate configured for NServiceBus, we can check SQL Server after we start the sample solution. Once we start the solution, NServiceBus will create the appropriate tables for saga and timeouts in the `nservicebus` database.

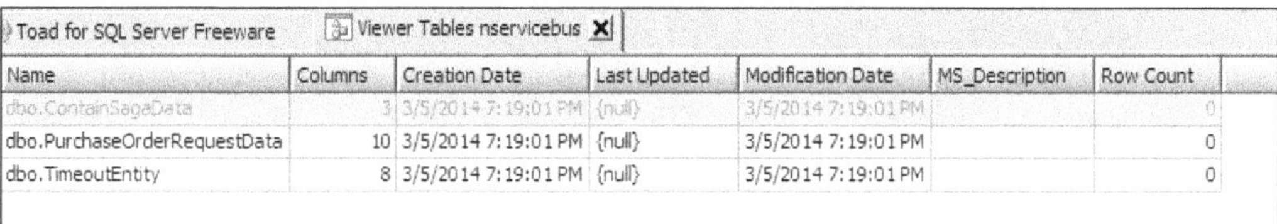

Name	Columns	Creation Date	Last Updated	Modification Date	MS_Description	Row Count
dbo.ContainSagaData	3	3/5/2014 7:19:01 PM	{null}	3/5/2014 7:19:01 PM		0
dbo.PurchaseOrderRequestData	10	3/5/2014 7:19:01 PM	{null}	3/5/2014 7:19:01 PM		0
dbo.TimeoutEntity	8	3/5/2014 7:19:01 PM	{null}	3/5/2014 7:19:01 PM		0

We see the base saga that is normally created called `ContainSagaData`, which has `Id`, `Originator`, and `OriginalMessageId`, to always be able to find the correct unique saga instance; it also has the originator information to reply to the client that sent this handler the message to start the saga.

It also created the `PurchaseOrderRequestData` saga where the table will match the object. The object will appear as follows:

```
namespace MySaga
{
    public class PurchaseOrderRequestData : IContainSagaData
    {
        /***
         * Gets/sets the Id of the process. Do NOT generate this value in your code.
           The value of the Id will be generated automatically to provide the
           best performance for saving in a database.
         * ***/
        public virtual Guid Id { get; set; }  // Required
        /***
         * Contains the return address of the endpoint that caused the process to run.
         * ***/
        public virtual string Originator { get; set; }  //Required
        /***
         * Contains the Id of the message which caused the saga to start.
           This is needed so that when we reply to the Originator, any
           registered callbacks will be fired correctly.
         * ***/
        public virtual string OriginalMessageId { get; set; }  //Required

        [Unique]
        public virtual Guid RequestId { get; set; }  // Unique ID to lookup Request message
        public virtual string Description { get; set; }
        public virtual decimal Cost { get; set; }
        public virtual bool RequiresApprovalByLevel1 { get; set; }
        public virtual bool RequiresApprovalByLevel2 { get; set; }
        public virtual bool ApprovedByLevel1 { get; set; }
        public virtual bool ApprovedByLevel2 { get; set; }
    }
}
```

The saga database data

So, the database table associated with the object will look like the following:

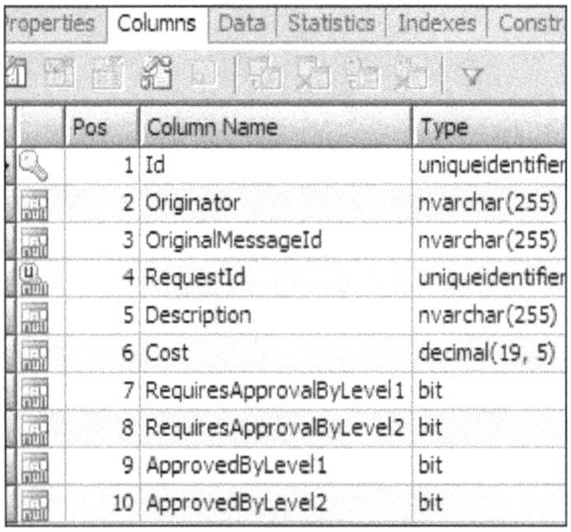

Pos	Column Name	Type
1	Id	uniqueidentifier
2	Originator	nvarchar(255)
3	OriginalMessageId	nvarchar(255)
4	RequestId	uniqueidentifier
5	Description	nvarchar(255)
6	Cost	decimal(19, 5)
7	RequiresApprovalByLevel1	bit
8	RequiresApprovalByLevel2	bit
9	ApprovedByLevel1	bit
10	ApprovedByLevel2	bit

Note that we neither needed to create any mapping files to do any of the mappings for NHibernate, nor create the table. We simply created the NSB configuration. NSB created the tables and performed the mapping. Look, no need to do SQL.

Likewise, I have a timeout message as an object, as follows:

```
using NServiceBus;

namespace MySaga
{
    public class TimeoutMessage : IMessage
    {
    }
}
```

However, since IBus keeps extra information to keep track of the correct saga and have IBus execute the timer separately from the current thread, there will be a lot of extra information in its timeout table for IBus' use.

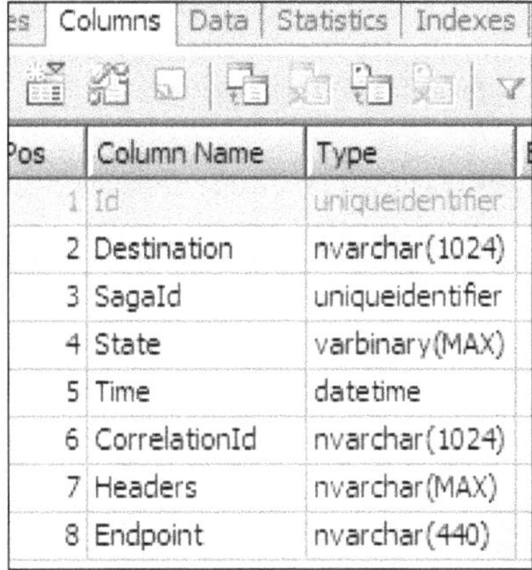

Pos	Column Name	Type
1	Id	uniqueidentifier
2	Destination	nvarchar(1024)
3	SagaId	uniqueidentifier
4	State	varbinary(MAX)
5	Time	datetime
6	CorrelationId	nvarchar(1024)
7	Headers	nvarchar(MAX)
8	Endpoint	nvarchar(440)

Logging

In this example, we also have to set the `app.config` file to use NLog. NServiceBus will support the common logging frameworks, common logging, NLog, Log4Net, and Serilog. Refer to `http://docs.particular.net/NServiceBus/logging-in-nservicebus` for more information.

For NLog, we need to add the Nlog Nuget reference to the project.

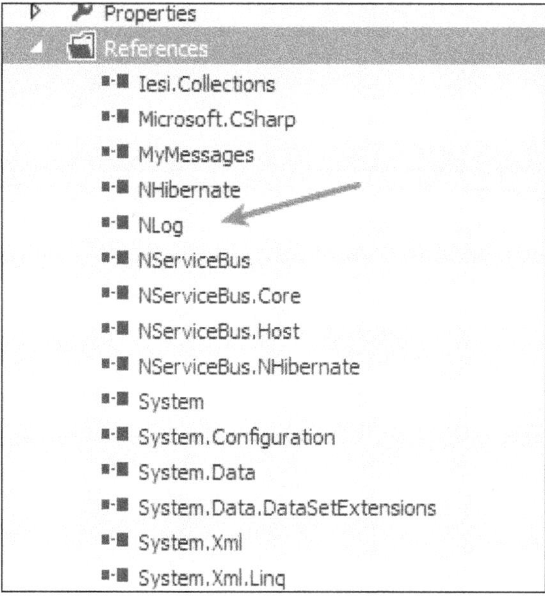

We need to set the logging levels and the location of where the logs are being sent to in the `app.config` file.

```
<!--          NLOG                          -->
  <nlog xmlns="http://www.nlog-project.org/schemas/NLog.xsd" xmlns:xsi="http://www.w3.org/2001/XMLSchema-instance">
    <targets>
      <target name="logfile" xsi:type="File" fileName="c:\logs\basicSaga_${shortdate}.log" layout="${longdate} ${level} ${message}" />
      <target name="console" xsi:type="Console" />
      <target xsi:type="EventLog" name="event" layout="${message}" source="MyProgram" eventId="555" log="Application" />
    </targets>
    <rules>
      <logger name="*" minLevel="Error" writeTo="event" />
      <logger name="*" minLevel="Info" writeTo="console" />
      <logger name="*" minLevel="Trace" writeTo="logfile" />
    </rules>
  </nlog>
  <!--          NLOG                          -->
```

The `app.config` file is set using Nlog in the same way like most applications do, the difference being that there needs to be a section name for NServiceBus to use Nlog, for example, `<section name="nlog" type="NLog.Config.ConfigSectionHandler, NLog" />`; for a tutorial on NLog, please see `https://github.com/nlog/nlog/wiki/Tutorial`. We also set the local configuration using `SetLoggingLibrary.NLog();`.

```
private static Logger logger = LogManager.GetCurrentClassLogger();
public void Init()
{

    // Log the Bus
    SetLoggingLibrary.NLog();
    logger.Info("--------Start-------");
```

From the `app.config` file, we are saving a lot of traceable information daily in the `C:\logs\` directory while creating a new file with a filename of the date.

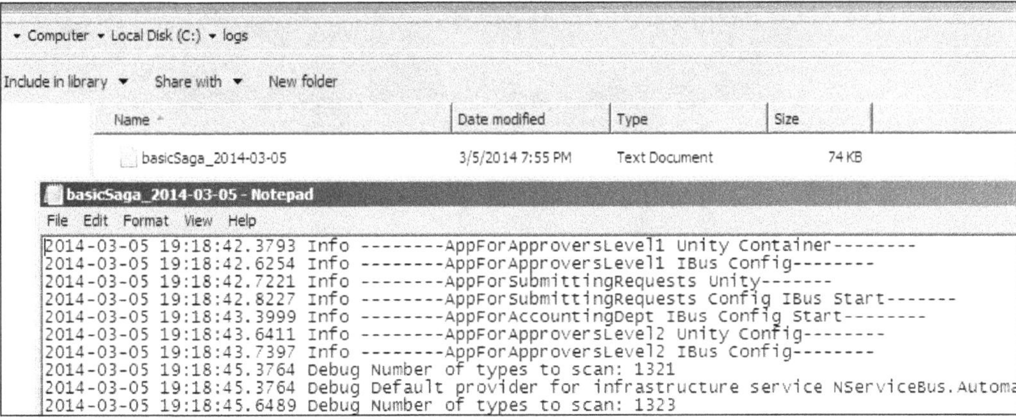

Logging becomes a necessity when trying to document the internal happening of messages, sagas, and persistence.

Buyer's remorse code walkthrough

We will walk through the sample for NHibernate that is found at `https://github.com/Particular/NServiceBus.NHibernate.Samples`. The reason that we keep choosing NHibernate for now is its ability to work with many different database products, including SQL Server and MySQL. We have also walked through a NHibernate example previously, so we are just extending those fundamental concepts.

This example will use SQL Server to store subscriptions, sagas, and timeouts. It will be a fictional video store with a web frontend, communicating with sagas and message handlers as before.

First, we have an e-commerce endpoint implemented as an ASP.NET MVC4 application that uses the following:

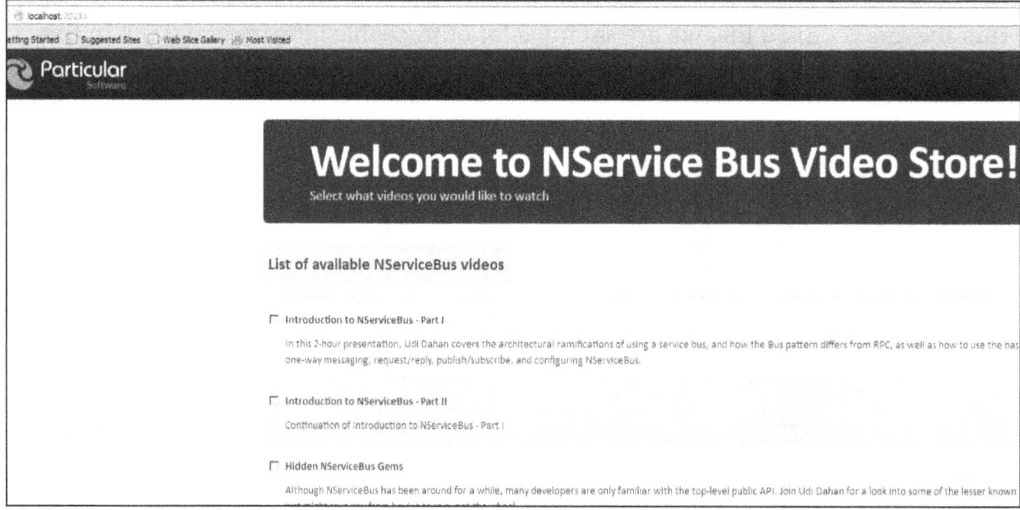

For Microsoft.AspNet.SignalR, see `http://www.asp.net/signalr` to know how to provide feedback to the user. SignalR allows you to have bidirectional communication between the server and client. ASP.NET MVC4 will provide a very generic home website to place orders for NServiceBus videos.

The MVC application will send `MvcApplication.Bus.Send(command);` to the bus with a command that contains the order information.

When the application starts, an `nservicebus` table is created with tables for `ContainSagaData` for IBus to store specific data that contains `Id`, `Originator`, and `OriginalMessageId` we have discussed before.

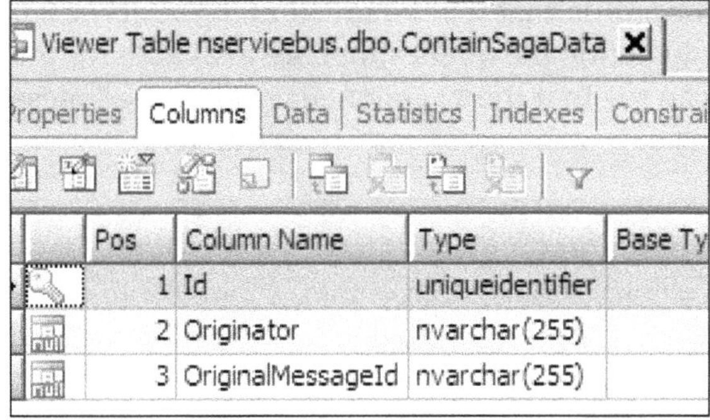

There will also be the sagas themselves, such as an instance of `ProcessOrderSaga` and a timeout record while it is saving `ProcessOrderSaga` on IBus.

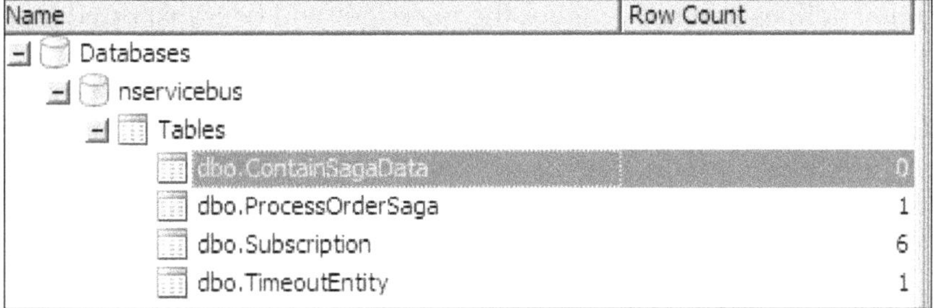

The timeout and sagas act as messages in the table because we set NHibernate from the code in the following screenshot in `InitializeNHibernatePersistence.cs`. To initialize the bus's sagas, timeouts, and subscriptions to NHibernate, this class needs to be in all the applications. This is because you want the subscriptions of all the applications to know the subscription definitions in order to transport the messages.

```
namespace VideoStore.Sales
{
    using NServiceBus;

    class InititalizeSubscriptionStorage : INeedInitialization
    {
        public void Init()
        {
            NServiceBus.Configure.Instance
                .UseNHibernateSubscriptionPersister() // subscription storage using NHibernate
                .UseNHibernateTimeoutPersister() // Timeout Persistance using NHibernate
                .UseNHibernateSagaPersister(); // Saga Persistance using NHibernate
        }
    }
}
```

The subscription information that will be saved in SQL Server will be in the `Subscription` table to define the queues that are available for the messages to be transported. We can see that the `ClientBecamePrefered` message will be placed on the `VideoStore.CustomerRelations` queue.

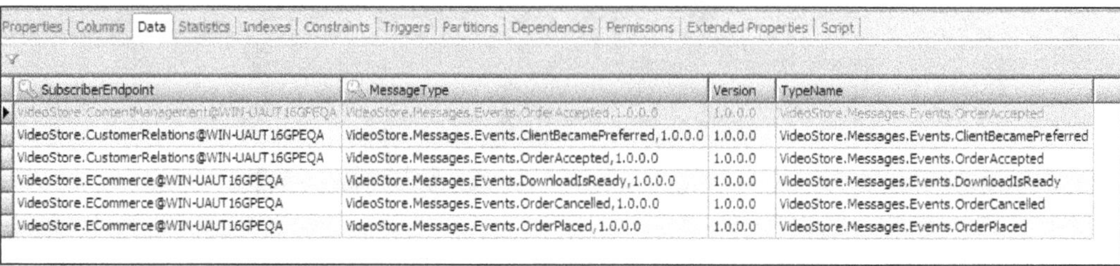

Properties | Columns | Data | Statistics | Indexes | Constraints | Triggers | Partitions | Dependencies | Permissions | Extended Properties | Script

SubscriberEndpoint	MessageType	Version	TypeName
VideoStore.ContentManagement@WIN-UAUT16GPEQA	VideoStore.Messages.Events.OrderAccepted, 1.0.0.0	1.0.0.0	VideoStore.Messages.Events.OrderAccepted
VideoStore.CustomerRelations@WIN-UAUT16GPEQA	VideoStore.Messages.Events.ClientBecamePreferred, 1.0.0.0	1.0.0.0	VideoStore.Messages.Events.ClientBecamePreferred
VideoStore.CustomerRelations@WIN-UAUT16GPEQA	VideoStore.Messages.Events.OrderAccepted, 1.0.0.0	1.0.0.0	VideoStore.Messages.Events.OrderAccepted
VideoStore.ECommerce@WIN-UAUT16GPEQA	VideoStore.Messages.Events.DownloadIsReady, 1.0.0.0	1.0.0.0	VideoStore.Messages.Events.DownloadIsReady
VideoStore.ECommerce@WIN-UAUT16GPEQA	VideoStore.Messages.Events.OrderCancelled, 1.0.0.0	1.0.0.0	VideoStore.Messages.Events.OrderCancelled
VideoStore.ECommerce@WIN-UAUT16GPEQA	VideoStore.Messages.Events.OrderPlaced, 1.0.0.0	1.0.0.0	VideoStore.Messages.Events.OrderPlaced

Now, to be clear, the preceding screenshot contains the message subscription's definition that defines in which queues the messages will be transported to; additionally, since we have not defined many other variables previously, we know that IBus will use `DafaultBuilder()`, XML serialization, and MSMQ transportation by default. If we want to use SQL Server as our method of transportation, then we will have to use the definition, `UseTransport<SqlServer>`. The `https://github.com/Particular/NServiceBus.SqlServer` link will demonstrate queuing across SQL Server.

As always, it is important to check out what the saga is doing. The saga will be located in the `VideoStore.Sales` project. This code may start to look very similar to the previous `BasicSaga` code, but as with most of ESB, it works in the same pattern and only adds minor differences. Here, we will be mapping `SubmitOrder` and `CancelOrder` to the saga through `OrderNumber`. This is to look up the saga at a later time by its unique `OrderNumber` that will keep the messages' mapping to the correct saga instance. Notice that when the saga is started by the `IAmStartedByMessages<SubmitOrder>` message handler, we start the timer; 20 seconds will be persisted to SQL Server after the end of this function call. We save the message information—specifically the uniqueness of the saga—and call `OrderNumber` and any information that we wish to save additionally, then off it goes to SQL Server to be grabbed later from the `CancelOrder` or `SubmitOrder` messages. This saga will be mostly used for a buyer's remorse period of 20 seconds to return to the order information and then publish it to process it if the user doesn't cancel it within 20 seconds.

```
VideoStore.Sales.ProcessOrderSaga                              Timeout(BuyersRemorseIs
    public class ProcessOrderSaga : Saga<ProcessOrderSaga.OrderData>,
                                    IAmStartedByMessages<SubmitOrder>,
                                    IHandleMessages<CancelOrder>,
                                    IHandleTimeouts<ProcessOrderSaga.BuyersRemorseIsOver>
    {


        /*****
         *
         * Configure how to find a daga by OrderNumber
         * for CancelOrder and SubmitOrder
         *
         * ***/
        public override void ConfigureHowToFindSaga()
        {
            ConfigureMapping<SubmitOrder>(m => m.OrderNumber)
                .ToSaga(s => s.OrderNumber);
            ConfigureMapping<CancelOrder>(m => m.OrderNumber)
                .ToSaga(s => s.OrderNumber);
        }

        /**
         * Saga Starter, save to Saga Data
         * Start a 20 second timer
         * ****/
        public void Handle(SubmitOrder message)
        {
            if (DebugFlagMutator.Debug)
            {
                Debugger.Break();
            }

            Data.OrderNumber = message.OrderNumber;
            Data.VideoIds = message.VideoIds;
            Data.ClientId = message.ClientId;


            RequestTimeout(TimeSpan.FromSeconds(20), new BuyersRemorseIsOver());
            Console.Out.WriteLine("Starting cool down period for order #{0}.", Data.OrderNumber);
        }
```

After the timeout period has elapsed, a `BuyersRemorseIsOver` object will be sent to the message handler of the timeout through the `IHandleTimeouts<ProcessOrderSaga.BuyersRemorseIsOver>` interface. Because this is part of the original saga, the saga will be pulled in as the data object.

The `public void Timeout(BuyersRemorseIsOver state)` function will be called to handle the message and a new `OrderAccepted` message will be created and populated from the saga instance, while the saga is being cleaned up. The `OrderAccepted` message will be published to the next endpoints for processing.

This seems like there is a lot of work, but as always, NserviceBus handles it using just a few lines of code.

VideoStore.Sales.ProcessOrderSaga — Timeout(BuyersRemorseIsOver state

```
/****
 *
 * Handle the Timeout
 * Publish that the order was accepted
 * because the buyer remorse period was overd
 * Delete the Saga for cleanup
 *
 * ****/
public void Timeout(BuyersRemorseIsOver state)
{
    if (DebugFlagMutator.Debug)
    {
        Debugger.Break();
    }

    Bus.Publish<OrderAccepted>(e =>
        {
            e.OrderNumber = Data.OrderNumber;
            e.VideoIds = Data.VideoIds;
            e.ClientId = Data.ClientId;
        });
    // Delete the Saga
    MarkAsComplete();
    Console.Out.WriteLine("Cooling down period for order #{0} has elapsed.", Data.OrderNumber);
}
```

What the user will see is the timing out of the order at the bottom. This is their chance to cancel the order if they change their mind, as it is in a pending state.

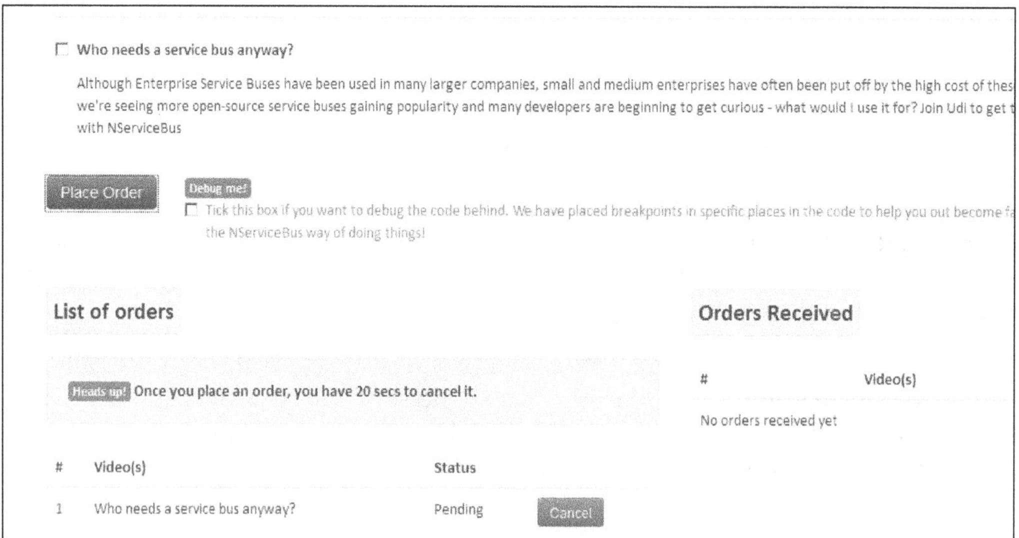

If the **Cancel** button isn't clicked, the timer will timeout and create a new message from a saga instance to publish a successful order; then, the saga will be cleaned up after the order is published. If **Cancel** isn't clicked, we will clean up the saga first and then publish the `OrderCancelled` message.

```
ieoStore.Sales.ProcessOrderSaga                                        Handl
        /*****
         * handle the CancelOrder message
         * ****/
        public void Handle(CancelOrder message)
        {
            if (DebugFlagMutator.Debug)
            {
                    Debugger.Break();
            }
            // Cleanup SAGA
            MarkAsComplete();

            Bus.Publish(Bus.CreateInstance<OrderCancelled>(o =>
                {
                    o.OrderNumber = message.OrderNumber;
                    o.ClientId = message.ClientId;
                }));

            Console.Out.WriteLine("Order #{0} was cancelled.", message.OrderNumber);
        }
```

Where are these messages published? By looking at the subscriptions table previously in SQL Server, we can see the map of the queues. See the previous picture, but it just shows the following:

- `VideoStore.Messages.Events.OrderAccepted`: `VideoStore.ContentManagement@MachineName` (just the local machine name)
- `VideoStore.Messages.Events.OrderAccepted`: `VideoStore.CustomerRelation@MachineName`
- `VideoStore.Messages.Events.OrderCancelled`: `VideoStore.ECommerce@MachineName`

If you have a look at MSMQ, you'll see that the messages for `OrderCancelled` are placed on `VideoStore.ContentManagement` and `VideoStore.CustomerRelation`.

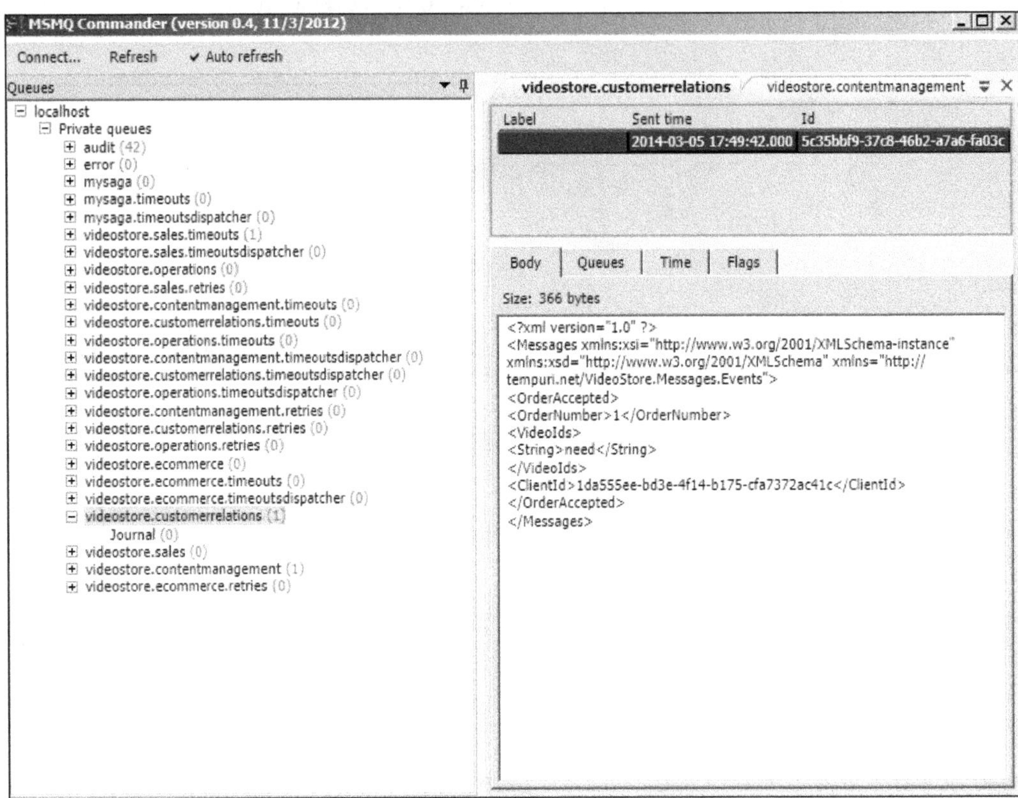

The customer relations application can then send coupons and special offers to the customer, and the content management application returns a link to be clicked on to download the video.

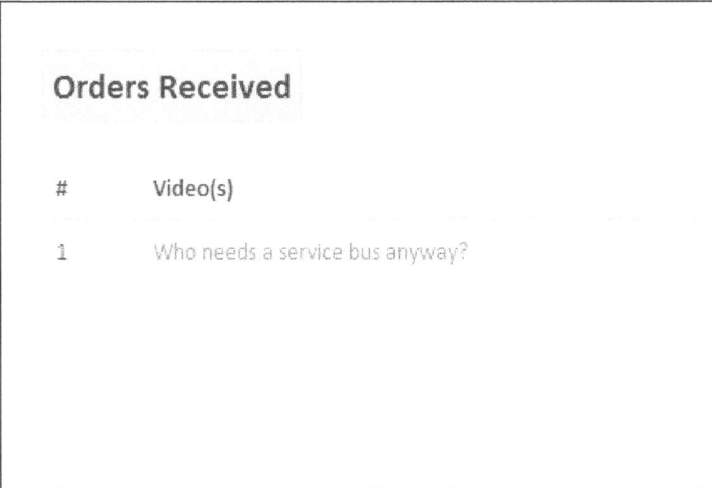

There are various pieces that could be added, and we would have gone into a lot more detail, but this is just to give you some understanding of the interaction between ESB and NHibernate. The messages can be observed and the endpoints, saga, and timeouts can be instrumented. Conditions can be added to the sagas and messages for errors beyond the default error queue that messages will be returned to if there are exceptions. There are many, many possibilities to extend this sample.

Message mutators

There was also a very handy utility to debug and watch this application get embedded into the ESB and messaging itself. Refer to a checkbox that appears at the bottom of the homepage, as follows:

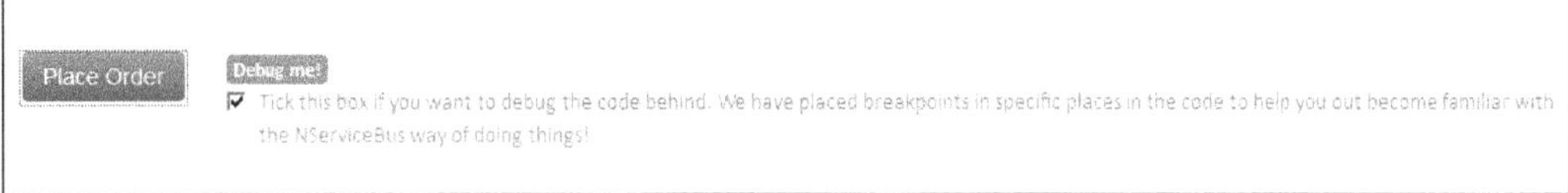

Checking this checkbox will allow breakpoints to be executed at the `Debugger.Break()` function.

```
VideoStore.CustomerRelations.OrderAcceptedHandler
namespace VideoStore.CustomerRelations
{
    using System;
    using System.Diagnostics;
    using Messages.Events;
    using NServiceBus;
    using VideoStore.Common;

    class OrderAcceptedHandler : IHandleMessages<OrderAccepted>
    {
        public IBus Bus { get; set; }
        public void Handle(OrderAccepted message)
        {
            if (DebugFlagMutator.Debug)
            {
                Debugger.Break();
            }
```

The class that is created in these samples is called `DebugFlagMutator.cs` that will incorporate the `IMutateTransportMessage` interface.

```
gFlagMutator.cs   EndpointConfig.cs   InitializeNHibernatePersistence.cs   ProvisionDownloadHandler.cs   ProvisionDownloadResponseHand
deoStore.Common.DebugFlagMutator                                                                                  Debug
namespace VideoStore.Common
{
    using System;
    using System.Threading;
    using NServiceBus;
    using NServiceBus.MessageMutator;

    public class DebugFlagMutator : IMutateTransportMessages, INeedInitialization
    {
        public static bool Debug { get { return debug.Value; } }

        public void MutateIncoming(TransportMessage transportMessage)
        {
            var debugFlag = transportMessage.Headers.ContainsKey("Debug") ? transportMessage.Headers["Debug"] : "false";
            if (debugFlag !=null && debugFlag.Equals("true", StringComparison.OrdinalIgnoreCase))
            {
                debug.Value = true;
            }
            else
            {
                debug.Value = false;
            }
        }
```

This class will use the interface `IMutateTransportMessage` as a message mutator. For more on message mutators, see `http://docs.particular.net/NServiceBus/nservicebus-message-mutators-sample`. Message mutators can change the message as it goes to and from the endpoint in transient. This happens in the transport header in most cases, without it affecting the rest of the message needed by the message handler.

Encryption

Also, please note that there are Rijndael Encryption configurations in the `VideoStore.ECommerce` project. In the `Global.asax` file, there is a confirmation according to which `RijndaelEncryptionService` can run on the bus:

```
protected void Application_Start()
{
    startableBus = Configure.With()
        .DefaultBuilder()
        .Log4Net(new DebugAppender {Threshold = Level.Warn})
        .UseTransport<Msmq>()
        .PurgeOnStartup(true)
        .UnicastBus()
        .RunHandlersUnderIncomingPrincipal(false)
        .RijndaelEncryptionService()
        .UseNHibernateTimeoutPersister()
        .CreateBus();

    Configure.Instance.ForInstallationOn<Windows>().Install();

    bus = startableBus.Start();

    AreaRegistration.RegisterAllAreas();
    FilterConfig.RegisterGlobalFilters(GlobalFilters.Filters);
    RouteConfig.RegisterRoutes(RouteTable.Routes);
}
```

The `SubmitOrder` message will have all the fields that start with the `Encrypted` word as defined in the `UnobtrusiveMessageConventions.cs` file via the `.DefiningEncryptedPropertiesAs(p => p.Name.StartsWith("Encrypted"));` configuration. This will encrypt the fields that start with `Encrypted`.

```
public class SubmitOrder
{
    public int OrderNumber { get; set; }
    public string[] VideoIds { get; set; }
    public string ClientId { get; set; }
    public string EncryptedCreditCardNumber { get; set; }
    public string EncryptedExpirationDate { get; set; }
}
```

We can verify this from the message being transported if the message has the encrypted values for credit card and expiration date:

Services and deployment

Many of the programs that we have shown in the examples thus far have been console applications that generally don't run in production.

There is a framework that is embedded in a lot of NserviceBus code called Topshelf; see `http://topshelf-project.com` for the Topshelf website. TopShelf is a framework used to build Windows services.

To deploy NServiceBus, a command script in Windows can be written to deploy the application via the `NServiceBys.Host.exe` command from NServiceBus; refer to `http://docs.particular.net/NServiceBus/the-nservicebus-host`. To see what the available installations are, simply run `NServiceBus.Host.exe /?`.

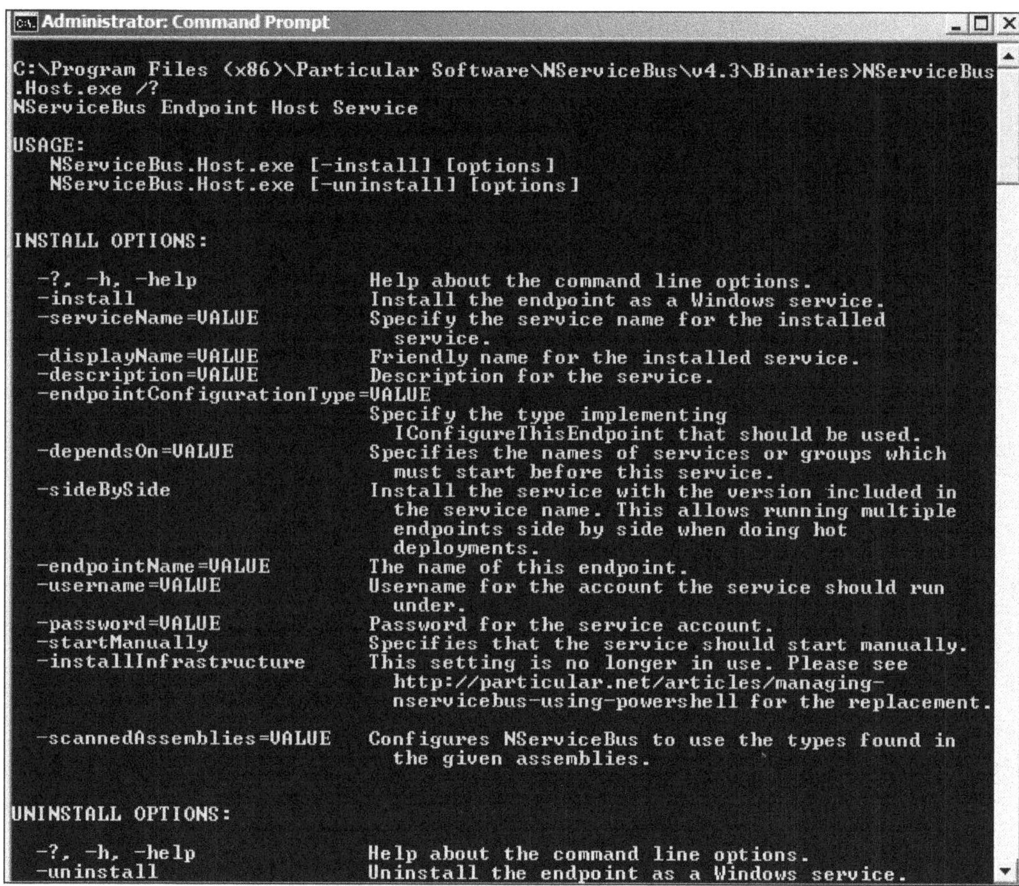
Administrator: Command Prompt
C:\Program Files (x86)\Particular Software\NServiceBus\v4.3\Binaries>NServiceBus.Host.exe /?
NServiceBus Endpoint Host Service
USAGE:
NServiceBus.Host.exe [-install] [options]
NServiceBus.Host.exe [-uninstall] [options]
INSTALL OPTIONS:
-?, -h, -help Help about the command line options.
-install Install the endpoint as a Windows service.
-serviceName=VALUE Specify the service name for the installed service.
-displayName=VALUE Friendly name for the installed service.
-description=VALUE Description for the service.
-endpointConfigurationType=VALUE Specify the type implementing IConfigureThisEndpoint that should be used.
-dependsOn=VALUE Specifies the names of services or groups which must start before this service.
-sideBySide Install the service with the version included in the service name. This allows running multiple endpoints side by side when doing hot deployments.
-endpointName=VALUE The name of this endpoint.
-username=VALUE Username for the account the service should run under.
-password=VALUE Password for the service account.
-startManually Specifies that the service should start manually.
-installInfrastructure This setting is no longer in use. Please see http://particular.net/articles/managing-nservicebus-using-powershell for the replacement.
-scannedAssemblies=VALUE Configures NServiceBus to use the types found in the given assemblies.
UNINSTALL OPTIONS:
-?, -h, -help Help about the command line options.
-uninstall Uninstall the endpoint as a Windows service.

A sample script to install a service can be created with something as simple as the following:

MyPayQueue.cmd

```
NServiceBus.Host.exe /install /serviceName:"MyPayQueue.dll" /displayName:"MyPayQueue"
/description:"Service for Payments" /endpointConfigurationType:"EndpointConfig,MyPayQueue"
```

As a note, besides Visual Studio 2012, I use Notepad++, Free Toad for SQL Server, and MSMQ Commander.

Summary

We have discussed many of the different configurations used to create IBus. Much emphasis has been put on both sagas and persistence. We walked through two similar but different examples and went through the `Init()` method, sagas, and message handlers. The goal is that the reader has enough references and knowledge about configurations to start configuring their own sagas and persistent examples going forward. We discussed the creation of services and endpoints, debugging through message mutators, and more. The NServiceBus IBus does the bulk of the work, so coding is kept to a minimal.

5
Persistence Architecture

For the ESB bus, persistence is the key element in storing messages that could be associated as business objects that run through the ESB workflow. There are other persistent elements that comprise the metadata that define how the messages and workflow are being handled in the ESB through configuration. Persistence can also be considered the feedback that the ESB gives to the system in the form of logging, errors, and audits. In this chapter, we will cover persisting items to the database, including messages and logging.

We will cover the following topics:

- Persistence basics
- Supporting frameworks for persistence
    - Introduction to Entity Framework
    - XML serialization
    - C# reflection
- The PayQueue sample
- The SQL queuing sample
- Database logging

Persistence basics

Up to this point, we have delved heavily into MSMQ. In later chapters, we will also cover RabbitMQ and ActiveMQ. If you know MSMQ very well, learning RabbitMQ and ActiveMQ will be simple, except that these technologies are not as tightly coupled to the Windows Server as MSMQ.

Let's face it: as a developer, and architect, you are likely reading this chapter to keep up your skills. Your skills get you jobs. If you are skilled in both Java and C#, your chances of getting employment is greater. The same logic applies if you know how to build enterprise systems not only using message queues, but databases as well. It will be easier to find server people who can administrate the databases rather than message queue systems simply because databases are prevalent in storing data for a multitude of desktop systems as well. Therefore, you may want to use databases for message queuing. Most projects spend a lot of time persisting data to the databases and building tables and databases, which we discuss through this chapter. However, we will not run SQL commands in this chapter; rather, we will build objects on top of C# frameworks to deal with SQL commands. In many modern technologies these days, such as NServiceBus, Entity Frameworks, NHibernate, and Spring Roo, the frameworks run a lot of SQL commands. We use objects in these frameworks, and the frameworks either generate DDLs, XML mapping, or scripting. NSB will take care of most of the mappings to the databases directly.

One of the reasons, besides heavily loading SQL Servers with stored procedures, for the **object relational mappers** (**ORMs**) being more and more popular and also NoSQL databases such as RavenDB and MongoDB, is not just to take advantage of having modern frameworks do the heavy lifting, but to have the tools in the frameworks do the heavy processing. SQL Server, and other databases, seem to always have enough load.

The concept is to create the objects in code, and the frameworks will take care of the SQL. This allows developers to code faster once they get used to the frameworks. Some of the fathers of agile processes developed frameworks such as Spring for all developers to glue frameworks as opposed to building everything from scratch. The other reason is SQL Injection. Feel free to go through some of my slides to understand some of this, `http://www.slideshare.net/rhelton_1/sql-injection-amp-entity-frameworks` and `http://www.slideshare.net/rhelton_1/asp-mvs3-rev009`. Here's a slide for a starting iPad development in C#, `http://www.slideshare.net/rhelton_1/the-ipad-monotouch`. Here's an older slide on NServiceBus, `http://www.slideshare.net/rhelton_1/nservicebus`. If SQL commands are in code, and used close to the frontend of an application, a hacker can try to inject SQL commands into the frontend pieces to see whether they can execute SQL commands directly into the database. For instance, a form may have SQL commands to access a database, and a hacker may inject SQL commands into the form to try to return passwords and users.

A typical scenario for injecting SQL into browsers would be to run the browser code in a Firefox debugger, look for any functions or JavaScript that looks like it may take SQL, and run a SQL Injection tool to try every combination of SQL through these commands. There are many off-the-shelf tools to test the browser code available to all. For those who hack or check hacking for a living, there are many, many freeware tools that assist in finding SQL Injection, and even training sites to train your skills in finding SQL Injection. If you practice hacking enough, such as SQL Injection, there are many official contests to try your hacking skills at. The ultimate way to get rid of SQL Injection is not to use SQL commands at all in code. With today's modern frameworks, with ORMs and NoSQL, there is not absolute need to use SQL commands. Also, the performance in NoSQL, and ORMs, to code, dependent on the code base, has been shown to increase performance, decrease development time, and decrease code.

Supporting frameworks for persistence

To familiarize you with SQL ORM's in Visual Studio, it would be negligent if I did not cover Entity Framework, XML serialization, and C# reflection as not only NSB, but many frameworks are based on these techniques. When working with SQL Server, it is not uncommon to have several Entity Framework tools for administration, monitoring, and synching data in SQL Server; otherwise, the alternative would likely be SQL scripting and stored procedures.

NServiceBus, as well as any ESB, is heavily reliant on XML serialization and object reflection, which will be covered as well.

In this section, we will be using the **PayQueue** solution:

- `MyMessages`: This is a payment message used for the projects
- `AppForWritingXML`: This is a project that writes payment XML files to a local `C:\` drive
- `AppForReadingXML`: This is a project to read XML files from the drive, which saves a copy to the local database through Entity Framework, using the routines from the `AppForWritingToTable` routines and sending them to MSMQ to process as messages
- `AppForWritinTables`: These are just the data access routines for `AppForReadingXML`

The `AppForWritingXML` creates 5 XML files into `C:\Load_XML_Files`. The `AppForReadingXML` will load the XML messages into the `Payment` table. The `Payment` table for sending payments, the `AppForReadingXML` table for receiving payments, the `unicastconfig` table and `auditconfig` tables need to be created. We see that the messages move from files to the `Payment` table to the `AppForReadinXML` table using various coding methods. A `PayQueue` database must be created in the `SQLExpress`. If the database is new and the tables need to be created, then run the `Model.edmx` to create the tables from the `Model.edmx` file of `AppForWritingForTables` using the "Generate Database from model". This will create a file called `Model1.edmx.sql` that when run will create the tables. This SQL script can be run to create the tables from Visual Studio 2012. These were ran in VS2012 in Windows Server 2012, with MSMQ, DTC, NServiceBus references, and SQL Server 2012 Express LocalDB installed. Ensure that DTC, MSMQ, and NServiceBus is set up per `http://docs.particular.net/nservicebus/preparing-your-machine-to-run-nservicebus`.

Run `ApprForWritingXML` to create XML files, and then `AppForReadingXML` to send them to the SQL tables and MSMQ using NServiceBus. These were run in VS 2012 in Windows Server 2012, with MSMQ, DTC, and NServiceBus references, and SQL Server 2012 Express LocalDB installed.

Introducing Entity Framework

Entity Framework (**EF**) has many tools designed to integrate well into Visual Studio. EF is an **object relational mapper** (**ORM**) where Visual Studio, through wizards into Visual Studio and SQL Server, takes care of a lot of the mapping effort and even creates entity objects from existing database. We will briefly touch upon Entity Framework for the needs of this book and working with SQL databases and MVC. It is neither a requirement to know EF at this point nor to be an EF expert to work with NSB; however, a developer should be familiar with EF so as to relate to Visual Studio and SQL Servers, especially as a Microsoft best practice. If further information is desired outside this book, feel free to visit my slides at `http://www.slideshare.net/rhelton_1/asp-mvc3-rev009`.

EF can be installed into your application when developing just using NuGet.

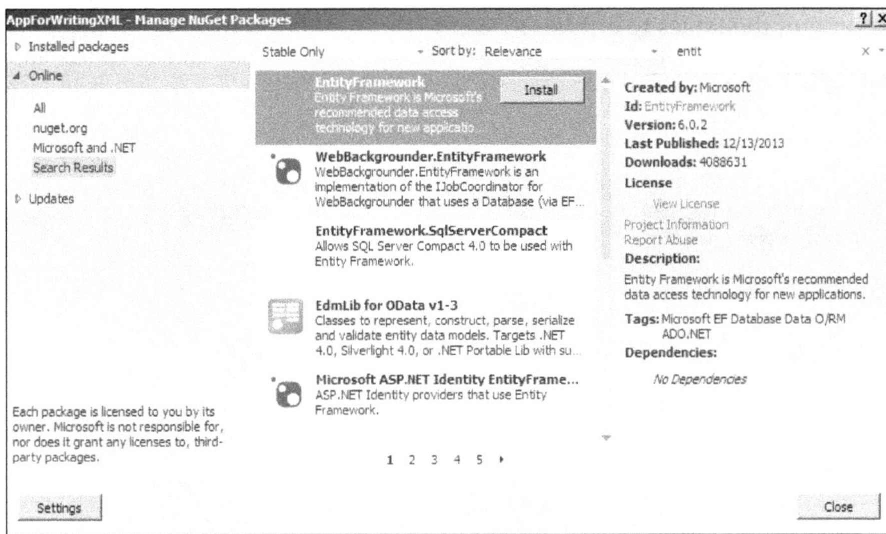

After downloading it, we can create model objects from tables and databases. The model will create the connection string for the entity models in the `app.config` file as well as establish mapping to the entity objects, and the entity objects themselves.

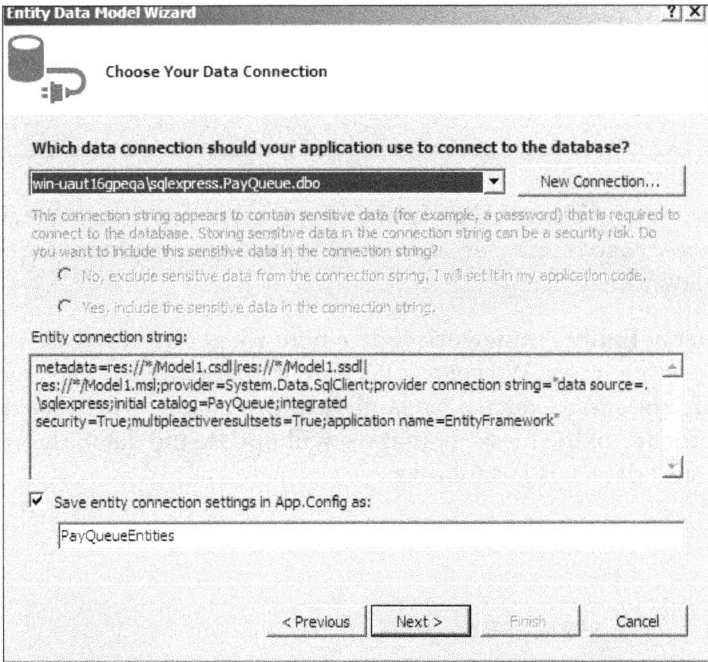

EF has the ability to update the tables to match any changes in the mapped models and even update the models from changes done to the tables. This is done to keep the mapping of the tables to entities synced.

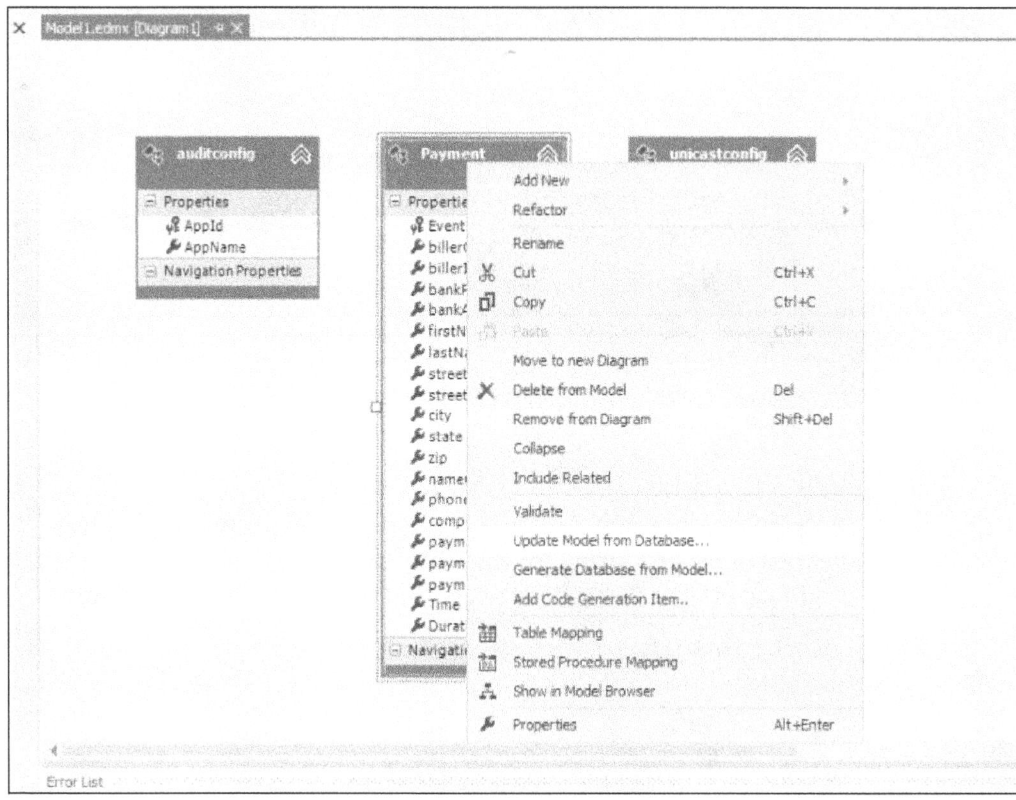

Entity Framework uses Fluent API's lambda expressions, as does NServiceBus; see `http://msdn.microsoft.com/en-us/data/jj591620.aspx` for more on this topic of Entity Framework.

Here's a snippet of Entity Framework code where we get the database context for the model, `PayQueueEntities`. We get a collection of all the rows in the `Payments` table called `payment_rows`. We exercise the lambda `Where` clause to retrieve the first row that has any primary of the message that we will update the database from; if none are found, we add the record as follows:

```
using (var context = new PayQueueEntities())
 {

        // Get the payment rows
```

```
            var payment_rows = context.Payments;
           // Fluent API, check to see if there already is a payment
with this EventId (PK)
           var payment = payment_rows.Where(x => (x.EventId == details.
EventId)).FirstOrDefault();
            /***
              * If no payment in rows
              * Add row
               * Otherwise update row
               * *****/
             if (payment == null)
             {
                 /**
                  * Walk through the details object
                  * Using Reflection
                  * ***/
                 Payment newPayment = new Payment();  // Create a new
payment row
```

Also, notice that a `newPayment` object was created to create a row in the database. This is some of the generated code from EF that already has mapping to the tables created through the Visual Studio wizard. It's nice not to have to create your own objects, but just to call the objects that match the database rows that were created with the Visual Studio ADO Entity class creation tools. The code, in the `Where` command, will find any matching `EventIds` keys matching the selected messages.

NServiceBus does not currently officially integrate into Entity Framework but uses NHibernate instead as a mapper to the SQL databases and creates the mapping for NServiceBus. There are people working in developing code who are starting to use Entity Framework as a persister, such as in a saga persister example at `https://github.com/Meksi/NServiceBus.Persistence`. However, almost every developer who executes MVC and C# has heard of, if not developed in, Entity Framework to some degree as it follows the Microsoft best practices in C# development.

Also, if you look in the examples discussed thus far, the Fluent API's lambda expression is used throughout NServiceBus. We can see it in pieces when we called `UnobtrusiveMessageConventions`:

```
class UnobtrusiveMessageConventions : IWantToRunBeforeConfiguration
 {
     public void Init()
     {
         Configure.Instance
```

```
                    .DefiningCommandsAs(t => t.Namespace !=
null && t.Namespace.StartsWith("VideoStore") && t.Namespace.
EndsWith("Commands"))
                    .DefiningEventsAs(t => t.Namespace !=
null && t.Namespace.StartsWith("VideoStore") && t.Namespace.
EndsWith("Events"))
                    .DefiningMessagesAs(t => t.Namespace !=
null && t.Namespace.StartsWith("VideoStore") && t.Namespace.
EndsWith("RequestResponse"))
                    .DefiningEncryptedPropertiesAs(p => p.Name.
StartsWith("Encrypted"));
        }
    }
```

Going forward, you may see many snippets of code in Entity Framework. Most of the code will be generated using the tools found in Visual Studio, mostly Visual Studio 2012.

XML serialization

NServiceBus, and ESBs in general, rely heavily on XML serialization and C# reflection as well as many other frameworks, such as EF. There are many books on XML serialization as well, but we will discuss it in brief as it applies to NSB messages. It is not a requirement of this book to have skills in EF, MVC, reflection, and XML serialization, so introductions will be provided. Working with NSB in general may not require these skills at first, but digging into any messaging and NSB code will start to require it; it will at least be beneficial for deeper understanding. Extending the Entity Framework example, let's retrieve, as an exercise, XML files that look like messages from a file directory, load them into a SQL Server table, and then send the messages through message queuing. Later, we will extend this example even more and load up the data through C# reflection. This example was derived from the need to automatically send test message—only a few now—but it could be extended to hundreds, through NSB into MSMQ. This is testing through console programs, so a MVC video store frontend could be added after the other pieces have been stress-tested. There are many applications that may not require a frontend, as many organizations still use batch processing, especially those associated with getting mainframe information, through the use of mainframe text files being parsed into XML files as they are passed from text into message forms. Messaging has evolved from various XML designs.

While many of the examples thus far have had simple messages, it is pretty normal that messages, just as with XML and databases, will have multiple parts to break down the messages:

```
namespace MyMessages
{
    public class EventMessage : IMessage
    {
        public Guid EventId { get; set; }
        public PaymentReq paymentReq { get; set; }
    }

    public class PaymentReq
    {
        public string billerGroupId { get; set; }
        public string billerId { get; set; }
        public string bankRoutingNumber { get; set; } // 9-digits
        public string bankAccountNumber { get; set; } // 9-digits
        public string firstName { get; set; }
        public string lastName { get; set; } // 9-digits
        public Address address { get; set; }
        public string nameOnAccount { get; set; }
        public string phone { get; set; }  // 10 digits
        public string companyName { get; set; }  // 50 characters
        public Guid paymentReferenceId { get; set; }
        public string paymentChannel { get; set; } // Usually WEB
        public string paymentAmount { get; set; } // of the form
201.10
    }

    public class Address
    {
        public string streetAddress1 { get; set; }
        public string streetAddress2 { get; set; }
        public string city { get; set; }
        public string state { get; set; }  // 2-chars
        public string zip { get; set; }  // 5-digits
    }
```

There are many mediums for XML messaging in NSB; we have mentioned SQL Server, MSMQ, ActiveMQ, RabbitMQ, Azure, and others, but NSB could also be used as the workflow for other endpoints, such as SFTP, WCF, and File I/O. However, when using custom endpoints, the developer now becomes responsible for the transactions and second-level retries. One way to handle these issues is the use of sagas. Here's a snippet illustrating writing the preceding message to an XML file using XML serialization.

```
        static void Main(string[] args)
         {

             string path = @"c:\Load_XML_Files\";

             /*****
              * Create 5 Sample XML Files
              * *****/
             for (int index = 0; index < 5; index++)
             {
                 string filename = @"temp" + (index + 1) + ".xml";
                 EventMessage details = new EventMessage();

    ...

                 SerializeEventMessage(path+filename, details);
             }


         }

         static public void SerializeEventMessage(string pathname,
EventMessage details)
         {
             XmlSerializer serializer = new XmlSerializer(typeof(Event
Message));
             using (TextWriter writer = new StreamWriter(pathname))
             {
                 serializer.Serialize(writer, details);
             }
         }
     }
```

We can read the XML data into the objects and then copy the data into the database.

```
class Program
    {
        static void Main(string[] args)
        {
            /*****
             * Open the temp files in this directory
             * *****/
            string[] dirs = Directory.GetFiles(@"c:\Load_XML_Files",
"temp" );
            foreach (string filename in dirs)
            {
                /***
                 * De-serialize the XML into the objects
                 * *****/
                EventMessage details = DeserializeEventMessage(filena
me);
                PaymentDAL payDAL = new PaymentDAL();
                /*****
                 * Save to the database
                 * *****/
                payDAL.writeEventMsg(details);

            }

        }
        static public EventMessage DeserializeEventMessage(string
filename)
        {
            XmlSerializer serializer = new XmlSerializer(typeof(Event
Message));
            using (TextReader reader = new StreamReader(filename))
            {
                EventMessage eventMsg = (EventMessage)serializer.
Deserialize(reader);
                return eventMsg;
            }
         }
    }
```

After we read and write data from files, we can process them as messages or save them to the database. This is a simple example of loading messages from files into the database using reflection and Entity Framework.

C# reflection

Reflection cannot be underestimated, especially when working with XML serialization and Entity Framework.

C# uses reflection mostly with the `System.Reflection` namespace; for further reading see `http://msdn.microsoft.com/en-us/library/system.reflection%28v=vs.110%29.aspx`. Reflection can be used to get information from assemblies, `http://msdn.microsoft.com/en-us/library/ms173183.aspx`, or to get information from object and classes, `http://msdn.microsoft.com/en-us/library/b05d559ty%28v=vs.110%29.aspx`.

So why does this help with all this development? Being able to walk through an object and copy fields to fields, as with a deep cloning of an object, can only be done with reflection. When copying from a message to a database row, it does not necessarily have to be a one-to-one copy, but it saves having to know all the fields of an object or changing the code when the fields of the objects change. Here's a snippet from the `PaymentDAL.cs` file that shows a copy of the address piece of the message object being copied into the `Payments` table address value with a payment row of data. In this piece of code, we are copying values from a one object to a different object with matching field names and putting in values, without calling these fields directly, which would involve a lot more code and work.

```
      /*****
        * Copy the values of the old Address object
         * to the address fields in the database
           * *******/
          Address address = (Address)payPropertyInformation.
GetValue(paymentReq, null);
                                      PropertyInfo[] addressProperty
= address.GetType().GetProperties();
        // Get each field from the address object
        for (int index4 = 0; index4 < addressProperty.Length; index4++)
         {
              PropertyInfo addressPropertyInformation =
addressProperty[index4];
              string addressName = addressPropertyInformation.Name.
ToString();
               // Get the address field value
              var addressField = addressPropertyInformation.
GetValue(address, null);
    // Find the same field in the database row
              var field3 = newPayProperty.Where(x => (x.Name ==
addressName)).FirstOrDefault();
```

```
            //Set the database row with the address field value
            field3.SetValue(newPayment, addressField, null);
        }
```

This code uses C# reflection to copy one field in an object created from XML to an object mapped in a table row and then saved.

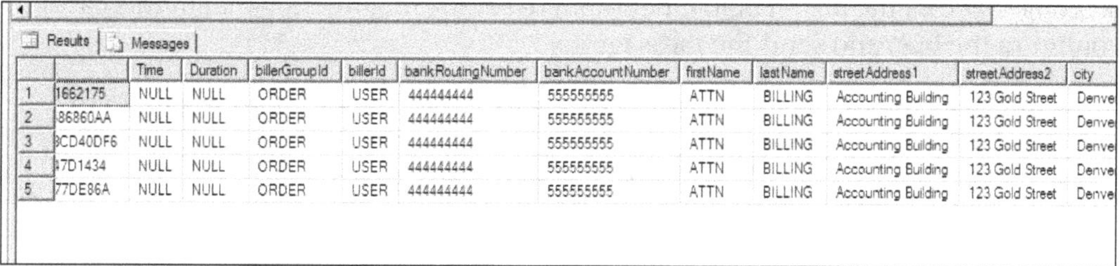

		Time	Duration	billerGroupId	billerId	bankRoutingNumber	bankAccountNumber	firstName	lastName	streetAddress1	streetAddress2	city
1	1662175	NULL	NULL	ORDER	USER	444444444	555555555	ATTN	BILLING	Accounting Building	123 Gold Street	Denve
2	86860AA	NULL	NULL	ORDER	USER	444444444	555555555	ATTN	BILLING	Accounting Building	123 Gold Street	Denve
3	CD40DF6	NULL	NULL	ORDER	USER	444444444	555555555	ATTN	BILLING	Accounting Building	123 Gold Street	Denve
4	7D1434	NULL	NULL	ORDER	USER	444444444	555555555	ATTN	BILLING	Accounting Building	123 Gold Street	Denve
5	77DE86A	NULL	NULL	ORDER	USER	444444444	555555555	ATTN	BILLING	Accounting Building	123 Gold Street	Denve

The PayQueue sample

From these frameworks and the use of SQL Queuing, we will be introducing a PayQueue sample that will be evolving over some of the following chapters.

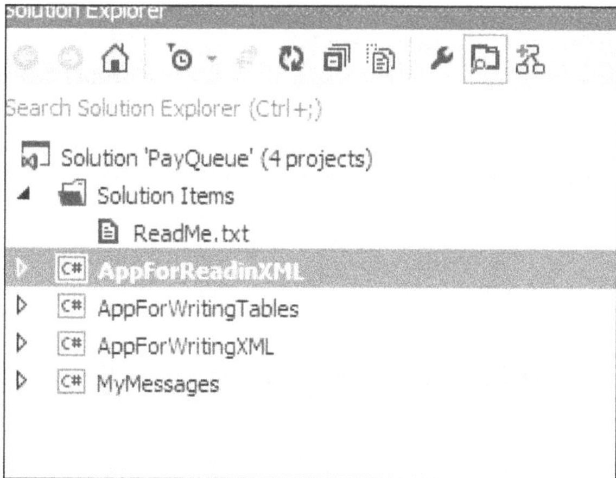

The solution will start with four projects:

- `MyMessages`: This contains the common messages—currently `EventMessage` given previously
- `AppForWritingXML`: This contains the application to write XML messages to disk

- `AppForWritingTables`: This contains Entity Framework and C# refection to populate the PayQueue `Payments` table with the event message data
- `AppForReadingXML`: This reads the sample XML files from disk, populates the `Payments` table, and sends the data through a SQL Queue

Many of the snippets have already been covered in part. The part that remains is sending it across the bus in SQL Queuing. We set the logging (log4net in this case), configure the bus, and send the message.

The installation piece creates the endpoints in SQL Server, and it knows to do this because the transport is set to `<SqlServer>`:

```
        // Set the log4net
          SetLoggingLibrary.Log4Net(log4net.Config.XmlConfigurator.
Configure);
          // Configure the Bus
          bus = Configure.With()
                  .DefaultBuilder()
                  .UseTransport<SqlServer>()
                  .UnicastBus()
                  .CreateBus()
                  .Start(() => Configure.Instance.
ForInstallationOn<NServiceBus.Installation.Environments.Windows>()
                                               .Install());
          /****
            * Send it to the Queue
            * ****/
          foreach (var msg in myXMLlist)
          {
              bus.Send(msg);
          }
```

However, this code is really a small piece of the recipe. The `app.config` file plays an important role in configuring the bus:

1. We will define `NServiceBus/Transport` that will give the SQL connection string for the queues, which will include the database and connection.
2. The Entity Framework connection string is used to perform other actions on the database to load tables with utilities outside NServiceBus.
3. The error and audit queues need to be set.
4. A log4net file appender was added to debug.
5. The queue has to be defined based on the messages namespace.

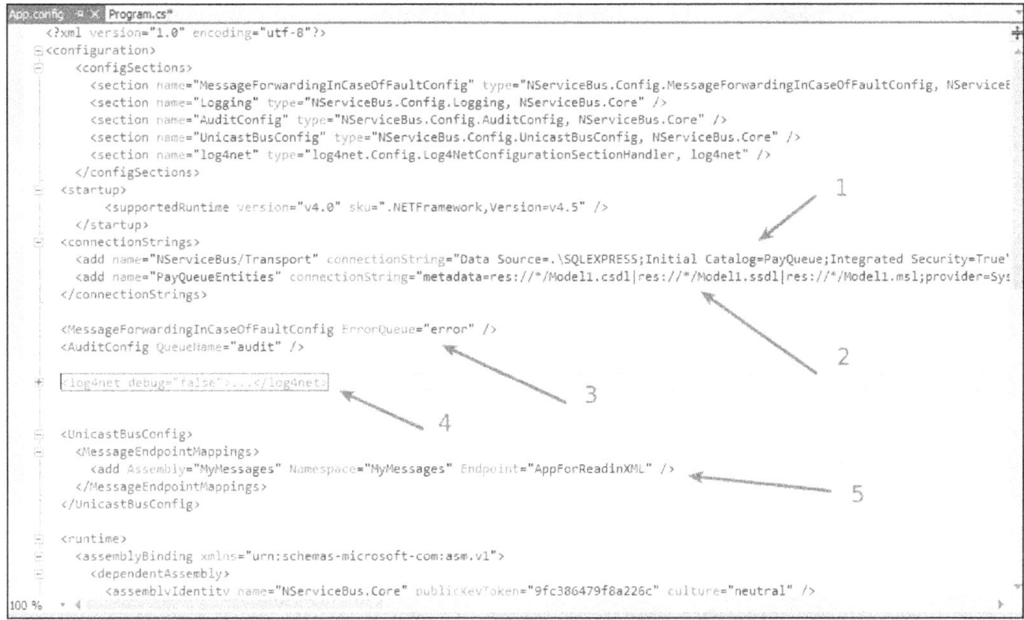

We can see that, when we started the program, the endpoints were created in the `PayQueue` table as follows:

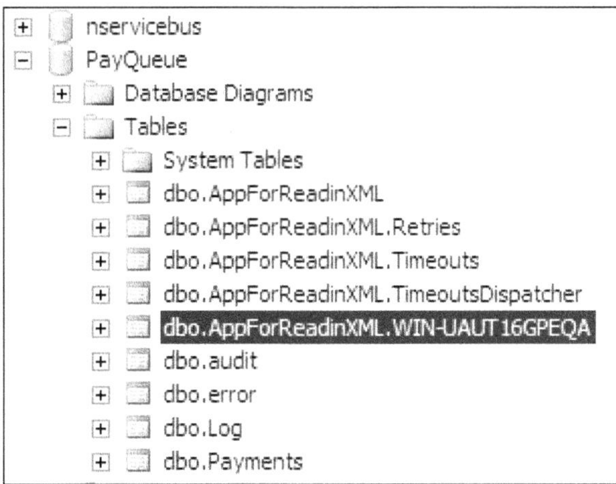

We can also see that, when the program runs, it creates messages in the queues, as shown in the following screenshot.

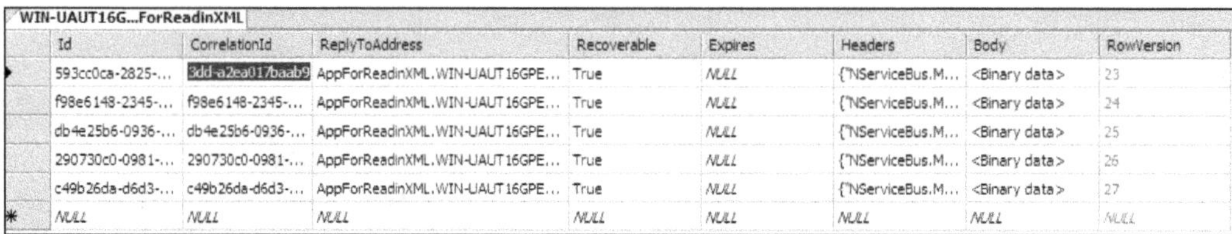

WIN-UAUT16G...ForReadinXML

Id	CorrelationId	ReplyToAddress	Recoverable	Expires	Headers	Body	RowVersion
593cc0ca-2825-...	3dd-a2ea017baab9	AppForReadinXML.WIN-UAUT16GPE...	True	NULL	{"NServiceBus.M...	<Binary data>	23
f98e6148-2345-...	f98e6148-2345-...	AppForReadinXML.WIN-UAUT16GPE...	True	NULL	{"NServiceBus.M...	<Binary data>	24
db4e25b6-0936-...	db4e25b6-0936-...	AppForReadinXML.WIN-UAUT16GPE...	True	NULL	{"NServiceBus.M...	<Binary data>	25
290730c0-0981-...	290730c0-0981-...	AppForReadinXML.WIN-UAUT16GPE...	True	NULL	{"NServiceBus.M...	<Binary data>	26
c49b26da-d6d3-...	c49b26da-d6d3-...	AppForReadinXML.WIN-UAUT16GPE...	True	NULL	{"NServiceBus.M...	<Binary data>	27
NULL	NULL	NULL	NULL	NULL	NULL	NULL	NULL

The SQL queuing sample

We have already explored MSMQ in previous chapters. Wouldn't it be nice to store the messages in MySQL or SQL Server instead, and not worry so much about tooling for MSMQ if the database is already tooled? Also, you can consolidate all the data into a database, thus not having multiple products to maintain. MSMQ is a product, and makes more used of database tools for these programs.

In this section, we will be using `NserviceBus.SqlServer.Samples-master\VideoStore.SqlServer`, which is described in the SQL Queuing sample. The sample runs a video store for SQL queuing to order videos.

The solution was run in VS 2012 in Windows Server 2012, with MSMQ, DTC, NServiceBus references, and SQL Server 2012 Express LocalDB installed.

Running the example, `https://github.com/Particular/NServiceBus.SqlServer.Samples`, we see that the queues are now created in the `nservicebus` table instead of the MSMQ.

Microsoft SQL Server Management Studio
File Edit View Debug Tools Window Community Help
New Query
Object Explorer
Connect ▾
.\SQLEXPRESS (SQL Server 10.50.4000 - WIN-UAUT16GPEQA\Administrator)
Databases
System Databases
nservicebus
Database Diagrams
Tables
System Tables
dbo.audit
dbo.ContainSagaData
dbo.error
dbo.ProcessOrderSaga
dbo.Subscription
dbo.TimeoutEntity
dbo.VideoStore.ContentManagement
dbo.VideoStore.ContentManagement.Retries
dbo.VideoStore.ContentManagement.Timeouts
dbo.VideoStore.ContentManagement.TimeoutsDispatcher
dbo.VideoStore.CustomerRelations
dbo.VideoStore.CustomerRelations.Retries
dbo.VideoStore.CustomerRelations.Timeouts
dbo.VideoStore.CustomerRelations.TimeoutsDispatcher
dbo.VideoStore.ECommerce
dbo.VideoStore.ECommerce.Retries
dbo.VideoStore.ECommerce.Timeouts
dbo.VideoStore.ECommerce.TimeoutsDispatcher
dbo.VideoStore.Operations
dbo.VideoStore.Operations.Retries
dbo.VideoStore.Operations.Timeouts
dbo.VideoStore.Operations.TimeoutsDispatcher
dbo.VideoStore.Sales
dbo.VideoStore.Sales.Retries
dbo.VideoStore.Sales.Timeouts
dbo.VideoStore.Sales.TimeoutsDispatcher

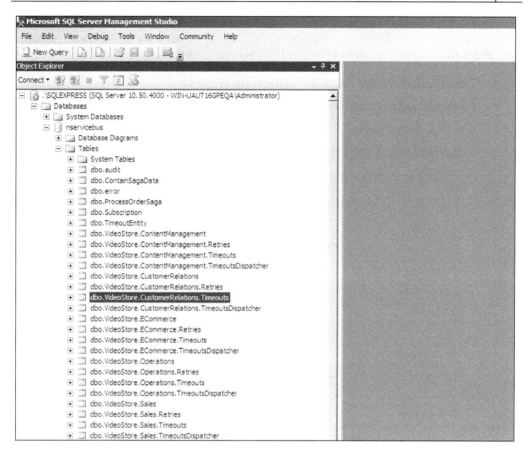

We can see that the audit message queue in SQL Server is filling up with messages; this is because audit logging is turned on via the registry and `app.config`. See `http://docs.particular.net/NServiceBus/auditing-with-nservicebus`.

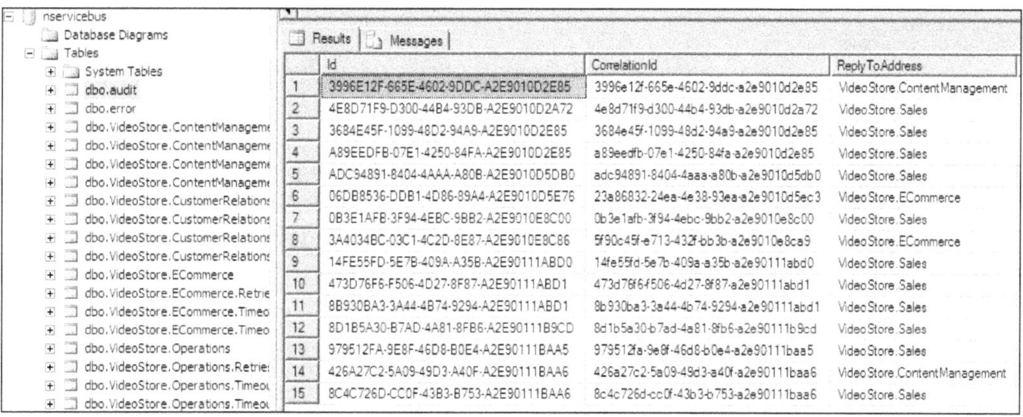

	Id	CorrelationId	ReplyToAddress
1	3996E12F-665E-4602-9DDC-A2E9010D2E85	3996e12f-665e-4602-9ddc-a2e9010d2e85	VideoStore.ContentManagement
2	4E8D71F9-D300-44B4-93DB-A2E9010D2A72	4e8d71f9-d300-44b4-93db-a2e9010d2a72	VideoStore.Sales
3	3684E45F-1099-48D2-94A9-A2E9010D2E85	3684e45f-1099-48d2-94a9-a2e9010d2e85	VideoStore.Sales
4	A89EEDFB-07E1-4250-84FA-A2E9010D2E85	a89eedfb-07e1-4250-84fa-a2e9010d2e85	VideoStore.Sales
5	ADC94891-8404-4AAA-A80B-A2E9010D5DB0	adc94891-8404-4aaa-a80b-a2e9010d5db0	VideoStore.Sales
6	06DB8536-DDB1-4D86-89A4-A2E9010D5E76	23a86832-24ea-4e38-93ea-a2e9010d5ec3	VideoStore.ECommerce
7	0B3E1AFB-3F94-4EBC-9BB2-A2E9010E8C00	0b3e1afb-3f94-4ebc-9bb2-a2e9010e8c00	VideoStore.Sales
8	3A4034BC-03C1-4C2D-8E87-A2E9010E8C86	5f90c45f-e713-432f-bb3b-a2e9010e8ca9	VideoStore.ECommerce
9	14FE55FD-5E7B-409A-A35B-A2E90111ABD0	14fe55fd-5e7b-409a-a35b-a2e90111abd0	VideoStore.Sales
10	473D76F6-F506-4D27-8F87-A2E90111ABD1	473d76f6-f506-4d27-8f87-a2e90111abd1	VideoStore.Sales
11	8B930BA3-3A44-4B74-9294-A2E90111ABD1	8b930ba3-3a44-4b74-9294-a2e90111abd1	VideoStore.Sales
12	8D1B5A30-B7AD-4A81-8FB6-A2E90111B9CD	8d1b5a30-b7ad-4a81-8fb6-a2e90111b9cd	VideoStore.Sales
13	979512FA-9E8F-46D8-B0E4-A2E90111BAA5	979512fa-9e8f-46d8-b0e4-a2e90111baa5	VideoStore.Sales
14	426A27C2-5A09-49D3-A40F-A2E90111BAA6	426a27c2-5a09-49d3-a40f-a2e90111baa6	VideoStore.ContentManagement
15	8C4C726D-CC0F-43B3-B753-A2E90111BAA6	8c4c726d-cc0f-43b3-b753-a2e90111baa6	VideoStore.Sales

This is accomplished because of the configurations on the IBus in the `VideoStore.ECommerce` project with the `Global.asax.cs` file. When reviewing the code, please note the following points as to how the IBus is configured:

- Ensures that we are using the same central queue
- Appends log events to the debug system through log4net
- Use SQL Server as queuing
- Install and configure the NServiceBus instance in the Windows environment

```
protected void Application_Start()
{
    Configure.ScaleOut(s => s.UseSingleBrokerQueue());          1

    bus = Configure.With()
            .DefaultBuilder()                                   2
            .Log4Net(new DebugAppender {Threshold = Level.Warn})
            .UseTransport<SqlServer>()
            .PurgeOnStartup(true)                               3
            .UnicastBus()
            .RunHandlersUnderIncomingPrincipal(false)
            .RijndaelEncryptionService()
            .CreateBus()
            .Start(() => Configure.Instance.ForInstallationOn<NServiceBus.Installation.Environments.Windows>()
                        .Install());

    AreaRegistration.RegisterAllAreas();
    FilterConfig.RegisterGlobalFilters(GlobalFilters.Filters);          4
    RouteConfig.RegisterRoutes(RouteTable.Routes);
}
```

Please see `http://docs.particular.net/NServiceBus/hosting-nservicebus-in-your-own-process-v4.x`, which covers some of this information.

The SQL queening is defined in the `web.config` file of the `VideoStore.ECommerce` project in the connection string section as the `NServiceBus/Transport` alias to define the database and table.

```
<connectionStrings>
  <add name="NServiceBus/Transport"
       connectionString="Data Source=.\SQLEXPRESS;Initial Catalog=nservicebus;Integrated Security=True" />
</connectionStrings>
```

In order for the `UseTransport<SqlServer>` form of queuing, the `NServiceBus.SqlServer` package must be installed. Log4net must be installed to use `Log4Net(new DebugAppender { Threshold = Level.Warn})`, which is discussed more in the next section.

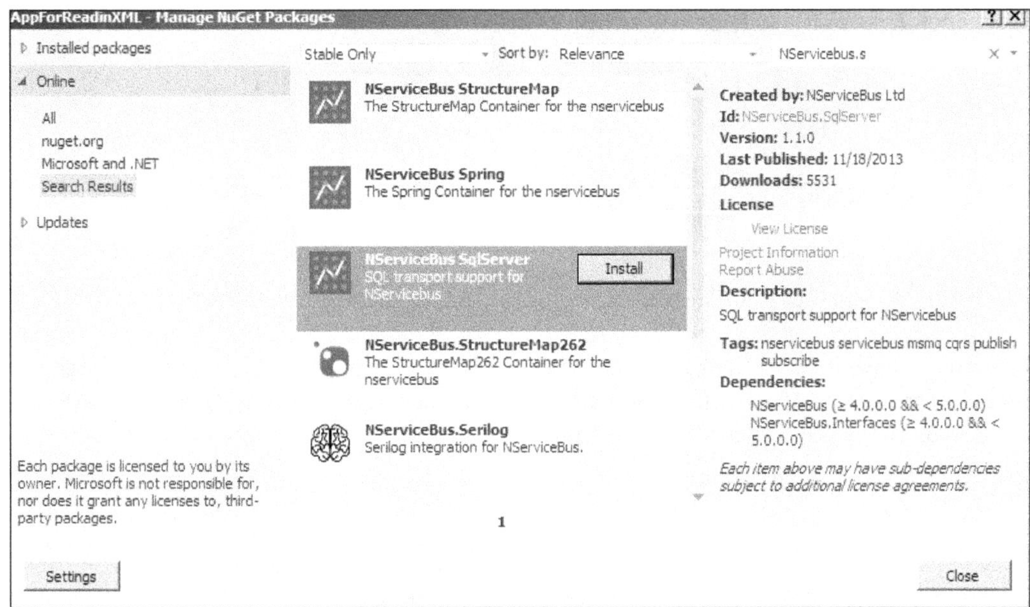

This sample is a video store sample, so we will have:

- `VideoStore.Ecommerce`: The MVC program that starts the bus with the installations in `Application_Start` given previously. A web page is used to select orders and the user is given 20 seconds to change their mind with feedback given to the page through SignalR.
- `VideoStore.Sales`: This has a saga, and handles the timeout and completion of the orders.
- `VideoStore.Message`: These are common messages for all the endpoints.
- `VideoStore.ContentManagement`: This returns the URL to be selected after the order is performed.
- `VideoStore.CustomerRelations`: This has the potential to send coupons to the customers for special offers.
- `VideoStore.Operations`: This has the potential to accept operational messages such as for errors and reporting at a later time.

This sample works very much like earlier samples discussed for MSMQ, except now all the pieces are in SQL Server. Or are they?

If we look in MSMQ, it appears empty.

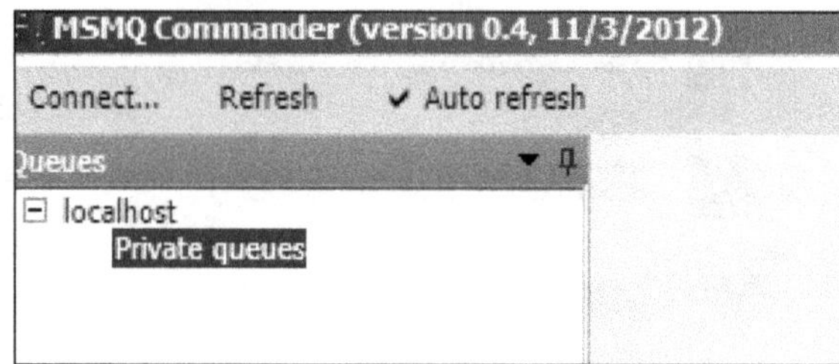

However, if we look in RavenDB for NServiceBus, we notice that tables have been created for the various endpoints as normal. They are not populated, but they are created as place holders for endpoint information.

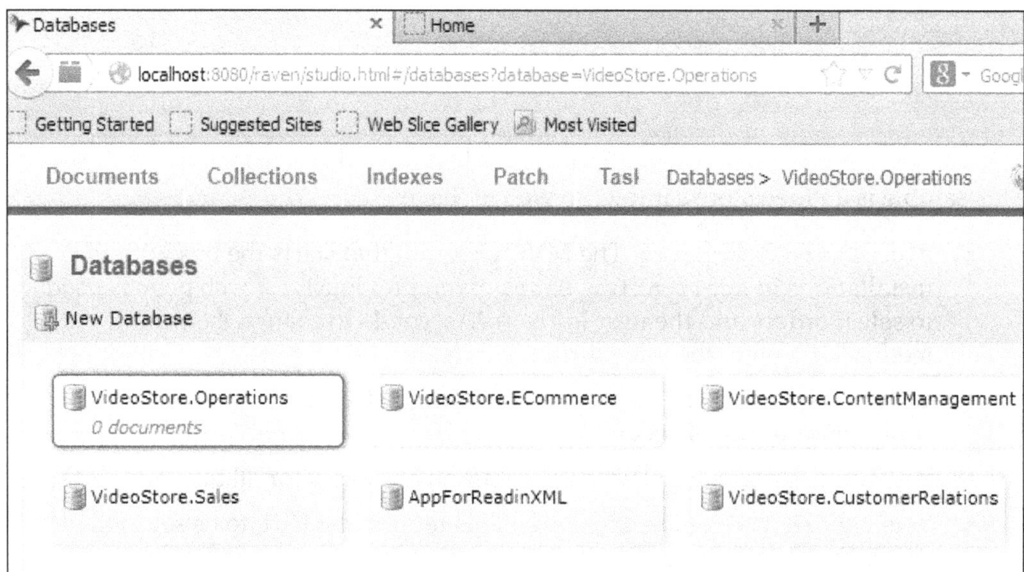

We want to ensure that, even though we are using SQL Server for practically everything in NServiceBus, for this example, we should still ensure that RavenDB, DTC, and MSMQ are set up as normal.

Database logging

In many organizations, there may be a security operations center, or network operations center. In such environments, it is normal to consolidate logs of applications for use in a syslog, `http://en.wikipedia.org/wiki/Syslog`, or for use in a security event manager, `http://en.wikipedia.org/wiki/Security_event_manager`. It could be that the developer will not be the person going through all the logs, but they have to be shared with other teams for keeping a record of hacking attempts to the system, for system reporting, for maintenance reporting, and more. Depending on clients' requirements, it may change from environment to environment. For this reason, logging and the consolation of logging become a line item and may be a section of the architecture documents, for the application's deployment in production.

There are many logging frameworks in both C# and Java that are common. For NServiceBus, there are the three logging frameworks that are supported out of the box:

- **Log4net**: This is a .NET port of Java's Log4J, the most popular logging framework in Java. It originated from the Apache Foundation; see `http://logging.apache.org/log4net/`
- **NLog**: This is a .NET logging framework; see `http://nlog-project.org/`
- **Serilog**: This is another .NET logging framework; see `http://serilog.net/`. This is written to store in NoSQL document database

For Log4net examples, please see `http://logging.apache.org/log4net/release/config-examples.html` and for NServiceBus, please see `http://docs.particular.net/NServiceBus/logging-in-nservicebus`.

We are going to use Log4net, and its `AdoNetAppender` to log in to SQL databases. The following steps will be accomplished:

1. Install Log4Net through NuGet.
2. Create a `Log` table in the `nservicebus` SQL database.
3. Configure the `app.config` file.
4. Configure NSB for Log4Net.

We will need to install Log4Net. Here, we are using the Package Manager Console that is a part of Visual Studio 2012. We are installing Log4Net Version 1.2.10 because this example was using NServiceBus Version 4.4. We will use the Package Manager Console to install the correct version.

```
100 %
Package Manager Console
Package source: nuget.org          Default project: VideoStore.Sales
PM> install-package Log4net -version 1.2.10
'log4net 1.2.10' already installed.
Adding 'log4net 1.2.10' to VideoStore.Sales.
Successfully added 'log4net 1.2.10' to VideoStore.Sales.

PM>
```

We will create the `Log` table in the `nservicebus` database by running SQL commands to create the `Log` table in the `nservicebus` table using Visual Studio 2012.

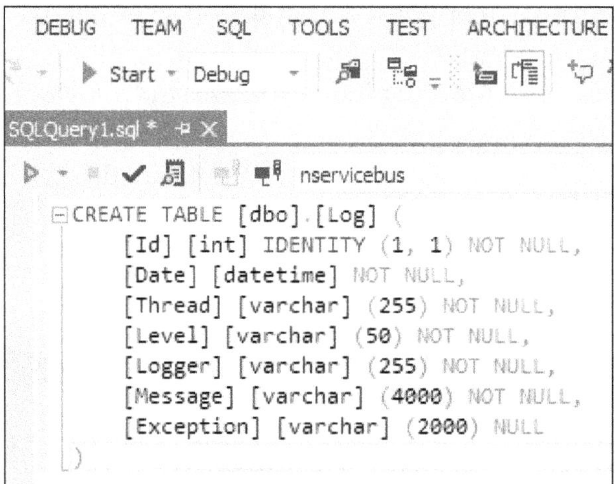

For the query, refer to the following code snippet:

```
CREATE TABLE [dbo].[Log] (
    [Id] [int] IDENTITY (1, 1) NOT NULL,
    [Date] [datetime] NOT NULL,
    [Thread] [varchar] (255) NOT NULL,
```

```
        [Level] [varchar] (50) NOT NULL,
        [Logger] [varchar] (255) NOT NULL,
        [Message] [varchar] (4000) NOT NULL,
        [Exception] [varchar] (2000) NULL
    )
```

The previous query created the `Log` table for `nservicebus`. SQL commands do have their uses in commands.

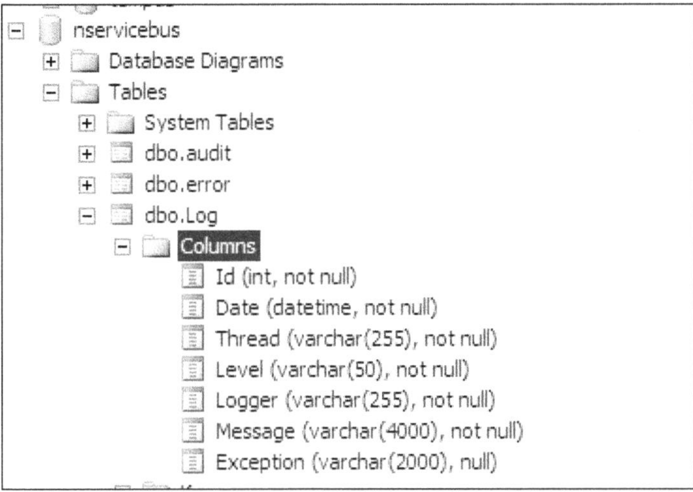

We will configure the `app.config` file. We will add several areas to the `app.config` file:

1. Log4net has to be included in the `configuration` section.
2. We will add an entire section for `AdoNetAppender` that will span many lines telling the system how to configure the table, with specific files to be added to each row in the table.

3. We will reuse the existing connection string. Using the same connection string several times in the same `app.config` file has a tendency to create deadlocks, so it is best to reuse the same alias name originally created for the connection string. In this case, `NServiceBus/Transport`.

```
<?xml version="1.0" encoding="utf-8"?>
<configuration>
  <configSections>
    <section name="MessageForwardingInCaseOfFaultConfig" type="NServiceBus.Config.MessageForwardingInCaseOfFaultConfig, NSe
    <section name="Logging" type="NServiceBus.Config.Logging, NServiceBus.Core" />
    <section name="RijndaelEncryptionServiceConfig" type="NServiceBus.Config.RijndaelEncryptionServiceConfig, NServiceBus.C
    <section name="AuditConfig" type="NServiceBus.Config.AuditConfig, NServiceBus.Core" />
    <section name="UnicastBusConfig" type="NServiceBus.Config.UnicastBusConfig, NServiceBus.Core" />
    <section name="log4net" type="log4net.Config.Log4NetConfigurationSectionHandler, log4net" />      1
  </configSections>
  <connectionStrings>
    <add name="NServiceBus/Transport" connectionString="Data Source=.\SQLEXPRESS;Initial Catalog=nservicebus;Integrated Sec
  </connectionStrings>
  <log4net debug="false">
    <root>
      <level value="DEBUG" />                                    3
      <appender-ref ref="AdoNetAppender" />      2
    </root>
    <appender name="AdoNetAppender" type="log4net.Appender.AdoNetAppender">
      <bufferSize value="100" />
      <connectionType value="System.Data.SqlClient.SqlConnection, System.Data, Version=1.0.3300.0, Culture=neutral, PublicK
      <connectionStringName value="NServiceBus/Transport" />
      <connectionString value="Data Source=.\SQLEXPRESS;Initial Catalog=nservicebus;Integrated Security=True" />
      <commandText value="INSERT INTO Log ([Date],[Thread],[Level],[Logger],[Message],[Exception]) VALUES (@log_date, @thre
      <parameter>
        <parameterName value="@log_date" />
        <dbType value="DateTime" />
        <layout type="log4net.Layout.RawTimeStampLayout" />
      </parameter>
      <parameter>
        <parameterName value="@thread" />
        <dbType value="String" />
        <size value="255" />
        <layout type="log4net.Layout.PatternLayout">
          <conversionPattern value="%thread" />
        </layout>
      </parameter>
```

We will configure NSB to log with Log4Net in code as follows:

```
public class EndpointConfig : IConfigureThisEndpoint, AsA_Publisher, UsingTransport<SqlServer>,
{
    public void Init()
    {

        SetLoggingLibrary.Log4Net(log4net.Config.XmlConfigurator.Configure);


        Configure.With()
            .DefaultBuilder()
            .RijndaelEncryptionService();
    }
}
```

After this, when running the NServiceBus SQL Server sample, we should start to get the following in the `Log` table.

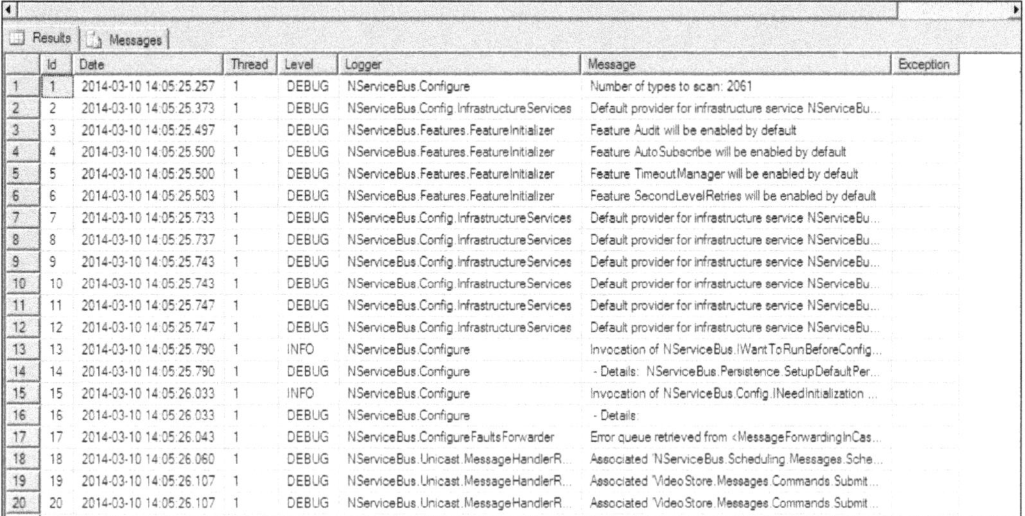

Results | Messages

	Id	Date	Thread	Level	Logger	Message	Exception
1	1	2014-03-10 14:05:25.257	1	DEBUG	NServiceBus.Configure	Number of types to scan: 2061	
2	2	2014-03-10 14:05:25.373	1	DEBUG	NServiceBus.Config.InfrastructureServices	Default provider for infrastructure service NServiceBu...	
3	3	2014-03-10 14:05:25.497	1	DEBUG	NServiceBus.Features.FeatureInitializer	Feature Audit will be enabled by default	
4	4	2014-03-10 14:05:25.500	1	DEBUG	NServiceBus.Features.FeatureInitializer	Feature AutoSubscribe will be enabled by default	
5	5	2014-03-10 14:05:25.500	1	DEBUG	NServiceBus.Features.FeatureInitializer	Feature TimeoutManager will be enabled by default	
6	6	2014-03-10 14:05:25.503	1	DEBUG	NServiceBus.Features.FeatureInitializer	Feature SecondLevelRetries will be enabled by default	
7	7	2014-03-10 14:05:25.733	1	DEBUG	NServiceBus.Config.InfrastructureServices	Default provider for infrastructure service NServiceBu...	
8	8	2014-03-10 14:05:25.737	1	DEBUG	NServiceBus.Config.InfrastructureServices	Default provider for infrastructure service NServiceBu...	
9	9	2014-03-10 14:05:25.743	1	DEBUG	NServiceBus.Config.InfrastructureServices	Default provider for infrastructure service NServiceBu...	
10	10	2014-03-10 14:05:25.743	1	DEBUG	NServiceBus.Config.InfrastructureServices	Default provider for infrastructure service NServiceBu...	
11	11	2014-03-10 14:05:25.747	1	DEBUG	NServiceBus.Config.InfrastructureServices	Default provider for infrastructure service NServiceBu...	
12	12	2014-03-10 14:05:25.747	1	DEBUG	NServiceBus.Config.InfrastructureServices	Default provider for infrastructure service NServiceBu...	
13	13	2014-03-10 14:05:25.790	1	INFO	NServiceBus.Configure	Invocation of NServiceBus.IWantToRunBeforeConfig...	
14	14	2014-03-10 14:05:25.790	1	DEBUG	NServiceBus.Configure	- Details: NServiceBus.Persistence.SetupDefaultPer...	
15	15	2014-03-10 14:05:26.033	1	INFO	NServiceBus.Configure	Invocation of NServiceBus.Config.INeedInitialization ...	
16	16	2014-03-10 14:05:26.033	1	DEBUG	NServiceBus.Configure	- Details:	
17	17	2014-03-10 14:05:26.043	1	DEBUG	NServiceBus.ConfigureFaultsForwarder	Error queue retrieved from <MessageForwardingInCas...	
18	18	2014-03-10 14:05:26.060	1	DEBUG	NServiceBus.Unicast.MessageHandlerR...	Associated 'NServiceBus.Scheduling.Messages.Sche...	
19	19	2014-03-10 14:05:26.107	1	DEBUG	NServiceBus.Unicast.MessageHandlerR...	Associated 'VideoStore.Messages.Commands.Submit...	
20	20	2014-03-10 14:05:26.107	1	DEBUG	NServiceBus.Unicast.MessageHandlerR...	Associated 'VideoStore.Messages.Commands.Submit...	

In this example, we have put as many different pieces into the SQL Server as possible.

Summary

In this chapter, we have discussed persistence as a whole, where we discussed supporting frameworks for XML, Entity Framework, and reflection in which we introduced a PayQueue sample used for more backed processing. We walked through a SQL Queuing example from NserviceBus while adding database logging.

In the next chapter, we will discuss saga architecture. Some may ask, "Why discuss sagas in a persistence book?" Sagas are a method of persisting message data, mostly state data, to a database. The difference is that the saga engine does a lot of the persistence work.

6
SQL Server Examples

In this chapter, we will be focusing on snippets of SQL Server examples. We will discuss queuing in SQL Server. In addition to this, more advanced features of **Entity Framework** (**EF**), as well as MVC-EF examples will be discussed. This chapter is for developers who work with SQL Server and Entity Framework with NServiceBus.

In this chapter, we will cover the following topics:

- The SQL Server example
- The MVC-EF example
- Entity Framework snippets
- Creating tables through EF
    - Creating tables from the EF code-first
    - Creating tables from the EF model-first
- Expanding the code
- Unit testing

The SQL Server example

One of the many benefits of using SQL Server to persist sagas, timeouts, logging, and messages is that Visual Studio has many capabilities if it's used in EF, such as wizards to create mapped objects from existing tables. So, when NSB is saving messages, sagas, timeouts, logging, and other NSB artifacts to SQL database tables, EF can be used in console applications to monitor these artifacts. We will look at monitoring messages, and we'll choose EF for these examples because of its ease of mapping in Visual Studio from existing SQL Servers. EF will generate the models from existing tables that NSB creates.

Let's start by building a simple publish or subscribe example from https://github.com/Particular/NServiceBus.Msmq.Samples/tree/master/PubSub. We have already walked through this in the previous example, so we will discuss just modifying the sample to save data in SQL databases to time. We will send the messages and subscription information to the nservicebus SQL database using NHibernate. This will be our **PubSub-SQL** solution.

This example will populate the SQL nservicebus database with the messages and subscription information from the original PubSub example by changing the transport type to SQL Server in the IBus configuration, that is,. UseTransport<SqlServer>(). Also, we will change the subscription persistence type to NHibernate. The app.config file will have to contain the connection information to point to the appropriate SQL Server database. We can study some articles from http://docs.particular.net/nservicebus/relational-persistence-using-nhibernate---nservicebus-4.x and http://docs.particular.net/NServiceBus/publish-subscribe-configuration to change the configurations to send the messages and map the subscriptions in SQL Server.

This will still be a PubSub example, except now the queues will be in the nservicebus database for the MyPublisher, Subscriber1, and Subscriber2 tables.

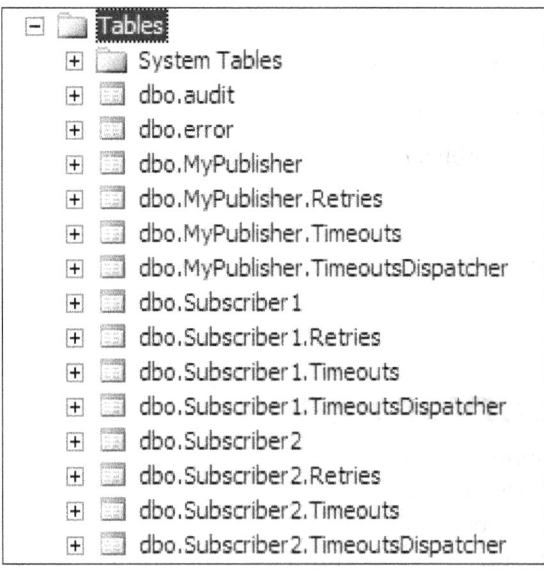

The subscription storage, using NHibernate for the local SQL Express database, will also be stored in the `nservicebus` database. First, we will install `NServiceBus.NHibernate` via NuGet. This will be the **PubSub-SQL** solution.

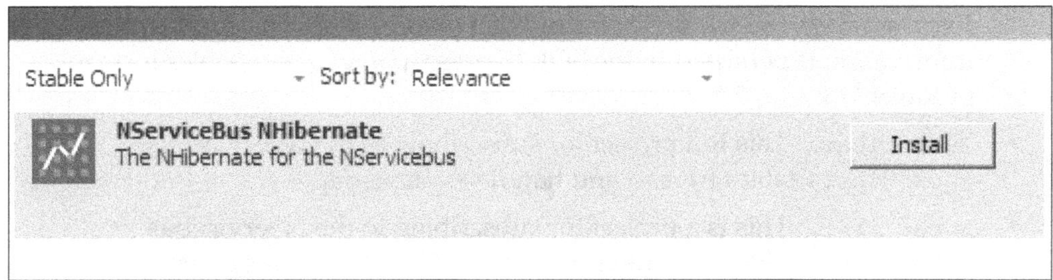

You will now have to put the subscription information in the SQL `nservicebus` table.

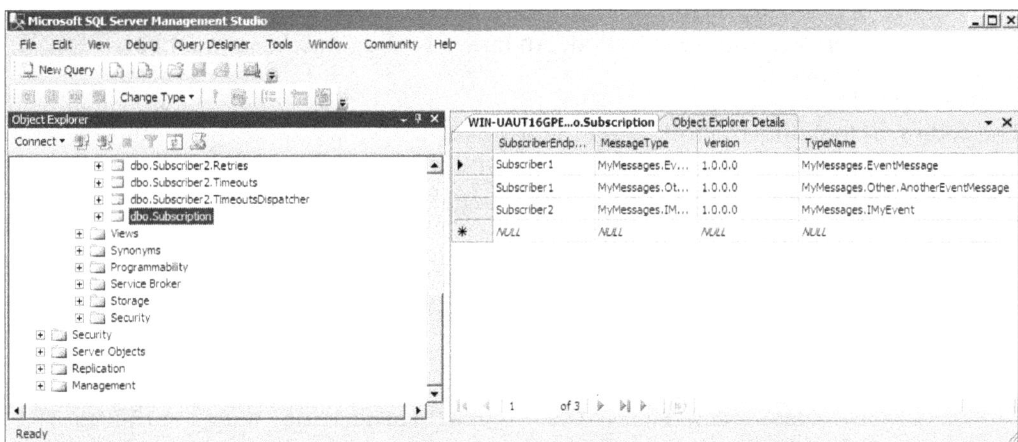

Even though the subscription table will now be in the SQL database, RavenDB will still require some of the internal information for NSB, so it must remain running as a service.

In this section, we will be using the **PubSub-SQL** solution:

- `MyMessages`: This is a payment message used for the projects.
- `MyPublisher`: This is a project that publishes `EventMessages` to the SQL Express `nservicebus` tables for publish or subscribe. The subscription information is persisted in the SQL Express `nservicebus` tables instead of RavenDB.
- `Subscriber1`: This is a project for subscribing to the NServicebus `Subscriber1` tables to read and handle `EventMessages`.
- `Subscriber2`: This is a project for subscribing to the NServicebus `Subscriber2` tables to read and handle the `IMyEvent` messages.

This is a publish or subscribe solution to publish messages that `Subscriber1` and `Subscriber2` handle. `Subscriber1` processes one type of messages, whereas `Subscriber2` processes a different type of messages. These were run in VS 2012 in Windows Server 2012, with MSMQ, DTC, NServiceBus references, and SQL Server 2012 Express LocalDB installed. An `nservicebus` database must be present in SQL Server.

The code will look like the following in the `MyPublisher`, `Subscriber1`, and `Subscriber2` projects. Note the addition of `.UseTransport<SqlServer>()` to send messages to SQL Server and `.UseNHibernateSubscriptionPersister()` to save the subscription data in SQL Server.

```
using NServiceBus;

namespace MyPublisher
{
    class EndpointConfig :  IConfigureThisEndpoint, AsA_Publisher,IWan
tCustomInitialization
    {
        public void Init()
        {
            Configure.With()
                .DefaultBuilder()   // Ensure the default builder is
there
                .UseTransport<SqlServer>()   // Use SQL Server Queues
               .UseNHibernateSubscriptionPersister() // Persist the
Subscription in SQL Server
```

```
                .DefiningEventsAs(t => t.Namespace != null &&
t.Namespace.StartsWith("MyMessages"));
            }
        }
    }
```

The `DefiningEventAs()` configuration is used to define the convention of the events that are used for pub/sub messaging, as messages starting with `MyMessages`. These messages are configured to process them as event messages for publish or subscribe.

We need to ensure that `app.config` is updated to send the messages and subscription information to the correct database. We will set this in the `NServiceBus/Transport` and `NServiceBus/Persistence/NHibernate/Subscription` sections of the `app.config` file.

Don't forget to change the `Subscriber1` and `Subscriber2` endpoints and to use `.UseTransport<SqlServer>()` in similar methods as well. Then, we will just generate some messages to populate the database.

To populate the `MyPublisher` table with examples, we need to run the program and create multiple messages.

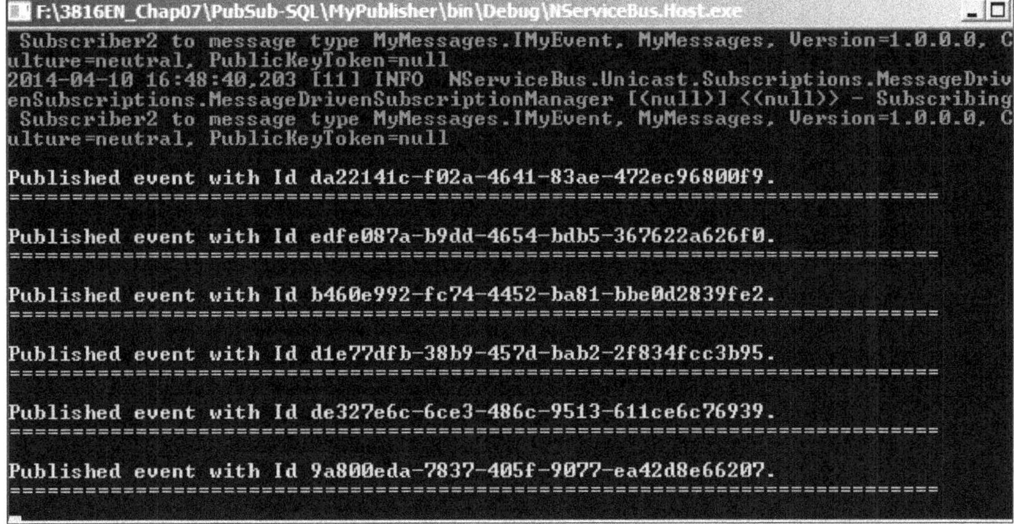

The MVC-EF example

Many C# developers create programs using MVC-EF as defined in Microsoft architecture best practices. We will look at the example enclosed in this book called `MVC-SQL` with an `MVCApp` project. This project will read the selected queues from the browser and display what they contain. We will read the available queues in the browser without the need to go through SQL Management Studio.

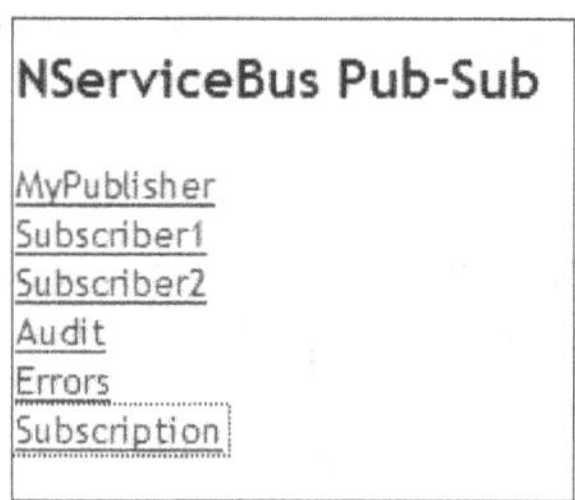

`MVCApp` is the main program that runs `MVC-EF` in SQL Server to view the tables created in the **PubSub-SQL** solution. However, the PubSub-SQL solution needs to be run first.

These examples were run in VS 2012 in Windows Server 2012, with MSMQ, DTC, NServiceBus references, and SQL Server 2012 Express LocalDB installed.

In order to get access to these tables in the `nservicebus` database, we need to create objects that map to the tables. In order to do that, we add the ADO.NET Entity Data Model, which will create the mapping to the tables.

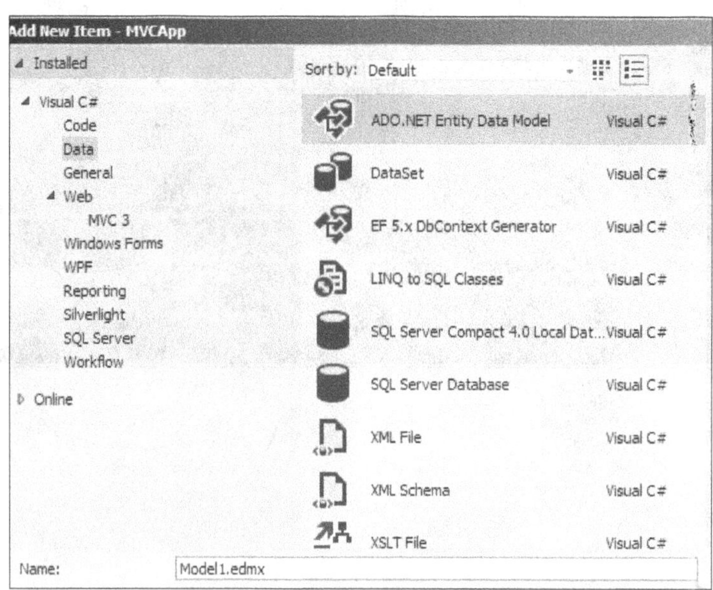

A database context will have to be added that will put a connection string in the `app.config` file or the `web.config` file for MVC. In this case, the connection string will be `nservicebusrnentities`.

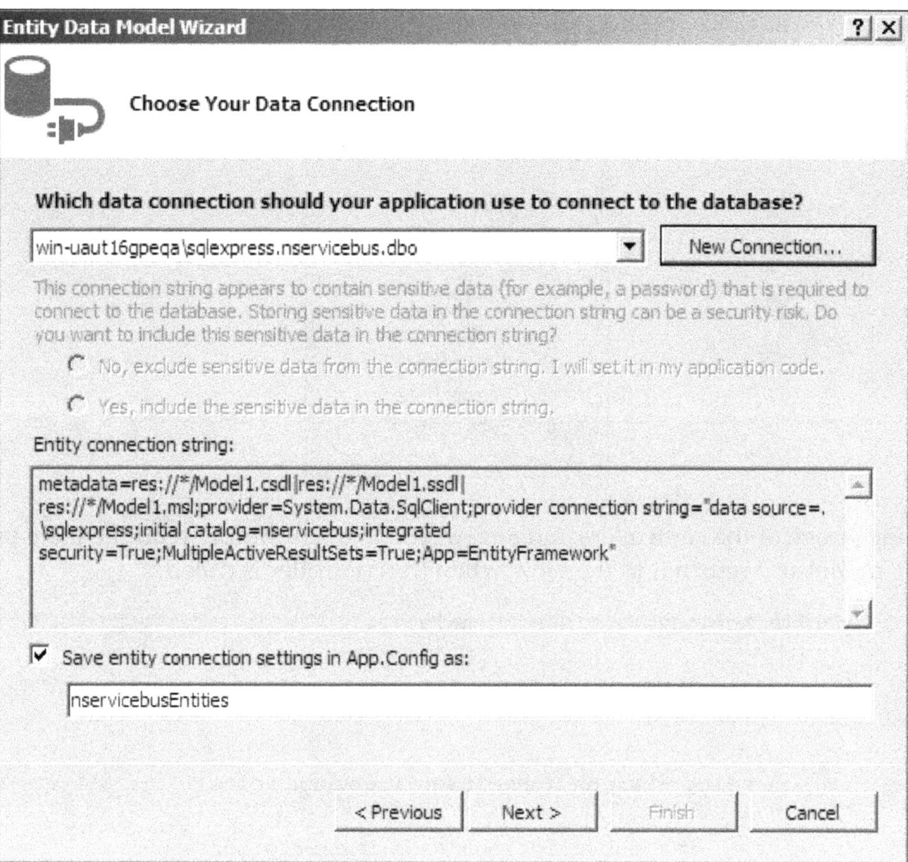

The `web.config` file will now contain the connection string:

```
<connectionStrings>
  <add name="nservicebusEntities" connectionString="metada
ta=res://*/DAL.Model1.csdl|res://*/DAL.Model1.ssdl|res://*/
DAL.Model1.msl;provider=System.Data.SqlClient;provider
connection string=&quot;data source=.\sqlexpress;initial
catalog=nservicebus;integrated security=True;MultipleActiveResul
tSets=True;App=EntityFramework&quot;" providerName="System.Data.
EntityClient" />
</connectionStrings>
```

In the `MVCApp` project, there will be models, views, and controllers to use the new EF models. The different controllers for reading the different queues will be in the `UserController`:

Looking at one of the controllers, `Subscription`, we will simply read the table using the EF model and return it to the view when the controller is called:

```
public ActionResult Subscription()
    {
        List<MVCApp.DAL.Subscription> models = new List<MVCApp.
DAL.Subscription>();

        using (var db = new nservicebusEntities())
        {
            var subscriptions = db.Subscriptions;
            foreach (var subscription in subscriptions)
            {
                models.Add(subscription);
            }
        }
        return View(models);
    }
```

The view will display the data that we match up from the EF model to display in `Subscription.cshtml`, which, in turn, will call the `Subscription` controller that will return the populated models from the database. The database context `nservicebusrnentities` is used to access the database, via the connection string, to populate the `MVCApp.DAL.Subscription` model, which is a property of the mapping in the `Models1.edmx` file. The sequence for the `Subscription` controller appears as follows:

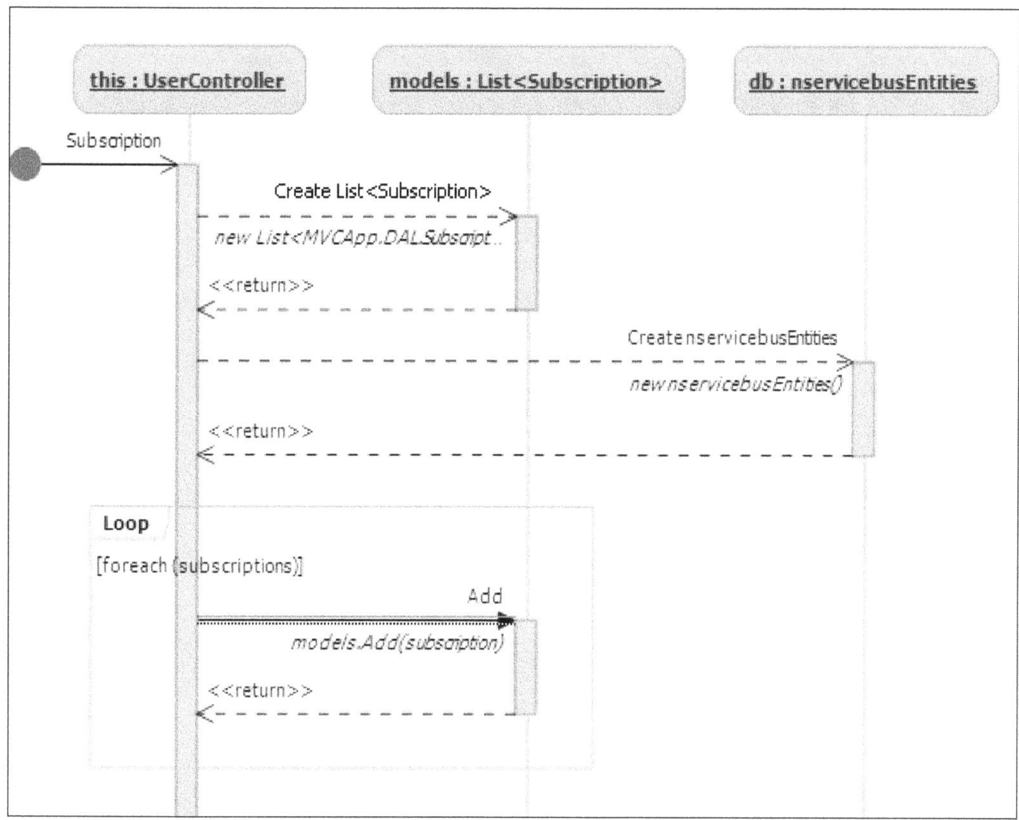

The `Models1.edmx` file is an XML file that defines a conceptual model, a storage model, and the mapping between these models for the `nservicebus` database. The `.edmx` file also contains the information that is used by the ADO.NET Entity Data Model Designer (Entity Designer) to render a model graphically. In the following screenshot, we can see some of the graphical renderings of the file:

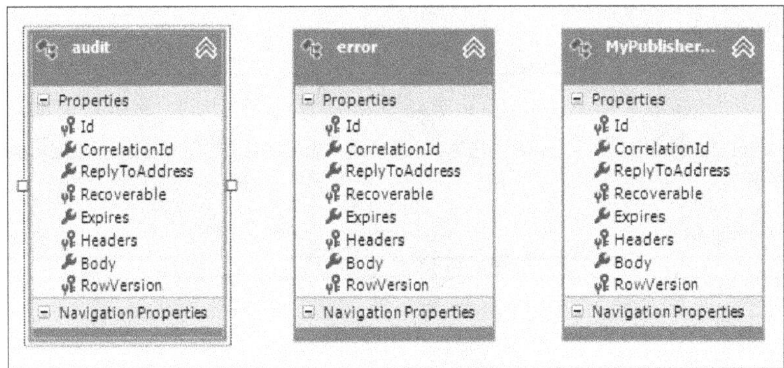

This file will contain not only the mappings but also the objects themselves that are translated, or mapped, to the table. In this example, we populated the `MVCApp.DAL.Subscription` model, which is not an object that we coded, but it was generated as the entity object to be mapped from the `.edmx` file. Here, we can see the code of the entity objects themselves; in this case, the `MVCApp.DAL.Subscription` entity is the entity object generated from the EF. Visual Studio generates all the mapping, including that of the entity objects on its own, such that we can use as models for both controllers and views.

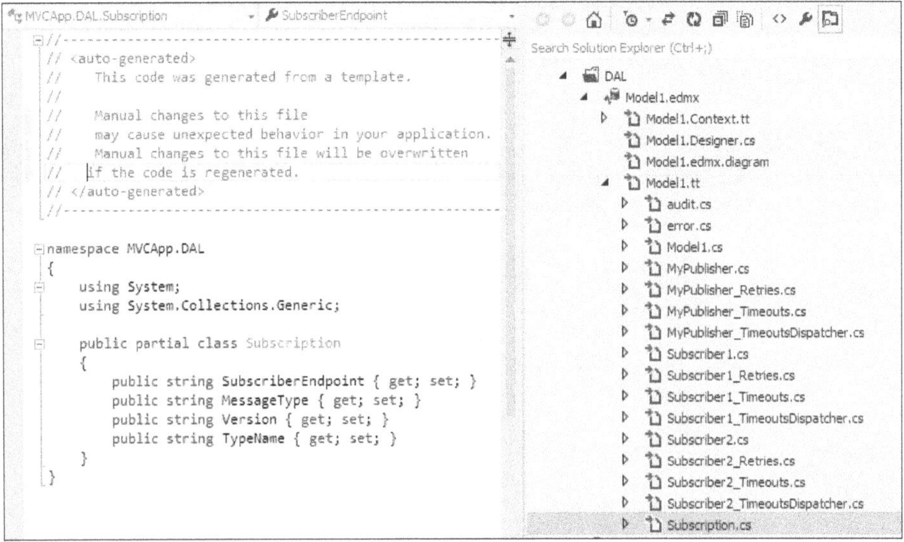

So, when the **Subscription** link is clicked, we will populate the `Subscription.cshtml` file with a collection of the table entries, as the entity models from the controller, to display all the entries in the browser.

In a similar manner, we can add the same for the `MyPublisher`, `Subscriber1`, `Subscriber2`, `error`, and `audit` queues to view their messages as well.

This is not a replacement for ServicePulse to get a pulse on NServiceBus, but this is an exercise of the power that NSB has to offer, and why ESB engines, such as NSB, are so powerful in using them. We just demonstrated through a simple program how to visually create an administration tool to view queues. Features could be added to send e-mails when there is a message in an error queue, to get an audit queue count of messages for today, and many more such tracking features. This demonstrates that not only are the message queues durable, but they can easily be tracked.

To recap MVC integration, MVC is the most common software design pattern used. In the `MVCApp` project, we have built models-views-controllers.

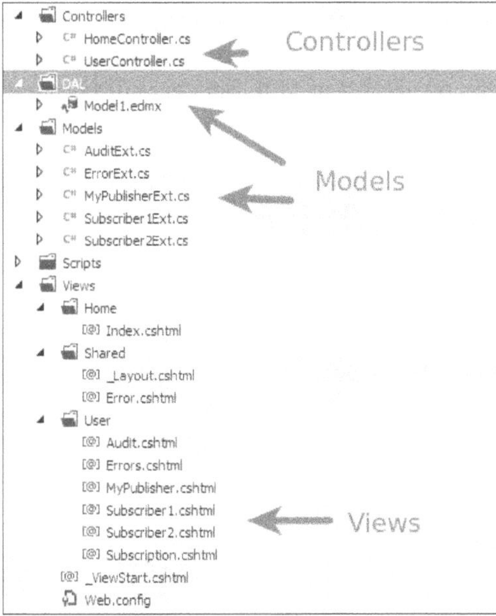

This example follows the MVC paradigm:

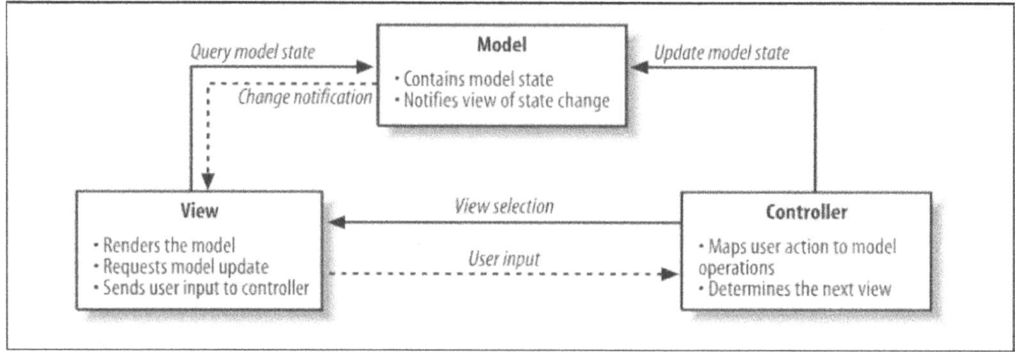

So, we have built a browser to review the publish or subscribe messages into the `nservicebus` SQL database.

Entity Framework snippets

We have ventured into creating models in MVC and EF from an existing database. There will be many cases where the database is not created. We listed previous examples and described in previous chapters how to manually create a database, but many ESB developers don't use SQL Server Management Studio, or SQL scripts, very often. We will get into some details on how to create tables from either EF code or models. There will be no SQL discussed here as we use objects to build tables and populate them. EF plays a major role in reading and writing to the SQL Server database. Since NSB will likely be deployed on a Windows Server machine to handle the enterprise objects, it is natural that SQL Server will be used as well for many of the Microsoft components.

Creating tables with EF

So far, the examples have shown us how to read messages in EF. We chose Entity Frameworks to monitor and build SQL Server tables as Entity Framework works well inside Visual Studio for modeling data. Also, using an ORM product eliminates SQL Injection as there is no SQL code to review. Refer to `http://www.slideshare.net/rhelton_1/sql-injection-amp-entity-frameworks` for more information on Entity Frameworks and SQL Injection. Besides security concerns, EF is a recommended platform for programming C# into SQL Server from Microsoft. Microsoft puts a lot of effort into both Visual Studio and the .NET frameworks to make it as easy as possible.

In the next two samples, we will show you how to populate sample messages into SQL Server tables to test some of our NSB deployments. EF is a very useful framework to generate code that will create tables and sample data, as well as read tables quickly for SQL Server. In the next two examples, messages will be generated through two means, one being code-first EF where a model does not have to be created from an existing database, and one via model-first where a model does have to created first from an existing database. In both examples, the frameworks will be creating pay messages in the `MVCApp1.AppContext` table as we go through a generic use. In the next chapter, we will create the same messages in `nservicebus`.

The goal of both these examples will be to create a pay message table and populate it:

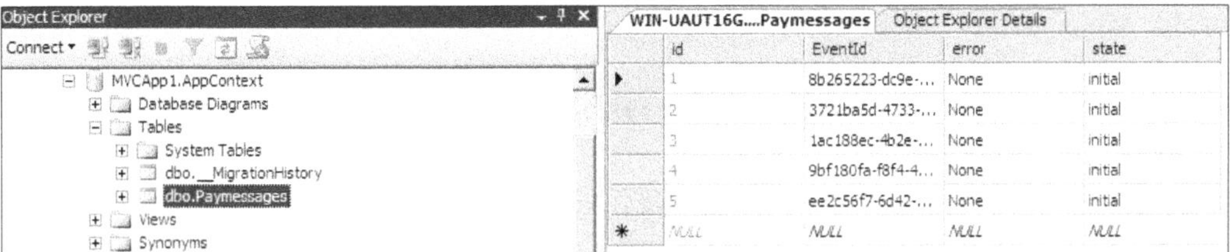

The `main` function in both programs to create the messages will also be the same, except they will be calling a different context that is used to create the database and tables from code-first or from the model-first.

The code-first program will be called from the `MVCApp1` solution and the model first example will be called from the `MVCApp1-ModelFirst` solution. The code-first solution is so named as the `MVCApp1` namespace is used in generating the database name.

We will start with the `Program.cs` file for both applications.

We will create a program to create the `AppContext` object, and use it to populate the table with the `Paymessage` objects.

```
namespace MVCApp1
{
    class Program
    {
        static void Main(string[] args)
        {

            int length = 5;
            using (var db = new AppContext())
            {
                for (int index = 0; index < length; index++)
                {
```

```
                    Paymessage message = new Paymessage();
                    message.id = index + 1;
                    message.error = "None";
                    message.state = "Initial";
                    if (index == 0)
                        message.EventId = new Guid("8b265223-dc9e-
4789-a6df-69d19f644ad7");
                    else if (index == 1)
                        message.EventId = new Guid("3721ba5d-4733-
4d98-a5e2-8e8afa3e61f4");
                    else if (index == 2)
                        message.EventId = new Guid("1ac188ec-4b2e-
436c-b989-db88c65db1fa");
                    else if (index == 3)
                        message.EventId = new Guid("9bf180fa-f8f4-
4b2b-8fac-cca73a4e2cab");
                    else if (index == 4)
                        message.EventId = new Guid("ee2c56f7-6d42-
4314-bce5-4825ed294437");
                    db.Paymessages.Add(message);
                    db.SaveChanges();
                }
            }
        }
    }
}
```

The following are the associated sequences for populating the five pay messages:

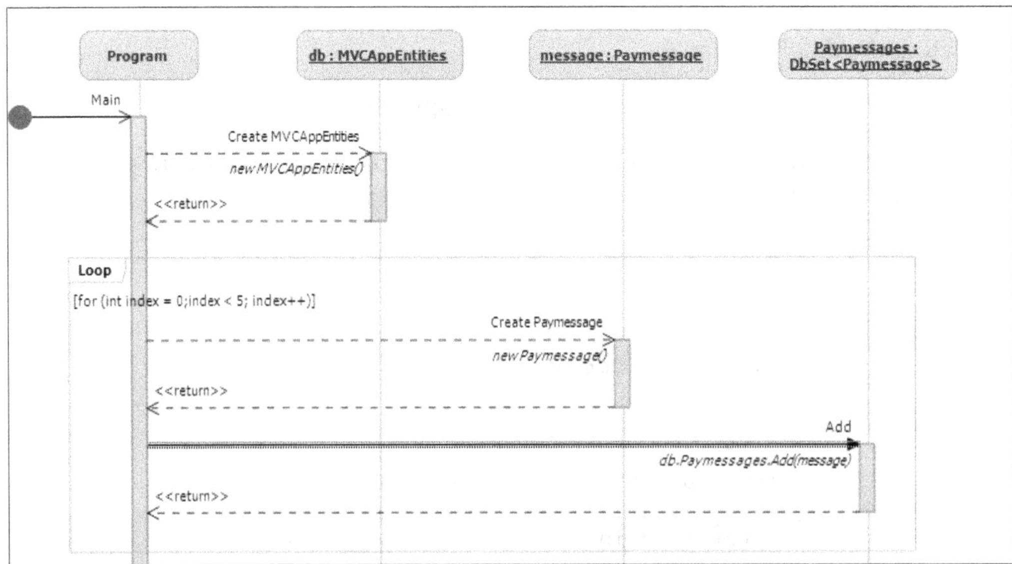

The namespace to the database context is `MVCApp1.AppContext`, which will be used to add messages inside the `Paymessages` database set. Another way this can be read as the sequence executes is create an `MVCApp1.AppContext` database and then a `Paymessages` table and populate it with the `Paymessage` object made up of `id`, `error`, `state`, and `EventId`. This was all that was needed to create our sample message data for testing and populating our SQL Server database into the following tables:

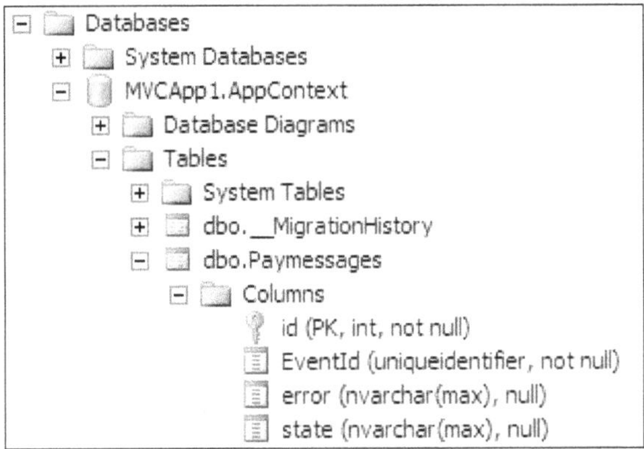

Creating tables from the EF code

In this example, we will be using the `MVCApp1` solution to create some sample messages. In this section, we will discuss using EF in code to create the tables with sample messages versus having the user or developer use SQL Scripting or develop the messages through the SQL Management Studio.

This will be a basic understanding of EF, and for more details, please refer to `http://www.slideshare.net/rhelton_1/asp-mvc3-rev009`.

To create tables in code through EF, the generic `DbContext` is used. The `DbContext` is a generic database context used to perform operations on the database. The best way to think of `DbContext` is a session database context created by a connection string, and no connection string will default to the local database. A `DbContext` article for working with the context can be found at `http://msdn.microsoft.com/en-us/data/jj729737.aspx`, but this example will work as it is.

In our example, we will extend the `DbContext` to tell it which sets of the database we will be creating a database to handle.

```
using System;
using System.Collections.Generic;
using System.Data.Entity;
using System.Linq;
using System.Text;
using System.Threading.Tasks;

namespace MVCApp1
{
    public class AppContext : DbContext
    {
        public DbSet<Paymessage> Paymessages { get; set; }
    }
}
```

You will see that the namespace is `MVCApp1`, the extended database context is `AppContext`, and the table is be filled with `Paymessage` objects; so, the namespace will be used as this is a lot of work. We will use `AppContext` to create the database and tables from code. When we run the code, without any model, we will get the tables and database filled.

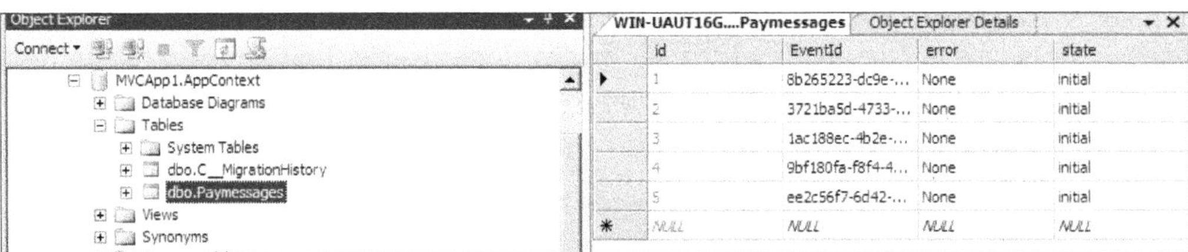

Creating tables from EF models

An alternative to creating sample messages in straight EF code is to have generated EF models create the sample messages table. Here are some basic steps from a current database.

1. The database name needs to be created first and have a connection string in the `app.config` file.
2. The model is created from an existing database through Visual Studio.
3. The model created from the database is used to create new databases, in cases where it is not already created through Visual Studio.

The `program.cs` will be the same in both files, the difference being the `AppContext` to map out the objects to the tables. First, we will add `Model1.edmx`.

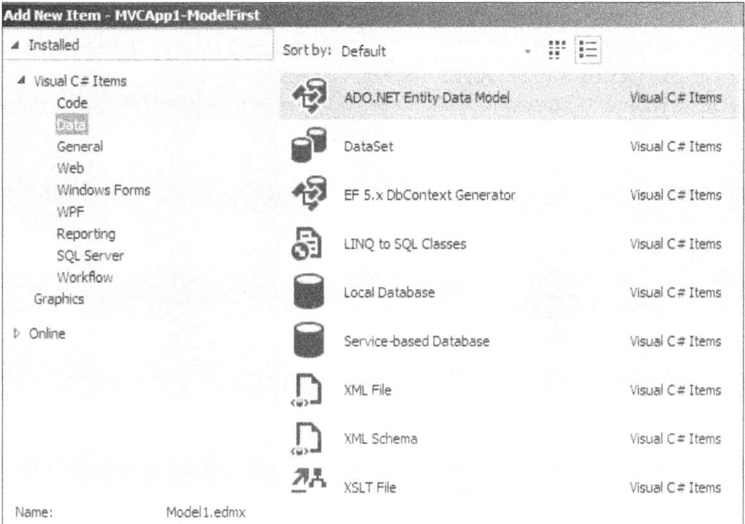

This will be created from the existing `MVCApp1.AppContext` database. Call `AppContext` to match the same code for the `main` function.

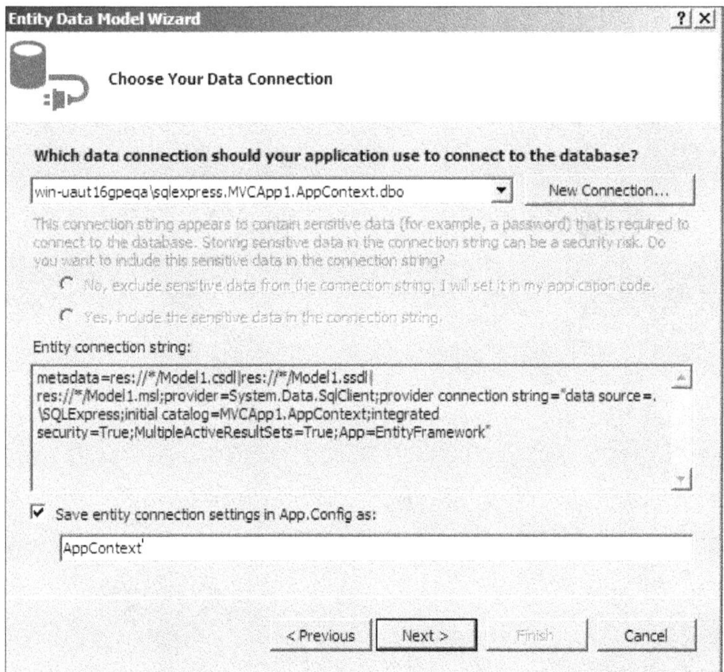

This mapping will also create the connection string in the `app.config` file to be associated with the database:

```
<connectionStrings><add name="AppContext" connectionString
="metadata=res://*/Model1.csdl|res://*/Model1.ssdl|res://*/
Model1.msl;provider=System.Data.SqlClient;provider connection
string=&quot;data source=.\SQLExpress;initial catalog=MVCApp1.
AppContext;integrated security=True;MultipleActiveResultSets=True;App
=EntityFramework&quot;" providerName="System.Data.EntityClient" /></
connectionStrings
```

Ensure that the database exists; if not, then create one.

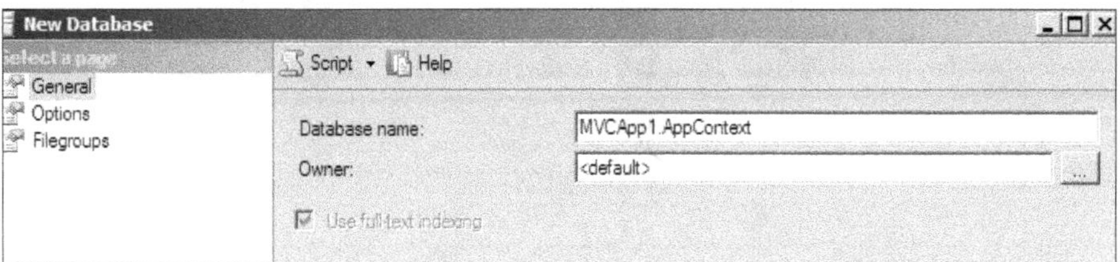

To create the tables, (in this case, the `MVCApp` table to populate with messages) simply right-click on **Generate Database from Model...** to create a DDL's SQL script to create the model's table.

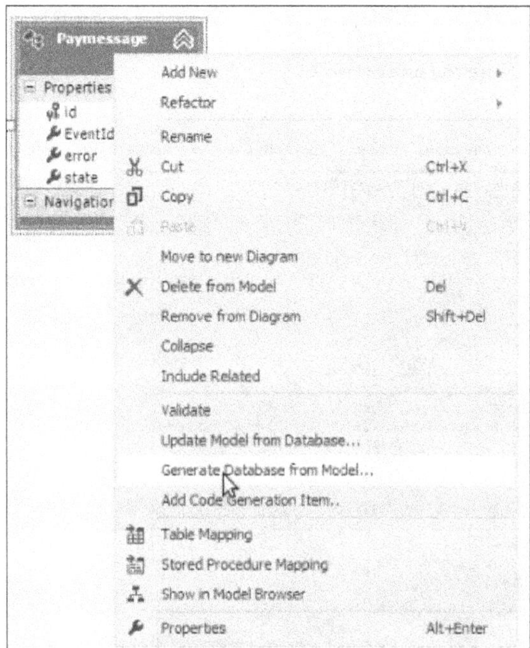

This will generate the DDL schema to be run by clicking on the **Finish** button.

Generate Database Wizard
Summary and Settings
Save DDL As:
Model1.edmx.sql
DDL
-- --
-- Entity Designer DDL Script for SQL Server 2005, 2008, and Azure
-- --
-- Date Created: 06/01/2014 11:56:16
-- Generated from EDMX file: F:\3816EN_Chap07\SAVE2\MVCApp1-ModelFirst\MVCApp1-ModelFirst\Model1.edmx
-- --
SET QUOTED_IDENTIFIER OFF;
GO
USE [MVCApp1.AppContext];
GO
IF SCHEMA_ID(N'dbo') IS NULL EXECUTE(N'CREATE SCHEMA [dbo]');
GO
-- --
< Previous
Next >
Finish
Cancel

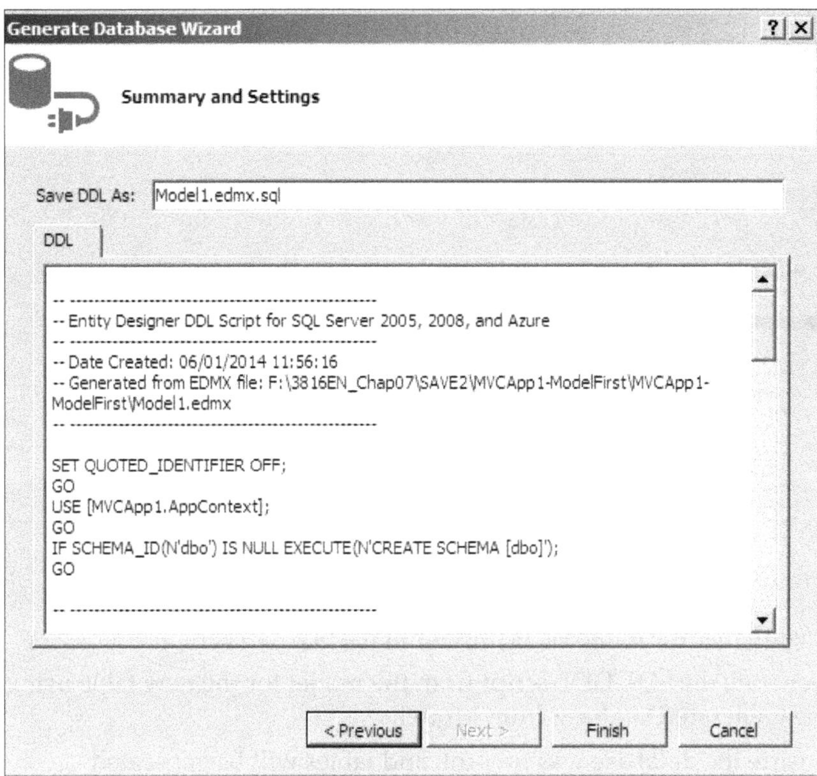

Once the DDL's SQL script is created, run the SQL script in Visual Studio.

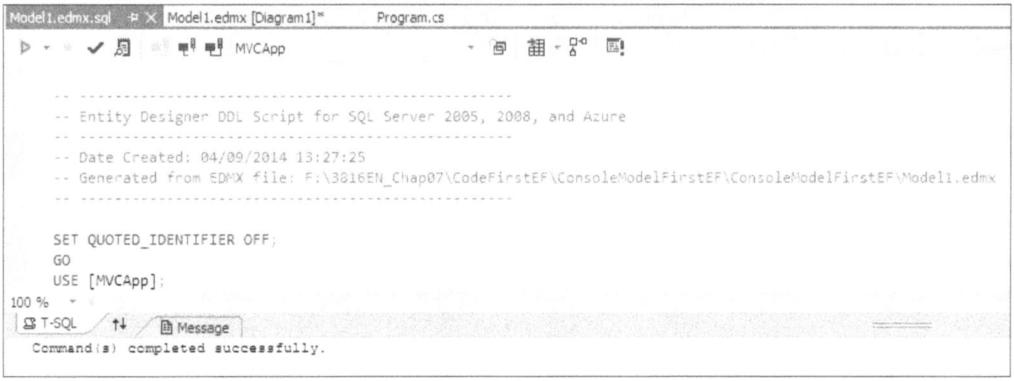

Model1.edmx.sql
Model1.edmx [Diagram1]*
Program.cs
MVCApp
-- --
-- Entity Designer DDL Script for SQL Server 2005, 2008, and Azure
-- --
-- Date Created: 04/09/2014 13:27:25
-- Generated from EDMX file: F:\3816EN_Chap07\CodeFirstEF\ConsoleModelFirstEF\ConsoleModelFirstEF\Model1.edmx
-- --
SET QUOTED_IDENTIFIER OFF;
GO
USE [MVCApp];
100 %
T-SQL
Message
Command(s) completed successfully.

After the SQL script is run and the Visual Studio is generated from the model, the table should be built.

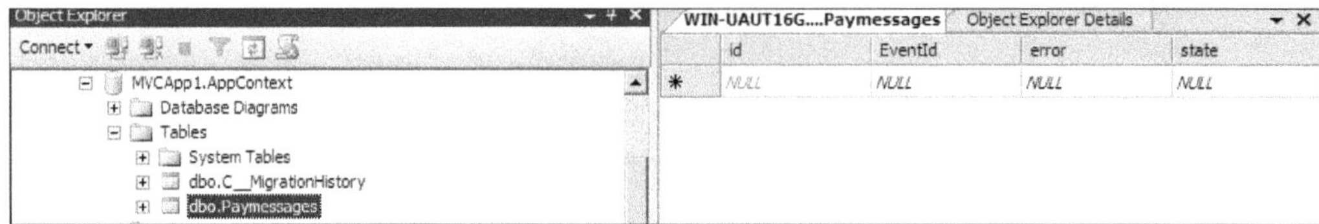

Then, we will run the program, and it will populate the pay messages.

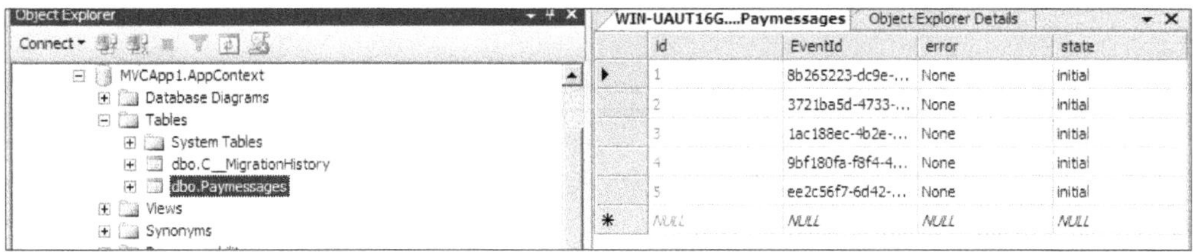

So, we simply had to do the following to create a table from a model:

1. Ensure that the database is present in the SQL Server.
2. Generate the SQL DDL script from the model for the new table using the **Generate Database from Model...**.
3. Ensure the database was present, and tables will be generated.
4. Run the generated SQL script in Visual Studio to create the new table from the table. The table should now match the current model.

Then, we have a populated table from a model without writing the SQL code ourselves.

Code-first EF

For many of the samples, data needs to be set up in the database. The preference in this book is to use ORMs than SQL Scripts and EF is a Microsoft framework that supports integration into Visual Studio. For some of the samples, we plan to read and write data to `nservicebus`, and other databases, using EF and MVC.

One of the tables that we will use is to load messages through the saga system. These messages would normally be the result of users populating MVC forms as they enter orders, payments, or more.

The table will appear as follows:

WIN-UAUT16GP....Paymessages

	id	EventId	error	state
▶	1	8b265223-dc9e-4789-a6df-69d19f64...	None	initial
	2	8b265223-dc9e-4789-a6df-69d19f64...	None	initial
	3	3721ba5d-4733-4d98-a5e2-8e8afa3...	None	initial
	4	1ac188ec-4b2e-436c-b989-db88c65d...	None	initial
	5	9bf180fa-f8f4-4b2b-8fac-cca73a4e2...	None	initial
	6	ee2c56f7-6d42-4314-bce5-4825ed29...	None	initial

We have discussed that there is no need to create many pieces manually, and we would use EF to perform some of these functions. We will log, audit, automate, and check things as much as possible.

Code-first EF utilizes the generic `DbContext` as we have mentioned in previous chapters. Here, we will extend it so that it is database specific. The `DbContext` is a generic database context used to perform operations on the database. A `DbContext` article for working with can be found at `http://msdn.microsoft.com/en-us/data/jj729737.aspx`. We will extend the `DbContext` so that it knows the sets of databases we will be creating to handle. To specify the connection string or base database, see `http://www.entityframeworktutorial.net/code-first/database-initialization-in-code-first.aspx` to create `DbSet`. We will create a project called `ConsoleDbContext` to populate the necessary tables.

```
namespace ConsoleDbContext
{
    public class AppContext : DbContext
    {
        public AppContext() : base("nservicebus") { }
        public DbSet<Paymessage> Paymessages { get; set; }
    }
}
```

We will extend the database context with `AppContext`; this will create a table called `Paymessage` to be filled with a set of `Paymessages` objects. To do all this manually is a lot more work, so we will rely on automating the filling of the table. The `base("nservicebus")` expression will dictate the code to put the table in the `nservicebus` database. By default, it will use the local SQL Express instance.

We will create the program to create the `AppContext` object and use it to populate the table with the `Paymessage` objects:

```
namespace MVCApp1
{
    class Program
    {
        static void Main(string[] args)
        {

            int length = 5;
            using (var db = new AppContext())
            {
                for (int index = 0; index < length; index++)
                {
                    Paymessage message = new Paymessage();
                    message.id = index + 1;
                    message.error = "None";
                    message.state = "initial";
                    if (index == 0)
                        message.EventId = new Guid("8b265223-dc9e-
4789-a6df-69d19f644ad7");
                    else if (index == 1)
                        message.EventId = new Guid("3721ba5d-4733-
4d98-a5e2-8e8afa3e61f4");
                    else if (index == 2)
                        message.EventId = new Guid("1ac188ec-4b2e-
436c-b989-db88c65db1fa");
                    else if (index == 3)
                        message.EventId = new Guid("9bf180fa-f8f4-
4b2b-8fac-cca73a4e2cab");
                    else if (index == 4)
                        message.EventId = new Guid("ee2c56f7-6d42-
4314-bce5-4825ed294437");
                    db.Paymessages.Add(message);
                    db.SaveChanges();
                }
            }
        }
    }
}
```

This will populate the database with the sample messages.

Code-first EF and configurations

As we have mentioned earlier, we can perform the configuration in code and outside the `app.config` file. The `app.config` file comes in very handy, but sometimes the technical or non-functional requirements may require encryption of the configuration, or that the configuration is more global by being entries in the database.

However, you may want to store this information in the database, as this shows user IDs and passwords in plain text. This code will be found in the `ConsoleDbContext-Config` directory.

We will walk you through a more extended example as it relates to NSB, just as we established a relationship in the case of the previous `DBContext` with the `app.config` file.

In this scenario, we want to store the `UnicastBusConfig` settings in the database. The unicast bus configuration is made up of a collection of message endpoints. So, we need a one-to-many relationship in the configuration in the database that appears similar to the following diagram:

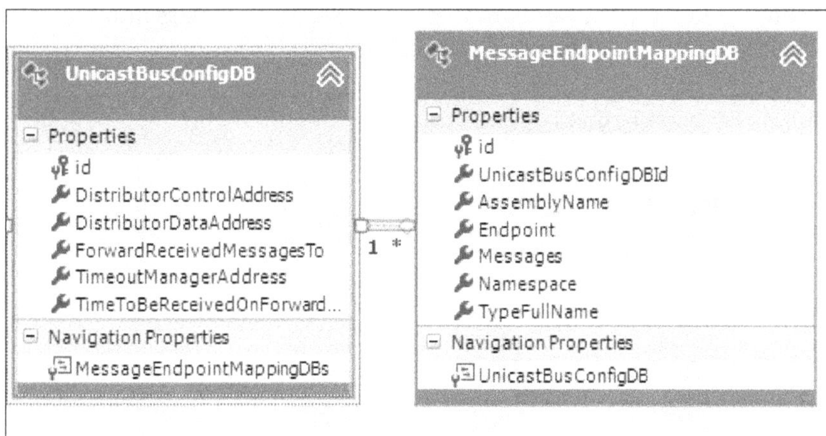

This shows a one-to-many mapping of the unicast configuration as it has a collection called `MessageEndpointMappingCollection` of `MessageEndpointMappings`. This is to allow many endpoint mappings in the `app.config` settings for unicast in the following code:

```
<UnicastBusConfig ForwardReceivedMessagesTo="MyAudits">
  <MessageEndpointMappings>
    <add Endpoint="MySFTPClient" Messages="MyMessages.SendCommand, MyMessages" />
  </MessageEndpointMappings>
</UnicastBusConfig>
```

We can add many message endpoints. In order to create a database to hold these name-value pairs, we will have to copy the `UnicastBusConfig` and `MessageEndpointMapping` classes to create the database tables that contain the same values. The reason that we cannot use the classes directly is that we need to add keys for data storage and the relationship of one-to-many in the tables. We will call these classes `UnicastBusConfigDB` and `MessageEndpointMappingDB` so that they are database compatible. We will add their keys.

```
public class UnicastBusConfigDB
{

    public UnicastBusConfigDB()
    {
        messageMaps = new List<MessageEndpointMappingDB>();
    }

    [Key]
    public int id { get; set; }

    public virtual ICollection<MessageEndpointMappingDB> messageMaps { get; set; }
```

We will create the key for the `MessageEndpointMappingDB` class and the relationship by going back to the `UnicastBusConfigDB` class.

```
public partial class MessageEndpointMappingDB
{
    [Key]
    public int id { get; set; }

    public int UnicastBusConfigDBId { get; set; }
    public UnicastBusConfigDB unicastBusConfigDB { get; set; }
```

This will create a relationship and the keys that we are aiming for in the Entity Framework table diagrams created previously.

```
public class AppContext : DbContext
{
    public AppContext() : base("nservicebus") { }
    public DbSet<UnicastBusConfigDB> unicastBusConfigs { get; set; }
    public DbSet<MessageEndpointMappingDB> messageEndpointMappings { get; set; }
    protected override void OnModelCreating(DbModelBuilder modelBuilder)
    {
        modelBuilder.Entity<MessageEndpointMappingDB>().HasRequired<UnicastBusConfigDB>(s => s.unicastBusConfigDB)
            .WithMany(s => s.messageMaps).HasForeignKey(s => s.UnicastBusConfigDBId);
        base.OnModelCreating(modelBuilder);
    }
}
```

To create the tables with a key that will relate the table of the endpoints to the unicast.

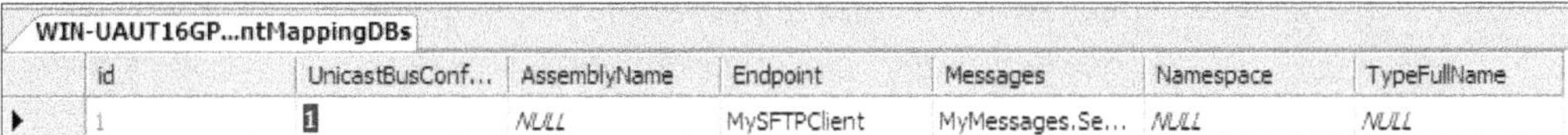

WIN-UAUT16GP...ntMappingDBs

	id	UnicastBusConf...	AssemblyName	Endpoint	Messages	Namespace	TypeFullName
▶	1	1	NULL	MySFTPClient	MyMessages.Se...	NULL	NULL

Then, we can read the endpoint and unicast tables to get the configuration instead of using the `app.config` file. This is a helpful exercise for those who do not wish to use the `app.config` settings:

```
        static void Main(string[] args)
         {
             /**************
              * Read the database fields
              * ************/
             using (var db = new nservicebusEntities())
             {
                 var unicasts = db.UnicastBusConfigDBs;
                 // Get the first UnicastConfig record for now
                 var unicastBusCfgDB = unicasts.FirstOrDefault();
                 /*****
                  * Get the message endpoints per unicast
                  * ****/
                 var messageEndpoints = db.MessageEndpointMappingDBs;
                 foreach (var endpoint in messageEndpoints)
                 {
                     if (unicastBusCfgDB.id == endpoint.
    UnicastBusConfigDBId)
                     {
                         unicastBusCfgDB.MessageEndpointMappingDBs.
    Add(endpoint);
                     }
                 }
                 /****
                  * Fill in normal unicast config from DB
                  * *****/
                 UnicastBusConfig unicastBusCfg = new
    UnicastBusConfig();
                 unicastBusCfg.DistributorControlAddress =
    unicastBusCfgDB.DistributorControlAddress;
```

```
                unicastBusCfg.DistributorDataAddress =
unicastBusCfgDB.DistributorDataAddress;
                unicastBusCfg.ForwardReceivedMessagesTo =
unicastBusCfgDB.ForwardReceivedMessagesTo;
                unicastBusCfg.TimeoutManagerAddress = unicastBusCfgDB.
TimeoutManagerAddress;
                unicastBusCfg.TimeToBeReceivedOnForwardedMessages =
unicastBusCfgDB.TimeToBeReceivedOnForwardedMessages;
                Console.WriteLine(unicastBusCfg);
                /**
                 * Add Message Endpoint Mappings
                 * ***/
                unicastBusCfg.MessageEndpointMappings = new
MessageEndpointMappingCollection();
                foreach (var endpointDB in unicastBusCfgDB.
MessageEndpointMappingDBs)
                {
                    MessageEndpointMapping endpoint =  new
MessageEndpointMapping();
                    endpoint.AssemblyName = endpointDB.AssemblyName;
                    endpoint.Endpoint = endpointDB.Endpoint;
                    endpoint.Messages = endpointDB.Messages;
                    endpoint.Namespace = endpointDB.Namespace;
                    endpoint.TypeFullName = endpointDB.TypeFullName;
                    unicastBusCfg.MessageEndpointMappings.
Add(endpoint);
                    Console.WriteLine(endpoint);
                }
            }

        }
```

Unit testing NServiceBus

Visual Studio 2012 has plenty of unit testing features. `NServiceBus.Testing` offers testing by sending messages through message handlers and sagas. This includes anything that a message handler and saga can do, including header manipulation and dependency injection. You can visit `http://docs.particular.net/NServiceBus/unit-testing` for some basic examples. For the source code of `NServiceBus.Testing`, visit `https://github.com/Particular/NServiceBus/tree/develop/src/NServiceBus.Testing`.

The very basics of starting unit testing is to create a unit test project in Visual Studio by adding a new unit test project to an existing solution. See `http://msdn.microsoft.com/en-us/library/hh598957.aspx/` for details.

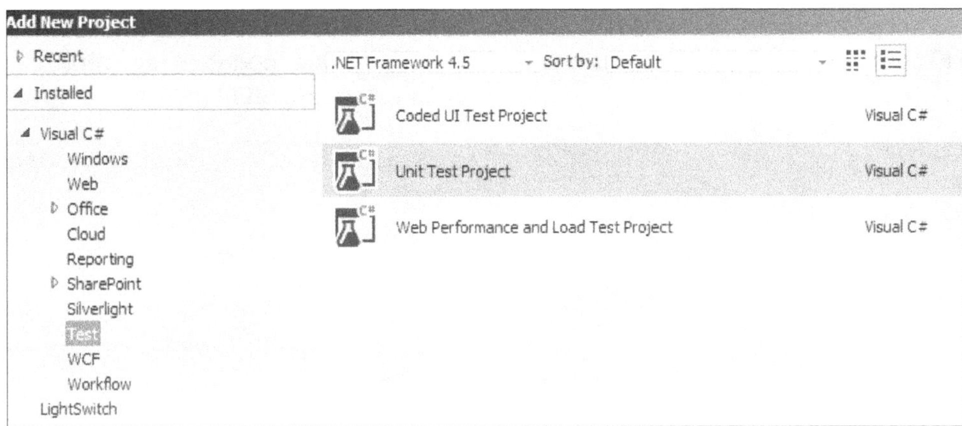

We will add `NServiceBus.Testing` from NuGet by visiting `http://www.nuget.org/packages/NServiceBus.Testing/`. We will initialize the tests using `Test.Initialize()`, which is calling `NServiceBus.Testing`, thus starting the tests with either `Test.Handler<HandleName>()` or `Test.Saga<SagaName>()`.

```
using NServiceBus;
using NServiceBus.Testing;

namespace UnitTestHandlers
{
    [TestClass]
    public class UnitTestHandler
    {
        /***
         *
         * Test the message handler for MYWCFClient
         * This will call the WCF Service for a completion
         *
         * ****/
        [TestMethod]
        public void Run()
        {
            Test.Initialize();

            Test.Handler<MyHandler>()
                .ExpectReply<ResponseMessage>(m => m.String == "hello")
                .OnMessage<RequestMessage>(m => m.String = "hello");
        }
```

When a test is built, we can run it or debug it. The test indicators will tell us whether anything failed. We can also put in rules and assertions that if the correct response does not happen, it will fail the test. This is a great feature of Visual Studio, and there are many samples: `http://msdn.microsoft.com/en-us/library/ms243176.aspx`, `http://www.visualstudio.com/en-us/get-started/create-and-run-unit-tests-vs.aspx`, and extensions such as `http://www.codeproject.com/Articles/22358/Visual-Studio-Unit-Testing-Extensions`.

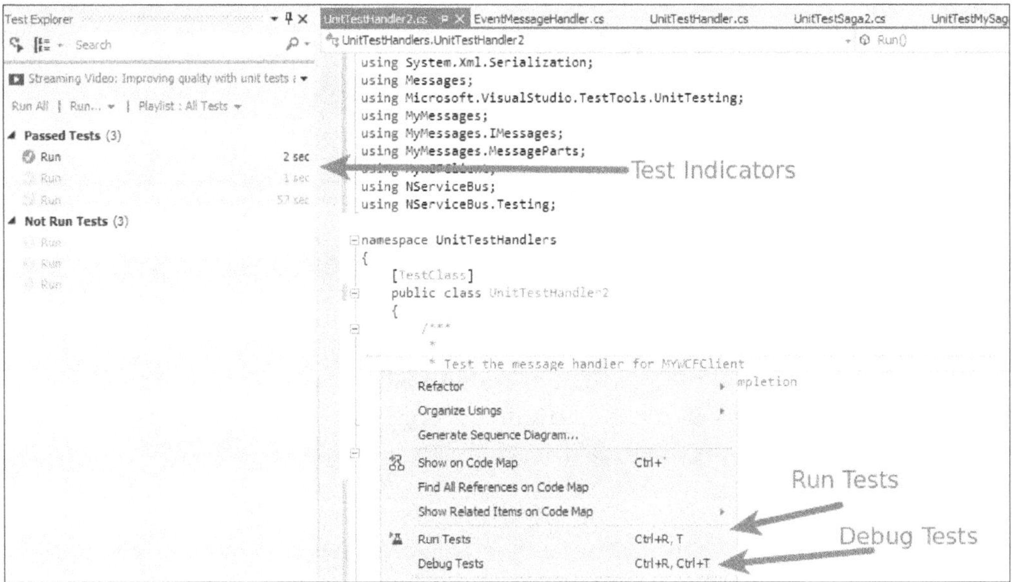

Message handler unit testing

The message handler code will be in the unit test itself. From our `\BasicWCF2\MVCApp - WCF\UnitTestHandlers\` project, where we have various unit tests, we will use this unit test, to debug, test, and walk through `EventMessageHandler`. The `EventMessageHandler` receives `SendCommand` from `MVCApp`, via the saga, loads XML messages, selects one if it has found one, and sends it to the WCF server, which will respond back to the saga.

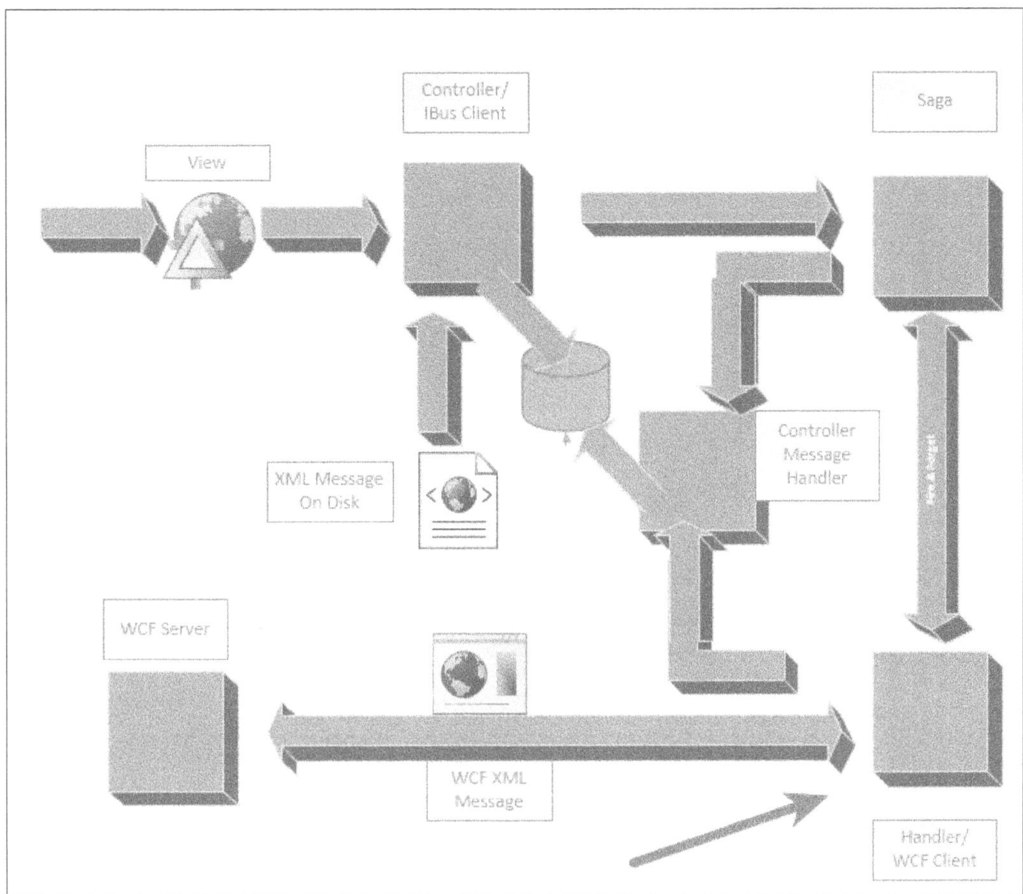

We proceed with creating `UnitTestHandler2.cs`, and then add the header information and `[TestMethod]`. This will be under `BasicWCF2` in the `UnitTestHandlers` project.

After the base of the file is created, we will create a normal message, `SendCommand`, with `GUID` and `state` that will inform where the message should be at before reaching the message handler called `command`.

```
namespace UnitTestHandlers
{
    [TestClass]
    public class UnitTestHandler2
    {
        /***
         *
         * Test the message handler for MYWCFClient
         * This will call the WCF Service for a completion
         *
         * ****/
        [TestMethod]
        public void Run()
        {
            Test.Initialize();
            /*****
             *
             *  Create a Command message
             *  used to look up an XML Message file
             *  on Disk, send to WCF Server
             *
             * ******/
            SendCommand command = new SendCommand();
            command.RequestId = new Guid("8b265223-dc9e-4789-a6df-69d19f644ad7");
            command.state = MyMessages.MessageParts.StateCodes.SentMyWCFClient;

            // The Test code
            Test.Handler<EventMessageHandler>()
                    .ExpectReply<ResponseCommand>(m => m.state == MyMessages.MessageParts.StateCodes.CompleteMyWCFClient)
                      .OnMessage<SendCommand>(command);
        }
```

We see that the command message is passed to `.OnMessage<SendMessage>(command)` and `ResponseMessage` in reply, with the state being set to `CompleteMyWCFClient`. When calling the unit test in Debug, we can even pass this message in the handler and see how it behaves.

```
StateCodes.cs    UnitTestHandler2.cs    EventMessageHandler.cs    UnitTestHandler.cs    UnitTest
UnitTestHandlers.UnitTestHandler2.EventMessageHandler                Handle(SendComm
        public class EventMessageHandler : IHandleMessages<SendCommand>
        {

            public IBus Bus { get; set; }

            public void Handle(SendCommand message)
            {

                ServiceReference1.WcfServiceOf_PayMessage_ErrorCodesClient clien
                     new ServiceReference1.WcfServiceOf_PayMessage_ErrorCodesCl

                // Create the response message
                ResponseCommand command = new ResponseCommand();
                command.RequestId = message.RequestId;
                /****
                 * Get the XML messages from the temp direcotry.
```

This allows us to design and debug the handler functionality in the unit test code. There are many rules that can be used when testing the handler or saga. For instance, `ExpectNotReply` where the handler does not reply with a specific message.

To get information on what is available in `NServiceBus.Testing`, we can:

- Try to enter something and hover the mouse over IntelliSense

- Read the documentation at `http://www.nudoq.org/#!/Packages/NServiceBus.Testing/NServiceBus.Testing/Handler(T)`

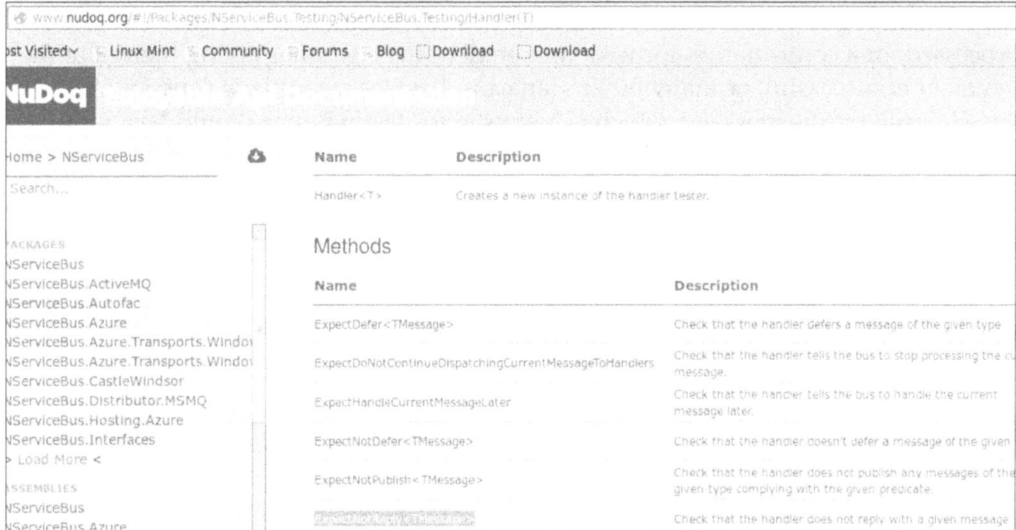

- To read the code in GitHub, refer to `https://github.com/Particular/NServiceBus/blob/develop/src/NServiceBus.Testing/Handler.cs`

https://github.com/Particular/NServiceBus/blob/develop/src/NServiceBus.Testing/Handler.cs

Community Forums Blog Download Download

```
/// <summary>
/// Check that the handler does not reply with a given message
/// </summary>
public Handler<T> ExpectNotReply<TMessage>(Func<TMessage, bool> check)
{
    expectedInvocations.Add(new ExpectedNotReplyInvocation<TMessage> { Check = check });
    return this;
}
```

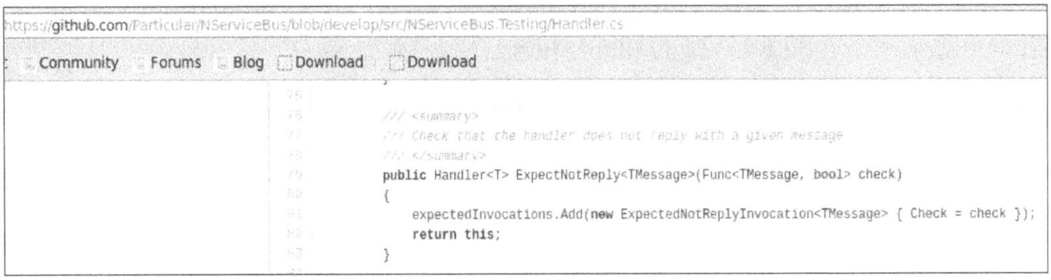

So, there are many possibilities to test the code. For the message handler, it will get the command with `GUID` and `state`, read the XML files to get a matching message, and send it to the WCF service, which will respond back to the saga. The saga keeps track of the message routing and states and will respond to `MVCApp`. The `MVCApp` project will update its state in the table. There could normally be multiple views that could read the state, maybe an admin utility to check on the state of the messages, the CSR talking to the customer and telling them whether the payment has been processed, or a confirmation form, or an e-mail to the customer telling them that the payment is successful, or many other scenarios. Besides a couple of functions to read the XML file for the message, which is just used for testing, there could be a number of scenarios added; however, the majority of the code is simply the following, which is simple enough:

```
/****
        * The message handler
        * Matches a XML message GUID from a file and the command sent
        * to it from MVC via the Saga
        * If found, sends it to the WCF  Server and responds
        * with the state of what happened.
        * The WCF Service must be running to complete.
        *
        * ****/
        public class EventMessageHandler :
IHandleMessages<SendCommand>
        {
            public IBus Bus { get; set; }
            public void Handle(SendCommand message)
            {
                ServiceReference1.WcfServiceOf_PayMessage_
ErrorCodesClient client1 =
                        new ServiceReference1.WcfServiceOf_PayMessage_
ErrorCodesClient();

                // Create the response message
```

```
                ResponseCommand command = new ResponseCommand();
                command.RequestId = message.RequestId;
                /****
                 * Get the XML messages from the temp direcotry.
                 * Find a match from the GUID
                 * ****/
                List<PayMessage> list = EventMessageHandler.
GetMessages();
                PayMessage payMessage = null;
                foreach (var temp_message in list)
                {
                    if (message.RequestId == temp_message.EventId)
                    {
                        payMessage = temp_message;
                    }
                }
                // if no XML, just fail
                if (payMessage == null)
                {
                    command.state = StateCodes.MyWCFClientFailXML;
                    Bus.Reply(command);
                    Console.WriteLine("No XML Found");
                }
                else
                {
                    ErrorCodes returnCode = client1.
Process(payMessage);
                    if (returnCode == ErrorCodes.None)
                    {
                        command.state = StateCodes.
CompleteMyWCFClient;
                    }
                    else
                    {
                        command.state = StateCodes.MyWCFClientFail;
                    }

                    Bus.Reply(command);
                    Console.WriteLine("Success");
                }
                Console.WriteLine("================================
========================================");
            }
```

After testing this code, we could use the tested code to create a class into a new project, minus the unit testing, and start using it as a message handler. It saves time by developing the code in a unit test, and putting the tested product into the applications' project. The unit test project also serves as a backup of knowing what it looked like during a good test.

Saga handler unit testing

We will start testing saga code from `\BasicWCF2\MVCApp - WCF\UnitTestHandlers\`, where we have various unit tests, including a copy of the `MySaga` code in `UnitTestSaga2.cs`. Again, a sample of some of the workings can be found at `http://docs.particular.net/NServiceBus/unit-testing`. Many of the same principles apply as we saw in unit testing the message handler, except now it will be saga handler, and our testing moves from `Test.Handler` to `Test.Saga`. Now, we can study the source code from `https://github.com/Particular/NServiceBus/blob/develop/src/NServiceBus.Testing/Saga.cs`.

One thing to note is that if a saga entity object is deleted in different function calls, with `MarkAsComplete()`, these should be tested separately because once we delete the object, we cannot delete them again. For example, in our tests:

```
[TestMethod]
public void Run()
{
    Test.Initialize();

     /**
     * State sent to Saga
     * ***/
    SendCommand command = new SendCommand();
    command.RequestId = new Guid("8b265223-dc9e-4789-a6df-69d19f644ad7");
    command.state = MyMessages.MessageParts.StateCodes.SentMyWCFClient;

    /**
      * Response from WCF and to MVCApp
      * ***/
    ResponseCommand resp = new ResponseCommand();
    resp.RequestId = new Guid("8b265223-dc9e-4789-a6df-69d19f644ad7");
    resp.state = MyMessages.MessageParts.StateCodes.CompleteMyWCFClient;


    Test.Saga<MyTestSaga>()
            .ExpectReplyToOrginator<ResponseCommand>()
            .ExpectSend<SendCommand>()
        .When(s => s.Handle(command))
           .ExpectReplyToOrginator<ResponseCommand>()
         .When(s => s.Handle(resp))
         .AssertSagaCompletionIs(true);

    Test.Saga<MyTestSaga>()
              .ExpectReplyToOrginator<ResponseCommand>()
               .ExpectSend<SendCommand>()
               .ExpectTimeoutToBeSetIn<SendCommand>((state, span) => span == TimeSpan.FromHours(3))
          .When(s => s.Handle(command))
             .ExpectReplyToOrginator<ResponseCommand>()
           .WhenSagaTimesOut()
           .AssertSagaCompletionIs(true);


}
```

In this snippet, we are testing the `IHandleMessages<ResponseCommand>` message handler in the first test case, and in the second test case, we are testing `IHandleTimeouts<SendCommand>` separately as they delete the saga object. We are passing in prefabbed messages in the code to see whether they work well with the normal messages.

The saga handler itself will act as an intermediate between the MVCApp and the WCF client. This is needed so that it can timeout after three hours in case there is no response from the WCF service.

Summary

We covered a lot of information in this chapter regarding persistence. This chapter has a lot of associated code. We covered the highlights of working with NSB and databases. NSB does take care of a lot of the workings with databases and mappings, but because of the flexibility of NSB, various pieces can be extended through C# to notify and monitor a variety of SQL Server pieces.

We covered how to create e-mail notifications by watching queues and notifying operations of the workings of NSB.

We created a SQL Server database from object code, we created one from EF models, we created MVC-EF code to read the tables for a PubSub that does most things in SQL Server, and we changed some of the pieces from EF to NHibernate and then from EF to RavenDB. We read the subscription tables of NServiceBus in code and displayed them in MVC for both RavenDB and SQL Server. We also offered a small sample on how to configure a daily check to send ourselves an e-mail if anything was populated in the MSMQ error queue. Wow! for a small chapter, the reader has a lot of information to build from.

The next chapter will be more into the code of general persistence. We will discuss NHibernate, RavenDB, and MongoDB. We will dive into the code to accomplish some database tasks since it relates to NServiceBus. This code can be applied to many tasks that are not ESB-specific.

7
Persistent Snippets

In this chapter, we will be focusing on snippets about persistence. We will discuss NHibernate, RavenDB, and MongoDB.

We will dive into the code to accomplish some database tasks since it relates to NServiceBus. This code can be applied to many tasks that are not ESB-specific. But this is a much-needed chapter on database code itself. We will create SQL Server databases without the use of SQL code and read tables that NServiceBus created in RavenDB. We will show how to create tables with code, read and display tables in NHibernate and RavenDB, and even send ourselves an e-mail with the error queue count. This will be the applied theory in this chapter.

In this chapter, we will cover:

- Entering NHibernate
- Using saga and NHibernate
    - Defining NHibernate
    - The saga database data
- Logging
- Entering RavenDB
- Entering MongoDB

Entering NHibernate

NServiceBus takes care of the mapping interface from the objects to relational databases. We will briefly cover how mapping occurs with NHibernate in a typical non-NSB application if the developer needs to walk through an NHibernate source in NSB or extend it.

Entity Framework is definitely the way to go for SQL Server, but there is a chance that you may have to deal with Oracle or MySQL. There are multiple ways to create the mapping from the objects to relations. One method is to code in the `hbm.xml` files and another is to use Fluent API. For more on Fluent API, see `http://en.wikipedia.org/wiki/Fluent_interface`.

We will use the Fluent API in NHibernate, which will utilize mapping in code instead of in XML. You may find more information on Fluent NHibernate at `http://www.fluentnhibernate.org/`. In order to use Fluent NHibernate, we will need to add it as a reference via NuGet.

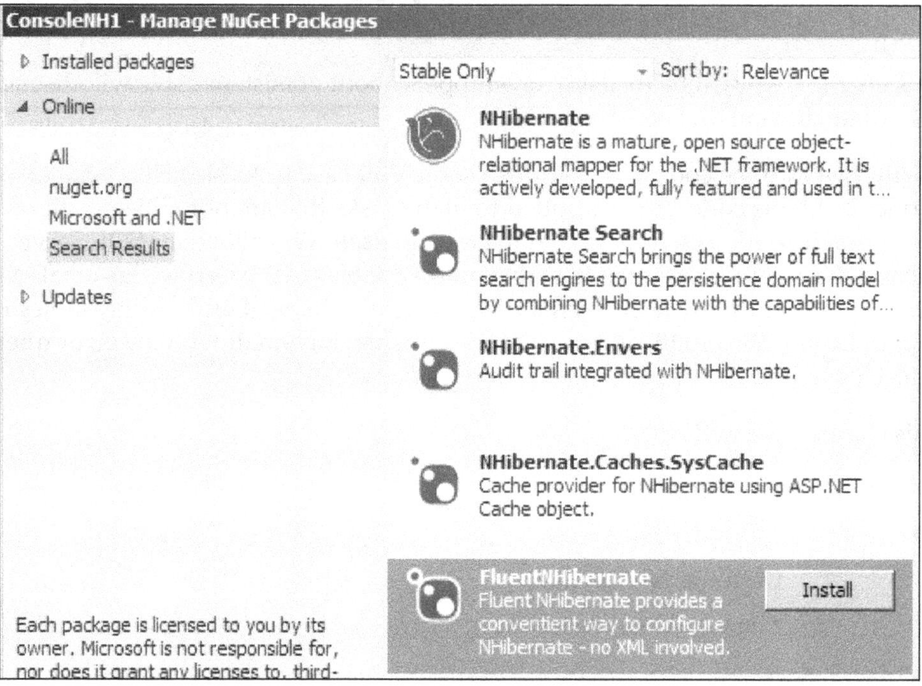

For the NHibernate pieces, there will be a `session` interface instead of an EF `context` interface, which works similarly. We will need the entity object, which is similar to the one created earlier, and the mapping that was created by EF. We will create a different entity object. Notice that it is very similar to creating an entity object except for the `virtual` keyword.

This will be the MVC-NHibernate solution:

```
namespace MVCApp.Models
{
    public class AuditExt2
    {
        public virtual System.Guid Id { get; set; }
        public virtual string CorrelationId { get; set; }
        public virtual string ReplyToAddress { get; set; }
        public virtual bool Recoverable { get; set; }
        public virtual Nullable<System.DateTime> Expires { get; set; }
        public virtual string Headers { get; set; }
        public virtual byte[] Body { get; set; }
        public virtual long RowVersion { get; set; }
    }
}
```

Then, we will create the mapping. A more detailed description can be found at `http://github.com/jagregory/fluent-nhibernate/wiki/Getting-started`.

The code snippet for mapping of `Id` and other variables will appear as follows:

```
using FluentNHibernate.Mapping;

namespace MVCApp.Mapping
{

    public class AuditExt2Map : ClassMap<MVCApp.Models.AuditExt2>
    {
        public AuditExt2Map()
        {
            Table("audit");
            Id(x => x.Id);
            Map(x => x.ReplyToAddress);
            Map(x => x.Recoverable);
            Map(x => x.Expires);
            Map(x => x.Headers);
            Map(x => x.Body);
            Map(x => x.RowVersion);
        }
    }
}
```

In this scenario, we are just providing a one-to-one mapping of the table values to the object values. We were able to take a shortcut as we already had the EF entity, so we could just copy and paste most of the pieces. So now we have an entity object and the mapping; however, instead of just calling the EF `context`, we actually have to code the NHibernate `session`. We will create `NhibernateHelper.cs`, which will contain the `connectionstring` that points to the correct database. Instead of SQL Server, we can easily use MySQL or SQLite on an iPhone or Android device. We will create a configuration for the session factory:

```
        private static void InitializeSessionFactory()
        {
            _sessionFactory = Fluently.Configure()
                .Database(MsSqlConfiguration.MsSql2008
                              .ConnectionString(
                                 @"Server=localhost\SQLExpress;Databa
se=nservicebus;Trusted_Connection=True;")
                              .ShowSql()
                )
                .Mappings(m =>
                           m.FluentMappings
                              .AddFromAssemblyOf<MVCApp.Models.
AuditExt2>())
                .BuildSessionFactory();
        }
```

Once we create the configuration, we will open the session and call the database objects in a way that is similar to how we do it in EF. Most of the code of the new function is made up by copying the NHibernate object into the previous EF object that is displayed on the screen. The screen won't have to change, just the entity object that NHibernate used:

```
public ActionResult Audit()
        {
            List<MVCApp.Models.AuditExt> models = new List<MVCApp.
Models.AuditExt>();
            using (var session = NHibernateHelper.OpenSession())
            {

                var audits = session.QueryOver<AuditExt2>().List();
                foreach (var audit in audits)
                {
```

```
                    AuditExt data = new AuditExt();
                    data.audit = new DAL.audit();
                    data.audit.Headers = audit.Headers;
                    data.audit.Id = audit.Id;
                    data.audit.ReplyToAddress = audit.ReplyToAddress;
                    data.audit.Recoverable = audit.Recoverable;
                    data.audit.Expires = audit.Expires;
                    data.audit.RowVersion = audit.RowVersion;
                    if (audit.Body == null)
                    {
                        data.reader = " ";
                    }
                    else
                    {
                        data.reader = System.Text.UTF8Encoding.UTF8.
GetString(audit.Body);
                    }
                    models.Add(data);
                }
            }
            return View(models);
        }
```

So what did we learn so far? We learned how to create objects from the NServiceBus tables to C# using EF, how to display these objects in MVC, and how to extend them into NHibernate so that we are not limited to just using SQL Server.

Using saga and NHibernate

We will walk through a modified example of a basic saga, originally from `https://github.com/jkillingsworth/NServiceBus-BasicSagas`. However, this example has been modified to use NHibernate, which uses a local SQL Express database. NHibernate was added using some of the steps from `http://docs.particular.net/nservicebus/relational-persistence-using-nhibernate---nservicebus-4.x`. We also added logging using the NLog framework to log functionalities as we go. The NHibernate ORM framework was chosen because it can connect to a multitude of different databases using the same code, the difference being the connection string in the `app.config` file for the different databases.

To elaborate on this saga example, there is a MySaga program that directs the messages while saving a saga instance as the messages are being moved. The saga persistence keeps track of the information that we defined to be saved in a saga entity object. The saga acts as an anchor that we can persist as we orchestrate messages moving across the bus. We can retrieve the instance of the saga associated with the message, update it, and keep it stored, since the original message morphs into different types of messages.

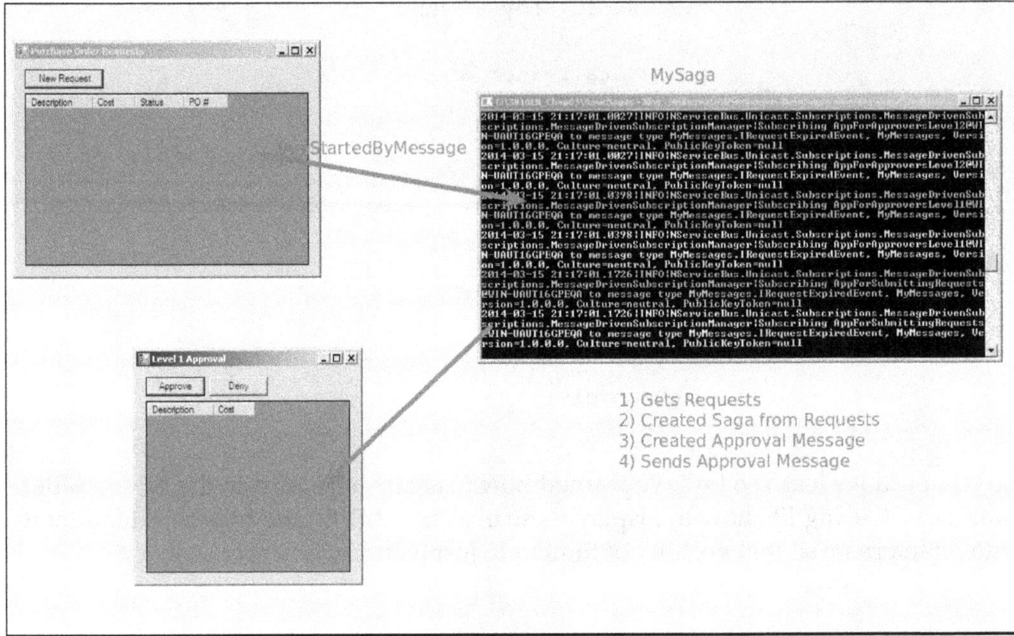

In this application, we sent IAmStartedByMessages<SubmitRequestCommand> from the AppSubmittingRequests application, seen here as **Purchase Order Requests**. It creates and submits SubmitRequestCommand, which takes the data from this message and creates a saga on the bus with a unique ID. It also sets a 60-second timer that will send a time-out message from the bus once the 60 seconds are completed.

```
public void Handle(SubmitRequestCommand message)
{

    logger.Info("--------MySaga Handle-------" + message);

    RequestTimeout<TimeoutMessage>(TimeSpan.FromSeconds(60));

    Data.RequestId = message.RequestId;
    Data.Description = message.Description;
    Data.Cost = message.Cost;
    Data.RequiresApprovalByLevel1 = message.Cost > 100.00m;
    Data.RequiresApprovalByLevel2 = message.Cost > 1000.00m;
    Data.ApprovedByLevel1 = false;
    Data.ApprovedByLevel2 = false;

    ProcessApproval();
}
```

Then, it sends an approval that creates **Level 1 Approval**, an application called `AppForApprovalsLevel1` and, after the **Approve** or **Deny** button is clicked, it creates a new message that is sent back to the saga; the saga handles the messages. Depending on the return message, it will either call the `IHandleMessages<ApproveRequestCommand>` or `IHandleMessages<DenyRequestCommand>` handler. The saga will be pulled up by the bus, since we used mapping code in this example to map the messages to `RequestId`.

```
public class PurchaseOrderRequestData : IContainSagaData
{
    /***
     * Gets/sets the Id of the process. Do NOT generate this value in your code.
       The value of the Id will be generated automatically to provide the
       best performance for saving in a database.
     * ***/
    public virtual Guid Id { get; set; }  // Required
    /***
     * Contains the return address of the endpoint that caused the process to run.
     * ***/
    public virtual string Originator { get; set; }  //Required
    /***
     * Contains the Id of the message which caused the saga to start.
       This is needed so that when we reply to the Originator, any
       registered callbacks will be fired correctly.
     * ***/
    public virtual string OriginalMessageId { get; set; }  //Required

    [Unique]
    public virtual Guid RequestId { get; set; }  // Unique ID to lookup Request message
    public virtual string Description { get; set; }
    public virtual decimal Cost { get; set; }
    public virtual bool RequiresApprovalByLevel1 { get; set; }
    public virtual bool RequiresApprovalByLevel2 { get; set; }
    public virtual bool ApprovedByLevel1 { get; set; }
    public virtual bool ApprovedByLevel2 { get; set; }
}
```

We can pull up the saga that matches the message and route it based on some logic, in this case, the cost, or return it to the originating client. The saga may contain most of the original message, so all of it doesn't need to be propagated through the messages.

```
public void Handle(ApproveRequestCommand message)
{
    logger.Info("--------MySaga Handle-------" + message);
    if (message.Approver == Approver.Level1)
    {
        Data.ApprovedByLevel1 = true;
    }

    if (message.Approver == Approver.Level2)
    {
        Data.ApprovedByLevel2 = true;
    }

    ProcessApproval();
}

public void Handle(DenyRequestCommand message)
{
    logger.Info("--------MySaga Handle-------" + message);
    var reply = new SubmitRequestReplyMessage
    {
        RequestId = Data.RequestId,
        Approved = false
    };

    ReplyToOriginator(reply);
    MarkAsComplete();
}
```

The saga is aware of its originator. It knows to match the `RequestId` because of the mapping, and the bus keeps an internal ID to keep all the sagas unique. All sagas must have the `Id`, `Originator`, and `OriginalMessageId` fields that the bus will use to keep track of the saga. Here, we also have the `[Unique]` attribute to ensure that `RequestId` is kept unique so that the map is made to return the correct saga.

```
public class PurchaseOrderRequestData : IContainSagaData
{
    /***
     * Gets/sets the Id of the process. Do NOT generate this value in your code.
       The value of the Id will be generated automatically to provide the
       best performance for saving in a database.
     * ***/
    public virtual Guid Id { get; set; }  // Required
    /***
     * Contains the return address of the endpoint that caused the process to run.
     * ***/
    public virtual string Originator { get; set; }  //Required
    /***
     * Contains the Id of the message which caused the saga to start.
       This is needed so that when we reply to the Originator, any
       registered callbacks will be fired correctly.
     * ***/
    public virtual string OriginalMessageId { get; set; }  //Required

    [Unique]
    public virtual Guid RequestId { get; set; }  // Unique ID to lookup Request message
    public virtual string Description { get; set; }
    public virtual decimal Cost { get; set; }
    public virtual bool RequiresApprovalByLevel1 { get; set; }
    public virtual bool RequiresApprovalByLevel2 { get; set; }
    public virtual bool ApprovedByLevel1 { get; set; }
    public virtual bool ApprovedByLevel2 { get; set; }
}
```

The `EndpointConfig.cs` file of the `MySaga` project contains the `Init()` method. This function contains the initial configuration for the endpoint of the IBus. The endpoint will default to the namespace of the project, for instance; in this case, `MySaga` will be the endpoint as it is associated with the namespace.

```
namespace MySaga
{
    public class EndpointConfig : IConfigureThisEndpoint, AsA_Server, IWantCustomInitialization, IWantToRunWhenBusStartsAndStops
    {

        private static Logger logger = LogManager.GetCurrentClassLogger();

        public void Init()
        {
```

However, you may explicitly define your endpoints of the IBus with `Configure.With().DefineEndpointName("MyEndpoint");`, where `MyEndpoint` is the IBus' endpoint to be defined.

As always, the NSB IBus will create the appropriate endpoints if defined correctly. Here, we have it based on the different project's namespaces in the solution. The different projects are `MySaga`, `AppforApprovalsLevel1`, `AppforApprovalsLevel2`, `AppForSubmittingRequests`, and `AppForAccountingDept`. Notice that NSB will create them in lowercase, and also create the appropriate time-out, error, and audit queues.

We are going to configure the IBus in `EndpointConfig.cs`, which in most cases is where the IBus will be configured to use the saga and time-out persistence in NHibernate.

```
Configure.With()
    .DefaultBuilder()  // Autofac Default Container
    .UseTransport<Msmq>()  // MSMQ, will create Queues, Defualt
    .MsmqSubscriptionStorage() // Create a subscription endpoint
    .UseNHibernateSagaPersister()
    .UseNHibernateTimeoutPersister()
    .UnicastBus(); // Create the default unicast Bus
```

Defining NHibernate

NHibernate is configured in the `app.config` file for the `MySaga` project, to configure the NHibernate interface in order to connect to the local SQL Express Server instance.

```
<!--  NHibernate Settings-->
<connectionStrings>
  <add name="NServiceBus/Transport" connectionString="cacheSendConnection=true" />
  <add name="NServiceBus/Persistence" connectionString="Data Source=.\SQLEXPRESS;Initial Catalog=nservicebus;Integrated Security=True" />
</connectionStrings>

<!-- specify the other needed NHibernate settings like below in appSettings:-->
<appSettings>
  <!-- dialect is defaulted to MsSql2008Dialect, if needed change accordingly -->
  <add key="NServiceBus/Persistence/NHibernate/dialect" value="NHibernate.Dialect.MsSql2008Dialect" />
  <!-- other optional settings examples -->
  <add key="NServiceBus/Persistence/NHibernate/connection.provider" value="NHibernate.Connection.DriverConnectionProvider" />
  <add key="NServiceBus/Persistence/NHibernate/connection.driver_class" value="NHibernate.Driver.Sql2008ClientDriver" />
</appSettings>
```

Here, we can see the NServiceBus NHibernate connection strings and app settings. Now that we have NHibernate configured for NServiceBus, we can check the SQL Server after opening the sample solution. After opening the solution, NServiceBus will create the appropriate tables for saga and time-outs in the `nservicebus` database.

```
namespace MySaga
{
    public class PurchaseOrderRequestData : IContainSagaData
    {
        /***
         * Gets/sets the Id of the process. Do NOT generate this value in your code.
           The value of the Id will be generated automatically to provide the
           best performance for saving in a database.
         * ***/
        public virtual Guid Id { get; set; }  // Required
        /***
         * Contains the return address of the endpoint that caused the process to run.
         * ***/
        public virtual string Originator { get; set; }  //Required
        /***
         * Contains the Id of the message which caused the saga to start.
           This is needed so that when we reply to the Originator, any
           registered callbacks will be fired correctly.
         * ***/
        public virtual string OriginalMessageId { get; set; }  //Required

        [Unique]
        public virtual Guid RequestId { get; set; }  // Unique ID to lookup Request message
        public virtual string Description { get; set; }
        public virtual decimal Cost { get; set; }
        public virtual bool RequiresApprovalByLevel1 { get; set; }
        public virtual bool RequiresApprovalByLevel2 { get; set; }
        public virtual bool ApprovedByLevel1 { get; set; }
        public virtual bool ApprovedByLevel2 { get; set; }
    }
}
```

We see that the base saga that is normally created, called `ContainSagaData`, has `Id`, `Originator`, and `OriginalMessageId` and is always able to find the correct unique saga instance and the originator information to reply to the client that sent this handler the message to start saga.

It also created the `PurchaseOrderRequestData` saga, where the table will match the object. The object will appear as follows:

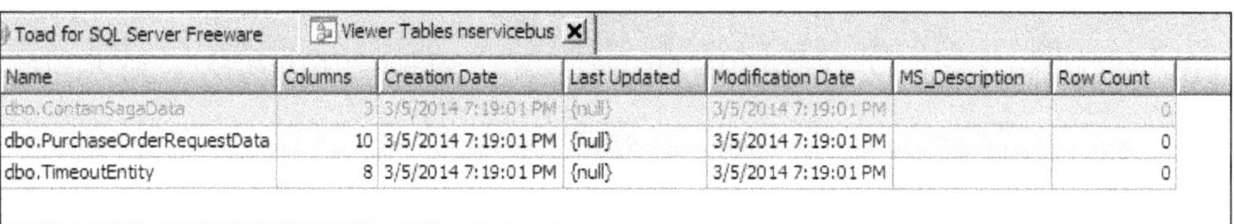

Toad for SQL Server Freeware | Viewer Tables nservicebus

Name	Columns	Creation Date	Last Updated	Modification Date	MS_Description	Row Count
dbo.ContainSagaData	3	3/5/2014 7:19:01 PM	{null}	3/5/2014 7:19:01 PM		0
dbo.PurchaseOrderRequestData	10	3/5/2014 7:19:01 PM	{null}	3/5/2014 7:19:01 PM		0
dbo.TimeoutEntity	8	3/5/2014 7:19:01 PM	{null}	3/5/2014 7:19:01 PM		0

The saga database data

So the database table associated with the object will look like the following:

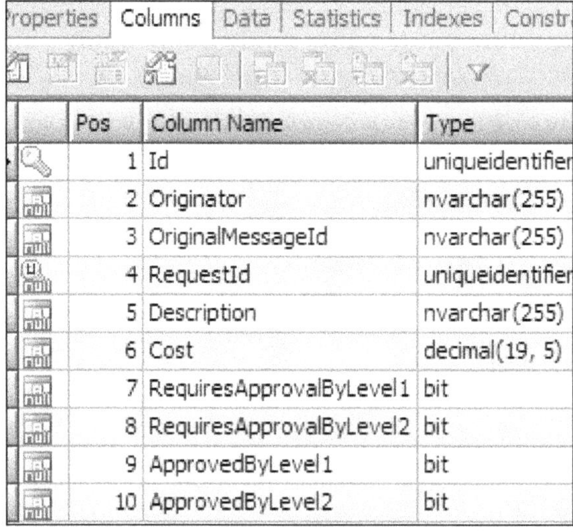

roperties | Columns | Data | Statistics | Indexes | Constr

Pos	Column Name	Type
1	Id	uniqueidentifier
2	Originator	nvarchar(255)
3	OriginalMessageId	nvarchar(255)
4	RequestId	uniqueidentifier
5	Description	nvarchar(255)
6	Cost	decimal(19, 5)
7	RequiresApprovalByLevel1	bit
8	RequiresApprovalByLevel2	bit
9	ApprovedByLevel1	bit
10	ApprovedByLevel2	bit

Please note that we did not need to create any mapping files for any of the NHibernate mappings, nor did we need to create the table. We simply created the NSB configuration. NSB created the tables and performed the mapping. Look! No need to use SQL.

Likewise, we have a time-out message as an object given as follows:

```
using NServiceBus;

namespace MySaga
{
    public class TimeoutMessage : IMessage
    {
    }
}
```

But since IBus retains extra information to keep track of the correct saga and has the IBus execute the timer separately from the current thread, there will be a lot of extra information in its time-out table for the IBus' use:

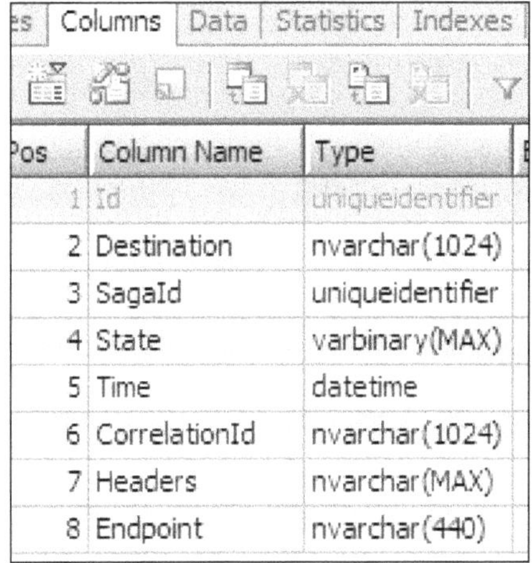

Pos	Column Name	Type
1	Id	uniqueidentifier
2	Destination	nvarchar(1024)
3	SagaId	uniqueidentifier
4	State	varbinary(MAX)
5	Time	datetime
6	CorrelationId	nvarchar(1024)
7	Headers	nvarchar(MAX)
8	Endpoint	nvarchar(440)

Logging

In the following example, we have also set the `app.config` file to use NLog. NServiceBus will support the common logging frameworks, common logging, NLog, Log4Net, and Serilog. Please see `http://docs.particular.net/NServiceBus/logging-in-nservicebus` for more information.

For NLog, we need to add the Nlog NuGet reference to the project:

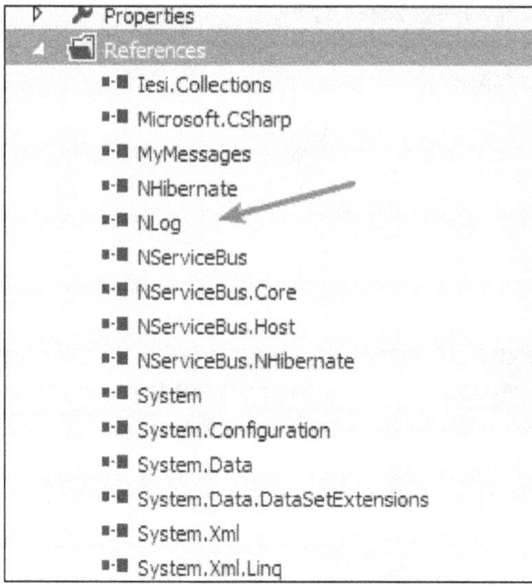

We need to set the logging levels and the location of where the logs are being sent to in the `app.config` file:

```
<!--        NLOG                    -->
  <nlog xmlns="http://www.nlog-project.org/schemas/NLog.xsd" xmlns:xsi="http://www.w3.org/2001/XMLSchema-instance">
    <targets>
      <target name="logfile" xsi:type="File" fileName="c:\logs\basicSaga_${shortdate}.log" layout="${longdate} ${level} ${message}" />
      <target name="console" xsi:type="Console" />
      <target xsi:type="EventLog" name="event" layout="${message}" source="MyProgram" eventId="555" log="Application" />
    </targets>
    <rules>
      <logger name="*" minLevel="Error" writeTo="event" />
      <logger name="*" minLevel="Info" writeTo="console" />
      <logger name="*" minLevel="Trace" writeTo="logfile" />
    </rules>
  </nlog>
  <!--        NLOG                    -->
```

The `app.config` file is set in a way similar to most applications, using Nlog.

```
private static Logger logger = LogManager.GetCurrentClassLogger();
public void Init()
{

    // Log the Bus
    SetLoggingLibrary.NLog();
    logger.Info("--------Start-------");
```

For a tutorial on NLog, please check out https://github.com/nlog/nlog/wiki/Tutorial. The difference is that there needs to be a section name for NServiceBus to use Nlog, <section name="nlog" type="NLog.Config.ConfigSectionHandler, NLog" />. We also set the local configuration by using SetLoggingLibrary.NLog();.

From the app.config file, we are saving a lot of the trace information in the C:\logs\ directory while creating a new file daily with a filename of the current date:

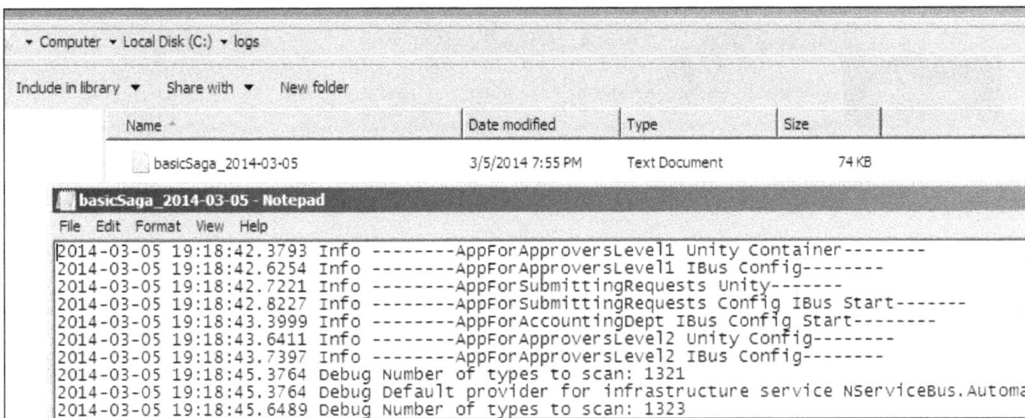

Logging becomes a necessity when trying to document the internal happenings of messages, sagas, and persistence.

Entering RavenDB

We have briefly discussed RavenDB in the earlier chapters of this book. NSB takes care of the document mapping in the RavenDB database; however, we will cover some of the basics of RavenDB in a typical C# program without NSB. I will remind you to review the RavenDB licensing when working with RavenDB.

RavenDB is a document-oriented store database that is used by many defaults in NServiceBus and makes use of the JSON format. See https://ravendb.net/ for more information. In our previous PubSub example, we took out most pieces of the persistence from RavenDB and put it in a SQL Server. Now, we will put the subscriptions back into RavenDB.

This is done by deleting `.UseNHibernateSubscriptionPersister()`, which we put earlier in the PubSub `MyPublisher` example. After deleting this piece of code, NServiceBus will default to storing the subscription information back into RavenDB. When running the PubSub example, we can see that the subscription information was generated in RavenDB.

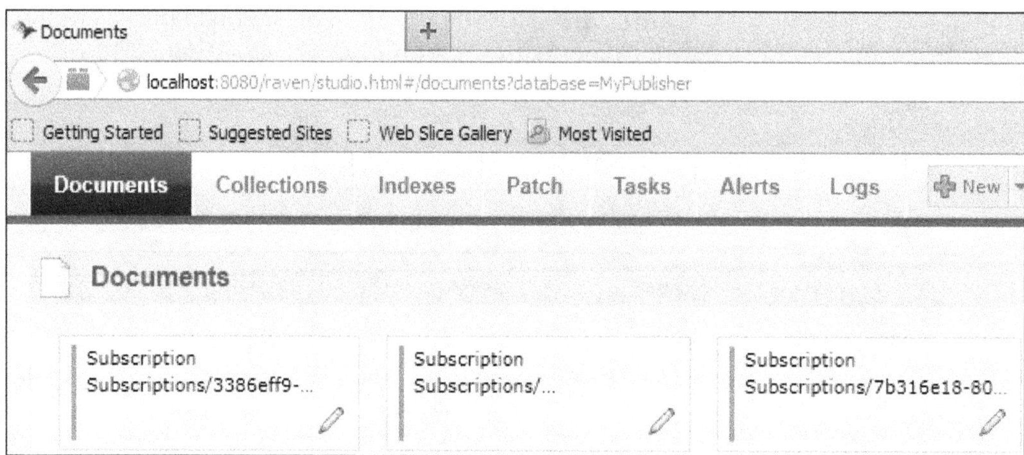

However, this section is about accessing RavenDB through snippets of code. Our end goal is to display the following screenshot through MVCApp by code so that we can later extend the persistence of NServiceBus to automatically log, monitor, and do more as we have been going through in this book. We wish to write the code to display it in the browser without the RavenDB admin tool to show the following screenshot:

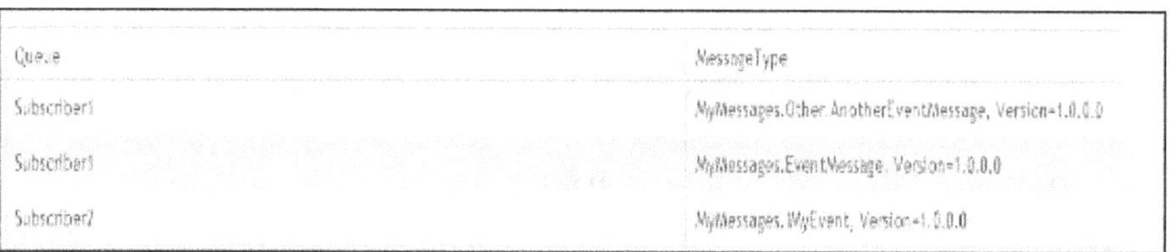

Queue	MessageType
Subscriber1	MyMessages.Other.AnotherEventMessage, Version=1.0.0.0
Subscriber1	MyMessages.EventMessage, Version=1.0.0.0
Subscriber2	MyMessages.MyEvent, Version=1.0.0.0

This is the subscription information of the `MyPublisher`, `Subscriber1` and `Subscriber2` queues. We could see this earlier in the SQL Server as the following:

	SubscriberEndp...	MessageType	Version	TypeName
▶	Subscriber1	MyMessages.Ev...	1.0.0.0	MyMessages.Ev...
	Subscriber1	MyMessages.Ot...	1.0.0.0	MyMessages.Ot...
	Subscriber2	MyMessages.IM...	1.0.0.0	MyMessages.IM...
*	*NULL*	*NULL*	*NULL*	*NULL*

To start developing with RavenDB, the RavenDB client will have to be installed from NuGet. This will be the **MVCApp - RavenDB** solution. For more information, see `https://www.nuget.org/packages/RavenDB.Client`.

Now, it is RavenDB's turn. RavenDB is a document oriented in the JSON format, meaning that the `string` values of C# will be used heavily. For more on JSON, see `http://www.json.org/`. We can see the record just by clicking on the icon on the RavenDB screen and viewing its details.

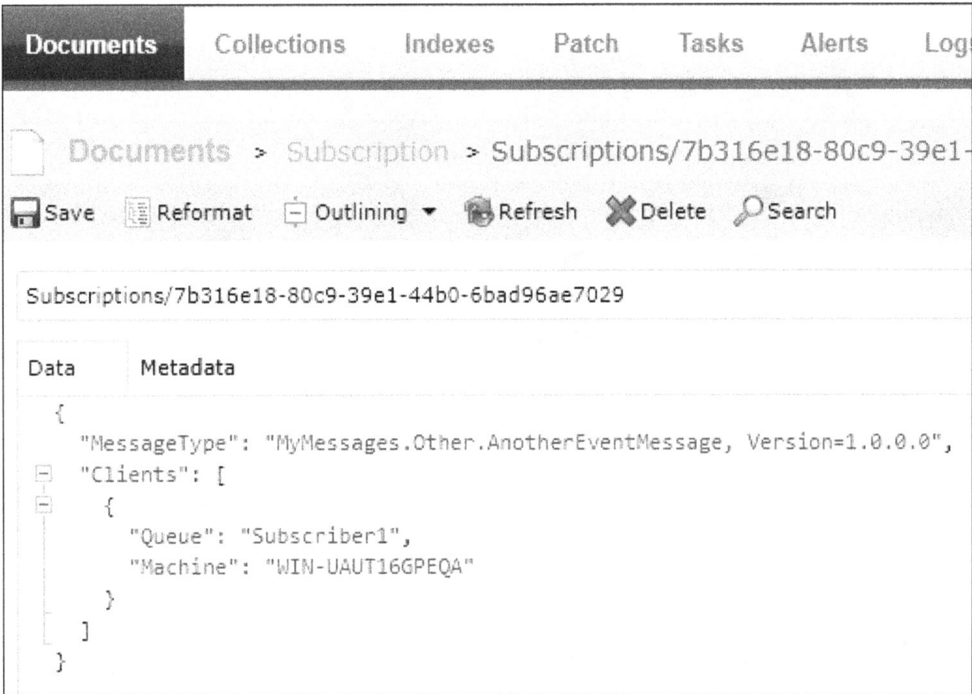

This is an object of two values: `MessageType` and a list of `Clients`. Inside the `Clients` list is `Queue` with the value of `QueueSubscriber1`, and `Machine` with the value of `WIN-.....` We will create an entity object to mimic the document data used previously to create our own list:

```
namespace MVCApp.Mapping
{
    public class SubscriptionExt
    {
        public string MessageType { get; set; }
        public List<Address> Clients { get; set; }
    }
    public class Address
    {
        public string Queue { get; set; }
        public string Machine { get; set; }
    }
}
```

We can see that there is a `MessageType` with a list of `Clients` containing `Queue` and `Machine`. We need to mention that this code snippet found at `https://gist.github.com/johannesg/7984309` was helpful.

To display a list in the view, I am going to use a simpler object where I don't have to worry about walking down multiple link lists until later, and just show the first client's values. This will be the object to populate my view:

```
public class SubscriptionExtView
 {
        public string MessageType { get; set; }
        public string Queue { get; set; }
        public string Machine { get; set; }
  }
```

So let's recap. We have the view and entity objects defined. We will populate a list of these objects that we read from a session to the database, as we did in the EF context and the NHibernate session. Now, we start a RavenDB session. The RavenDB session uses a URL as a connection string to the database. Once we open the session, we are going to search for the data. One of the many features of RavenDB, especially in searching is that RavenDB uses Lucene. Lucene is an open source Apache search engine software; for more information, see `https://lucene.apache.org`. For building Lucene queries in RavenDB, see `http://ravendb.net/docs/2.0/client-api/querying/query-and-lucene-query`. So, now we will execute the following code:

```
public ActionResult Subscription()
{
    List<SubscriptionExtView> models = new List<SubscriptionExtView>();

    using (var ds = new DocumentStore { Url = "http://localhost:8080", DefaultDatabase = "MyPublisher" })
    {
        ds.Initialize();
        using (var session = ds.OpenSession("MyPublisher"))
        {
            var len = session.Advanced.LuceneQuery<SubscriptionExt>("Raven/DocumentsByEntityName").QueryResult.TotalResults;
            for (int index = 0; index < len; index++)
            {
                var foo = session.Advanced.LuceneQuery<SubscriptionExt>("Raven/DocumentsByEntityName").QueryResult.Results[index];
                var bar = JsonConvert.DeserializeObject<SubscriptionExt>(foo.ToString());
                // Copy the entity object into the view object
                MVCApp.Mapping.SubscriptionExtView view = new SubscriptionExtView();
                view.MessageType = bar.MessageType;
                MVCApp.Mapping.Address addr = bar.Clients.First();
                view.Machine = addr.Machine;
                view.Queue = addr.Queue;
                models.Add(view);
            }
        }
    }
    return View(models);
}
```

We will perform the following steps:

1. Open the session with the URL of RavenDB. We will need the `MyPublisher` database.
2. We will perform a Lucene search in the table to find our entities using the entity object format.
3. We will copy the entity object into the view object to display the results.

This will display the subscription storage from RavenDB.

Entering MongoDB

A very popular NoSQL database that is being used more and more in the NoSQL community is MongoDB. MongoDB is a document-oriented database system that uses JSON-like documents with dynamic schemas. For more information on MongoDB, see `http://en.wikipedia.org/wiki/MongoDB`. MongoDB can be found at `http://www.mongodb.org/` and the installation instructions for Windows can be found at `http://docs.mongodb.org/manual/tutorial/install-mongodb-on-windows`. MongoDB is written in C++, is open source, uses the Apache open source license that most Apache Foundation products run under, and is cross-platform.

To install MongoDB on Windows, download the installation file, which will install it today at `C:\Program Files\MongoDB 2.6 Standard`. To start the installation, open a command prompt, change the directory to `C:\Program Files\MongoDB 2.6 Standard\bin`, create the database directory using `md \data\db`, and start the database via `mongod.exe`.

```
Administrator: Command Prompt - mongod
C:\Program Files\MongoDB 2.6 Standard\bin>md \data\db

C:\Program Files\MongoDB 2.6 Standard\bin>mongod
mongod --help for help and startup options
2014-04-29T14:05:50.905-0600 [initandlisten] MongoDB starting : pid=232 port=270
17 dbpath=\data\db\ 64-bit host=WIN-UAUT16GPEQA
2014-04-29T14:05:50.906-0600 [initandlisten] targetMinOS: Windows 7/Windows Serv
er 2008 R2
2014-04-29T14:05:50.906-0600 [initandlisten] db version v2.6.0
2014-04-29T14:05:50.906-0600 [initandlisten] git version: 1c1c76aeca21c5983dc178
920f5052c298db616c
2014-04-29T14:05:50.906-0600 [initandlisten] build info: windows sys.getwindowsv
ersion(major=6, minor=1, build=7601, platform=2, service_pack='Service Pack 1')
BOOST_LIB_VERSION=1_49
2014-04-29T14:05:50.907-0600 [initandlisten] allocator: system
2014-04-29T14:05:50.908-0600 [initandlisten] options: {}
2014-04-29T14:05:50.948-0600 [initandlisten] journal dir=\data\db\journal
2014-04-29T14:05:50.965-0600 [initandlisten] recover : no journal files present,
 no recovery needed
2014-04-29T14:05:51.012-0600 [FileAllocator] allocating new datafile \data\db\lo
cal.ns, filling with zeroes...
2014-04-29T14:05:51.013-0600 [FileAllocator] creating directory \data\db\_tmp
2014-04-29T14:05:51.048-0600 [FileAllocator] done allocating datafile \data\db\l
ocal.ns, size: 16MB,  took 0.031 secs
2014-04-29T14:05:51.050-0600 [FileAllocator] allocating new datafile \data\db\lo
cal.0, filling with zeroes...
2014-04-29T14:05:51.170-0600 [FileAllocator] done allocating datafile \data\db\l
ocal.0, size: 64MB,  took 0.118 secs
2014-04-29T14:05:51.171-0600 [initandlisten] build index on: local.startup_log p
roperties: { v: 1, key: { _id: 1 }, name: "_id_", ns: "local.startup_log" }
```

We can check on the database by running many MongoDB tools listed at `http://docs.mongodb.org/ecosystem/tools/administration-interfaces/` or `http://stackoverflow.com/questions/3310242/do-any-visual-tools-exist-for-mongodb-for-windows`. One of the many tools is UMongo, which is cross-platform and built in Java; for more information see `http://edgytech.com/umongo/`. We can see the `MyPublisher` subscription tables in the publish/subscribe example.

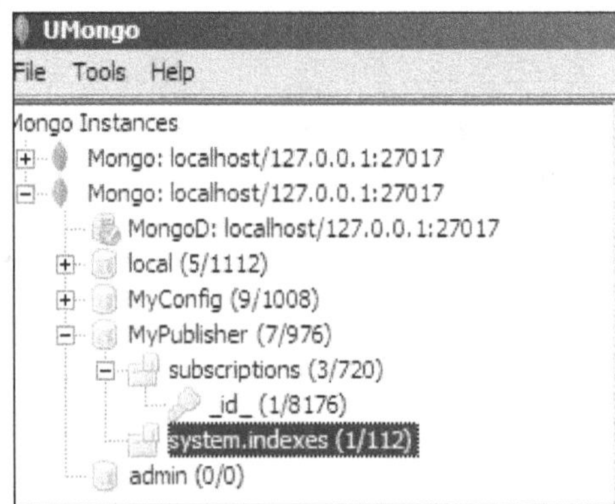

For developing in C#, `mongocsharpdriver` will need to be installed in the project through NuGet using `PM> Install-package mongocsharpdriver`. For more information, see `https://www.nuget.org/packages/mongocsharpdriver/`.

We will run through a small sample of C# MongoDB to get acclimatized to MongoDB before diving into it with NServiceBus. In this example, we will place configurations in the MongoDB local database.

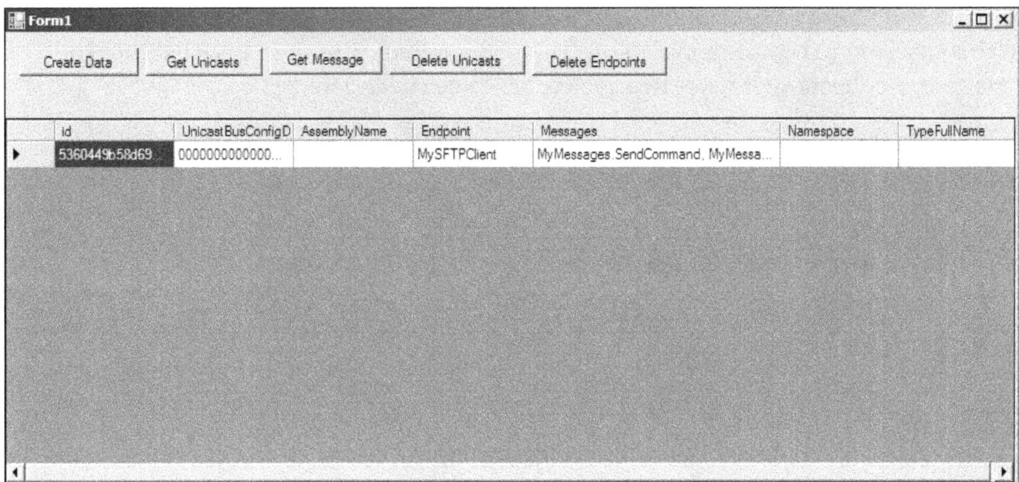

In order to build data, we need to define the object in a form of `BsonDocument`, to which we will add the collection of objects in the database table. BSON is Binary JSON. For more information, see `http://en.wikipedia.org/wiki/BSON`. The `BsonDocument` is the name-value pair of the data field to the data value that is added to the database. An in-depth discussion can be found at `http://docs.mongodb.org/ecosystem/tutorial/use-csharp-driver/`. We will connect to the database by setting the connection string in the `app.config` file to `Server=localhost:27017`:

```
private static void CreateMessageMaps(MessageEndpointMappingDB
mapping)
        {
            var client = new MongoClient(ConnectionString);
            var server = client.GetServer();
            MongoDatabase myConfig = server.GetDatabase("MyConfig");

            MongoCollection<BsonDocument> endpoints = myConfig.GetColl
ection<BsonDocument>("MessageEndpointMappingDB");
            BsonDocument endpoint = new BsonDocument {
                        { "AssemblyName", mapping.AssemblyName },
                        { "Endpoint", mapping.Endpoint },
                        { "Messages", mapping.Messages },
```

```
                    { "Namespace", mapping.Namespace },
                    { "TypeFullName", mapping.TypeFullName }
                    };

            endpoints.Insert(endpoint);
        }
```

We create the `BsonDocument`, which contains the field names of the database, for instance `Server AssemblyName`, and sets the associated string value in that field, in this case, `mapping.AssemblyName`. The `BsonDocument` is then inserted into the database, a collection of rows in `endpoints.Insert(endpoint)`.

To retrieve the collection of objects, we return the `MongoCollection` of objects and transform the collection into an object list:

```
public static List<MessageEndpointMappingDB> GetMessageMaps()
      {
            List<MessageEndpointMappingDB> endpointList = new List<Messa
geEndpointMappingDB>();

            var client = new MongoClient(ConnectionString);
            var server = client.GetServer();
            MongoDatabase myConfig = server.GetDatabase("MyConfig");

            MongoCollection<MessageEnd
pointMappingDB> endpoints = myConfig.
GetCollection<MessageEndpointMappingDB>("MessageEndpointMappingDB");
            foreach (var endpoint in endpoints.FindAll())
            {
                endpointList.Add(endpoint);
            }

            return endpointList;
      }
```

To delete the table, we simply perform `Drop` on the table, which is a `MongoCollection` of objects related to the table itself. MongoDB is not an ORM. It is a document-oriented database, meaning it handles the database as a collection of documents, in this case, BSON documents (a collection of documents). Think of each document as a row in the database and each field in the row as a name-value pair:

```
public static void DeleteMessageMaps()
        {
            var client = new MongoClient(ConnectionString);
            var server = client.GetServer();
            MongoDatabase myConfig = server.GetDatabase("MyConfig");

            MongoCollection<MessageEnd
pointMappingDB> endpoints = myConfig.
GetCollection<MessageEndpointMappingDB>("MessageEndpointMappingDB");
            endpoints.Drop();
        }
```

This was a simple introduction into MongoDB.

NServiceBus MongoDB persistence

For the NuGet installation of the MongoDB persistence NServiceBus references, they can be found at `http://www.nuget.org/packages/NServiceBus.Persistence.MongoDb/` and the associated source code can be found at `https://github.com/tekmaven/NServiceBus.Persistence.MongoDb`.

In order to create the MongoDB subscription information for applications such as `MyPublisher`, place the MongoDB configurations in `IBus` after installing the references through NuGet, for instance, `MongoDbSubscriptionStorage()`:

```
namespace MyPublisher
{
    class EndpointConfig :  IConfigureThisEndpoint, AsA_Publisher,IWantCustomInitialization
    {
        public void Init()
        {
            Configure.With()
                .DefaultBuilder()
                //this overrides the NServiceBus default convention of IEvent
                .DefiningEventsAs(t => t.Namespace != null && t.Namespace.StartsWith("MyMessages"))
                .MongoDbPersistence()
                .MongoDbSagaPersister()
                .MongoDbSubscriptionStorage()
                ;}


    }
}
```

Summary

We covered a lot of information in this chapter regarding persistence. This chapter has a lot of associated code. We covered the highlights of working with NSB and databases. NSB does take care of most of the workings of databases and mappings however, because of the flexibility of NSB, various pieces can be extended through C# to notify and monitor a variety of SQL Server pieces.

The next chapter will dive into the working of the Cloud. We will discuss the coding practices we have learned so far to produce more end-to-end systems.

8
The NSB Cloud

In this chapter, we will be focusing on snippets of NServiceBus in the cloud after a very brief introduction to the cloud and some of its services. While NServiceBus has support as a service bus for the Microsoft Cloud of Azure, it is also a beneficial tool to integrate into other cloud technologies as well, as all clouds have support for third-party integration to pass data through web services.

In this chapter, we will cover the following topics:

- Introducing the cloud and NSB
- Introducing PaaS, IaaS, and SaaS
- Cloud vendors
- Using Microsoft Azure
- Adding NServiceBus
- NSB in the mobile world
- Questions that were answered

Introducing the cloud and NSB

At the beginning of this chapter, NSB Version 5.0 for Azure is in beta. This chapter will explain how to use NSB without DTC. NSB is getting integrated more and more into the Azure queues and Azure SQL Server, but the evolution will likely involve Big Data as well. Just as computers were using 4 MB of RAM in the past, and now more than 16 GB of RAM is pretty normal, queuing of data will increase as well. Basic Big Data through databus has been around for some time; however, payment engines and customer databases are always in the need of processing large files to transfer data and funds. To understand the cloud is to understand the offloading of queuing, small data, and large data into cloud servers, which are managed through cloud wizards. This results in a loss of the on-premise viewing of fine details to some degree, as the remote servers are dependent on the cloud wizards.

The NSB tools are also adapting. ServiceInsight has grown to handle more details with sequence diagrams for debugging outside of Visual Studio and MSMQ as well. The tools are moving from being integrated locally into a physical server to being integrated into a remote server where many of the details of the server itself may be less important as servers are virtualized offsite. For instance, in the future, ServiceInsight will add saga sequence diagrams to add more detail than the current flow diagrams. The following sequence diagram shows what is in store for ServiceInsight:

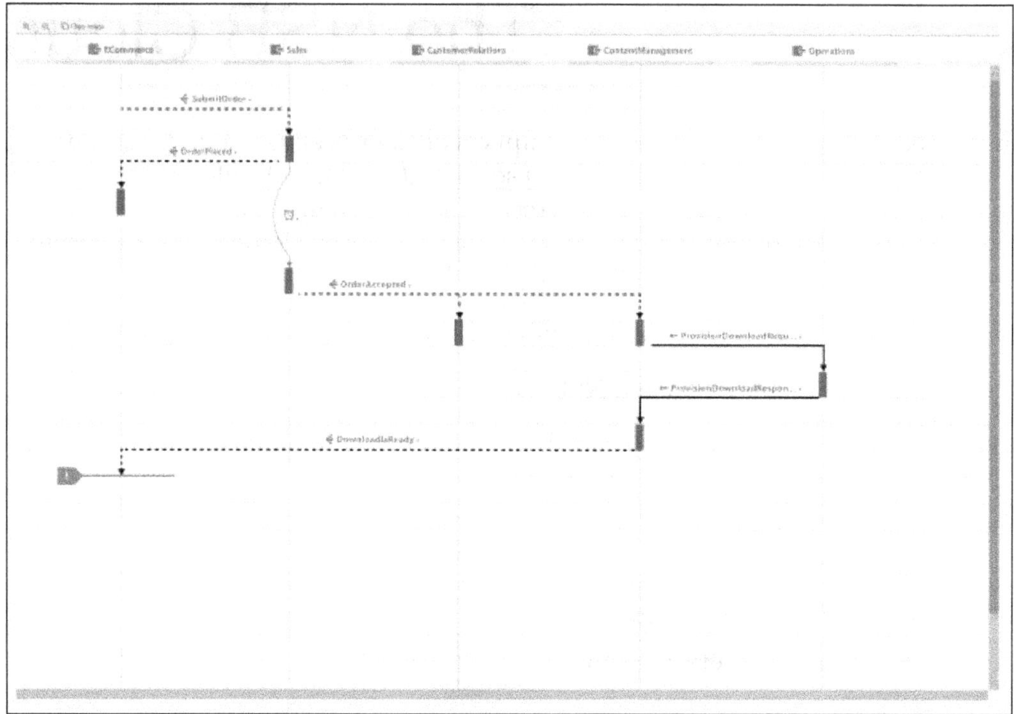

However, DTC is not supported in many cloud technology queues and RabbitMQ, but enhancements are being made in NSB Version 5 and above to compensate this, mostly by keeping track of messages that have either already been processed or about to be processed in the transactional integrity of tables.

Introducing PaaS, IaaS, and SaaS

In the evolution of cloud computing, there are the concepts of **Platform as a Service** (**PaaS**), **Software as a Service** (**SaaS**), and **Infrastructure as a Service** (**IaaS**).

PaaS is the cloud computing service that provides a computing platform and a solution stack as a service. In PaaS, the cloud solution provider provides the operating systems, databases, web servers, development tools, and other services that are required to host the consumer's application. IaaS is at a level below the PaaS, as it provides the virtual (as well as physical) machines, servers, storage options, load balancers, networks, and more basic components. SaaS is at a higher level than PaaS, as it is the software distribution model in which the applications themselves are hosted by a vendor or service provider and made available to customers over a network, typically the Internet. Here is an image that shows how Windows Azure supports IaaS and PaaS:

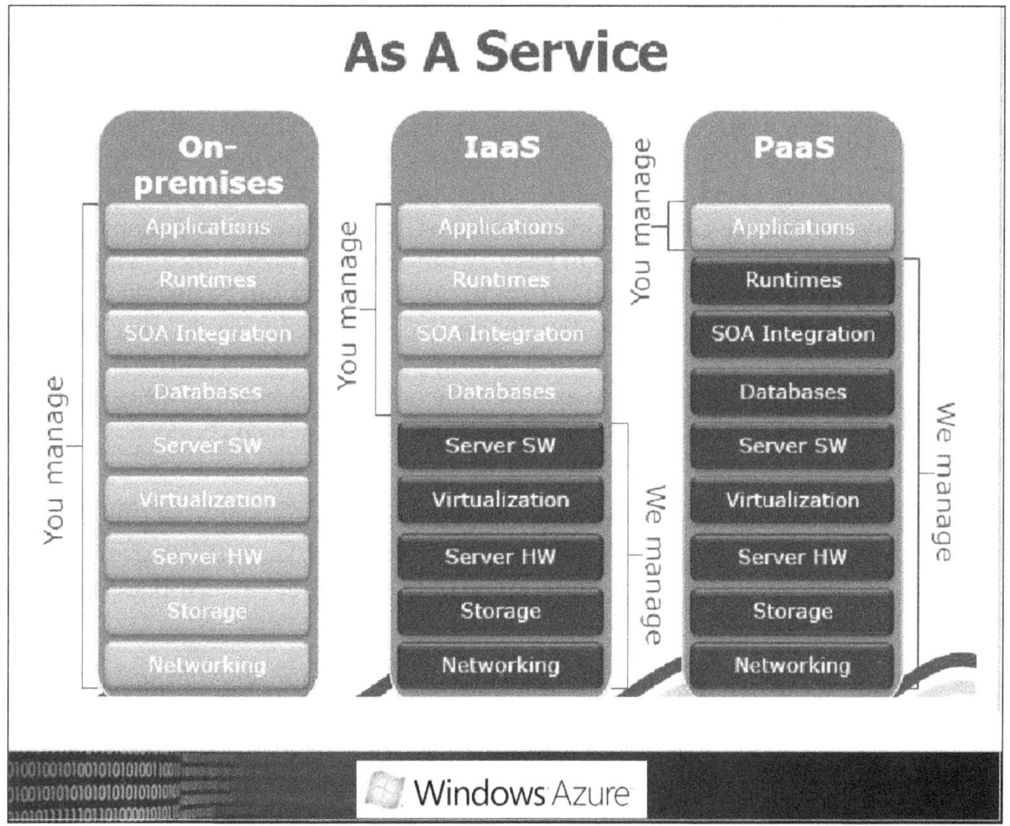

Depending on the cloud vendor, some of these terminologies may be termed slightly different. While all cloud vendors support these components, they differ on the level of abstraction for these components. For example, Windows Azure will allow you to configure a virtual machine in the cloud, while Salesforce clouds will not allow you to know which infrastructure you are running on. The cloud vendor that is selected, as well as licensing, will dictate your throttling level of transactions and the limitation of your resources. There will be many limitations on resources and transactions as you are sharing resources that other companies may be using as well and paying more to utilize those resources. In the cloud world, consumption of resources and transactions is based on licensing. There are many resources available by all cloud vendors to develop in their cloud, and there is a lot of help available as their goal is to get you to utilize their cloud as much as possible as that is their revenue stream.

Cloud vendors

There are many cloud vendors, for example, Salesforce.com, Microsoft Azure, **Google App Engine** (**GAE**), and **Amazon Elastic Compute Cloud** (**EC2**). Salesforce uses a Java-like language called Apex. The GAE uses Java, Python, PHP, and Go. Microsoft Azure uses .NET but also supports SDKs for Java, Python, PHP, and NodeJS. Amazon uses Java, Python, PHP, Ruby, and .NET. NServiceBus supports both the Microsoft Azure Cloud and the Amazon Cloud. The cloud solutions have many templates that are considered to have an **out-of-box** (**OOB**) functionality to build the cloud solution. There are also extra modules that can be installed; many are free, and some require a subscription, such as Salesforce's AppExchange, `https://appexchange.salesforce.com`. The supporting engines and programming languages are used to extend none of the OOB functionalities. These are additional modules or applications, for example, which connect additional Salesforce features into Android or use Google mail.

While many cloud vendors, such as Amazon and Azure, can use NServiceBus to interface directly into their queuing solution, other vendors, such as Salesforce, which has its own language Apex, built on top of Java, cannot have NSB access its queues as an ESB engine.

As Salesforce has connectors into other products such as Android APIs and Google mail, connectors would have to be used to queue through external ESBs such as NSB as well. Most connectors are built through the use of web services. Some of this methodology is described at `http://www.ramonsmits.com/2013/04/08/receiving-salesforce-notifcations-with-nservicebus.html`.

Developing an application from scratch seems easier when developing in the cloud as many cloud vendors have templates and wizards to create data from scratch. The complexity increases if an on-premise solution has to be migrated to an off-premise cloud solution that is language dependent. For instance, if you have a .NET solution, moving to Microsoft Azure may be relatively easy, but moving to Google Apps may require a migration to Java first. Moving to Salesforce may require multiple migrations to the data first, and then building the GUI through VisualForce, the Salesforce visual interface, as most of the underlying infrastructure of the Salesforce cloud, Force.com, is not exposed. For this reason, there are several tools to move data into Salesforce objects, such as the data loader tool, `https://developer.salesforce.com/page/Data_Loader`.

The following screenshot shows a sample VisualForce screen:

For the Salesforce Apex language, there is a Developer Console that can be used in the Force.com cloud to develop any code-specific application; however, the thought with Salesforce is to get away from coding a lot of the data and visual objects. An example of the Developer Console is shown in the following screenshot:

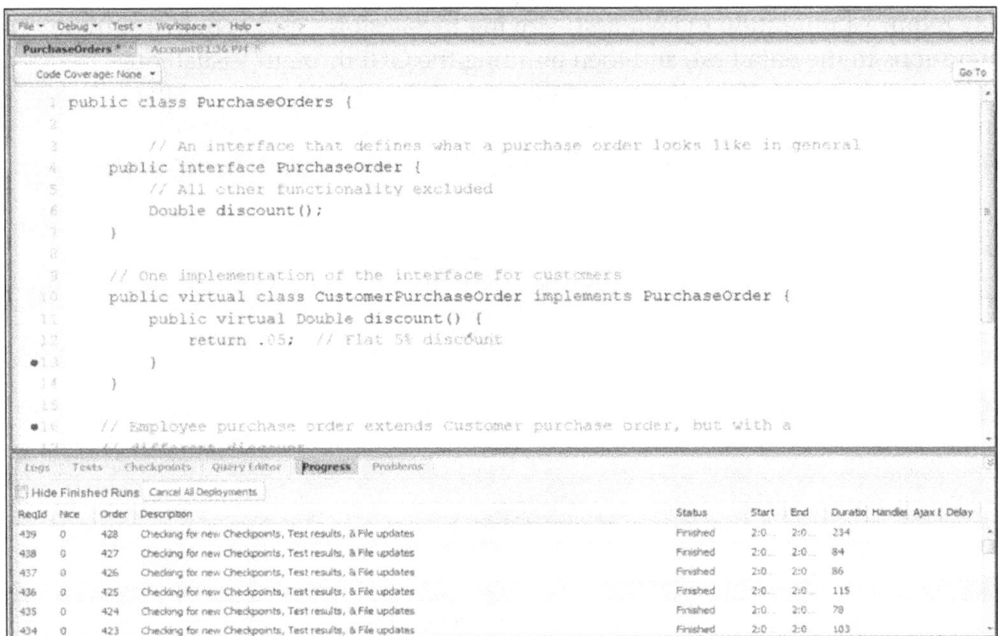

The issue with many off-premise scenarios is that while developing in the cloud, if a current solution is currently working on-premise, there has to be a period of time for turnover from on-premise to off-premise systems during which the data has to be synched to both systems at the same time, and outages have to be scheduled. The data has to be synched not only on a legacy system and a new system, but also on the GUI and business logic as well. The switch from a legacy system to a new system needs to be as seamless as possible to keep the customers of the system happy.

One of the problems frequently overlooked when moving from old systems to new systems is that while new systems are being built, old systems may also be updated with enhancements, which have to be updated in the new system as well before it is completed. There are myriad issues involved while creating a new system, which are beyond the scope of this book, but it will suffice to say that the more complex the older system is, the more it can affect a new system. For the many reasons of jumping from an old solution from an on-premise data center to a new solution off-premise in the cloud, some of the changes can be eased with creating hybrid solutions where an on-premise data is shared to the new cloud solution until a complete migration is accomplished. For this purpose, NSB is a great solution for marshaling data and business logic from an on-premise solution for an off-premise solution.

Let's not say that this is a replacement for data warehousing where a central repository is used for data, but when we update one system with a response of a completed message, error, or another message that is performing an action through SOA, we update the other system with the same message as well. The following diagram shows a simple example where the on-premise contains most of the logic to update a payment through a third-party service, but the response is sent to the cloud as well that is duplicating some of the services to update not only the data but the business processes as well:

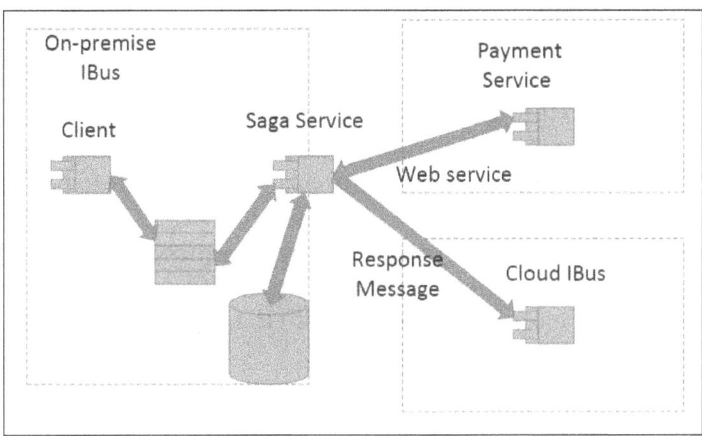

This example shows the distribution of the ESB messages to the cloud through the message queues. The Azure and Amazon Clouds would easily support this design. However, some cloud vendors will not expose their queuing mechanisms, and for this reason, WCF integration could be used as a connector to update the services inside more proprietary clouds such as Salesforce.

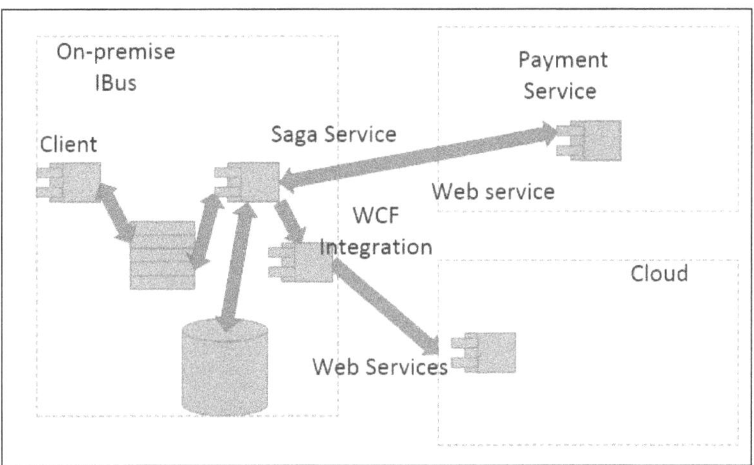

The service method of transferring data is a semi-real-time method of transferring small amounts of data from one system to another through a secure pipe of HTTPS using digital certificates. We also know that we can transfer messages through a secure HTTPS gateway using NServiceBus. A lot of these messages have very small limits by default; for MSMQ, we have 4 MB, and the default for WCF is roughly 64 KB. Some of these limits can be changed by using an NSB databus to set new limits in WCF. However, it will not be sending very large files for a daily upload of files. For this reason, Salesforce has a data loader.

In many systems, there are similar processes that derive from the **Extract-Transform-Load (ETL)** process. See `http://en.wikipedia.org/wiki/Extract,_transform,_load`. An ETL process will extract data from a system, say a SQL Server table that had changes for that day; it will transform into data that can be loaded into the system that needs the daily data, say an XML data file, and then load it into another system, say a Salesforce Cloud system. Some systems may simply need a daily load of the information instead of a second-by-second replay of the data that has changed. The thought is that instead of sending web services or messages to cloud queues, a daily snapshot can be taken from the on-premise MSMQ, or a SQL table, and sent securely to the cloud to be uploaded through SFTP, a secure version of FTP. The diagram will be similar to this picture:

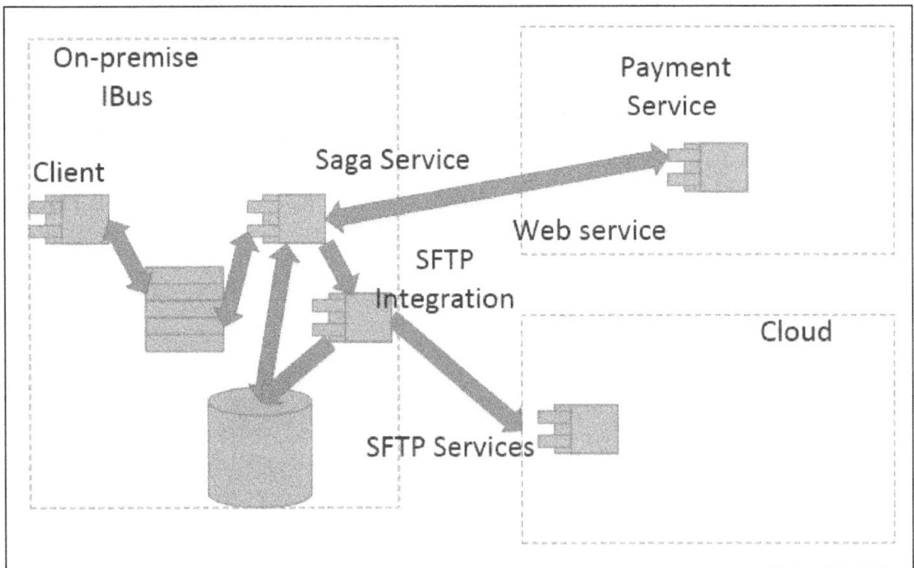

We could exponentially come up with a variety of ways to update the cloud with local data or to load data to a new cloud system. Auditing and reporting should be one of the characteristics of any form of sending data to the cloud, as any organization may be called one day from an organization, such as the IRS, to show that the customers were initially loaded and validated into the cloud solution. For this reason, using the saga design pattern would be of a great benefit for taking a snapshot of messages that were sent to the cloud solution through many of these means. Even in the SFTP solution, we could take a snapshot of which records were put into a file and verify the sending of the data to be uploaded into the cloud database. The benefit of NSB is that we can take snapshots of messages, and audit through queues and report on the interaction and endpoints.

Using Microsoft Azure

The benefit of Azure is that it can be used in Microsoft data centers around the world. The purpose of Azure is to have a Software Development Kit for websites, virtual machines, and cloud services for either the cloud, on-premise, or a hybrid between the two. Some cloud technologies, such as Salesforce, are cloud-centric and not on-premise-centric. The Windows Azure SDK is considered open source from Microsoft, yes, open source, and it can be found at `https://github.com/Azure`. There are Power Shell tools for Windows to deploy (see `https://github.com/Azure/azure-sdk-tools`) and even command-line tools for the Linux and Mac operating systems (see `http://research.microsoft.com/en-us/projects/azure/windows-azure-for-linux-and-mac-users.pdf` and `http://azure.microsoft.com/en-us/documentation/articles/command-line-tools/`).

Just as in Salesforce and other cloud technologies, there are galleries with pre-created applications and modules (see `http://azure.microsoft.com/en-us/gallery/store/`), and there are wizards to build the sites and samples (see `http://azure.microsoft.com/en-us/develop/net/samples/`). Once you access Azure, you have the ability to create various applications and services. There are many applications and services on the left that can be created. All clouds use a pay-for-what-you-use model, mostly in production, for licensing. In Azure, there is an Azure calculator to calculate the costs, `http://azure.microsoft.com/en-us/pricing/calculator/`.

In Azure, there are three Execution models, meaning, there are normally three different ways to deploy end-to-end applications:

- You can create a website, meaning, you can add backend storage, messaging, and other pieces to it.
- You can create a virtual machine, meaning, you could add various pieces as you would in a Linux or Windows Server to also deploy applications and a website.

- You can create cloud services, such as web service, which also contains backend storage, messaging, and other pieces.

The websites can be created in PHP, ASP.NET, Node.js, or Python. The website can be created so that the platform, patches, and all the platform pieces are handled for you. Since it is ASP, it could be built locally and even deployed through the source control. You can even create a domain, other than the cloud domain, for this website to be accessed on the Internet.

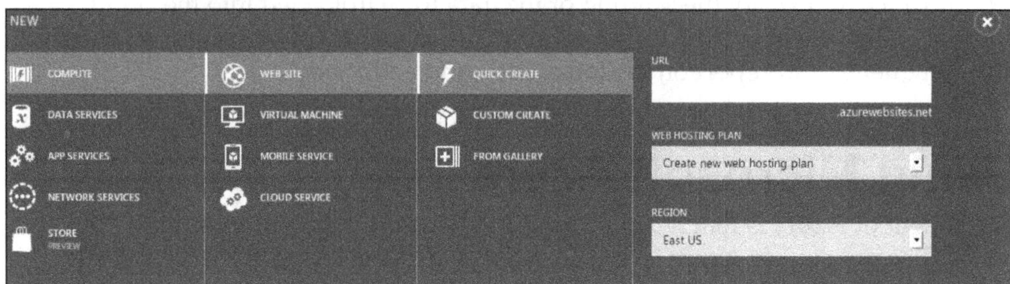

After a website is created, it can be edited in the cloud or locally through WebMatrix (see `http://www.microsoft.com/web/post/how-to-edit-a-site-hosted-on-windows-azure-with-webmatrix`). Using WebMatrix is similar in nature to some of the previous MVC examples, and Microsoft MVC can still be used in Microsoft Azure. A simple page can be done in HTML with WebMatrix to build a website in Azure in the following screenshot:

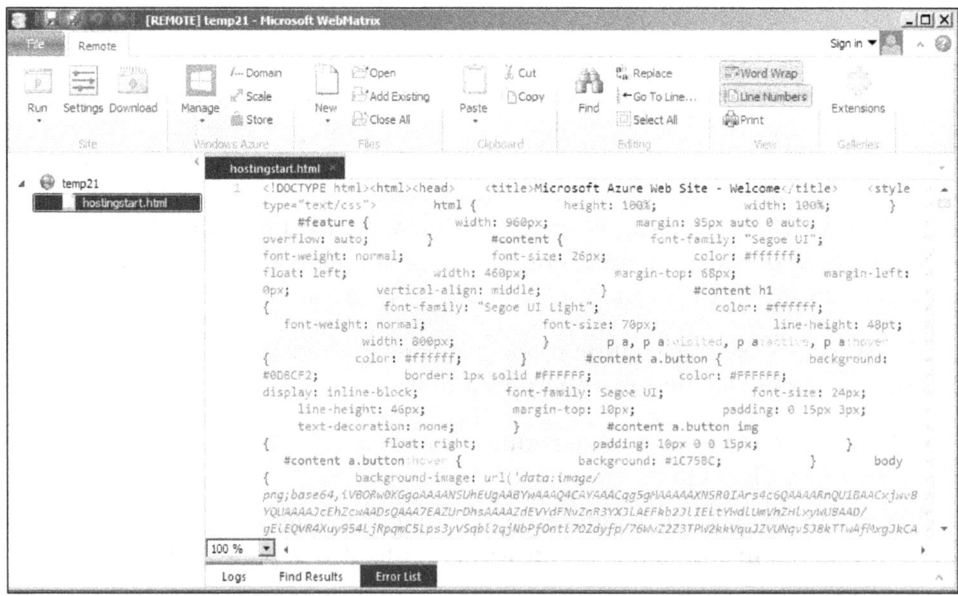

More complex websites can be created using MVC-EF in Visual Studio and then deployed to Azure using the publish interface in Visual Studio. So, we can use the previous chapter's MVC-EF examples as well in Azure. However, WebMatrix is a nice tool to create a sample Azure website quickly, and combinations of MVC with Razor and WebMatrix can be used to create HTML5 pages.

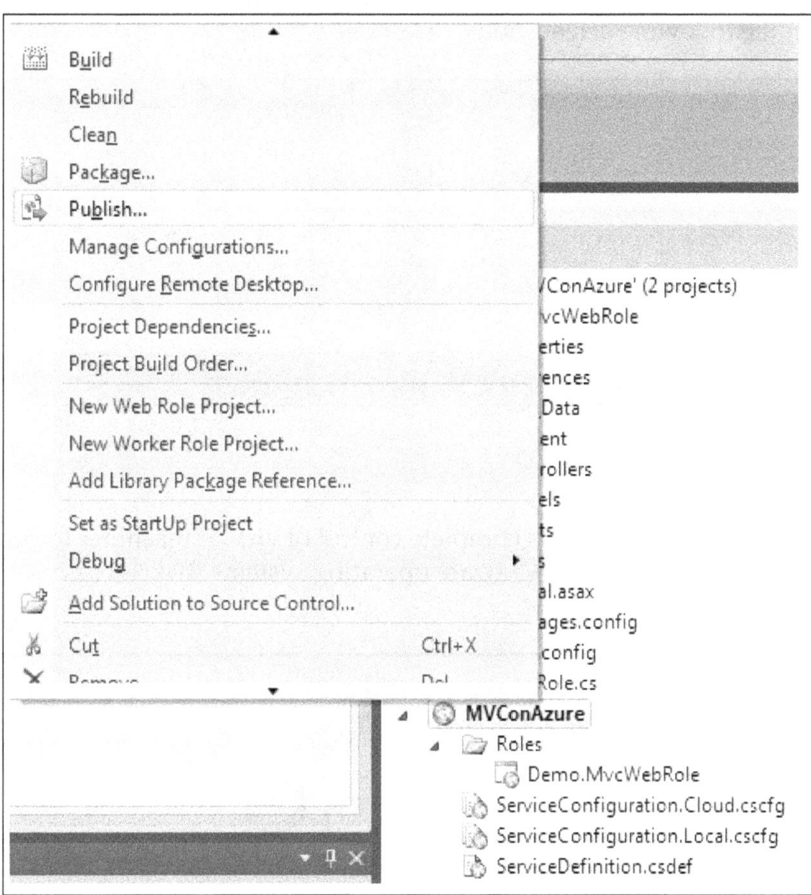

The Azure SDK is integrated into Visual Studio. The differences will be that Azure Cloud services, such as the cloud website, storage, SQL database, active directory, and other Windows services can be used instead of the local on-premise ones. A point to note is that NServiceBus is integrated into Visual Studio as well. We can install the Azure SDK 2.3 for Visual Studio 2012 using the Microsoft Web Platform Installer from `http://www.microsoft.com/web/downloads/platform.aspx`. This is shown in the following screenshot:

Virtual machines

Microsoft Azure gives customers complete control of virtual machines to run in the cloud. There are many base VMware operating systems that can be created in the cloud.

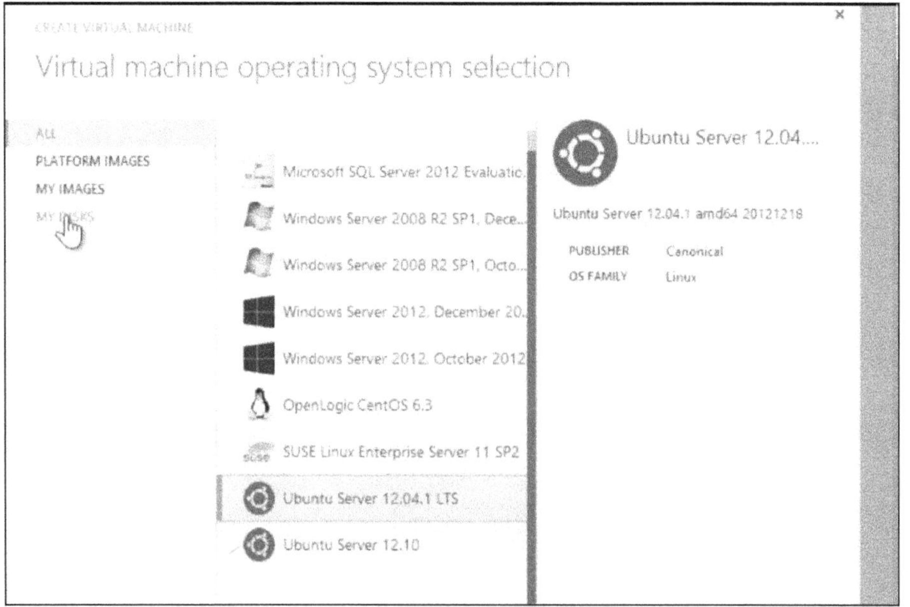

We could easily create a virtual machine for Windows Server 2012, and utilize many of the features that we would use locally in creating an application. The difference would be that the licensing and administration would be based on cloud-based tools and wizards.

Utilizing virtual machines off-premise is very much like having one on-premise, except that you are paying for someone else to maintain it off-site. Therefore, if MSMQ and SQL Server are configured on the virtual machine, they could be used in a way similar to on-site NSB examples.

Not only can you deploy websites and virtual machines, but you can deploy other applications as well, such as services that live in the cloud, which are called cloud services. These can be servers or other types of services that a person would normally deploy on a server. For instance, a backend process such as NServiceBus could be considered a cloud service. IIS running in the cloud is considered a cloud service. Many of the web services running in the cloud will be considered cloud services.

The cloud service also must have a role to run the service. There are two main roles to run cloud services: one is the web role to run IIS, and websites built in PHP and CGI, and the other is the worker role that is more geared to run backend processes or backend cloud services. Both roles can run the .NET framework services, native code, and the Windows Server services.

A cloud service can be published or packaged from Visual Studio. To publish a cloud service, built in the Azure SDK, it will package and deploy the cloud service to your Azure cloud services.

Another method to deploy a cloud service is to package it locally and upload the pieces into the Azure cloud services to deploy it interactively with Azure.

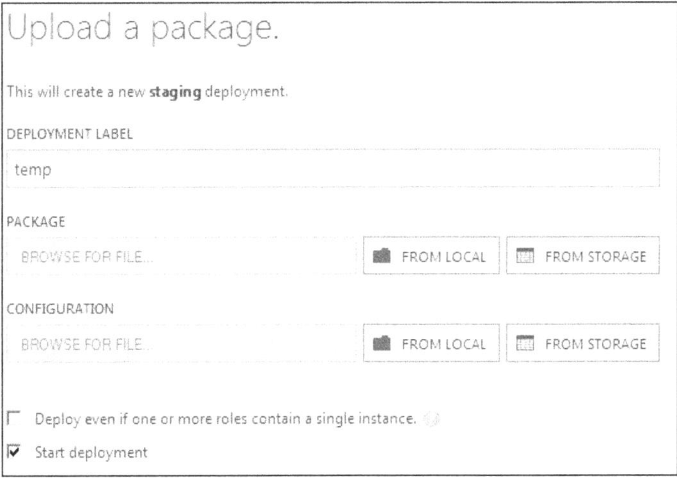

Depending on the cloud vendor, you can determine your development methodology. We have provided some small examples for developing in Salesforce. While developing in Google Apps, you can use the Eclipse IDE in Java, Apache Tomcat, and the Mule ESB on-premise, and then upload it to the Google Cloud. For Azure, you can develop your solution on-premise as well as in Visual Studio, and then upload it and run it from Azure Cloud. However, for Azure, you will need cloud development packages. There is a cloud service package, which is a development ZIP file that will be deployed in a `.cspkg` format. It will need to be deployed with a cloud configuration file as well, which is in the `.cscfg` file format.

However, in order to interact with the cloud services of Azure, and work with Azure services locally, the Azure SDK has to be installed into the local machine mentioned earlier.

For storage service's data management, we can create a SQL database in the cloud, and use a SQL database on-premise from the cloud, or a hybrid thereof. The main difference is that the connection string in the SQL Server database points towards an on-premise or off-premise server. A virtual network can be set up between the cloud and an on-premise LAN to provide a secure network connection. When connecting to SQL Servers, IPs have to be explicitly allowed through the firewall to the cloud database. There is a lot of built-in security to protect the cloud services. The Azure SDK interfaces through Visual Studio so that there are tools to build SQL tables, stored procedures, and more, from Visual Studio to the Azure cloud SQL database.

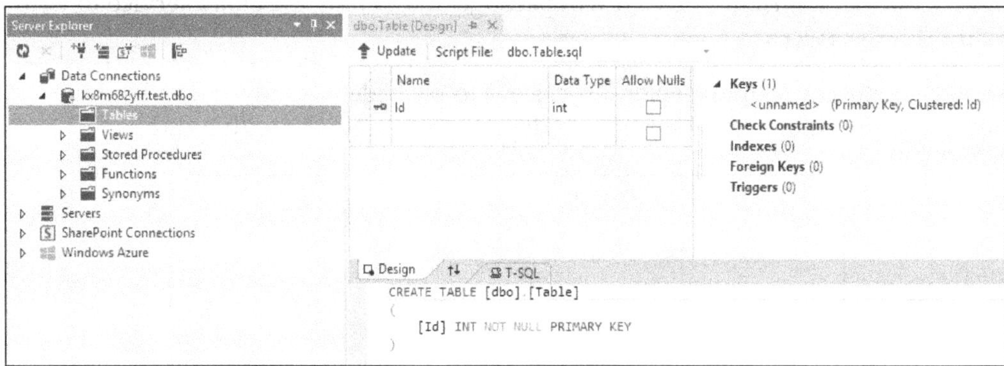

We can even manage the SQL database in the Azure Cloud from SQL Management Studio.

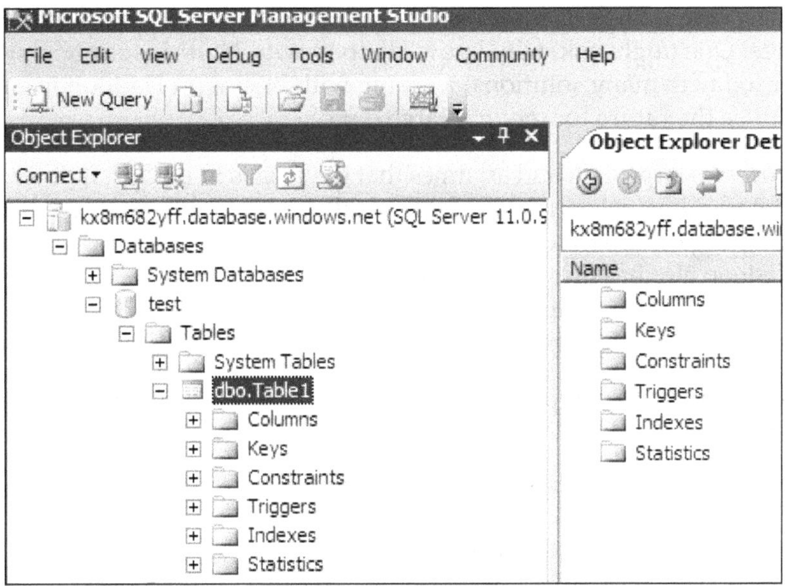

This, in turn, means that we can use it to create entity models, and use the remote SQL database for NServiceBus persistence as we would in a local SQL database, and any other coding that we would do in a local SQL database. The only difference is that it is living in the Azure cloud. Here, we are developing entities from the cloud database.

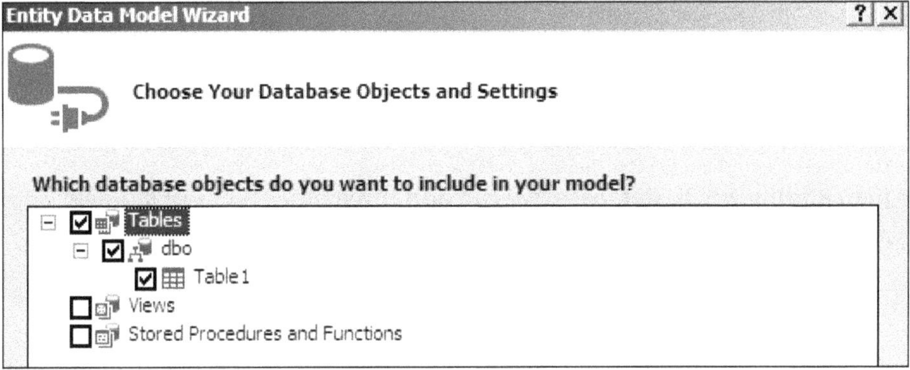

For business analytics and reporting, normal SQL Server tools can be used in the cloud, such as **SQL Server Reporting Services** (**SSRS**); there is reporting on the SQL database that normally comes with the SQL Server as well as Hadoop. The SQL reporting can be to the off-premise in similar manner to the on-premise SQL reporting with SSRS. In the off-premise cloud, there are additional Azure management tools that can be used.

However, working with SQL Server is for medium-size data in the cloud. There is also Big Data. One might ask, why know Hadoop with NSB? Just as NSB works with SQL Server today in many solutions, working with NSB with Hadoop in a databus solution will be the future for moving large data.

Hadoop processes large data and assumes that the data is in BLOBs. It processes data in parallel by running logic across multiple parallel machines by MapReduce jobs. By processing large chunks independently using **Hadoop Distributed File System (HDFS)**, Hadoop also has its own SQL-like query language called Apache Hive Interface (see `http://hive.apache.org/`). For non-SQL-like query languages, there is the Pig Latin Hadoop language called Apache Pig (see `http://pig.apache.org/`).

HDInsight is Microsoft's 100 percent compatible distribution of Hadoop that is managed in Azure or on the Windows Server, as shown in the following screenshot:

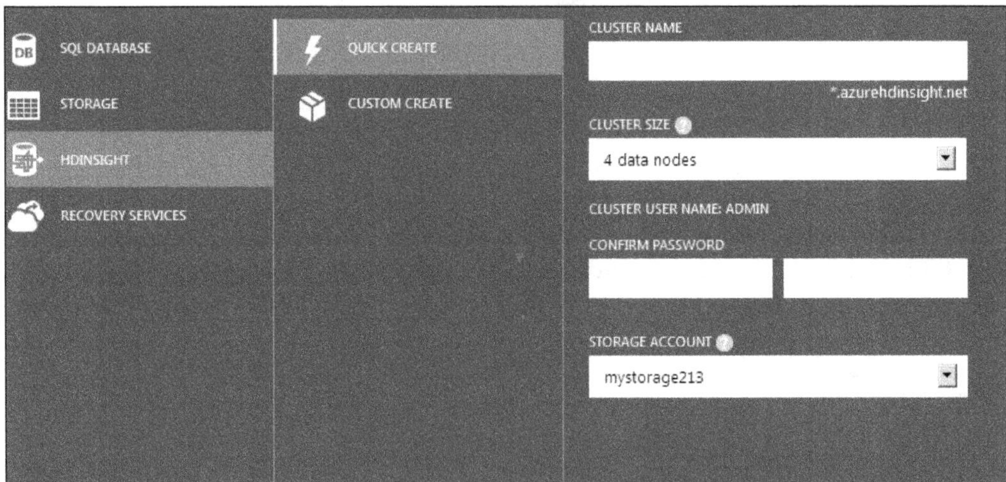

Other than adding a SQL database, we can add three other types of storage:

- A table storage that is based on a key-value No-SQL table format
- A **Binary Large Object** (**BLOB**) storage for binary storage, such as video files
- A queue storage to store messages

A BLOB is a group of containers, which is just unstructured data, such as a video or audio file stored as binary storage in a data store.

Table storage is a No-SQL solution instead of the relational SQL database. It can store data across multiple machines. Each table can contain partitions across multiple machines. These tables have entities with partition and row keys to access the entity. Access to the table data uses a key-value pair to access the data store. These tables do not enforce a SQL table schema that a SQL server would do for storage. Since there is very little enforcement to create a table, the objects are loosely coupled to the access, as there are just key-value pair references. This helps in access speed as management of the data is minimal, and requires less storage as various SQL schema pieces for table management are not used. Thus, it can take less storage, resulting in less cost for the data. For table storage, there is a partition key, row key, and a timestamp:

- **Partition key**: This is a unique key associated with a partition as a collection of all associated rows. This is defined to specify which partition to access. An example is the name of the table.
- **Row key**: This is a unique key to identify the row in the partition, and is usually a unique ID.
- **Timestamp**: This is the time at which the row was updated, and is updated by Azure.

Queue storage is very similar to storing messages in MSMQ, except that the management tools are in Azure Cloud. NSB uses Azure queues in a manner similar to MSMQ and SQL Queues. However, Azure queues do not use DTC. There is a lot of support from NServiceBus for both Azure queues and Azure service bus queues.

Just as many of the Azure Cloud items can be managed through the Azure SDK and Visual Studio, storage queues can also be managed through the Visual Studio 2012 Server Explorer.

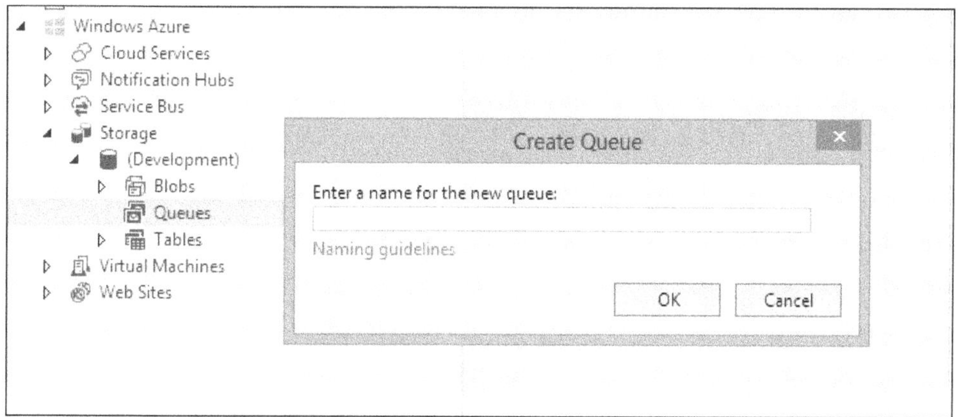

Besides using Visual Studio, there are many open source tools such as Azure Storage Explorer, found at `http://azurestorageexplorer.codeplex.com/`.

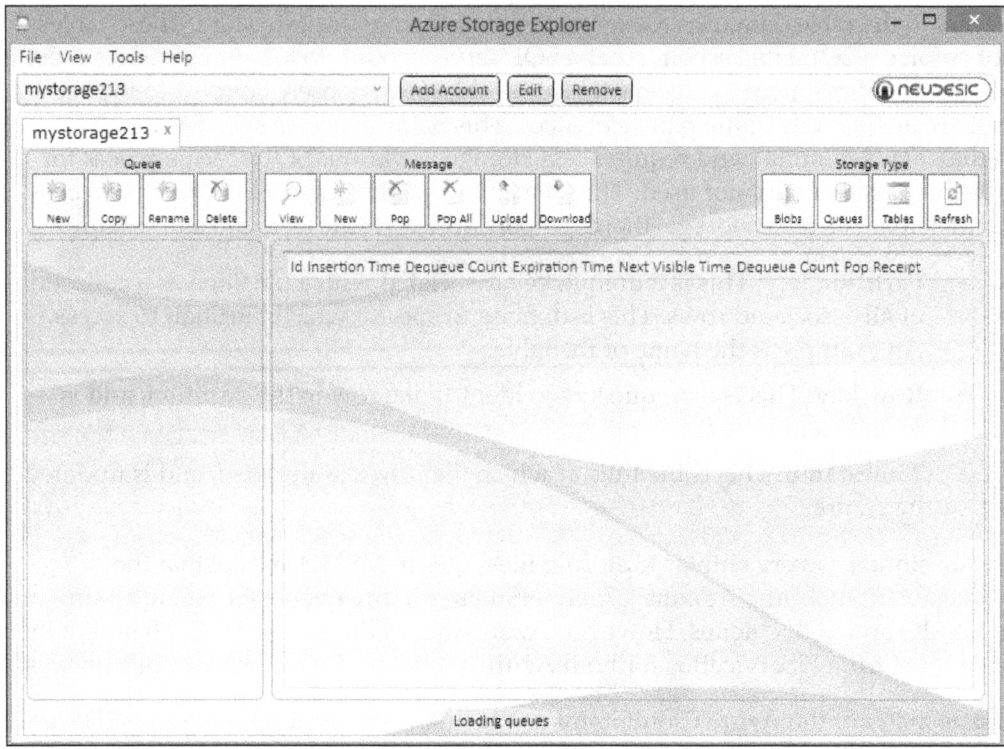

These are just some of the local tools working through the Azure portal in the Azure Cloud that allow a person to monitor, log, send notifications, and more, on the storage being allocated for use.

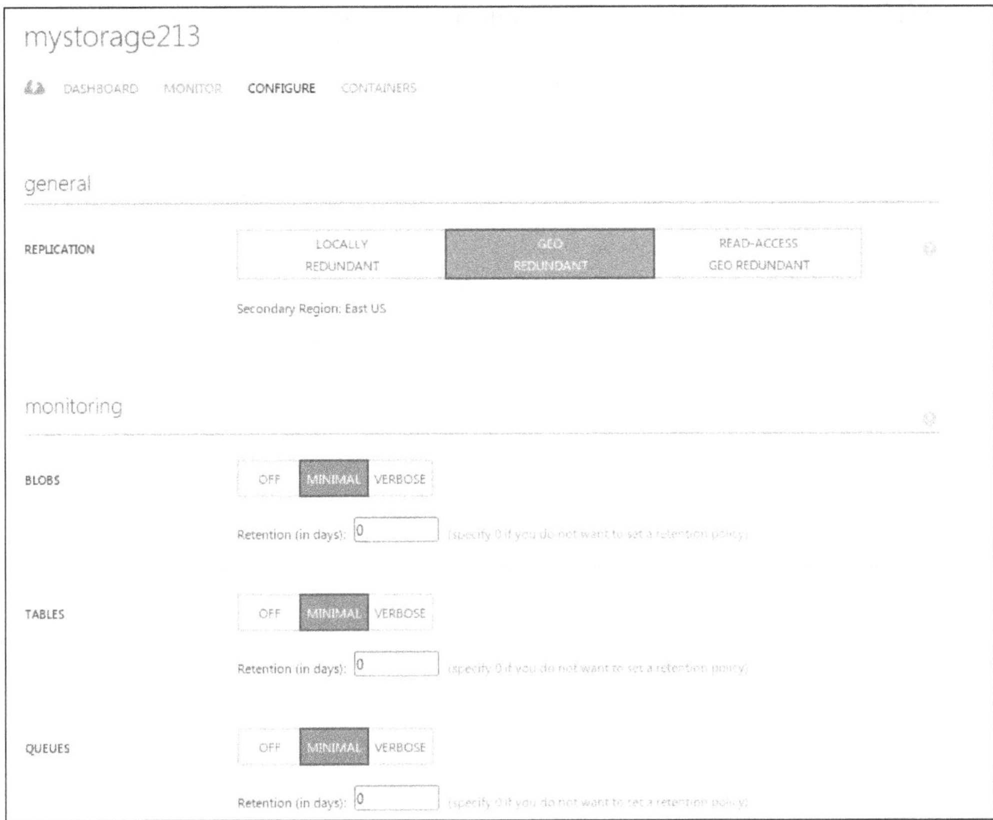

Azure Service Bus

The Windows Azure Service Bus provides a hosted, secure, and widely available infrastructure for widespread communication between different messaging endpoints to include web services. The service bus communicates via three methods:

- **Queues**: You can perform one-to-one messaging through queues
- **Topics**: You can send one-to-many publish/subscribe messages from one publish endpoint to many subscriber endpoints
- **Relays**: One-to-one requests-replies that will not be queuing passed between endpoints

Microsoft.ServiceBus.dll will be used to connect to the service bus, extend the service bus, as well as work with the WCF and Windows workflow when interacting with the service bus. The Azure Service Bus can be created in the Azure portal by first creating the service bus namespace.

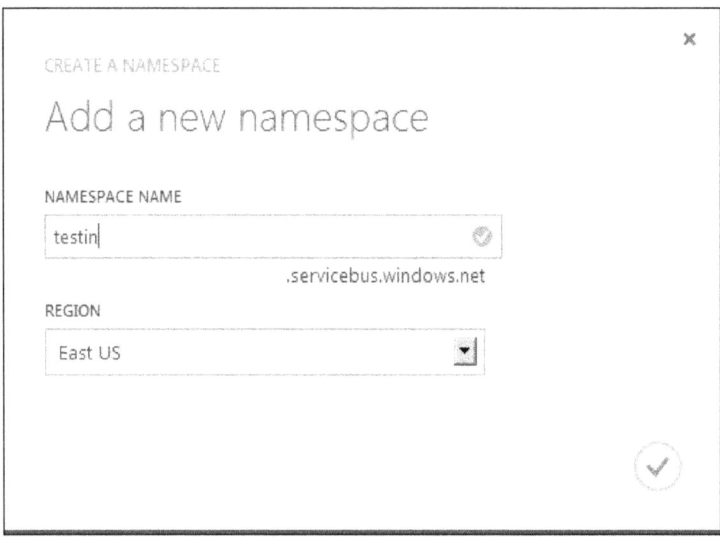

We can create the service bus queues, topics, and relays in the Azure portal, and we can also manage the service bus through Visual Studio after it was initially created in the Azure portal. The service bus will use a primary key and a connection string (which is not too dissimilar from a connection string to a SQL database) to be accessed.

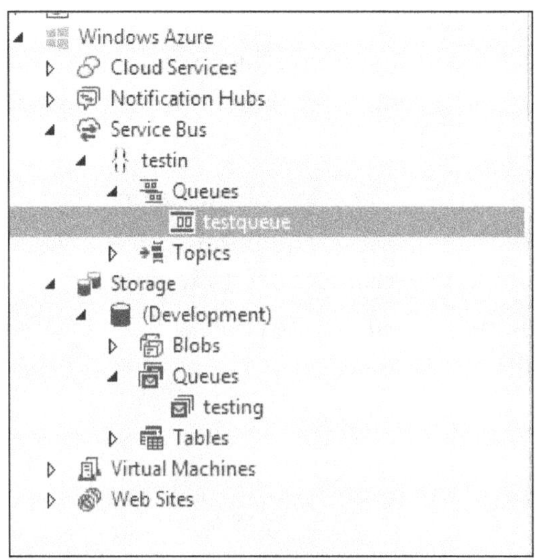

Also note that there is a difference between storage queues and service bus queues. Note the different names in this example. Service bus queues have more features for management such as guaranteed FIFO, while Azure Queues have less manageability built in. See `http://msdn.micosoft.com/en-us/library/hh767287.aspx`.
I contrast the differences as the service bus queues have some features such as NServiceBus, while Azure Queues are more generic in nature, such as SQL Queues. When creating an Azure service bus queue, we can see the granularity that is offered during the creation.

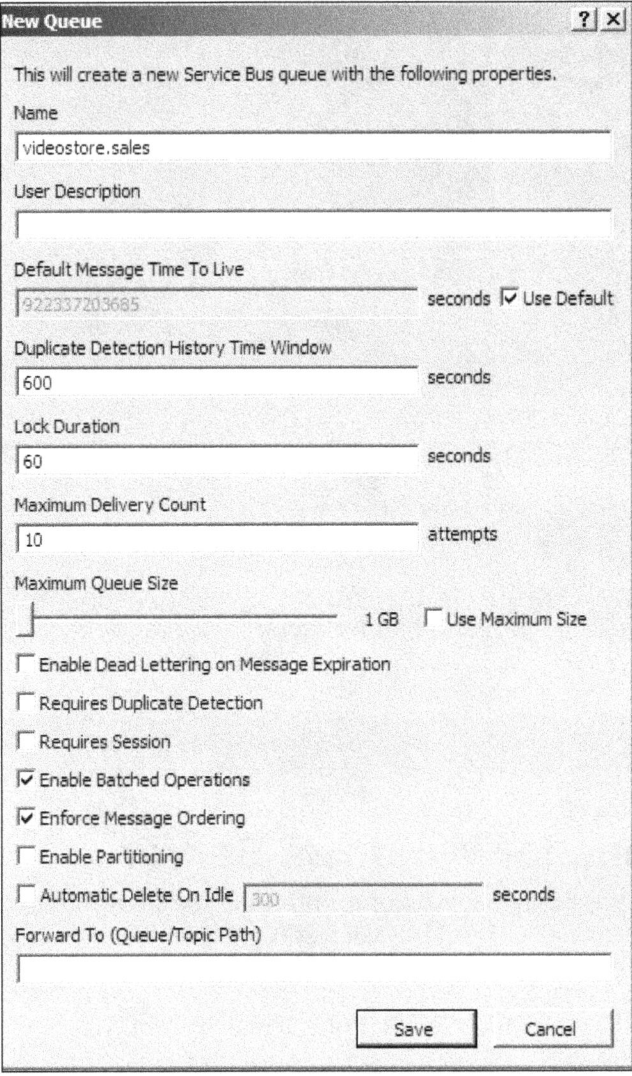

There are additional tools for exploring the Azure service bus, such as the Server Bus Explorer found at `http://code.msdn.microsoft.com/windowsazure/Service-Bus-Explorer-f2abca5a`.

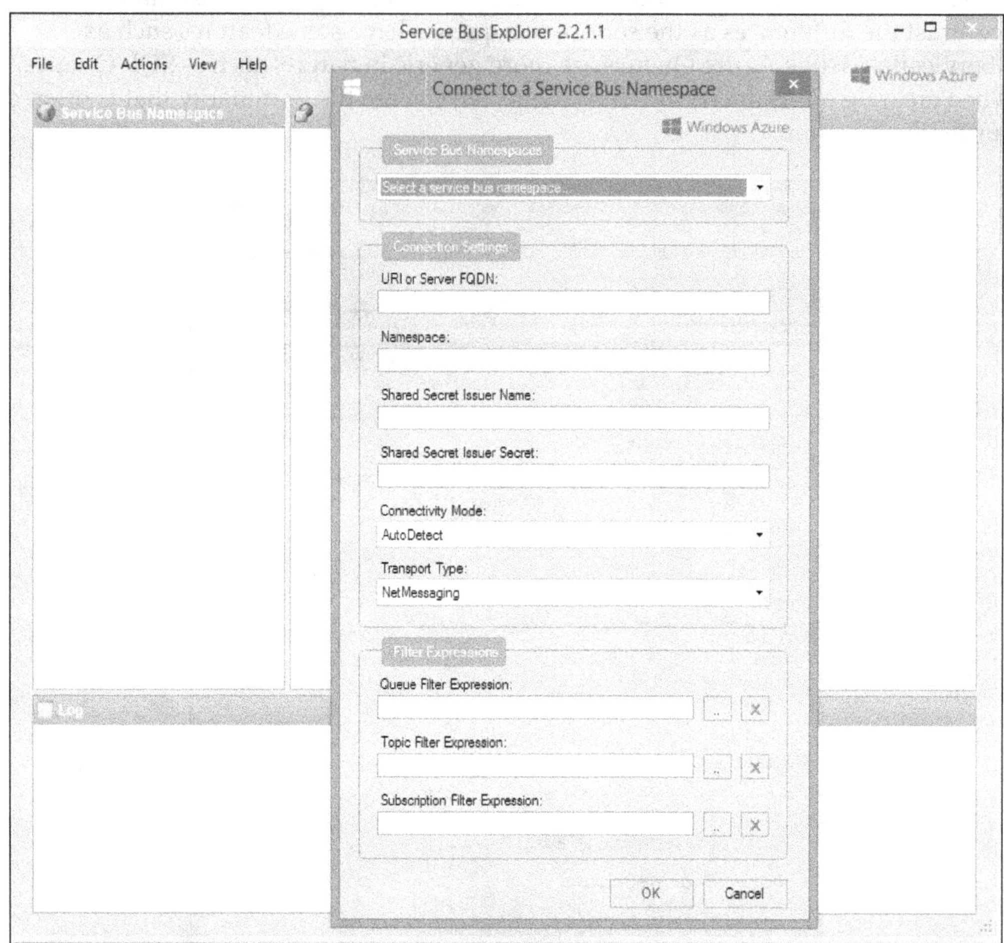

Service bus for Windows Server

To develop with the Azure service bus on-premise, the service bus for Windows Server needs to be installed from the Microsoft website; one download link is at `http://msdn.microsoft.com/en-US/library/jj193004.aspx`.

We can also install it from the Web Platform Installer from `http://www.microsoft.com/web/downloads/platform.aspx`.

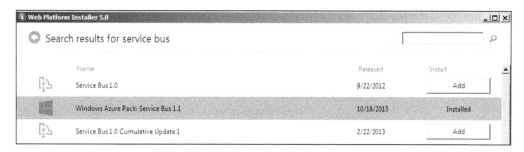

After installation of the Azure service bus to a Windows server, a configuration must take place with the service bus tools.

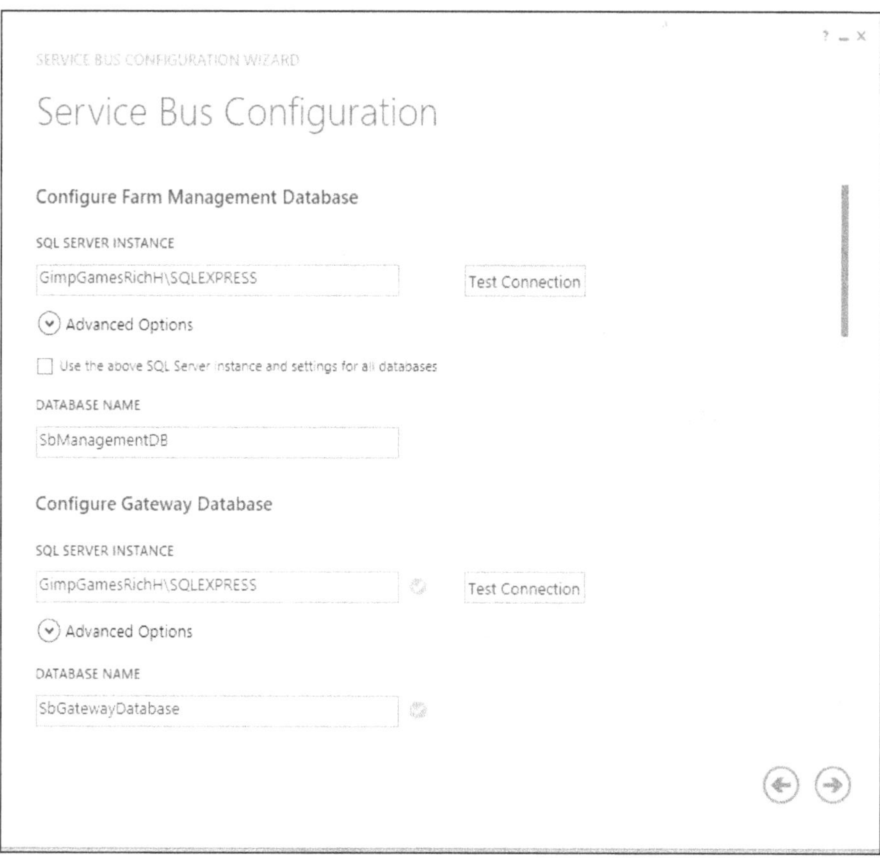

The configuration for this service bus will create a "farm" in the SQL database, which is normally local, but depending on the instance and database name entered in the configuration, it could even be a cloud database instance as we discussed before. The database will create three tables.

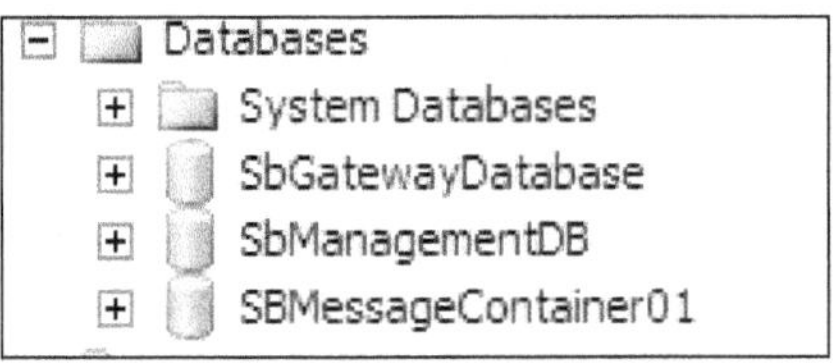

It will also create either two services, for Version 1.0, or four services, for Version 1.1, to send and receive the service bus messages, excluding the Windows Fabric service.

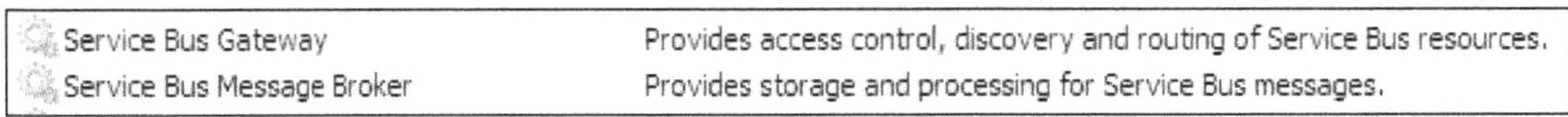

The breakdown of the services is as follows:

- **Windows Fabric**: This is the core clustering technology that manages a "ring" of the nodes in a farm.
- **Service Bus Message Broker**: This manages the send and receive operations from service bus queues, topics, and subscriptions.
- **Service Bus Gateway**: This serves as the protocol head for supported service bus protocols. The gateway also performs security validation on incoming requests.
- **Service Bus Resource Provider**: This handles management requests from the Windows Azure Pack Portal.
- **Service Bus VSS**: This discovers and automates backup and restore operations using Microsoft's **Volume Shadow Copy Service** (**VSS**).

To view the logs of any event in the service bus for Windows Servers, the application installs its own event log area.

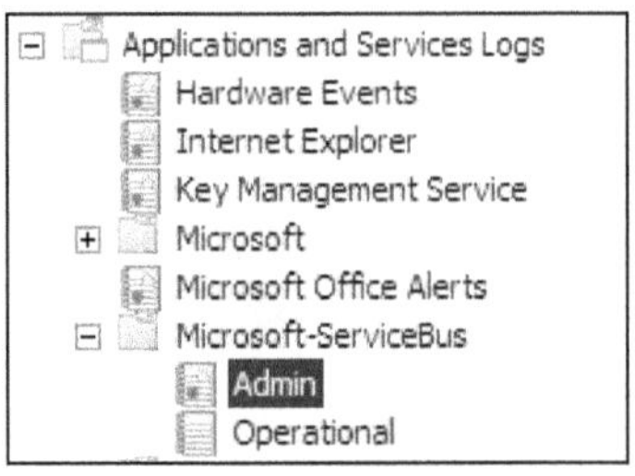

There are many PowerShell commands that can be used to administrate the Windows service bus for the Windows Server. They can be found at `http://msdn.microsoft.com/en-us/library/jj659882.aspx`. Some of the commands include:

- `get-sbclientconfiguration`: This gets the client configuration to connect to the server
- `get-sbfarm`: This gets the configuration of the farm
- `get-sbfarmstatus`: This gets the current status of the farm connected
- `get-sbnamespace`: This gets the details of the namespace

There are many more. The following screenshot shows a small example of `get-sbfarm`:

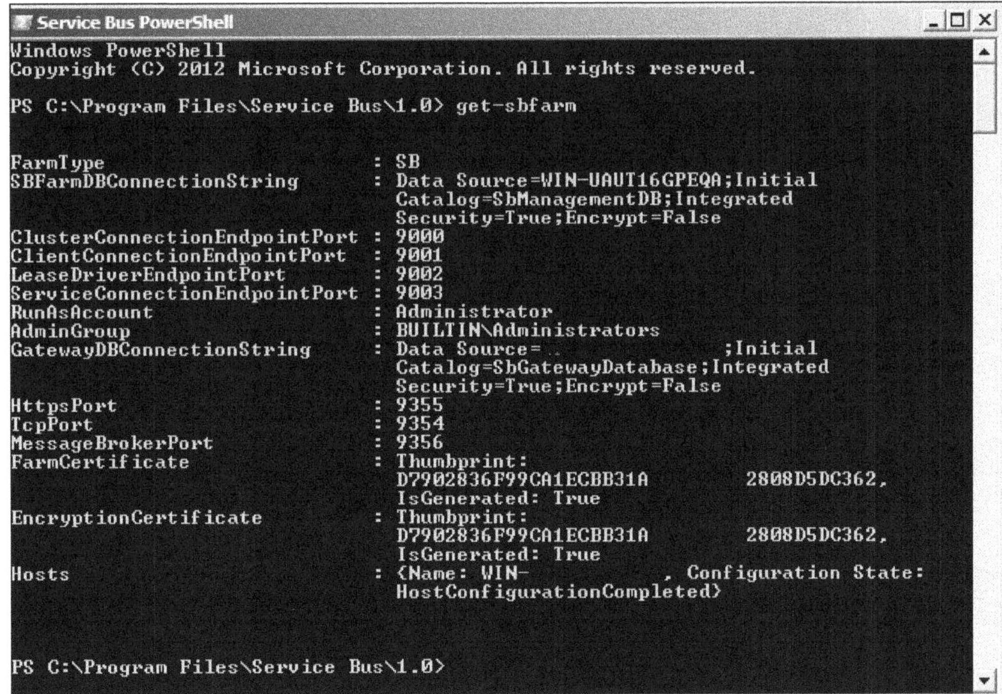

After we create the configuration for the Azure service bus, I copy the logs during the creation process; they will contain the connection string and other information that created the service bus. By using the connection string from the creation process while running the configuration tools, we are able to connect to the service bus through Visual Studio using the Server Explorer for the Service bus.

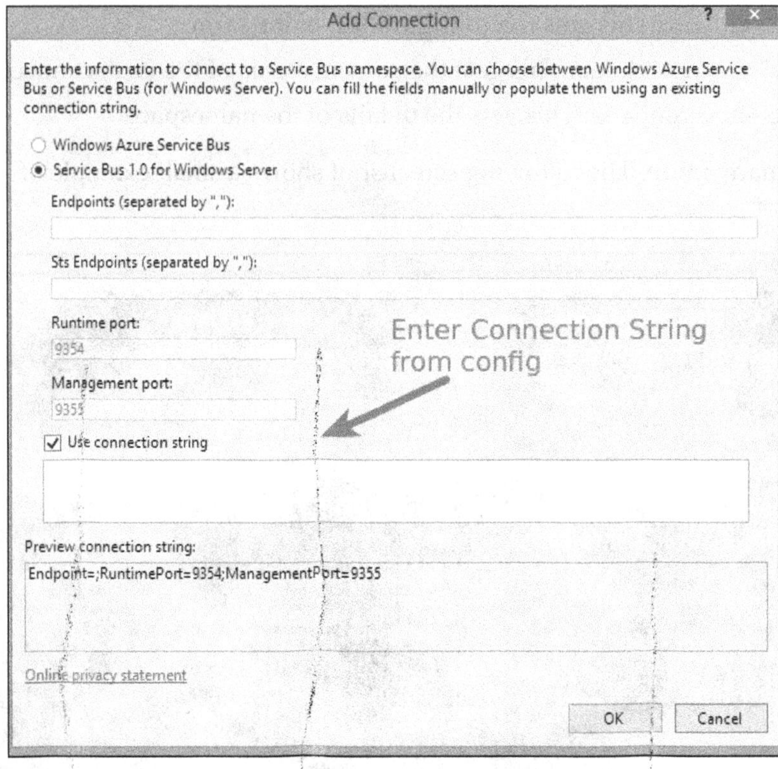

Then, we can manage it in Visual Studio's Server Explorer.

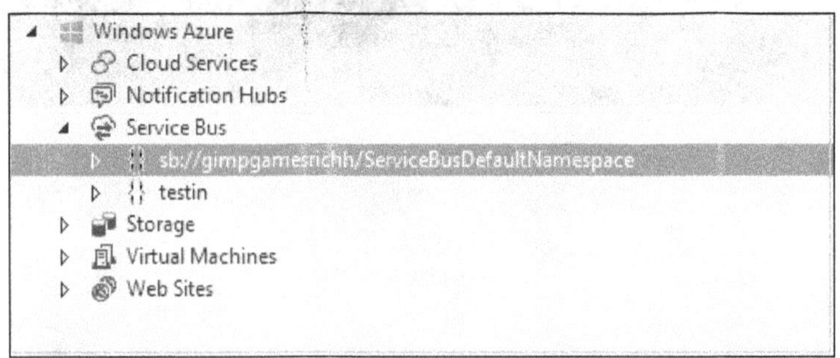

Now, we have Azure Service bus running on-premise.

Other Azure services

Windows Azure Active Directory is designed to be used with cloud applications such as SaaS applications. It also provides a **Single Sign On** (**SSO**) technology to work with Windows Server Active Directory, Facebook, Google, and many other technologies.

Windows Azure Messaging allows applications to talk to other applications. The Azure technologies provided for this are Windows Azure Service Bus and Windows Azure Queues. The Azure Service Bus can have applications communicate with each other through the cloud, on-premise or both. It communicates via queues, topics, or relays. Queues are one-to-one messaging, topics are one-to-many publish/subscribe messaging, and relays are bidirectional messaging. Relays do not store messages in between. Windows Azure Queues provide the ability for queues to exist between the web and worker roles to separate roles and responsibilities in passing messages between cloud queues. This allows messages to be stored between the responsibilities of applications. However, queuing in the cloud is not exactly the same as queuing on-premises because the worker role is responsible for deleting the messages, so there may be no guarantee that the message is used once.

Windows Azure provides different network connection configurations, such as virtual network, connect, and traffic management. The virtual network can use a static VPN through IPSec for an always-on connection to the cloud to continuously connect on-premise to the cloud. This is for users and developers who need continuous network access from on-premise to the cloud. It will appear to be on the same network. There may be a need to connect specific on-premise machines to specific cloud virtual machines. For this reason, we use Windows Azure Connect. Specific cloud services connect to specific on-premise connections. This is to specify developers and users to specific applications, for instance, connecting an on-premise DBA to a cloud SQL database. Windows Azure Traffic Manager helps in routing specific users to specific clouds, for instance, connecting Asian customers to the Asian cloud. This is based on policies defined in the Traffic manager.

Windows Azure provides mobile and media services as well. Media service has components to help deploy media to users, which includes content protection, using different media types and formats to assist in streaming media. Windows Azure mobile services allow the backend development for mobile services. While mobile devices have native programming done in Objective-C, Android, Java, PhoneGap, and Mono, mobile services allow a user to log in and access data and applications to sync their devices through resources and web services. They also allow SSO authentication and the ability to push to their devices when they log in to receive updates.

Adding NServiceBus

All cloud services communicate via web services to on-premise data or to other cloud services. Even though products such as the Salesforce cloud is normally kept in the cloud versus on-premise, there may still be data sent to Salesforce and kept on-premise. There could be many reasons why some data could be kept on-premise and not stored in the cloud; some reasons may be that there is proprietary data that a company wishes not to store off-premise, or data for security reasons may need to be kept on-premise.

Salesforce provides WSDL interfaces to their cloud by downloading their WSDL and client certificate guide, `https://help.salesforce.com/HTViewHelpDoc?id=dev_wsdl.htm&language=en_US`. A workflow rule in Salesforce would have to be created to define the data fields that have to be defined. See the tutorial found at `http://www.ramonsmits.com/2013/04/08/receiving-salesforce-notifcations-with-nservicebus.html` as an example. We have already covered setting up NServiceBus with WCF in previous chapters.

NServiceBus for Azure

Azure has queuing and subscription services just as a local on-premise Windows Server has MSMQ, but it is different. For this reason, NServiceBus has built interfaces to use the Azure pieces in the IBus interface as well. See `http://docs.particular.net/nservicebus/windows-azure-transport`. The examples can be found on GitHub at `https://github.com/Particular/NServiceBus.Azure.Samples`.

We can develop using NServiceBus to manage the Azure service bus and Azure queues in the following scenarios:

- NServiceBus managing an Azure service bus on-premise
- NServiceBus managing an Azure service bus in the Azure Cloud
- NServiceBus managing the Azure queues in the Azure Cloud
- NServiceBus managing the Azure queues in the Azure Cloud with multiple endpoints hosted in the same role instance

Azure support for NServiceBus

Let's work with the MSMQ publish/subscribe example that we have worked with multiple times. There will have to be multiple steps for either the Azure service bus or Azure queues to be used with NServiceBus. These steps include:

1. A reference for the NuGet reference for NServiceBus transport needs to be installed for Azure Service Bus; we use NServiceBus.Azure.Transports. WindowsAzureServiceBus, `http://www.nuget.org/packages/NServiceBus.Azure.Transports.WindowsAzureServiceBus/`, and for the Azure queue, we use NServiceBus.Azure.Transports. WindowsAzureStorageQueues, `http://www.nuget.org/packages/NServiceBus.Azure.Transports.WindowsAzureStorageQueues/`.
2. The `app.config` or `web.config` needs to contain the new `NServiceBus/Transport` configuration. For the Azure Service bus, it will be of the form:

   ```
   <connectionStrings>
       <add name="NServiceBus/Transport"
   connectionString="Endpoint=sb://{namespace}.servicebus.windows.net
   /;SharedSecretIssuer=owner;SharedSecretValue={key}" />
     </connectionStrings>
   ```

   For the Azure queue, it will be of the form:

   ```
    <connectionStrings>
       <add name="NServiceBus/Transport" connectionString="UseDevelop
   mentStorage=true" />
     </connectionStrings>
   ```

3. The transport of the IBus needs to change appropriately. For the Azure service bus, the transport needs to be set to `UseTransport<AzureServiceBus>()`. For Azure queues, the transport needs to be set to `UseTransport<AzureStorageQueue>()`.

By running the NServiceBus video store example for the Azure queues found at `https://github.com/Particular/NServiceBus.Azure.Samples/tree/master/VideoStore.AzureStorageQueues.Cloud`, and creating the `videostore-sales` queue to write to, we can see that the transport queues are created in a similar manner as NServiceBus would do for MSMQ.

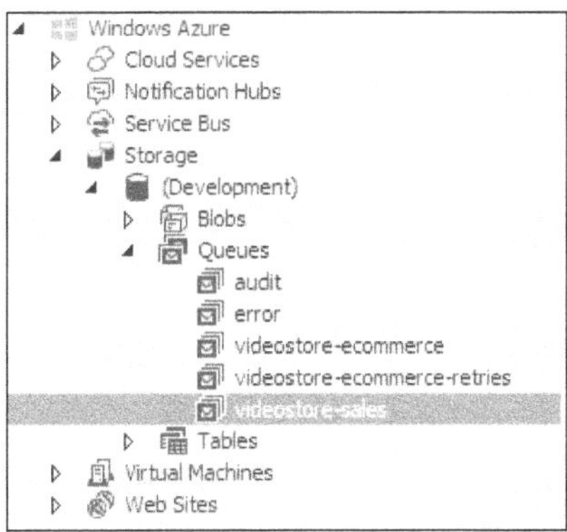

After submitting several orders through the e-commerce site, we can see the messages passed into the storage queue.

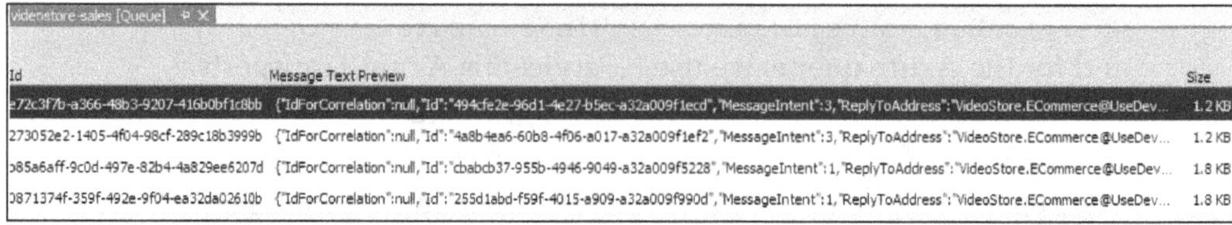

We can also use the NServiceBus example for the Azure Cloud service bus queues from `https://github.com/Particular/NServiceBus.Azure.Samples/tree/master/VideoStore.AzureServiceBus.Cloud`. We can get the Azure service bus connection string from Azure in the connection information.

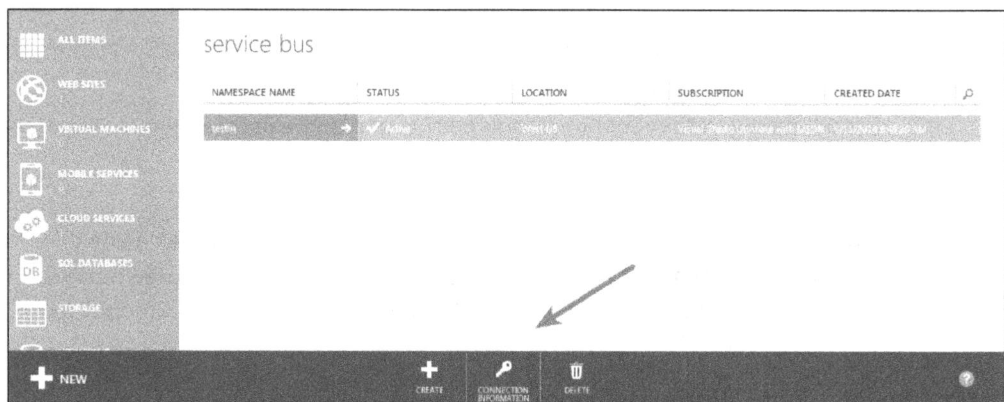

We copy the connection information into the `app.config` or `web.config` file:

```
  <connectionStrings>
    <add name="NServiceBus/Transport" connectionString="Endpoint=sb://
testin.servicebus.windows.net/;SharedSecretIssuer=owner;SharedSecretValue=NBXXXXXXXXXXXXXXXXFI6lS6i8DUyWY7eh2fjIpmf44=" />
  </connectionStrings>
```

Then, we send the order through the `videostore.ecommerce` project. Ensure that the `videostore.sales` queue is created in the Azure service bus.

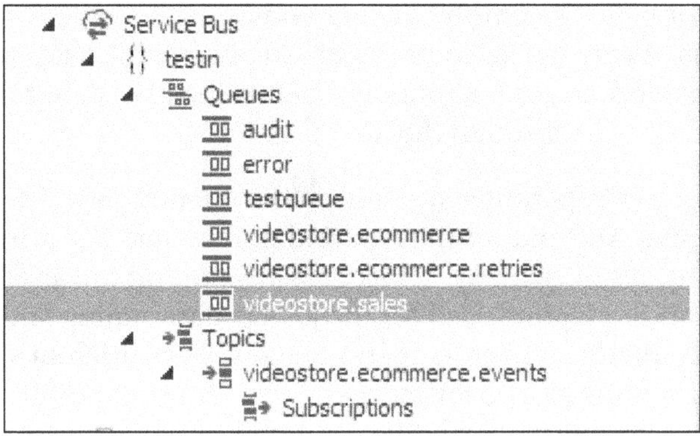

Using the Service Bus Explorer, we can see that the message was sent to the Azure service bus queue.

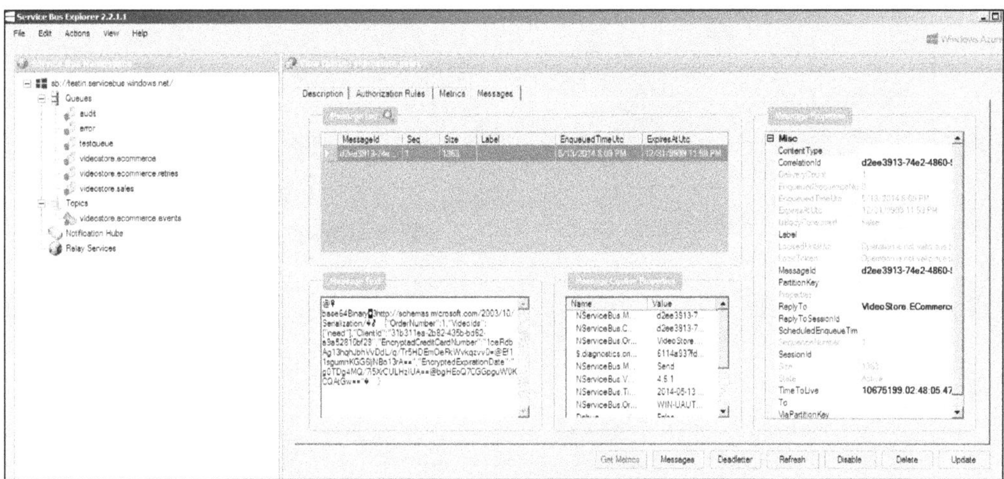

So, we have just tested the Azure service bus. To test the on-premise solution, it is done in a similar manner, except that an on-premise emulator must be present. The emulator is installed by installing a service bus for Windows Servers.

NSB in the mobile world

While, one day, there may be the possibility of using MSMQ on the Windows Phone operating system or using RabbitMQ queues and MySQL inside Android devices as native applications, it may not seem practical as ESBs handle backend processing. These may be possible features for running NSB on the phone, but the purpose of NSB is to establish an SOA through the use of a C# ESB.

With the rise of different operating systems on the phones, be it iOS for the iPhone and iPad, or be it Java Android for the Android phones and the Windows Phone and tablet operating systems, many developers are turning towards "write-once run-anywhere". This is a tagline used for the Java programming language, the Mono development platform from Xamarin to use C# on different systems, to more recently the use of writing games for the web browser using HTML5 and PhoneGap. In HTML5, many of the native capabilities of mobile devices are available. In PhoneGap, you can tap into more native mobile phone capabilities better than HTML5. With HTML5, you can leverage Microsoft MVC as we have done in many examples; the difference is now that you are upgrading your HTML to Version 5, and using JavaScript APIs to support phone functionality.

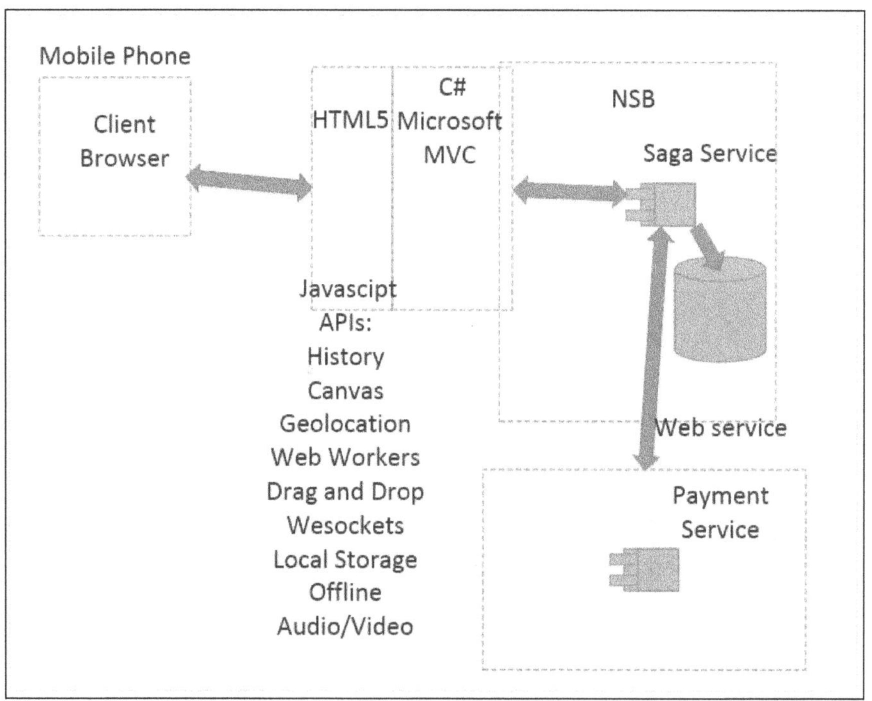

In this scenario, NSB is interacting with Microsoft MVC as it has in many examples in this book, but now, Microsoft MVC is utilizing HTML5 for mobile development in Visual Studio. There are many extensions to assist in HTML5 development with Visual Studio for MVC, such as Mobile Ready HTML5 MVC.NET at `http://visualstudiogallery.msdn.microsoft.com/9df9c61c-4d90-43e5-9aa1-a58786b7a1e4`.

NSB becomes an even more valuable framework for decoupling the frontend interaction from the backend processing. For instance, you may be playing a game, and want to pay for the game. Decoupling the frontend will allow you to make a payment for the game inside HTML5, during a pause of the game, and continue with the game as the payment is being processed to the credit card service. Without the NSB decoupling, the continuation of the game may be an issue while the payment is being processed with the frontend processes. Imagine the pizza order scenario with **Do not Refresh this page while we are processing your order**. This scenario may be extended without the benefit of decoupling with NSB, for a game being played in HTML5 as **Do not Refresh this page on your phone while we are processing your payment for the game**. How embarrassing, but there are many popular websites that have these warnings as they are processing orders and payments.

PhoneGap is an HTML5 application platform that allows you to author native applications with web technologies and get access to APIs and application stores. PhoneGap is basically used for developing working code for iPhones, Androids, Blackberries, and WebOS devices that contain HTML, **cascading style sheet**(**CSS**), and JavaScript. It can be found at `http://phonegap.com/`. PhoneGap is also supported in Visual Studio and C#.

Recap

Here are some of the benefits of NSB that we have demonstrated in this chapter:

- NSB can send messages to some vendor queues such as access queues through some cloud vendors such as Azure service bus queues
- Azure service bus can be used for on-premise testing by using ServiceBus for Windows Servers, and the current version is Version 1.1
- For cloud vendors that do not expose their message queues, NSB services can connect to them using web services, such as WCF
- For mobile phones, HTML5 can be used to extend MVC for mobile applications to use NSB as it would normally be used for MVC
- NSB is a good solution for marshaling messages between on-premise and off-premise data and business logic

Questions that were answered

Here are some of the questions answered throughout this chapter:

1. What is the emulator for the on-premise service bus?

A. Service bus for Windows Servers.

2. What are two frameworks that could be used in C# to provide HTML browser clients for mobile devices?

A. HTML5 and PhoneGap.

3. What is one of the tools to create Microsoft Azure websites?

A. WebMatrix.

4. What does HDFS stand for?

A. Hadoop Distributed File System (HDFS).

5. What is the Azure service bus pattern that is similar to MSMQ publish/subscribe?

A. Topics.

6. What SDK has to be installed for Visual Studio 2012 to use Azure Server Explorer?

A. Visual Studio 2012 for Web and Windows Azure SDK-2.3.

7. What's one way to install the Azure SDK and Service Bus for Windows Server?

A. By using the Microsoft Web Platform Installer.

8. Name one of the ways to use SQL Reporting in Azure.

A. SSRS.

9. Does NSB support Azure service bus and Azure storage queues?

A. Yes.

10. What is one of the ways to connect NSB to SalesForce?

A. WCF.

11. Does RabbitMQ support DTC?

A. No.

12. Are future versions of NSB adding support for Azure and the cloud?

A. Yes.

13. Is ServiceInsight supporting more sequence diagrams for sagas?

A. Yes.

Summary

In this chapter, we took a deeper dive into **Software as a Service** (**SaaS**) and how NServiceBus ties into cloud computing. We gave a very brief introduction to the cloud and some of its services.

We discussed how NSB will be useful as well in the mobile device world going forward by utilizing C# technology into HTML5 and PhoneGap. We know that NServiceBus is a framework that is quickly adapting to the software industry mobile and cloud trends going forward.

Index

A

B

C

J

L

M

Q

R

S

T

U

V

W

X

Thank you for buying
Mastering NServiceBus and Persistence

About Packt Publishing

Packt, pronounced 'packed', published its first book "Mastering phpMyAdmin for Effective MySQL Management" in April 2004 and subsequently continued to specialize in publishing highly focused books on specific technologies and solutions.

Our books and publications share the experiences of your fellow IT professionals in adapting and customizing today's systems, applications, and frameworks. Our solution based books give you the knowledge and power to customize the software and technologies you're using to get the job done. Packt books are more specific and less general than the IT books you have seen in the past. Our unique business model allows us to bring you more focused information, giving you more of what you need to know, and less of what you don't.

Packt is a modern, yet unique publishing company, which focuses on producing quality, cutting-edge books for communities of developers, administrators, and newbies alike. For more information, please visit our website: `www.packtpub.com`.

About Packt Enterprise

In 2010, Packt launched two new brands, Packt Enterprise and Packt Open Source, in order to continue its focus on specialization. This book is part of the Packt Enterprise brand, home to books published on enterprise software - software created by major vendors, including (but not limited to) IBM, Microsoft and Oracle, often for use in other corporations. Its titles will offer information relevant to a range of users of this software, including administrators, developers, architects, and end users.

Writing for Packt

We welcome all inquiries from people who are interested in authoring. Book proposals should be sent to `author@packtpub.com`. If your book idea is still at an early stage and you would like to discuss it first before writing a formal book proposal, contact us; one of our commissioning editors will get in touch with you.

We're not just looking for published authors; if you have strong technical skills but no writing experience, our experienced editors can help you develop a writing career, or simply get some additional reward for your expertise.

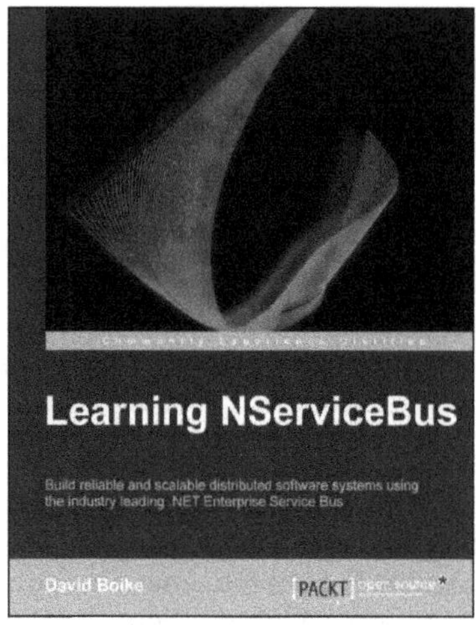

Learning NServiceBus

ISBN: 978-1-78216-634-4 Paperback: 136 pages

Build reliable and scalable distributed software systems using the industry leading .NET Enterprise Service Bus

1. Replace batch jobs with a reliable process.
2. Create applications that compensate for system failure.
3. Build a message-driven system.

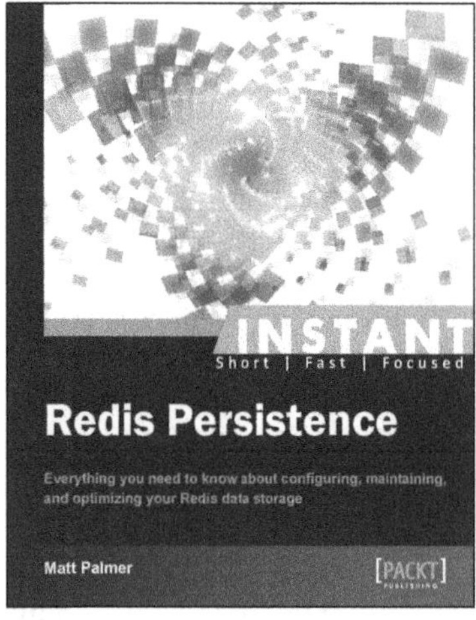

Instant Redis Persistence

ISBN: 978-1-78328-021-6 Paperback: 50 pages

Everything you need to know about configuring, maintaining, and optimizing your Redis data storage

1. Learn something new in an Instant! A short, fast, focused guide delivering immediate results.
2. Configure and manage how Redis stores your data.
3. Optimize performance and ensure data security with backups and encryption.

Please check **www.PacktPub.com** for information on our titles

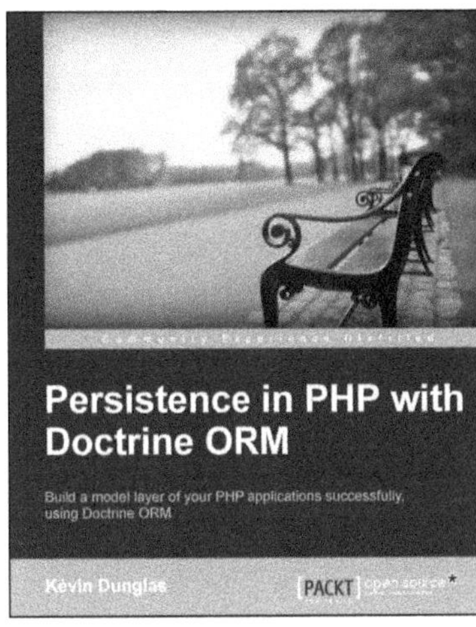

Persistence in PHP with Doctrine ORM

ISBN: 978-1-78216-410-4 Paperback: 114 pages

Build a model layer of your PHP applications successfully, using Doctrine ORM

1. Develop a fully functional Doctrine-backed web application.
2. Demonstrate aspects of Doctrine using code samples.
3. Generate a database schema from your PHP classes.

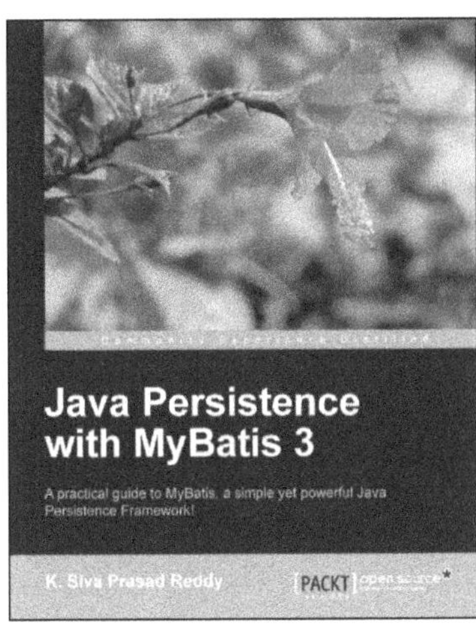

Java Persistence with MyBatis 3

ISBN: 978-1-78216-680-1 Paperback: 132 pages

A practical guide to MyBatis, a simple yet powerful Java Persistence Framework!

1. Detailed instructions on how to use MyBatis with XML and annotation-based SQL mappers.
2. An in-depth discussion on how to map complex SQL query results such as one-to-many and many-to-many using MyBatis ResultMaps.
3. Step-by-step instructions on how to integrate MyBatis with a Spring framework.

Please check **www.PacktPub.com** for information on our titles

www.ingramcontent.com/pod-product-compliance
Lightning Source LLC
Chambersburg PA
CBHW060523060326
40690CB00017B/3371

* 9 7 8 1 7 8 2 1 7 3 8 1 6 *